Scriptures, Shrines, Scapegoats, and World Politics

The effect of religious factors on politics has emerged as a key issue in political inquiries since the end of the Cold War and the rise of religious terrorism. However, much of the work on these matters is inconclusive, marred by controversies and polemics. The systematic investigations of these topics have been partial, focusing primarily on the effects of religious factors on—domestic and international—conflict. *Scriptures, Shrines, Scapegoats, and World Politics* offers a comprehensive evaluation of the role of religion in world politics, broadening the scope of investigation to such topics as the relationship between religion and international cooperation, international conflict, civil war and the quality of life. Zeev Maoz and Errol A. Henderson argue that religion is often manipulated by leaders to advance their political interests. They find that no specific religion is either consistently more bellicose or consistently more cooperative than other religions. However, religious similarity between states tends to decrease the propensity of conflict and increase the propensity for security cooperation. Finally, the authors find a significant relationship between secularism and human security.

Zeev Maoz is Distinguished Professor of Political Science at the University of California, Davis and Director of the Correlates of War Project.

Errol A. Henderson is Associate Professor of Political Science at Pennsylvania State University.

Scriptures, Shrines, Scapegoats, and World Politics

Religious Sources of Conflict and Cooperation in the Modern Era

Zeev Maoz and Errol A. Henderson

University of Michigan Press
Ann Arbor

First paperback edition 2021

Copyright © 2020 by Zeev Maoz and Errol A. Henderson
Some rights reserved

This work is licensed under a Creative Commons Attribution-NonCommercial-NoDerivatives 4.0 International License. Note to users: A Creative Commons license is only valid when it is applied by the person or entity that holds rights to the licensed work. Works may contain components (e.g., photographs, illustrations, or quotations) to which the rightsholder in the work cannot apply the license. It is ultimately your responsibility to independently evaluate the copyright status of any work or component part of a work you use, in light of your intended use. To view a copy of this license, visit http://creativecommons.org/licenses/by-nc/4.0/

Published in the United States of America by the
University of Michigan Press
Manufactured in the United States of America
Printed on acid-free paper
First published in paperback December 2021

A CIP catalog record for this book is available from the British Library.

Library of Congress Cataloging-in-Publication data has been applied for.

ISBN 978-0-472-13174-7 (hardcover : alk. paper)
ISBN 978-0-472-12643-9 (e-book)
ISBN 978-0-472-90123-4 (OA)

ISBN 978-0-472-03875-6 (pbk. : alk. paper)

http://dx.doi.org/10.3998/mpub.11353856

This book is freely available in an open access edition thanks to TOME (Toward an Open Monograph Ecosystem)—a collaboration of the Association of American Universities, the Association of University Presses, and the Association of Research Libraries—and the generous support of the University of California, Davis, and the Pennsylvania State University. Learn more at the TOME website, available at: openmonographs.org.

Preface

Religion is one of the most persistent resins that forms and maintains communal bonds. Almost all recorded historical sources—anthropological, archaeological, textual or oral—document this fact. It is also an important force defining intercommunal interaction since the dawn of recorded history. Yet, until quite recently, most mainstream students of world politics did not pay much attention to the role of religion in conflict and cooperation, explicitly. Just when religious factors seemed to play a smaller role in political and social affairs—with growing numbers of secular people and more states practicing separation between religion and government—mainstream scholars of world politics began to focus on the interplay between religion and international relations.

We have some ideas about this peculiar piece of intellectual history, which we discuss in the first chapter. Notably, however, the surge in studies on religion and world politics started in the early 1990s, just after the end of the Cold War. Since then, a number of important theories have emerged connecting different aspects of religion to conflict and cooperation—between and within nations—and focusing on religion's impact explicitly or implicitly. Several of the hypotheses stemming from such theories have been subjected to rigorous empirical analyses. The results, however, are inconclusive at best. Some theories linking religion to conflict and cooperation have received empirical support; others have not. Yet, neither the supportive nor the disconfirming evidence is sufficiently robust to allow unequivocal assessment of the validity of these theories. Moreover, most studies of religion and world politics are partial and scattered. The studies focusing on the linkages between religion and international conflict have ignored the relations between religion and international cooperation and vice versa. Other studies have focused on the domestic political implications of religion, e.g., its effect on civil conflict, political stability, and democracy. While all these studies offer interesting—if inconclusive—insights, we still lack a comprehensive account of the overall role of religion in world politics. The present study offers such an account.

Utilizing a new and comprehensive dataset on world religions, we study the effect of religion on (a) international conflict, (b) international cooperation, (c) domestic conflict, and (d) human security and welfare. These analyses combine to form a more general understanding of the role religion has played in world politics since the end of World War II. They also enable us to examine the implications of these results for the future of the international system.

Our approach is more extensive than most studies on the subject in several important respects. First, we examine the effect of religion on politics among and within nations. We also examine how religion influences the interaction between domestic and international politics. Second, most studies focus on a single unit of analysis—either the individual state or the dyad (i.e., pair of states)—whereas we examine the interrelations between religion and politics across multiple levels of analysis. We focus on individual states, pairs of states, groups of states and regions, and the international system as a whole. This enables us to reach far more generalizable conclusions than most previous studies on the subject.

Third, we focus on a far wider array of behaviors than most previous studies. Again, this leads to broader and more reliable generalizations. Finally, the scope of our empirical analyses is considerably wider, and methodologically more innovative than most studies on the subject. This makes our results much more robust than previous investigations. We not only replicate what others have done but also improve and expand on the theoretical treatment of these topics, offer higher-resolution data, and improve on the methods and analyses linking religion to world politics. In short, this is possibly the most comprehensive empirical study of its kind.

The authors came to this topic from two different perspectives. Maoz's interest in religion arises from his focus on international networks. The motivating idea stems from a belief that culture plays an important role in shaping the structure of conflictual and cooperative networks. Henderson came to this topic from his interest in the role of culture in world politics. His earlier work on the subject focused on tests of one of the most visible arguments in the field—Huntington's (1993, 1996) clash of civilizations

(CoC) thesis. However, we both felt that the literature and the data on our respective areas of interests were quite problematic. So we decided to collaborate in order to make things better.

This interest coincided with an existing project on religion and society, led by Professor Roger Finke at Pennsylvania State University. With the collegial support of Finke, director of the Association of Religion Data Archives (ARDA), as well as colleagues in the United States and Israel, and generous support through a grant from the Templeton Foundation, we developed the World Religion Project (WRP) dataset. This dataset enabled us to launch a set of empirical investigations into the role of religion in world politics.

We wish to thank a number of people who have helped with this project. First, our coders, graduate and undergraduate research assistants: Carl Palmer, Aimee Tannehill, Anisha Chikarmane, Molly Sweeny, Paul Johnson, Katherine Unger, Jaime Jackson, Tatiana Lukoianova, Jaime Harris, Tamara Tur, Samantha Gallardo, Brad Middleton, Phil Schafer. Second, we thank Scott Bennett, Robert Martin, and Gail Ulmer for helping us format and reformat our datasets so that they can be included in the ARDA and COW websites.[1] Third, we want to thank Roger Finke for his insights and his support. Last, but not least, the Templeton Foundation supported the collection of the WRP through grant #1342. Any errors of omission and commission, however, are ours alone.

Table of Contents

Chapter 1 Religion and World Politics—Theory and Evidence 1
Chapter 2 Scholarship on Religion and World Politics: A Critical Review of the Literature 25
Chapter 3 Religion and World Politics: An Integrated Theoretical Perspective 62
Chapter 4 The Religious Landscape of the World 1945–2010 115
Chapter 5 Religion and International Conflict 146
Chapter 6 Religion and International Cooperation 224
Chapter 7 Religion and Civil War 283
Chapter 8 Religion and Quality of Life 344
Chapter 9 Conclusion: The Complex Role of Religion in World Politics 370

Notes 387

Bibliography 397

Index 419

Digital materials related to this title can be found on the Fulcrum platform via the following citable URL: https://doi.org/10.3998/mpub.11353856

CHAPTER I

Religion and World Politics—Theory and Evidence

1. Introduction: What Is Religion, Why Does It Matter for World Politics?

Religion, in its simplest form, is a belief in the existence of some divine authority/ies. This belief translates to a set of values and moral codes and a set of rituals and practices that are presumably prescribed by such deities to humans. This interpretation of religion may imply that religion is a private affair. A person either possesses these beliefs or he/she does not; a person either follows these values and codes of conduct and rituals or he/she does not. A person is either "religious" or he/she is not.

While this simple definition may be valid, the implication that religion is only a private affair is inaccurate. If religions were only private affairs, then individuals would hardly care about the belief systems of others. Religious persons would not try to convert other people. The notion of righteousness would be purely individual: I am a true believer regardless of whether other people are. If rituals were private affairs, we would have no churches, temples, mosques, pagodas, or holy burial sites. We would need no priests, rabbis, mullahs, monks, gurus, or shamans. Holy places would have been sacred to one individual and meaningless to others. If religions were private affairs, every person or every other person would have his/her own scripture: a document that stipulated the existence of different God(s) and prescribed different moral codes, values, and righteous behaviors.

If religion were an individual trait, and if every person derived a different set of beliefs and norms from his/her religion, there would be no reason to search for the links between religion and world politics. What makes religion so relevant to social life and to international relations is that most religions—certainly the more popular ones—form and sustain communal institutions. They contain tangible elements that bind people together in profound ways. Virtually all religions prescribe collective rituals and directives for communal behaviors. These principles define not only the identity of individual believers (or nonbelievers) but also distinguish between communities of believers and communities of nonbelievers. The moral codes of many religions not only entail rituals, practices, and values that define righteous relations and behaviors among believers but also contain codes of conduct for believers toward nonbelievers or toward believers of different religions.

Virtually all religions are institutionalized to one degree or another. Religious institutions may be as formal, centralized, and hierarchical as the Roman Catholic Church, or they may be as informal and decentralized as an African *sangoma* or a Native American shaman. These institutions define or interpret the principal values, rituals, and moral codes that constitute a specific religion. They also define the identity of believers and differentiate between believers and nonbelievers; between religious in-group and out-groups. These institutions typically ordain religious officers (priests, rabbis, mullahs, etc.). Religious institutions offer key evidence of religions as communal structures.

Not all religions have scriptures, but many do. Scriptures are the fundamental sources of religious beliefs. They contain stories about the origins of religion—typically a story where the superior being(s) revealed itself/themselves to one or more human beings, the founder(s) of that religion. They contain the basic directives that guide the rituals and moral codes of believers. Religious institutions are the formal interpreters of these scriptures. And many splits and divisions within and between different religions are centered either on the status of these scriptures or on their interpretation by different institutions.

The history of religions traces their origins, development, and change. History tells us where, when, and how a religion was established and reveals the relationship between different religions. For example,

Christianity developed from Judaism. Likewise, Muhammad, the founder of Islam, was influenced by Judaism and Christianity, and incorporated elements of both into Islam. The history of religion is also a tale of religious infighting and of the rise of religious families within the same religion. History tells us how Eastern Orthodoxy and Protestantism split from the Roman Catholic Church. It tells us how Islam split into Sunnis, Shi'ites, Alawites, Ahmadis, and other religious families. It tells us how Buddhism split into the Mahayana and Theravada families. In short, history tells us when one community of people formed a new religion or split into a separate family of the same religion. The historical record of most major religions and their branching into religious families and denominations suggests a common pattern of community formation, community development, and intercommunal conflict and cooperation. This transformational record offers additional evidence of religion as a communal institution.

In quite a few cases the development of religion and its history involved conflict—sometimes extremely bloody conflict—within and between communities. This tale of religious conflict suggests a strong connection between religion and world politics. Leaders of communities, whether they were prophets, kings, warlords, presidents, or prime ministers, often used religion to promote their interests. Wars in the name of one God against infidels—believers in other Gods—seem to be a common theme in world history. But religion also has been a source of cooperation within and between communities. Most religions define codes of moral conduct. These help establish common norms among disparate communities. Communities that shared similar religious values may have found it easier to communicate and cooperate than communities that practiced different religions.

World politics is also a story of conflict and cooperation between and within communities. Since religion was such a central driver in the formation and sustainability of communities, it played an important role in—domestic and international—political processes. The story of the formation, transformation, and impact of religions is intertwined with international history. In fact, the linkages between religion and world politics are at the center of some of the most profound controversies in the contemporary study of world politics.

2. Religion in the History and Theory of World Politics— A Brief Overview

A brief and, admittedly cursory, review of the relationship between religion and international conflict in history underlines this duality. It illuminates the ways in which religion has been a source of both conflict and cooperation, of intracommunity strife and intracommunity solidarity, of intracommunity decline and development.

Religion in premodern societies often had an important unifying role. It added some evolutionary advantage to primitive communities, which organized for utilitarian reasons such as common defense, the pooling of hunting resources, and reproductive efficiency. Religious rituals and symbols served as a unifying factor that added cohesion to such communities. As such, religion may have played a unifying role in fostering cooperation and intracommunal welfare. However, once different groups of *Homo sapiens* organized around religious symbols, the relative advantage of religion as an organizing force in warfare diminished significantly (Gat 2006, 100–5). Gat's extensive review of war in primitive societies suggests that religion was an "added" motive to the fundamentally materialist causes of warfare, but it was not an independent one. Such communities often believed that sorcery—committed by members of other communities—was the source of ills and misfortunes that befell one's community. Such beliefs often served as a mobilizing instrument for subsequent raids and attacks.

The earliest recorded history suggests the salience of religion in the earliest civilizations. For example, arguably one of the factors contributing to the civil war (that marked the tumultuous First Intermediate Period of ancient Egypt, from 2181 to 2055 BCE, and the end of the Old Kingdom) was a religious dispute between Upper Egypt, which advocated the supremacy of Amun, and Lower Egypt, which advocated the supremacy of Ra (Shaw 2003). The reunification of the country and the hegemony of Amun-Ra may have reflected a religious compromise to help resolve at least that aspect of the dispute. Religious texts themselves also provide narratives that suggest the influence of religion on the international interactions of antiquity, but these are primarily narratives of *faith* rather than *fact*.

The Old and New Testaments juxtapose historical episodes, legends, and religious directives. Stories about the role of religion in shaping intercommunal conflict and cooperation suggest a mixed effect. The treatment of the Israelites by the Egyptians and the Pharaoh may have been based on religious difference and suspicion, but from what the Old Testament tells us, it is no less likely a story about ethnic and economic exploitation. Since the Old Testament focuses on the history of the Israelites, we cannot infer from this story whether other ethnic communities were treated similarly by Egyptian royalty. However, there is archaeological evidence suggesting that this was indeed the case (Kemp 2006).

The conquest of ancient Palestine by the Israelites could also be construed as a story of religious warfare. But it is just as likely that it was a typical raid of one tribe against others. Since the Old Testament is told from the perspective of Jewish religious leaders, every incident of conflict between the Israelites and "pagan" communities could be construed as a tale of religious warfare. However, most of these stories of conflicts between Jews and their neighbors can be easily attributed to other issues—economics, territory—just as easily as they can be attributed to religious differences.[1]

Homer's *Iliad* and Thucydides's *Peloponnesian Wars* are two stories of conflict and diplomacy in the ancient Greek city-state system. The entire Greek peninsula and its surroundings (and later the Roman Empire) practiced the same polytheistic religion. Their many gods were believed to engage in human activities such as conflict and love affairs. Nevertheless, both Homer's and Thucydides's accounts of the era and its politics—while mentioning locations such as Zeus's temple or certain religious rituals—assigned religion a marginal role in the politics of these periods.

The Roman Empire was fairly liberal when it came to religious practices in its protectorates (Luttwak 1979). The imperial administrative style was quite simple: the Romans allowed their protectorates to be ruled by autonomous local leaders. As long as a given protectorate paid its taxes and did not rebel, local communities were left pretty much to their own devices. Rebellions that took place in the empire (e.g., the Judean rebellion, Flavius [75] 2014) were driven by economic factors, not by religious differences. The collapse of the Roman Empire was also not due to religious competition.

More explicitly religious wars become central to the international politics of the region marked by the intersection of Europe, North Africa, and Southwest Asia largely bordering the Mediterranean during the medieval period. First, the Islamic conquests of the Middle East and North Africa were driven by both political and religious ambitions, and were accompanied by the forced conversion of the occupied populations to Islam (Rogan 2009). These motivated the Crusades, and the ensuing conflict between Christians and Muslims in Palestine is an early example of clash of civilizations (Huntington 1993, 1996) warfare. This conflict was about religious control of the holy places in Palestine, Jerusalem in particular.

It would be a mistake to portray the Middle Ages as an era of interreligious conflict, however. Both within Islam and Christendom, wars involved both traditional contests over resources—for example, territory—and competing succession claims as well as religious differences. Islam split into Sunni and Shi'a families originating in the Hussayni rebellion and its suppression by the Ummayads in 680 CE (Rogan 2009). This was accompanied by recurring conflicts between Sunni and Shi'a communities. In Europe, most of the medieval wars were between adherents of the same religion. The Reformation and spread of Protestantism in Europe were intimately related to interreligious warfare—this time between several families of the same religion. However, the lack of well-defined state structures in Europe makes it difficult to distinguish such cases as the Wars of Religion in France or the Eighty Years' War in the Netherlands—primarily civil wars—from the Thirty Years' War that was a combination of intrastate wars (i.e., civil wars) and interstate wars (Dunn 1979).

The aftermath of the Thirty Years' War—arguably one of the longest and bloodiest wars in history (Wilson 2011)—brought at least a temporary respite from "religious" warfare in Europe. This is not to say that subsequent wars did not occur between states of different religions or within states between different religious communities. Rather, religion was typically not a prominently stated issue over which many people fought in the eighteenth, nineteenth, and most of the twentieth centuries. At the same time, wars between religiously dissimilar societies—primarily in imperialist and colonial contexts—continued to take place across the world.

The story of Eastern religions and of Asian civilization has similar undertones. There are obvious differences between Far Eastern religions and the Abrahamic (Judaism, Christianity, Islam) religions (Smart 1998). Yet the relationship between religion and politics in many Asian societies was not all that different from the history of the West. Communities organized around common religious beliefs and followed religious leaders. Strictly within-community marriages yielded class systems that were more internally homogeneous and externally diverse in terms of religion.

Geography also shaped the distribution of religious beliefs. Consequently, conflictual or cooperative relations among different communities were also affected by religious similarity or dissimilarity. Even before East-West trade began to facilitate Western influence on Asian societies, conflict between communities in South and East Asia could be described both on religious grounds and on material grounds. The relations between European imperialists and local societies were increasingly shaped by the imperial activities of European powers and missionaries in Asia in the late eighteenth and nineteenth centuries. The European sense of white supremacy rested both on tangible factors—such as superior economic and military power and technology—and on the notion that Christianity was spiritually superior to other religions and had to be spread in order to bring modernity to the "primitive" societies of Asia, America, and Africa (Du Bois 1915, Furedi 1998, Mazrui 1988, Abernethy 2000). This added another—ideological—layer to the social, economic, and political/military exploitation of indigenous societies by European imperialism.

The most destructive interstate wars in human history—the two World Wars—were not focused on religion. To be sure, Russian support for Serbia was expressed in part as a result of the former's view of itself as the protector of Orthodox allies, in this case Serbia, against Catholic Austria-Hungary. The July–August Crisis of 1914 was the spark on a powder keg traced in large part to the continued decay and breakup of the Islamic Ottoman Turkish Empire and competition among the Catholic, Protestant, and Orthodox European states over the spoils of this process as well as the competition for new imperial domains especially in Africa (Du Bois 1915). Not surprisingly, major parts of World War I were fought between religiously dissimilar states, for example, between the Ottoman Empire and the Western powers. But the center of the conflict was a struggle between religiously similar Christian states (Catholic, Protestant, Orthodox, Anglican states). The population of most combatants included a mix of several religious families of Christianity. Similarly, in World War II, the armed conflict between Japan and the United States and its allies, or Nazi Germany and the USSR involved religiously dissimilar states, but religion was not a major issue in the war. During the Cold War era, a significant number of wars broke out between religiously dissimilar states. These included the Korean War, the Vietnam War, the Arab–Israeli wars, and the Indo–Pakistani wars. However, there is little evidence that religious factors played a key role in these wars. The Korean, Vietnam, and Cambodian wars pitted initially religiously similar communities against each other. Only later did these civil wars expand to interreligious conflict. Importantly, the issues over which these wars were fought were primarily political, not religious. There are certainly strong religious aspects to the Arab–Israeli and Indo–Pakistani conflict. However, religion was not a single, and most likely not a central, issue at stake in these wars.

The complex role that religion has played in the political history of the world has had only few traces in both ancient and modern theories of world politics. The classics of International Relations (IR) theories—writings by historians, philosophers, military strategists, legal scholars, and economists—focus only marginally on the role of religion in world politics. For example, Sun Tzu's *The Art of War*, written sometime in the sixth century BCE is probably one of the first treatises on military strategy. It mentions off and on some Confucian and Taoist concepts, but in essence it is about rational management of force (Johnston 1995). There is virtually no place for divine intervention in military affairs, as far as his ideas are concerned (Sun Tzu 1994 [circa 512 BCE]).

Thucydides's history of the Peloponnesian Wars (Thucydides 1943 [circa 413 BCE]) is a story of realpolitik. Religion plays a very minor role in these wars; the Peloponnesian Wars are about power, dominance, and prestige, but not about religion. Polytheistic beliefs were common to both Athens and Sparta as well as to the other city-states in the Greek Peninsula. If anything, the Peloponnesian wars were clearly intrareligious conflicts.

The political and legal theory of the Enlightenment era—including Hugo Grotius and the Enlightenment political philosophers (e.g., Adam Smith, Jean-Jacques Rousseau, Thomas Hobbes, Charles Montesquieu, John Locke, and later, Immanuel Kant) was predicated on the conception of political systems built on rational foundations. This conception relied on a notion that political order rests on a social contract among people rather than on a divine directive. These theorists also viewed the relations among political communities as either regulated or unregulated by the same rational logic. God plays no role in the brutish Hobbesian state of nature. Nor does God play a role in Rousseau's version of the fragility and instability of the more harmonic relations among states. Nor does God play a role in the vision of a cooperative system in Comte's notion of peace through trade or in Kant's notion of peace among liberal republics (Waltz 1958, Hoffmann

1964, Knusten 1994, Doyle 1986). Importantly, religious institutions, religious beliefs, and rituals do not play a significant role in liberal thinking about the state and international relations.

An exception to this view in nineteenth-century political philosophy is Karl Marx's treatment of religion as an instrument that both the traditional elites and the bourgeoisie in industrialized states use to sustain the class structure and the submissiveness of the proletariat (Elster 1985, 504–10). This conception is an important element of what we characterize as the instrumentalist perspective of religion and political theory. However, even in Marxism, religion plays only a supporting role. It is but one instrument, not even the most central one, by which elites maintain the class structure of industrialized societies. Indeed, Marx's historical analysis emphasizes the emergence of capitalist societies due to separation of religion from politics and economics. Religion in and of itself is not an element of the social structure of capitalist states; rather, it is a convenient weapon that capitalists have adapted from medieval societies and have used efficiently in a new class structure. Marx's followers—Lenin, Trotsky, Mao Zedong, and modern Marxist scholars in the West—have continued this interpretation of religion as an instrument of class domination.

The critique that mainstream political scientists and IR scholars seem to have downplayed the role of religion in world affairs is not a baseless claim. Whether motivated by modernization, secularization, or some other impetus, it seems clear that most IR scholars appeared reticent to highlight the role of religion in their published work. We discuss this point in more detail in chapter 2. For now, however, we can document the marginalization of religion in IR research by examining the scholarly publications on various topics related to world politics. We examined the number of publications with the word combination "religion" and "international relations," "international politics," or "world politics" using two search engines: Google Scholar and Web of Science.

Table 1.1 provides data on the number of studies with the word combinations "religion and world/international relations/politics" in their titles. These studies cover the period 1945–2018. We compare the number of studies with these word combinations across two subperiods: 1945–90 and 1991–2018. Such a comparison requires us to take into account the expansion in the number of publication outlets and the significantly better documentation of publication sources during the latter period. In order to

Table 1.1. Titles on religion and international (world) politics (relations), 1945–2018

Word Combination	1945–1990 (1)		1991–2018 (2)		Pct. Change (3)		Relig./Power Ratio[4]	
	WOS	GS	WOS	GS	WOS	GS	WOS	GS
Religion—International Relations	0	5	67	218	–	4,360%		
Religion—International Politics	1	9	40	111	4,000%	1,230%		
Religion—World Politics	32	58	109	247	309%	341%		
Power—International Relations	53	174	182	828	340%	476%	Inf.	9.16
Power—International Politics	72	216	174	596	242%	276%	16.53	4.46
Power—World Politics	85	207	193	637	227%	308%	1.36	1.38

Note: WOS: Thompson/Reuters Web of Science, GS: Google Scholar.
– Undefined because of division by zero, or division of infinity by a real number.
Relig./Power Ratio is measured by:

$$R/P = \frac{pct.chg(religion_{1 \to 2})}{pct.chg(power_{1 \to 2})}.$$

This is the ratio of the percentage change in the number of religion-titled publications (e.g., religion and world politics) to the percentage change in the number of power-titled publications (e.g., power and world politics).

$$pct.chg = \frac{No. Publications_{1991-2016} - No. Publications_{1945-1990}}{bNo. Publications_{1945-1990}}$$

avoid biases stemming from such changes, we compared these figures to the number of publications using the combination of power and international/world relations/politics over the same periods, which was among the most common combinations in the scholarly literature in the field across both subperiods.

The increase in the number of publications including the word "religion" in their title (combined with various international/world relations/politics) terms is substantially higher than the increase in the number of publications including the concept of "power" in the same combination. The difference between the number of religion-IR combinations and power-IR combinations are of orders of magnitude, as seen by the R/P ratio scores, and not merely a marginal increase in the centrality of religion as a topic of inquiry in the field.[2]

Why were IR scholars reticent to focus on religious factors during the Cold War era? One hypothesis is that prominent IR scholars were inclined, for professional and personal reasons, to concentrate on matters that were consistent with the stated national security policies and preferences of their countries' leadership. This may have also been part of a prevalent academic subculture (Oren 2003). It is possible that "the role of religion in international affairs has not so much been neglected and overlooked as misrepresented and under-theorised" (Pabst 2012, 997). As this table suggests, the post–Cold War era witnessed a dramatic shift in publications about the role of cultural factors, in general, and religious factors, in particular, in world politics. Two watershed events seem to account for this shift: the end of the Cold War and the terrorist attacks on the United States in September 2001.[3] The reality of two superpowers competing in an anarchical international system dominated international thinking during the Cold War, but this was not separate from, or uninformed by, a framing of the competition in terms of a Christian West and an atheistic Communist bloc. The management of this competition was the principal domain of realist and neorealist political thought. The reality of economic and institutional cooperation was the principal domain of liberal and neoliberal institutionalist theorizing. Both schools of thought—paradigms—of IR focused on rational and material motivations of states and on the structural constraints imposed by international anarchy.

When the Eastern European states abandoned communism, and more so after the collapse of the Soviet Union, theorists started asking questions about the kind of structures that would replace bipolarity. Some viewed the world moving toward unipolarity under the "benign" leadership of the United States (Nexon and Wright 2007); others saw the world deteriorating into chaos (Mearsheimer 1990/91). However, a new conception emerged, one that shifted the fundamental paradigm from the Cold War focus centered on the distribution of power in the context of the ideological confrontation between West and East to a revised conception based on cultural divides. Samuel Huntington's clash of civilizations (CoC) thesis contended forcefully that the struggle between superpowers would be replaced by a struggle among civilizations (Huntington 1993, 1996). The fundamental conflicts of interest, perspectives, and ideas embedded in different civilizations had been submerged by the superpower standoff during the Cold War. According to Huntington, civilizational conflicts would rise to the surface and dominate world politics in the post–Cold War era. Religion plays a pivotal role in Huntington's conception of civilizations and civilizational identity. Hence, his clash of civilizations is fundamentally a clash of religions.

Huntington's ideas created a relatively large splash in the scholarly community, but had little effect on the policy community initially. International wars that broke out in the 1990s, such as the first Gulf War, the Armenia–Azerbaijan war, the Kosovo war, and the Indo–Pakistani Kargil war, even though they were wars between states with fundamentally different religious identities, were not interpreted as such. However, the terrorist attack on the World Trade Center and the Pentagon (and the abortive attack leading to the downing of United Flight 93 near Shanksville, Pennsylvania) on September 11, 2001, revived the CoC thesis. Huntington's ideas were adopted by politicians—principally by the neoconservative community then in power in the United States. The revived interest in terrorism in the scholarly community also focused on radical Islam and on the presumed influence of religious ideas and religious institutions on violent behavior. A similar focus emerged in Judaism when a religious fanatic assassinated Israeli prime minister Rabin in 1995, and has continued with the growing violence on the part of radical Jewish settlers against Palestinians in the West Bank over the last two decades.

The convergence of rightist evangelical Christian thought, rightist evangelical groups and think tanks, and neoconservatism in the United States played an important role in the mobilization of public support for the Afghanistan and Iraq wars. It also served an important role in the move to increase the infringement on personal liberties by security institutions via such legislation as the Patriot Act, the formation of detention centers, and the legitimation of torture in interrogations of suspected terrorists. The "global war on terror" was framed—sometimes implicitly and sometimes explicitly—as a war of the Western world against radical Islam. But the distinction between what constituted "radical" Islam and what constituted "nonradical" Islam was vague; and simultaneously terrorism associated with adherents of Western religious traditions was more likely to be associated with the individual actors rather than the religions themselves, as is often done with Islamists. The Brexit referendum in England and the election of Donald Trump as president of the United States in 2016 are also indications of the growing anti-Islamic sentiments in the Western democracies.

The revived intellectual discourse on religion and world politics has both explicit and implicit elements. These are derivative from various theories of IR. The explicit elements consist of such ideas as the CoC thesis, and the focus on the linkages between specific religions (e.g., Islam) and particular violent strategies (e.g., terrorism, suicide bombings). The implicit ideas are embedded in the key tenets of a relatively new paradigm of IR: constructivism. Constructivism highlights issues of identity, ideational factors, and socially constructed realities. It argues that these concepts have a strong impact on world politics. Constructivist scholars do not generally award religion an explicit role in their ideas about what makes IR work. Yet, religious factors are logical derivatives of the ideas emerging from this paradigm.

This survey of historical and intellectual trends linking religion to world politics serves to highlight two important issues. First, it suggests that religious factors played an important role in international history. This was the case even when they were not considered important or central to the development of international interactions. It is certainly the case at present when the significant role of religion in world politics seems to have been vindicated both in theory and in practice. However, we still have a long way to go if we are to gain better knowledge of the kind of roles religious factors play in the formation, evolution, and structure of states, and in the manner in which they interact with each other.

Second, the empirical validity of different ideas about religion in world politics has yet to be established. Many ideas about these issues are just that: abstract notions. We survey below the empirical studies of religion and world politics. This survey shows that many hypotheses that emerge from these abstract theories have not been subjected to empirical analysis. The jury is still out on other ideas that have received relatively serious empirical scrutiny, such as some aspects of the CoC thesis. Empirical scientific research that attempted (or purported) to test the CoC thesis has more often refuted its main empirical claims regarding civilizations per se. At the same time, these studies have simultaneously provided some supporting evidence regarding the increased salience of cultural factors—and religion, in particular—in world politics. We argue that part of the reason for this state of affairs has to do with incomplete or flawed specifications of the theories linking religion to world politics. Another cause of the problems and disagreements in the literature is related to methodology: how these abstract notions are tested; what kind of evidence is brought to bear on these issues; and the kind of methods that are employed to test them.

3. What Is New and Different about This Study?

Our study addresses several questions.

1. What is religion?
    a. How do we classify world religions and religious families?
    b. How do we measure the religious characteristics of states, the religious similarity between states, and the religious characteristics of broader international structures (such as cooperative groups or regional groupings)?
2. What are the religious characteristics of the world?
    a. What are the religious characteristics of the international system as a whole?
    b. What are the religious characteristics of regions?
    c. How have these characteristics changed over time?
3. What role do religious factors play in international conflict?
    a. How do the religious characteristics of states affect their conflict behavior?
    b. How do the religious characteristics of dyads affect the probability and magnitude of conflict between members?
    c. How do the characteristics of the international system and of regional subsystems affect degrees of stability and instability in these structures?
4. What role do religious factors play in various aspects of international cooperation?
    a. How do the religious characteristics of states affect their cooperative practices?
    b. How do the religious characteristics of dyads affect the type, level, and scope of cooperation between members?
    c. What role does religion play in the emergence of cooperative international structures?
    d. What role do religious factors play in shaping cooperation across different regions?

e. How does religion affect levels of cooperation at the global level?
   f. Do religious factors play different roles across different cooperative domains? For example, are religiously similar states more likely to cooperate in security affairs than in economic affairs? Is religion a factor in state membership in international institutions?
5. To what extent do religious factors affect internal conflicts?
   a. Do the religious characteristics of a state affect the likelihood of civil war outbreak? Do they affect the magnitude and severity of civil wars?
   b. Does the religious similarity between a state and its relevant international environment affect the probability of external intervention in civil wars?
   c. Do civil wars represent a domestic variant of the clash of civilizations?
6. Is there a relationship between the religious characteristics of states and the quality of life of their members?
   a. To what extent do religious factors, compared to other factors, play a role in economic, social, political, and cultural development of states?
   b. To what extent does the religious homogeneity or heterogeneity of a society affect the quality of life of its members?
   c. Is there a relationship between the religiosity of a society and the quality of life of its members? Are different religions associated with a better or worse quality of life?

These questions cover rather complex issues. We discuss both the questions and the underlying ideas that drive them in the following chapters. However, in this chapter we provide a brief outline of the structure of the book as it addresses each of these questions. Before doing this, we point out what is special about our study. Given the significant revival of the study of religion and politics, in general, and of religion and world politics, in particular, it is incumbent on any new study such as ours to explain how it differs from, and how it contributes to the literature on these topics. We argue that the present study innovates on at least six dimensions.

1. *Scope.* The scope of the current study is considerably wider than virtually all previous studies analyzing religion and world politics. The same applies to the combination of issues the study covers. While many studies address specific questions similar to those listed above, we know of no study that covers all of these questions. This makes the present study the most comprehensive empirical work on religion and world politics that exists to date. We have cast a wide net of issues connecting religion to various aspects of international and domestic politics because many of these issues are linked. They are connected by common theoretical arguments on how religion affects politics. They are also joined by the fact that international and internal conflict are connected, and by the notion that international conflict and cooperation are interrelated. All these factors also affect human security and social welfare. Because these issues are inherently connected, they may all be affected by religious factors and structures.
2. *Theory.* We offer a novel and integrative theoretical framework for studying the relationship between religion and politics. We integrate different theoretical approaches that address the interrelations between religion and world politics. Our theoretical framework builds on existing theories but also reinterprets them in a way that enables us to develop a more sophisticated understanding of the manner in which religion operates as an identity marker of societies and states, and of the ways in which political elites manipulate religion to advance their aims.
3. *Methodology.* We believe—and will document in the coming chapters—that many of the empirical analyses that address the above topics are methodologically flawed. This raises serious questions about the validity of their substantive inferences. This book is not about political methodology. We relegate the more complex methodological presentations to appendices at the end of the relevant chapters so that readers who wish to focus on the substance can do so without getting bogged down by technical details. Nevertheless, given the complexity of the issues covered in the book, we innovate on a number of levels. First, we employ methods that enable us to overcome the problems that

have plagued existing empirical studies of religion and politics. Second, we rely on network analytic approaches—some of the more sophisticated and innovative methodologies that deal with social interactions—to develop new and more sensitive measures of religious similarity. Third, network analysis allows us to detect and analyze new units of analysis that have not been investigated in previous research on these topics. We refer to these units as "endogenous groups." An endogenous group is an emergent social grouping characterized by highly dense within-group interactions, and by sparse between-group interactions. These groups are "emergent" in the sense that their size, numbers, and memberships are determined by the degree and nature of interactions, not by some—more or less arbitrary—assignment of external observers. Fourth, we conduct an extensive set of robustness checks. Robustness checks are analyses that examine the degree to which substantive inferences from these analyses are sensitive to variations in measures, methods, or specific control variables. Accordingly, such analyses employ different variations of measures, methods, and combinations of variables. Taken together, these methodological innovations help establish far more nuanced and far more reliable inferences about the interrelations between religious factors and political processes.

4. *Multiple Relational Domains.* In contrast to many other studies that cover snippets of the possible linkages between religion and world politics, we offer a more general set of analyses that cover (a) the relationship between religion and international conflict, (b) the relationship between religion and international cooperation—across different cooperative domains, (c) the relationship between religion and domestic conflict, and—an aspect that has not been studied extensively—(d) the relationship between religion, human security, and quality of life in societies. In this respect, the empirical evidence presented in this study goes well beyond most of what has been reported in the speculative or scientific literature on these topics.

5. *Generalizability.* Our analysis covers the entire globe and extends over a period of nearly seventy years. Here, too, we go well beyond what has been studied in much of the literature. Such a broad scope

is possible due to the comprehensive dataset on world religions that we collected. We discuss this dataset in chapter 3. Our study also employs several other datasets on the international relations side of the equation, some of which have been collected by us, and some by other scholars. These datasets enable us to generalize about the various linkages between religion and world politics well beyond what others have done in the past. In this sense, we may be able to provide a broader empirical picture of trends, relationships, and implications than has been available before.

6. *Multiple Levels of Analysis.* One of the difficulties of providing general insights about the interrelations between religion and various aspects of world politics has been the partial nature and limited scope of most empirical studies on these topics. One aspect of this limited scope has been that different studies focused on different units of analysis: some examining the behavior of individual states, others focusing on relationships between pairs of states (dyadic analyses), and very few going beyond this level of analysis. By contrast, we study multiple levels of analysis. Specifically, we consider the behavior, external and internal, of individual states; we examine dyadic interactions; and we study emergent groups (e.g., cooperative communities) and regional politics as well as characteristics of the international system as a whole. This multilevel perspective enables us to examine whether and to what extent empirical results that are observed at one level of analysis generalize to other levels of analysis. This is an important contribution because it provides an assessment of the robustness of the empirical results across levels of analysis.

These innovations enable us to provide a more general, rich, and reliable understanding of how religious factors and processes affect domestic and international political interactions. The picture that emerges from the integrated theoretical perspective and the empirical analyses is far more nuanced but also more interesting than some of the more simplistic approaches that have captured the headlines—in both popular discourses and scholarly journals—thus far. We hope that the combination of theoretical, empirical, and methodological innovations will add an important layer to this discourse. We now turn to a brief overview of the book.

4. Overview of the Book

Chapter 2. This chapter provides a critical review of the literature on religion and world politics. It discusses the key critiques of students of religion and politics. These critiques are aimed primarily at modernization and secularization theories. More broadly, however, students of religion and politics criticize the key paradigms of IR, tying these paradigms to secular conceptions of politics. Our focus in this review is on the key theoretical arguments of the extant literature, linking religious factors to various aspects of politics. The modern literature on religion and international relations has some interesting and innovative ideas. At the same time, however, this literature is marred by controversy, vague conceptions, logical conundrums, and methodological problems. It is also plagued by a disconnect between the more general arguments it makes and the empirical work that builds on it. We find that the ratio of polemical to analytical work in this field is very high. Moreover, the more analytical work—much of which we review in the empirical chapters that follow—is limited in scope, focuses on a restricted set of units, and rests on different theoretical foundations in different contexts. This suggests a need for a more coherent and unifying analytical framework that could yield testable propositions about religion and politics.

Chapter 3. In this chapter we outline the theoretical framework that guides this study. This framework builds on several perspectives that are prevalent in the literature, but it offers a broader set of ideas covering the issues addressed in the key research questions. Our framework focuses on two key elements that link religion to domestic and international political processes: the religious structure of society, and the relations between religious and political institutions. We offer a causal mechanism that links religion to various processes of conflict and cooperation within and among states. This causal mechanism, in our view, is based on the ability and willingness of political elites to use religious values and ideas as political weapons and key instruments of social mobilization. We suggest that political elites seek to maximize political survival—to attain political power if they do not have it (or do not have enough), and to retain their leadership position if they have one. To accomplish this goal, they need to put together and sustain a winning coalition that helps them fend off or defeat internal or external opposition. One of the key tools of political mobilization is the use of religious ideas in support of some policies or in opposition to some enemies.

We argue that political elites will use religion as a tool of political mobilization when they need to and if they can. The manipulation of religious ideas as a strategy of political mobilization is more feasible in some societies, under certain circumstances, and against some enemies. Our theory attempts to spell out the contexts in which such manipulation is more feasible, and under which structural or situational conditions political elites may not be able to use religion to attract support or fend off enemies.

Chapter 4. In this chapter we provide a systematic description of the religious characteristics of the international system since the end of World War II. This draws on our major data collection project, the World Religion Project (WRP). We discuss the underlying logic of this project, starting with the search for a definition of religion and a set of observable indicators and criteria for classifying religions. We then discuss the religious taxonomy that serves as a foundation for the data collection process and explain how we validated this taxonomy before discussing various challenges during the data collection process.

These data allow us to provide systematic evidence on changes in the characteristics of the international system in terms of the rise and decline of religious adherence since 1945. This discussion is all the more important in light of various theories and speculation about trends toward or away from secularization. We provide data on regional distributions of the major world religions and religious families. And, as a prelude to the more analytical discussions in subsequent chapters, we provide some preliminary data on religious similarity across regions and in the international system as a whole.

Chapter 5. This chapter explores the interrelations between religion and international conflict. Our theory suggests that political leaders can—and usually do—use religious factors and identities to mobilize support for foreign adventures. However, the use of religion to support dangerous conflict initiatives is done selectively. Leaders of states that are characterized by high religious homogeneity can and typically do use religion to support conflict against religiously dissimilar adversaries. This is even more common in cases where the political survival of leaders is at risk.

Consequently, the argument that drives the empirical analyses in this chapter centers on several factors. First, the key to understanding the linkage between religious characteristics and conflict rests with the degree of similarity between and among states. At the national level of analysis, the similarity between the religious makeup of the state and its politically relevant environment—the potential or actual enemies of the state—has a significant impact on its conflict behavior. Specifically, states surrounded by religiously similar states are less likely to engage in international conflicts than states that are surrounded by religiously different states. Likewise, religiously similar states are less likely to fight each other than religiously dissimilar states. Further, the level of conflict in religiously heterogeneous regions is significantly higher than in religiously homogeneous ones.

Second, the effect of similarity on conflict is mediated by the relationship between political institutions and religious institutions. We suggest that religion has little or no effect on the conflict behavior of states that separate religious from political institutions. By contrast, we expect religious factors to play a significant role in shaping the conflict behavior of states in which religious and political institutions are closely linked.

We conduct multiple analyses using different specifications of religious attributes and different specifications of conflict behavior. We examine the religion-conflict linkages at different levels of analysis, covering individual state behavior, dyadic conflict, and regional patterns. The results of these analyses offer a nuanced picture of the relationship between religious factors and international conflict behavior.

Chapter 6. Given that states cooperate across a wide array of issue areas, in this chapter we focus on three general dimensions of international cooperation: security, economic, institutional. Our theory suggests that the religious foundations of international cooperation differ significantly across domains. Specifically, states that are religiously similar are more likely to cooperate in security affairs—principally through formal alliances and international security institutions. However, religious similarity plays little or no role in economic transactions across states. We also suggest that there may be fundamental differences between the cooperative choices of "new" states, that is, states that have just gained their independence, and "old" states, that is, states that have been independent for much longer.

This chapter offers a general argument about international cooperation that expands considerably on existing theories on the subject. We develop the concept of "endogenous cooperative communities," that is, emergent groups of highly cooperative states. We show that these communities have a number of structural determinants, and that religious factors play an important role in their emergence and persistence. The results of these analyses enable us to make some interesting—and in some cases, counterintuitive—points about the factors that serve to increase or impede international cooperation in security, economic, and institutional affairs.

Chapter 7. This chapter focuses on the relationship between religious factors and domestic political conflict. It examines the effects of the religious structure of a society on political stability and instability. Our argument is that religious factors play an important role in political stability and instability, but the causal mechanism that determines when, why, and how they do so is more complicated than the notions proffered in previous academic forays into this subject.

Studies of civil violence have focused on religious (or ethnic, which typically subsumes religious, ethnic, racial, and linguistic characteristics) factionalism. Religious factionalism plays an important role in political instability, but not in isolation. Rather, societies that are religiously diverse tend to exhibit instability when religious minorities are discriminated against by the regime, and when they anticipate support from outside groups. This is more likely when neighboring countries are composed of religiously similar groups, and it suggests a link between domestic instability and international conflict. Here, too, we offer a range of evidence based on a large number of empirical analyses supporting these arguments.

Chapter 8. This chapter examines the effects of the religious structure of a society on the quality of life enjoyed by citizens within the state. There is a growing literature on human security. Human security typically refers to the degree to which individuals are free from risks to their lives, property, and welfare, and the extent to which they enjoy fundamental individual and collective liberties. There are different ways to measure human security, and we focus on a modification of the UN Human Development Index (HDI).

Human security encompasses a number of factors ranging from the economic and physical to the spiritual and social. Taken together these factors facilitate and sustain effective and self-fulfilling functioning of individuals in society, and promote efficient social and political institutions. Since religion is a communal institution, and since all religions contain prescriptions for moral and righteous behavior, it is reasonable to expect religion to be one of the factors that promotes and sustains the quality of life.

We argue that it is not religion per se that helps improve or reduce the quality of life in societies. Rather, it is the interaction between religion and politics that is at work. Both religiously heterogeneous and religiously homogeneous societies in which governments place severe restrictions on religious freedoms and activities tend to have far lower levels of quality of life than states in which religious freedom is an important norm. Religious freedom, which includes the freedom not to practice religion, is part of a broader range of values that embraces diversity, tolerance, and pluralism. Religious freedom allows people to act in a relatively free and egalitarian fashion as members of society, hence promoting the general quality of life. In contrast, restrictions on religious beliefs and practices tend to be a source of discontent and frustration, leading to protest and violence or alienation. This tends to have dampening effects on the quality of life. Here, too, we offer original evidence that emerges from a wide range of analyses in support of these arguments.

Chapter 9. This chapter reviews the empirical results and discusses the implications of our analysis for future research and policy. We emphasize the nuanced and complex nature of the relationship between religion and world politics. The relationship between religion and international behavior is not simple and straightforward as anticipated by some of the more central theories on these subjects. We suggest that the religious impact on world politics is neither linear nor simple. This impact is clearly inconsistent with many simplistic notions about religion and international conflict and cooperation that have been propagated in some scholarly and popular writings on these subjects.

For example, we find consistently that religiously similar states are less likely to fight each other while religiously dissimilar ones are more likely to, but that these relationships hold across time and are not more salient in the post–Cold War era as they were during the Cold War era. Thus, we also argue with some degree of confidence that most empirical results challenge the key expectations of the CoC thesis. We also find only weak evidence supporting the hypotheses derived from the primordialist and instrumentalist perspectives, and even more limited evidence for the hypotheses derived from the constructivist perspective.

Perhaps the most salient empirical result across all the empirical analyses of international and internal conflict, international cooperation, and human security is that many notions about the bellicose nature of specific religions and about the cooperative nature of others are misplaced and flawed. *Our results suggest quite decisively that there is no relationship between a specific religion or religious group and conflict or violence. Nor is there any evidence linking a specific religion or religious group to cooperation.* For example, Huntington's popular notion that "Islam has bloody borders" is patently untrue.

We find more concrete and general evidence for the hypotheses derived from our integrative theory of religion and politics. Specifically, we find support for the argument linking social structure and the political circumstances to the ability and willingness of political leaders to use religious factors as an instrument of political mobilization. This combination of social structure, political circumstances, and the manipulation of religion by political leaders applies both to conflict and cooperation. We also find a consistent relationship between religious freedom and human security. Finally, we find that, with a few exceptions, the linkages between religious factors and world politics has not changed substantially over time. The post–Cold War era is not "God's Century," as some authors have claimed.

We believe that some of the negative results—particularly those that challenge the notion of a linkage between a specific religion and conflict, whether external or internal, and between a specific religion and cooperation—offer some policy insights. These, unfortunately, but unsurprisingly, challenge the policy orientation of some key actors in the international system—including those of the United States and some NATO members as well as other states in the Middle East that treat each other as friendly or hostile due to their religious affiliations. We also challenge the false attribution of conflictual or cooperative orientations to states based on the level of religiosity or secularism that characterizes their policies—for both democratic and nondemocratic states. However, most importantly, our key policy recommendation is that policy makers need to be circumspect when it comes to devising policies on presumed linkages between religion and international relations. It is not that such linkages do not exist; rather, it is that they are all but simple and straightforward. On a more general level, attentive publics need to be aware that religion can and often is manipulated by political leaders, sincerely or in a strategic fashion, to advance goals that may have little to do with the content and values of such religions or their adherents.

CHAPTER 2

Scholarship on Religion and World Politics: A Critical Review of the Literature

1. Introduction

This chapter provides a critical review of some of the more central studies connecting religious factors to international conflict and cooperation as well as to matters of domestic political conflict and stability. Much of this literature is quite recent; the study of religion and world politics was a fairly marginal topic in the mainstream IR literature up to the early 1990s. The focus on cultural factors, in general, and on religious factors, in particular, as explanatory variables in the study of conflict, cooperation, and internal political processes did not attract much attention during the Cold War era.

Studies using religion as an explanatory variable of international and domestic processes in the post–Cold War era produced many important insights. However, as is the case with any emerging trend in the study of complex issues, this literature involves multiple polemical and theoretical debates, a great deal of diversity in terms of scope, quality, and rigor, and— as we demonstrate in the following chapters—largely mixed results. Our focus here is on the central theoretical insights into the linkages between religion and international political processes. We discuss the key ideas and identify some logical and methodological weaknesses that characterize this literature. More focused reviews of specific aspects of these linkages—for example, the linkage between religion and international or internal conflict, and between religion and international cooperation—are provided in the analytical chapters on these topics.

Before we go into the substance of this literature, we point out some of its more general features. First, it is important to note that the proliferation of the religion and politics literature has yielded a large number of writings, many of them polemical or works of advocacy. There are numerous calls to introduce more religion-related concepts, theories, and empirical works into the study of IR (Fox and Sandler 2004, Sandal and James 2011, Snyder 2011 and several of the articles in that volume). Other publications debate whether religion influenced the writings of various IR scholars, whether religious factors were missing or present from key paradigms of IR, or whether they could be integrated into one or more of the existing paradigms (e.g., the writings of the authors in Troy 2014, Sandal and James 2011, Snyder 2011). These are useful but do not really add to our knowledge about when, how, and why religious factors help explain key aspects of world politics. They tell us where to look, but they do not tell us how to find what we are looking for. These writings lack a clear theory of the linkages between religious factors and international or domestic political behavior. Nor do they contain empirical results concerning such linkages.

Still other treatises question whether religion can be classified or quantified (Fitzgerald 2011), criticizing both empirical and more philosophical writings on religion and international relations. Other studies question whether it is possible to generalize the concepts of secularism, religiosity, and the relations between religion and state (Hurd 2008), casting them in a postmodernist context where everything is blurred and socially manipulated in a hierarchical power structure. Some may think such polemics are useful and enlightening; we do not. Logically, one cannot use terms like Christianity, Islam, Buddhism, political institutions, power, or state without defining them. Once these terms are defined, the boundaries of such concepts are set. There are things that fall into the parametric structure of the definition, and things that do not. This is inherent in definitions. Such definitions may not establish a metric that has lower and upper bounds (or left and right ends of a continuum), and units of measurement that divide this continuum into parts. They do, however, include a conceptualization that allows distinguishing genders, individuals by family name or school enrollment, streets by street names, and so forth. Logically, one cannot deny something can be done, and at the same time do that very thing one asserts cannot be done simply by using the concepts that one says cannot be used.

Another class of "theories" of religion and politics entails general arguments about how religion enters local, national, regional, and global politics

(Hanson 2006). The general argument is that religion influences politics and societies at all these levels, and that, moreover, religion interacts with four different systems that characterize global politics: the political system, the economic system, the military system, and the communications system. This is an interesting "grand" paradigm. The problem is that it does not allow meaningful deduction of testable propositions about how exactly religion interacts in each of these contexts. There is a sense that the only aspect of religion that allows it to influence those levels of analysis and operate within each of the four systems is identity. This is an important observation, but hardly a novel or surprising one. We will discuss religion as an identity marker at greater length in the next chapter.

Given this discussion of quasi-theoretical polemics in the literature, our biases are rather clear. Our approach is decidedly positivist. We wish to understand if, how, when, and why religious factors affect specific types of international and domestic political processes. We seek guidance in the literature about these issues. If the literature offers some guidance—even if we think there are problems and flaws in certain arguments—then it is useful from a scientific point of view. This principle guides our review. Therefore, we focus in this chapter on theories of religion and international relations that yield testable statements—statements which can be verified or refuted by facts. Such testable statements specify whether, how, when, and why religious factors affect the behavior of states, of groups within states, and of groups of state and nonstate actors.

2. Straw Men in the Religion and Politics Literature—Modernization and the Classical Paradigms of IR

The received wisdom is that IR theory discounted the role of religion as an independent factor in world politics. There is more than a little merit to this claim. The focus in the key theories that dominated the study of IR in the first half of the twentieth century was on concepts such as national self-determination, transparency, and governance through international institutions (idealism), or power, interest, and balance (realism). These ideas were, in many respects, extensions of Enlightenment philosophy—and often had religious justifications and rationales subsumed under considerations of the imperialist project of "Western civilization," which connoted Western Christendom. Idealist and realist approaches contain empirical and analytical adaptations of different philosophical ideas to the realities of the first and second half of the twentieth century (Waltz 1958, 1979), but religious rationales were at times just below the surface (Guilhot 2010).

The second half of the twentieth century was dominated by realist, neorealist, and Marxist theories on the one hand, and by liberal and neoliberal theories on the other. Neorealist theories continued the tradition of classical realism with their focus on power, survival, and top-down systemic approaches that left little room for presumably nonsystemic forces such as culture or religion. Marxist approaches were avowedly non-religious or even anti-religious, and except for Gramscian approaches (e.g., Gill 1993) were largely dismissive of cultural factors even with the emergence of cultural theses of anticolonial struggles epitomized in Cabral's (1972) analyses. Mainstream liberal theorists also marginalized the cultural dimension of world politics, focusing on economic interests and institutional structures (Keohane 1984). When they did talk about culture, this was typically restricted to democratic values and norms (Maoz and Russett 1993, Russett and Oneal 2001, Doyle 1986). As Shah and Philpott (2011) argue, modern IR theory was (and still is) fundamentally secular.[1]

Even more to the point, the claim of widespread acceptance of modernization arguments among IR theorists prophesizing a secular decline in religion in world politics is overstated at minimum. This point is typically accompanied by the ubiquitous allusion in the literature to Berger's (1968) contention in a *New York Times* article that by "the twenty-first century, religious believers are likely to be found in small sects, huddled together to resist a worldwide secular culture." His renunciation of this view thirty years later, presumably demonstrates the "resurgence" of religion as a factor in IR (Philpott 2002, Shah and Philpott 2011, Toft, Philpott, and Shah 2011, Fox 2015). Shah and Philpott (2011, 24) are hardly alone among scholars of religion and politics in asserting that Berger's original contention "spoke for intellectuals across the West." Absent from many of these analyses is consideration that even as modernization became prominent, a rival "modernization revisionism" (Huntington 1971, 293) emerged from arguments of Samuel Huntington, Reinhard Bendix, S. N. Eisenstadt, Joseph Gusfield, Milton Singer, and Lloyd and Suzanne Rudolph, among others.

Randall (1999, 45) notes that "it was modernization theory, or a particularly crass version of it, which encouraged expectations that the general salience of religion in our lives and more specifically its place in politics would diminish with progressive modernization and notably with secularization and rationalization." However, modernization revisionists challenged or rejected such claims. For example, they rejected the simplistic dichotomy between "tradition" and modernity, which suggested a zero-sum relationship between the two, recognizing that "traditional institutions adapt to and co-exist with modern institutions, specifically the nation-state," while "the process of modernization may actually revitalize dormant traditional institutions and practices" (Randall and Theobald 1985, 35).

Revisionist scholars challenged the teleological assumptions of the modernization literature that assumed "underdeveloped" states were compelled to "modernize" to a Western ideal. Haynes (2008, 24) agrees that "modernization revisionism not only exposed early modernization theorists' simplistic and ethnocentric assumption about tradition and modernity but also underlined that various so-called 'traditional' phenomena," including religion, "continued to have developmental salience over time." In fact, "the impact of modernization has been uneven; in more remote and traditional communities religious feelings and practice continue largely unchanged." In some cases "rather than straightforwardly undermining religion, modernization has served in some ways to enhance its relevance" (Randall 1999, 48–49).

Generally, the modernization/secularization view of religious decline was often inattentive to the multidimensionality of religious adherence. Predicting a decline in the influence of religious institutions does not necessitate decline in the cognitive, normative, or experiential dimensions of religion. These informal dimensions of religion allowed religious influence to persist in "modern" societies (Ireland 1988). No later than 1971, political scientists such as Huntington (1971, 297) were asserting that "each of the assumptions which underlay the original, simple image of modernization could also be called into question," yet the view persists among many scholars of religion and IR that modernization/secularization arguments held sway over the field.

Despite the challenges to modernization/secularization theories in the sociological, political development, and dependency theories, modernization theory has become a favorite straw man of the religion and politics literature in the last two decades. Almost any recent study that seeks to establish a connection between religion and political processes challenges the modernization thesis. A typical example is Shah's (2012, 3) argument:

> Much classical thinking and practice [in politics] is . . . concerned with policing and strengthening the fence between two worlds. The first world is the "secular" and "public" world in which international actors . . . are presumed to make rational choices in the pursuit of political and economic power. The second world is the "spiritual" and "private" world in which religious actors—everything from church hierarchies to clerical councils to violent organizations such as Al Qaeda and Hizbollah—are presumed to make faith-based choices in the pursuit of nonrational or irrational goals. . . . [T]he factual assumption about these two worlds is that they are two separate universes, with little or no mutual contact or interaction.

Fox and Sandler (2004, 12) make an even more radical claim about modernization and religion:

> Ironically, this reassessment of the role of religion in society has resulted in an argument that is nearly exactly opposed to the argument made by modernization and secularization theory: *modernization, rather than causing religion's demise, is responsible for its resurgence.* . . . While modernization and secularization theorists posited that modernity had made religion a primordial remnant that was fading away as an important social and political factor, the central argument of this reassessment is that modernity is increasing the role of religion in society and politics. [Italics added for emphasis.]

Fox and Sandler argue that peoples' expectations emanating from modernization processes toward greater welfare, peace, and security were largely unfulfilled. This disappointment with modernization was particularly acute in the third world. In these countries, unfulfilled expectations were converted into basic—or even fundamentalist—religious beliefs and practices. The growing opposition to colonialism and imperialism—and its replacement by authoritarianism and oppression—also led people to return to their religious roots. Western secular ideas were associated with imperialism, while religious beliefs were again associated with tribal, national, or communal roots. Finally, modernization has "allowed both the state and religious institutions to increase their spheres of influence, thus resulting in more clashes between the two" (p. 12).

Similarly, Philpott (2007) and Toft, Philpott, and Shah (2011, 9–19) also make far-reaching claims about the role of religion in politics. Philpott (2007, 505) argues that "religion has waxed in its political influence over the past generation in every region of the globe except perhaps Western Europe." Toft, Philpott, and Shah (2011, 3) contend: "Earlier confined to the home, the family, the village, the mosque, synagogue, temple, and church, religion has come to exert its influence in parliaments, presidential palaces, lobbyist offices, campaigns, militant training camps, negotiation rooms, protest rallies, city squares, and dissident jail cells."

Hurd (2008, 134) also argues that secularism has failed, and that religion has experienced a significant resurgence over the past few years.

> For at least three reasons, it has now become impossible to maintain that religion is irrelevant to international outcomes, as most conventional accounts would have it. First, the United States and others have had a hard time imposing their vision of secular democracy around the world. Second, there has been the advent of a U.S. foreign policy model in the George W. Bush administration that is officially secular but inspired by a kind of Christianity. Third, over the past several decades there has been a rise in religious movements and organizations with broad bases of national and transnational influence.

Several things can be deduced from these statements. First, they rest on a temporal view of the role of religion in politics. These arguments suggest that religious factors became more important in both international and domestic politics—as well as in modern theories of IR—recently much more than they had been in the past. Several authors who have suggested that religious actors and religious matters can be relegated to the private or subpolitical domains, have come to recant their previous arguments (e.g., Henir 2012). Others (e.g., Hurd 2008, 2012) claim that secularism was a social construction of a political and intellectual elite that dominated both the practice and study of world politics in the Western world. In fact, this dominant view of world politics was always contested and challenged in other parts of the world and in other scholarships, but these latter challenges became prominent only in the post–Cold War era.

Second, another assertion is that religious factors and religious actors have always played an important role in practical world politics. Yet, the key scholarly paradigms of IR (and consequent empirical investigations) have largely ignored them. Even key proponents of these paradigms seem to acknowledge this point. Robert Keohane, a central theoretician of neoliberalism, argued: "The attacks of September 11 [2001] reveal that *all mainstream theories of world politics are relentlessly secular with respect to motivation.* They ignore the impact of religion despite the fact that world-shaking political movements have so often been fueled by religious fervor."[2] Snyder (2011), a realist theorist, makes a similar argument.

Third, some argue that IR theories have acknowledged the role of religious factors in shaping politics, but this was buried or rather not taken seriously in approaches such as classical realism (Henne and Nexon 2014, 165–66). In the same volume, Mollov (2014) suggests that Morgenthau's "liberal" realism was influenced by his Jewish heritage. Likewise, Carlson (2014) points out the "Christian" nature of Reinhold Niebuhr's realism. The common thread of these arguments is that even when a theory is presented as fundamentally secular, its insights are influenced by the religious beliefs of its authors. A related argument asserts that mainstream IR of the postwar era was heavily influenced by and attentive to issues related to religion. Guilhot (2010, 224) argues that "while nobody would deny that international relations theory is a secular social science . . . the search for a theory of international relations was permeated by theological themes." Not only do a number of IR scholars employ "religious metaphors" and "eschatological or theological references" in analyzing "core features" of world politics (e.g., "Wizards of Armageddon," "Theologians of War," "New Leviathan") but also such "references are too pervasive, too ubiquitous to be treated as mere coincidences. They point at a theological substratum that once provided an explicit background against which a number of central concepts of IR theory resonated" (p. 224).

As a result, the scholarship on religion and international relations holds to the view that IR ignored the role of religion in world affairs, but this is more apparent than real. Nonetheless, there is a persistent view that secularization was a largely unquestioned "sacred canopy" over postwar IR.[3] While this may have been evident in sociology, it was much less evident in IR, and even less in the subfield of comparative politics, which was home to the modernization arguments in political science.

On another plane, the prevalence of religious influences in international affairs was evident among policy makers and analysts even if their language often adopted the more ideological and basic force arguments of the national security regimes in Western states and their Cold War adversaries. Preston (2012, 7) asserts that religion is the "missing link, a vital but unrecognized, even undiscovered," aspect of US foreign relations. It was not the only factor, but at times "it was a critically important factor; other times, it played a relatively minor role." Religion "acted as the conscience of American foreign relations;" and popular religious pressure led foreign policy elites to "merge the moralism and progressivism of religion with the normally realist mindset of international politics." Moreover, "Protestant exceptionalism helped breed American exceptionalism and led to a consistent belief in America as a chosen nation and Americans as a chosen people" (p. 13), which inspired and served to justify American imperialism and interventions abroad. Similarly, Muehlenback (2012, viii) asserts that "religion played a significant role in determining the scope and stratagems of the Global Cold War," though he is careful to add that "it was a factor in the Cold War, not *the* factor." [emphasis added]

We do not seek to adjudicate among these interpretations of the clash between modernization theories and studies on religion and politics. We agree, as we showed in chapter 1, that the role of religion in accounts of modern world politics took off after the end of the Cold War and peaked following the terrorist attacks of September 11, 2001. Our focus is not on this debate, but rather, we focus on the extent that the extant literature on religion and world politics challenges the key assumptions of the central paradigms of IR.

First, religious "theories" challenge the notion that states are the principal actors in world politics. This notion is basic to realism, but liberalism and constructivism abandoned it long ago. The key point of religious theories is that—in addition to the type of nonstate actors that are the focus of liberal or constructivist approaches—such as international organizations, multinational corporations, or nongovernmental organizations—we should focus on religious actors. These actors can be formal institutions such as the Catholic Church, or informal and diffuse transnational groups like Al Qaeda, local religious leaders, or cults. These actors can act within or across states. Ignoring them and their impact on politics comes, according to these theories, at great cost.

Second, religious theorists share the constructivist criticism of the "materialist" focus of the realist and liberal paradigms. The argument that national and international processes are driven by material interests is empirically and theoretically tenuous. Constructivists focus on ideational factors and identity without always specifying the exact nature of these factors. By contrast, scholars of religious politics emphasize the role of religion as an identity marker of groups, communities, and even nations. Religion is also seen as a socially constructed phenomenon that defines individual and collective belief systems (Fox and Sandler 2004, 176–77; Sandal and James 2011, 6–7; Hurd 2008, 149–50).[4] The idea that both constructivist and religionist scholars advance is that individuals, communities, and political organizations, such as states, are driven by their belief systems. Religion, according to this conception forms a central, ideational factor distinct from material factors such as power, interests, or wealth.

Third, some religious scholars challenge the distinction (or dichotomy) between religion and secularism (Hurd 2008; Fitzgerald 2011). Such a distinction, attributed primarily to secularist theories, creates a false impression that religious actors and political actors are separate entities, or, alternatively, that secularists imply that religion is inexorably detached from politics. This may be the case in some places and it may be true for some periods. However, in a more general sense this is a flawed dichotomy. It helped sustain paradigms in IR that focused on secular, material, and "objective" factors rather than on subjective (or intersubjective) ideational sources of national and international behavior.

These criticisms seem quite fair. Most of the targets of such critiques are the central paradigms of IR. Yet similar arguments can be leveled against key theories of domestic politics, like various versions of political development, theories of regime change and regime persistence, and so forth. But this raises several questions. If we are to account for religious actors, incorporate religious ideas, and we are to avoid the religious-secular dichotomy in explaining international phenomena and processes, then what theoretical ideas follow? How do religious actors operate? How do religious ideas and identities influence different aspects of world politics? What is the relationship between religious actors, religious ideas, and religion-state continua and international relations? Here is where the essence of religion and politics theories needs to be examined.

3. Central Themes of the Religion and IR Literature

Most of the studies reviewed in this chapter make a key substantive argument: religious factors have a profound impact on world politics. What that impact is and how it works are less clearly specified, however. Most importantly, as we argue below, very few of these studies offer a coherent theory of religion and international relations. This is evident when we compare the polemics about religion and politics in the literature to the more systematic arguments that are derived from the theoretical writings. In particular, it is hard to find a comprehensive framework that contains a body of specific and refutable propositions about such things as the relationship between (a) religion and international conflict, (b) religion and international cooperation, (c) religion and internal political order, and (d) religion and human security.

In most cases, when scholars attempt to articulate some potentially testable arguments about the relationship among religious actors, religious ideas, and domestic or international relations, the evidence they provide for these arguments is primarily anecdotal. These anecdotal pieces of evidence focus on an important but selective sample of cases, mostly from the so-called third world. Little systematic quantitative evidence exists, and that which does suffers from significant methodological problems. And when we find examples of quantitative "tests" of such hypotheses, these often are based on truncated and biased samples, and/or on tenuous empirical assumptions.

We document these arguments by discussing some of the central themes of this literature. Fox and Sandler (2004) offer a comprehensive argument for the incorporation of religion into the study of world politics. They suggest that religion can serve three principal functions in international relations. First, it can provide ideational legitimacy for certain foreign policy actions. It allows policy elites to "legitimate" both violent actions and peaceful ones. Second, religion is a communal identity marker. Specifically, within a primordial context, religion can provide a communal raison d'être—a reason for being. It can justify the claim of a community to territory, resources, and holy spaces by uniting individuals into defined communities. Third, it can provide the key foundations and elements of political belief systems, thus affording both policy makers and mass movements normative justifications for action or inaction. People—whether they are political leaders or followers—may choose actions because they are consistent with their religious beliefs, or refrain from those that contradict the normative dictates of their religion.

Fox and Sandler provide numerous examples to support their claim, including references to empirical studies of inter-ethnic conflict and a detailed case study of the Israeli–Palestinian conflict. However, we are left with a general argument of the underlying importance of religion, but we do not get from this study a set of specific hypotheses about how, when, and under what conditions these forms of linkage between religion and politics translate into specific actions, processes, and outcomes. The discussion of the Israeli–Palestinian conflict is illuminating, but it could be presented in alternative terms couched in secular theories of nationalism, and the result would be equally convincing.

Another theoretical treatment that addresses multiple aspects of the relationship between religion and politics is provided by Toft, Philpott, and Shah. Philpott (2007) focuses on the relationship between religion and democratization. In the broader work, Toft, Philpott, and Shah (2011) apply similar ideas to a wider array of political processes including civil war and terrorism.

The puzzle that these authors address concerns the dual role of religion in domestic conflict and cooperation. Religious actors can be a powerful force in the struggle for democratization. But religious actors can also be a powerful force pushing theocracy or authoritarianism. Likewise, religious actors can have a strong pacifying presence, but there are, at the same time, religious actors that advocate violence and practice terrorism.

Their theory of religion and politics is based on two principal factors: religious ideology (or what Philpott [2007, 507] calls "political theology") and the relationship between religious and political institutions ("differentiation"). The political theology of a given religion can be more or less active, or an influential part of the religion. In some cases, the political theology requires religious principles to influence legal, social, political, and economic affairs. In other cases, the political theology may be minimalist in nature—requiring basic liberties or spaces for religious practice. When the political theology focuses on moderation and openness, religion can be a force for democratization, civil liberties, and cooperation. However, when the political theology is introverted, legitimizing violent behavior to promote religious values, and when it preaches the domination and supremacy of religious principles over civil ones, then religion can be a force for autocracy, terrorism, and violence.

The relationship between religion and politics can also vary considerably, according to this framework. On one end of this continuum, religion and politics can be one and the same, or very closely linked. On the other end, these two sets of institutions represent different and largely separate realms. In the real world, however, relations between religious and political institutions are distributed widely along this continuum. This relationship also can be differentiated in terms of the extent to which religious and political actors accept an existing level of separation/integration between religious and political or legal institutions. At one extreme, this relationship can be consensual; both religious actors and political actors are perfectly happy with the existing state of affairs. At the other extreme, this state of affairs may be conflictual. Either religious actors want to change the existing degree of independence (that is, to exert more influence on political processes), or political actors want to increase the separation between religion and politics. Consensual relations typically sustain the political status quo. Conflictual relations induce pressure for change that may involve instability and violence (Toft, Philpott, and Shah 2011, 39–47). The combined effect of political theology and the independence of religious actors from political institutions influences the religious actors' activities and political outcomes (Toft, Philpott, and Shah 2011, 46).

Nexon's (2009) study of the role of religion in the Reformation and the Thirty Years' War offers a slightly different theoretical perspective on the role of religion in international relations. Nexon argues that religion can become a transnational movement that sweeps both public and political leaders into processes that revolutionize politics. Specifically, in the context of the medieval structure of power, the Reformation triggered several processes that undermined the existing social and political structure of Europe. Specifically, the transnational nature of the religious revival during the Reformation

1. converted localized resistance into a cross-local force for rebellious mass mobilization;
2. undermined the ability of rulers to use discrete identities of local communities as a mechanism of support and loyalty;
3. created new opportunities for intermediaries to enhance their autonomy vis-à-vis dynastic rulers;

4. introduced new trade-offs (or conflicts) between political and religious objectives; and
5. created new channels for the "internationalization" of domestic disputes.

The interplay between religious actors and political actors—that can range from conflict to close collaboration—defines the structure of relations between and within political units. This relationship is a central aspect of the causal mechanism that drives political processes. The role of religious actors—as transnational movements—in Philpott (2007), Toft, Philpott, and Shah (2011) and Nexon's (2009) theses—is central to political processes such as conflict and cooperation. The irony is, of course, that while Protestantism posed a transnational challenge not only to the Catholic Church but also to different local rulers in Europe, the emergent structure from the Reformation was a state system dominated by political elites, not a group of theocratic states (arguably with the prominent exception of Henry VIII's establishment and rulership of the Church of England).

There are some insightful ideas in these frameworks. They offer a lens into the goals and belief systems of religious actors and into the ways they manage (accept or challenge) relations with political institutions. Yet, politicians do not play a key role in their theory. Religious actors are certainly important, and religion-state interactions feature as a key component in most theories of religion and politics. However, they provide little evidence that the leading actors are religious groups or institutions. They largely ignore the power of political actors. Some religious actors with a militant theology who are oppressed by states may want to act forcefully to change the status quo. However, even though they may have a great deal of legitimacy and influence at the grassroots level—such as the Muslim Brotherhood had and (possibly) continues to have in Egypt—the ability to convert their will to action is rather limited if political elites control effective means of coercion and monopolize the use of force.

When religious actors have taken over political institutions and political power, they have become—for all practical purposes—political actors. Such actors, ostensibly guided by religious beliefs, are no different from other political actors. They are eager to retain power, deal with internal and external constraints on the exercise of power, and tolerate or negotiate with enemies. Like all other non-religious political actors, they use whatever instruments they have at their disposal, religious or non-religious, to accomplish their goals. The behavior of Iranian leaders is a prime example of this process. Ayatollah Khomeini's Iran incited Iraqi Shi'ites to rise up against the "infidel" regime of Saddam Hussein. It labeled the United States the "Big Satan" and Israel the "Little Satan." However, once the Iran–Iraq war broke out, it had no compunction about reaching a deal with both "Satans" to purchase TOW antitank missiles, to help it fight the Iraqis. The current Iranian regime—still an Islamic Republic, unofficially run by Supreme Leader Ali Khamenei—again reached an agreement with the United States and other powers that was supposed to limit (or suspend) its ability to develop a nuclear weapon system, thus enabling a host of economic interactions with the Western world.

The focus on religious actors also discounts the importance of non-religious actors outside formal political institutions. Organized groups can take on a wide array of forms. People may be bound together by economic interests, political ideologies, geographic attachments, and so forth. These bonds may overlap or trump religious affinities. Regardless of the political theology or independence of religious actors, non-religious actors may compete not only with political actors but also with other social groups and institutions. Political elites facing internal or external threats may manipulate such competitions to fit their own goals. Here, too, Egyptian politics following the ouster of Hosni Mubarak are a case in point. The electoral victory of the Muslim Brotherhood and the Salafi party in the parliamentary and presidential elections of 2011 and 2012 resulted in a conflict between these religious parties, liberal groups, and the military. The military took advantage of large-scale demonstrations by liberal groups opposing the imposition of Sharia law as part of the Egyptian constitution to reestablish an authoritarian system (Brownlee, Masoud, and Reynolds 2015).

The focus on religious actors also obscures the fact that many states are religiously diverse, with a multitude of religious actors. In some cases these actors may work in harmony, but in many other cases they actually compete with one another. Religious competition often becomes zero-sum, especially in diverse societies where each group wants to impose its rules, norms, and beliefs on others. This is the essence of the work on religious discrimination (Fox 2016; Grimm and Finke 2011).

An important approach that actually addresses these issues is the religious economy model (Innaccone 1990, 1998; Gill 2001, 2007, 2013).

This model analogizes religious activity to economic activity. Religious institutions are seen as equivalent to economic firms, and their activity as principally self-interested activity. From the perspective of individuals, religion fulfills some fundamental needs. It offers answers to basic philosophical questions and dilemmas, and it also offers communal participation and association. This explains why individuals (a) allocate time and resources to religious activity—sometimes at the expense of activities that can produce material benefits, and (b) follow religious regulations.

Religious institutions are also utility-maximizing organizations. The function of these institutions is to provide adherents with responses to basic philosophical (but also practical) questions and dilemmas. But these institutions must also sustain themselves. Their well-being and prosperity is a function of the willingness of adherents to contribute funds and to follow their directives. Religious institutions use rules, rituals, and principles as mobilization devices, and as strategies to overcome free-riding dilemmas (in which people benefit from "free" public goods, without contributing to the maintenance of these goods). Strict rules and regulations, and stringent religious rituals "dissuade free-riders from joining the organization and diluting its resources. Moreover, because strict religions tend to dissuade participants from partaking in activities outside the religious organization, more time and monetary resources can be directed toward the group goal" (Gill 2001, 131).

The religious economy model treats religion as a market and focuses on the relationship between religious freedom and political, social, and economic development (Gill 2007, 2013). By operating within a competitive market structure, religious groups and religious organizations work to attract membership and sustain their social and economic position. However, governments are also actors in that market. They can work with or against certain religious institutions. They can allow the religious market to be open and competitive by guaranteeing and safeguarding religious freedom; they can regulate religious activity so that they can monitor it more efficiently; they can display favoritism toward a subset of religions or religious organizations and discriminate against others; or they can curtail religious activity across the board. Gill (2007, 2013) argues that the key motivation of political leaders is to ensure, extend, and safeguard their political survival. Religious actors and politicians play in the same marketplace—both try to mobilize, influence, and serve people. They can cooperate, or they can compete. Gill (2007, 53–57) suggests some conditions that affect the degree of religious freedoms or restrictions in a political and religious competitive market. The relationship between political institutions and religious groups therefore defines the ability of these groups to operate, and, as Philpott and his associates (Philpott 2007; Toft, Shah, and Philpott 2011) argue, determine to a large extent the cooperative or conflictual relations between religion and state.

The central argument of the religious economy model is that a competitive religious marketplace—aided by high levels of religious freedom—contributes to general aspects of the quality of life. It has a positive effect on economic development, democracy, and, indirectly, on other aspects of human development such as health indicators, education, and gender equality. By contrast, religious hegemony aided by government discrimination and a high level of cooperation between religious and political institutions typically reduces the level of human development. Specifically, Gill (2007) argues that religious hegemony typically drives religious actors to strive for high levels of government regulation, whereas religiously diverse societies will strive toward religious freedom.

The focus of the religious economy model is on the relations between religion and state; therefore it has little to offer when it comes to IR. However, it has important implications for theories of religion and politics. We return to some of these ideas in the next chapter. Nevertheless, the focus on the relationship between religion and state is at the center of Jonathan Fox's work on religion and politics. Based on a comprehensive dataset on religion discrimination—which explores a wide array of relationships between political and legal institutions, on the one hand, and religious groups, on the other hand—his work explores systematically the causes and consequences of such relations. The principal importance of this work lies in the descriptive aspects of the data. From a more analytical perspective, the studies focusing on the relations between religious discrimination and civil war are methodologically problematic, and any inferences drawn from these studies are dubious. We discuss these studies in more detail in chapter 7. Here, however, we point out the general ideas driving these analyses.

Fox (2004a, 2012c) lists several factors that affect the relationship between religion and civil war. The first is a primordial argument. Religion is an integral part of a community's identity. As such, communities define friends and foes on the basis of religious similarities or differences. Groups that reside within the same region that differ significantly in terms of their religion are likely to view each other with suspicion and mistrust. The pressure to separate and govern themselves is apt to increase. This becomes all the more important if one group feels discriminated against by the political elites. Such discrimination fuels its suspicion and sense of frustration and drives it to rebel.

The second element of this religion and civil war model centers on the notion of religion as a belief system. It is not clear how this argument is different from the basic primordial argument, but Fox (2004a, 18–22) argues that perceptions of threat to religious values (including threats to holy places, Hassner 2009)—threats to certain rituals and practices, or general threats to religion emanating from secularization, modernization, or globalization trends) can affect group mobilization around this common threat. If this threat is seen as associated with government policies, rebellion may arise.

Third, Fox (2004a, 2012a), like Toft, Philpott, and Shah (2011) (as well as the sources he cites therein as specific examples), argues that religious institutions offer a source of legitimacy and mobilization, but this can work both as an engine for change (e.g., via rebellion) or for sustaining a status quo that may be authoritarian, exploitative, and abusive. There is no clear indication when religious institutions inspire mobilization for change and when they legitimize a given political, social, or economic status quo.

Finally, fundamentalism is typically a source of conflict. Religious fundamentalism is a particular source of violence because fundamentalists typically embrace violence as a legitimate method, both against different religious groups and against moderates of their own religious group. Also, the distinction between combatant and noncombatant does not pose a moral dilemma to fundamentalists. Thus, with the rise of fundamentalist elements among religious groups—typically inspired by religious leaders or religious institutions—the likelihood of a resort to violence of any kind increases.

These ideas offer interesting insights into possible linkages between religion and civil war, but, as Fox (2004a) shows, religious factors (e.g., religious grievances) do not have an independent effect on the attributes of civil wars. Rather, it is only the combination of religious grievances and demands for separatism—which may be due to economic causes (not included in his models)—that have a significant impact on rebellion (not clearly defined in any meaningful operational manner). That, on top of some fairly serious methodological issues with Fox's statistical analyses (which we discuss in chapter 7), casts serious doubt on the validity of this argument.

Threats to belief systems as a cause of civil uprising might be important if there were a clear way of separating religious grievances from political and/or economic grievances. These combinations are often prevalent in societies characterized by substantial communal inequalities, and it is unclear whether the spark that ignites a civil uprising is religious, social, economic, or a combination of these. Hassner's (2009) insightful analysis of sacred spaces suggests that threat to control of such spaces may be a critical issue and can cause punctuated mobilization as certain policies and events pose a threat to the ability of a community to worship via a certain holy site. There are two problems with these insights, however. First, the generalizability of these concepts beyond a few—well-selected—cases is quite limited. What constitutes a threat in these terms is rather subjective, typically mediated by other factors (for example, how religious leaders interpret a given policy or act), and varies from one case to another, from one religion to another, and from one policy to another.

For example, Hassner (2009) argues persuasively that both the Palestinians and the Israelis have reacted violently to threats to their holy sites due to actions of the other side. Jerusalem has been a hotbed of trouble in this regard. However, Jerusalem is not only the third-holiest site in Islam and the holiest site to Judaism but also contains some of the holiest sites to Christians. However, the Christian world did not display any kind of significant religious reaction to the transfer of power in Jerusalem after the 1967 war. Nor did the Christian world have any religious reaction to the various ideas about partitioning Jerusalem in the context of an Israeli–Palestinian peace settlement.

Consequently, the likelihood of finding a common denominator of "threats to religious values" across situations, religions, governments, or policies is rather low. But without such a common denominator, measurement and systematic analysis may be difficult to carry out. Thus, credible insights about how groups react to threats to religious values are rather limited.

Second, the theoretical argument is rather specific to domestic conflict. When diverse religious communities are governed by political leaders or institutions affiliated with a specific religion, competition over religious laws, religious customs, and sovereignty over holy places is apt to arise. However, how does this generalize to relations among states? How does it affect international conflict and cooperation? How do threats to religious beliefs affect conflict and cooperation among different states? These writings do not offer meaningful answers to these questions.

Perhaps the most interesting effort to provide a theory of religion and world politics is the work of Sandal and Fox (2013). In this research, the authors suggest a strategy for integrating religious factors into the traditional paradigms of world politics. They discuss several avenues by which religion affects international relations. They also tie these to more conventional ideas about the way international politics operate. Their list includes several issues:

1. *Religious worldviews.* A worldview constitutes a set of principles consisting of a descriptive theory of how the world works and of normative principles that guide the believer's behavior given such a theory. Religious worldviews are grounded in beliefs about the role divine authority has granted to a certain individual and community. This role defines what such an individual or community seeks to accomplish and the strategies and behaviors they can and should pursue to accomplish that goal. A religious worldview can be part (or the whole) of a leader's belief system or a collective socially constructed belief system of one or more community.
2. *Religious legitimacy.* Following Hurd (1999), they define legitimacy as "the normative belief by an actor that a rule or an institution ought to be obeyed." They argue that religion is a principal source of legitimacy for actions in the international system. Principles that define permissible or unacceptable international behavior are often derived from basic religious directives. Hence, they serve to define both internal and international norms.
3. *Religious states.* States ruled by religious principles and doctrines structure their internal legal and political system according to theological dictates. They also fashion their foreign policy according to those dictates. Religious states identify friends or foes in terms of whether or not these actors follow similar or different religious dictates. They act to protect or support religious communities that share the same beliefs in other states. And they often seek to spread their religious beliefs and practices beyond their borders.

4. *Nonstate religious actors.* Religious institutions may have global or regional reach capacity, and serve as a source of mass mobilization for certain policies or ideas. As such they serve to support or constrain political behavior beyond a single state or region. Substate religious actors such as religious terrorist organizations have engaged in both mobilization and action across international borders. In the post–September 11, 2001 period they have substantially influenced the international behavior of both nation-states and international organizations.

5. *Local religious issues that propagate across borders.* These involve internal conflicts with a religious bent in one country that spill over to the relations of that country with other countries or communities. These religious issues may also spill over to other types of issues—social, political, or economic—whereby religious-based conflict may have economic, political, or social implications.

6. *Transnational religious movements.* Religious fundamentalism can form movements and actors that spread across multiple borders. The same may apply to religious discourses on matters of human rights, the management of sites that are holy to several religions or religious groups within a single religion, and missionary action across international borders and communities.

7. *Religious identity.* Identity defines an actor's (person, community, or country) inherent nature with respect to its religious beliefs (both the type of religion and the degree or strength of religious adherence). But it also defines the relative position of that actor vis-à-vis other actors. As such, it defines the affinity or suspicion that an actor harbors towards other actors in terms of religious similarity or dissimilarity.

These are interesting and important ideas about religion's influence on international relations. Sandal and Fox also do a creditable job in tying these factors to key elements in a number of central IR theories, including classical realism and neorealism, neoliberalism, the English School, and constructivism. In some cases these efforts are insightful and surprisingly successful. In other cases, especially with respect to classical realism, neorealism, and neoliberalism, these efforts seem forced and superficial. Nevertheless, this work is an important, albeit undercited, effort to integrate religious issues and themes into the more traditional IR discourse.

There are several problems with this work that limit its usefulness as a foundation for theorizing about religion and international behavior. First, like other studies that seek to insert religion into largely "secular" theories, their focus is on religious issues, actors, and beliefs. As such they tend to discount the role of religion as a political instrument, and the manipulation of religious ideas and beliefs by both political and religious actors. Clearly, religion is an important ideational glue, binding together people into cohesive communities. However, it is not an autonomous one. Religion has always been an instrument of power and mobilization.

In some cases, political and religious leaders are guided by beliefs based on scriptures, religious dictates, fatwas, and the like. These beliefs, as Sandal and Fox (2013) argue persuasively, shape their treatment of their own people and of other people, institutions, or countries. At the same time, many political or religious leaders manipulate religious beliefs and ideas to mobilize support for actions that are designed to serve rather "secular" goals, such as ensuring security, acquiring or sustaining power, accumulating wealth, or eliminating enemies. A key question arises as to when international behaviors, norms, or institutions are motivated by genuine religious beliefs, and when religion is an instrument that serves to advance "secular" goals. Not only do Sandal and Fox (2013) offer little insight into this cardinal question, but they sidestep it completely.

Second, religion is discussed in terms that almost black box it completely. Religious worldviews, identities, legitimacies, and state or nonstate actors are certainly important factors. They need to be considered as important factors in both domestic and international discourses and interactions. Yet, almost each religion, and almost at each stage of its history, is a hub of multifaceted ideas and debates. For example, what constitutes a Christian worldview is highly debatable. Is it the creationist theory embedded in evangelical Protestantism that the world was formed by God some 5,700 years ago, or is it the allegorical interpretation of creation of Catholicism that affords some acceptance of Darwinian evolution?

Which interpretation of Islam is the right one? Is it one advocated by groups such as ISIS and Al Qaeda that views concepts of jihad as a holy war that legitimizes any form of violence against infidels and internal enemies? Or is jihad taken to be a concept of cultural war in which Islam is spread and implemented through education, persuasion, and charity? As we discuss in chapter 4, one of the observable features of all religions has to do with their historical evolution. This history often involves conflicts between communities that belong to the same (macro) religion. Such communities derive their principles from the same scriptures and practice similar prayers, ceremonies, holidays, and rituals. Yet, they often view the other religious group or denomination with suspicion or disdain.

The interaction between religious ideas, institutions, and actors, on the one hand, and political actors and behavior, on the other, is a two-way street. Moreover, religion interacts with other processes: changes in social norms, technological advances, and economic changes (Hanson 2006). In some cases, religion influences social processes. In other cases, politics, science, and technology influence religion. The debate between Galileo Galilei and the Catholic Church about the position of the earth and the sun is the historical incarnation of contemporary debates about abortion, gay marriage, science (e.g., evolution), and religion (creationism) in education. These have become issues in the discourse between religious actors and secular or political ones as a result of the influence of medical technology, social norms, and scientific advances. They have forced religious leaders and institutions to delve into questions that had not been part of the religious discourses of the past.

Many scholars who advance the idea that religious factors have a significant influence on international relations, and who criticize modernization and secularization ideas or "traditional" IR paradigms for ignoring them, commit the very same sin they attribute to their straw men. Specifically, they minimize or discount the role and effect of "secular" factors on religion. Religious actors, religious states, and religious worldviews and identities are taken to be important independent variables in the contemporary literature on religion and politics. These also are outcomes of other social processes.

Finally, integrating religious factors into the more traditional IR paradigms does not do much beyond suggesting some general concepts that should be considered when examining contemporary aspects of international politics. There are no clear testable propositions we can infer from such concepts on the causes and consequences of international or internal conflicts, patterns of international cooperation, or human security. Sandal and Fox (2013) suggest some general ways in which religious factors affect political processes, but they do not offer a clearly articulated theory.

4. Empirical Evidence on Religion and Politics

We discuss some of the empirical evidence in support of the role of religion in international relations in more detail in the coming chapters. Here we focus on some examples illustrating our point that much of this evidence is based on questionable inferences from flawed methodologies.

For example, Ellingsen (2006) examines several hypotheses related to religion's resurgence. Using the World Values Survey (WVS) data and the PRIO armed conflict data, she asks several questions about the significance of religion in politics. First, she analyzes the WVS responses at the country level, inferring that religion has always been important, and that this has not changed fundamentally over the period of 1981–96. Then she analyzes the factors that affect national religiosity levels. She finds that gross domestic produce (GDP) per capita has a significant negative impact on religiosity, while certain regions tend to have higher levels of religiosity than others. Likewise, she finds that Islamic and African (not clear how she classifies this category) "civilizations" tend to be more religious than others. This raises a number of fundamental issues.

First, this is a classic case of the ecological fallacy. Survey results are based on individual responses; aggregating them into national averages and correlating these averages with macro—national or "civilizational"—characteristics leads to the flawed inference that countries that have a higher per-capita GDP tend to have lower levels of religiosity. While this may be the case, the level of religiosity in a society ignores the variance in societies. A society that has 15 percent of its population defined as "religious" may have the remaining 85 percent still believe in God, pray occasionally, and consider religion as an important guide to their lives. Another country with 15 percent religious may have all the other 85 percent as atheists. More serious is the omission of religious diversity in societies. Two societies with the same level of religiosity may be fundamentally different in that one is religiously homogeneous, that is, virtually all of its citizens practice the same religion (albeit with varying levels of commitment), while another society may be evenly split among several religions.

Second, the partition into "civilizations" is arbitrary, lacking any clear classification criteria, and therefore appears to be ad hoc. How is "African" civilization membership determined, and what makes it "African" as opposed to the major cultures on the continent and its diaspora (Mazrui 1988)? What is a Latin American "civilization" and how does it differ from European civilizations in countries such as Spain, Portugal, and Italy, also relatively homogeneous Catholic states?

More disturbing are mathematical puzzles in the results. For example, Ellingsen (2006) uses the natural log of the Polity score. However, as noted in the footnote, this score varies between −10 and +10. Unfortunately, there are no base-two logarithms for negative numbers. So it is not clear how to interpret the lack of relationship between regime score and religiosity.

In another set of analyses, she examines temporal variations in "identity" conflict using the Uppsala Conflict Data Program (UCDP) domestic and international conflict data. A conflict in the UCDP dataset is defined as a set of engagements between two or more actors—at least one of them a government of a state—that results in a minimum of 25 battle-related deaths per year. Focusing on intrastate conflicts, she points out that "since the 1960s identity conflicts have been the dominant form of conflicts in the world" (p. 29). Again, while this may be true, it tells us little about religious resurgence. There are several problems with such inferences. For one, identity conflicts (even if their coding is credible—in itself a questionable issue), include ethnic, racial, religious, linguistic, and other types of identity issues. Religious issues may be a small fraction of what constitutes "identity" groups. Second, there is an inherent assumption that "identity" conflicts involve a group with one type of identity fighting a group with another type of identity. Again, this may be the case, but the data do not allow such an inference—especially in terms of religion.[5]

The most important inferential issue there has to do with the fact that these figures do not control for "identity interaction opportunities." What we mean by that is that the expansion in identity conflict may be simply because there are more interaction opportunities between different ethnic groups in the post-1960s era than before. Several factors and processes account for such an inference. First, the 1960s, and again the late 1980s and early 1990s, witnessed two major waves of state formation. The first wave was dominated by independence for multiple African (and a few Middle Eastern) formerly colonial states, most of whom were characterized by significant ethnic diversity. The second wave occurred primarily in Eastern Europe, the Balkans, and Central Asia following the dissolution of the Soviet Bloc. Many of these new countries were ethnically diverse as well. Therefore, it is quite possible that structural causes rather than religious resurgence are responsible for the rise in the frequency of identity conflicts.

Another set of analyses focuses on the outbreak of intrastate conflict. Two key religious factors are included in an attempt to explain such conflicts: religious differences and level of religiosity. Ellingsen (2006) codes religious differences as a binary variable that is assigned a score of one if the country is split among two or more religious groups and zero otherwise. Of course, this immediately suggests that the number of religious groups and the distribution of adherents in a society do not matter, which really defeats the whole notion of differences. Second, and more important, once her analyses control for time dependence, the effect of these religious factors on intrastate conflict becomes statistically insignificant. This contrasts with her argument that "religious differences again indicate a positive—and this time *significant*—effect on the probability of armed conflict incidence" (p. 23) (italics in original). This is true only if one is willing to accept a $p = 0.066$ given a sample of N = 1,193, but with such a large N, any effect that has a type I error probability of higher than 0.05 suggests that the lower end of the 95 percent confidence interval is below zero. The implication is that the marginal effect of religious differences on intrastate conflict (that is, the difference in the probability of conflict between a religiously homogeneous and a religiously heterogeneous society) is negligible.

In the same volume, Pearce (2006; also see Pearce 2005) examines the intensity of religious conflict, using the UCDP dataset of armed (domestic and international) conflicts. She concludes her papers with the statement "Based on the statistical analysis of 278 interstate and intrastate territorial conflict phases occurring worldwide between 1946 and 2001, the evidence indicates that conflicts involving religion are significantly more intense than other types of conflict, though the evidence is much weaker than expected" (p. 55). Her definition of religious conflict is a conflict involving two states or two groups that belong to different religions. We discuss the problem in identifying a conflict as "religious" below. For now, we do not challenge this definition, but merely examine the methodological problems of this analysis.

A careful examination of the results suggests that the empirical analysis does not show any significant relationship between religion and intensity, and the inferences of a relationship between "religious conflict" and intensity are fundamentally flawed. Some of the points we made above with regard to Ellingsen's work apply here as well, albeit even more. First and foremost, since this analysis includes only conflict that actually took place, it is impossible to infer how the opportunity for conflict was distributed between religious and non-religious groups. Therefore, it is impossible to infer whether the actual occurrence of conflict of any type—religious or non-religious—was more likely. For example, the key evidence for her argument is shown in her Table 1 (Pearce 2006, 48) that tabulates the level of intensity of the conflict by its type (religious or non-religious, where the former is observed when the actors on both sides of the conflict share a different religious affiliation). Below is the table drawn from her essay (we present frequencies rather than percentages for reasons discussed below).

The top number in each cell provides the actual number of conflicts (rather than the percentages presented in her Table 1). The bottom row in each cell is the expected number of conflicts by chance alone. When calculating the chi-square statistic with actual frequencies (as opposed to percentages, which is not a proper way to calculate this), the statistic is actually higher than reported: 8.428, which, with 4 degrees of freedom is significant at the $p = 0.06$ level, slightly above the 0.05 level accepted as significant in the social sciences. A few issues arise. First, the actual association between conflict intensity and religious/non-religious conflict type is quite low. The more permissive coefficient of ordinal association, gamma is 0.09, just marginally higher than zero.

Second, when examining the relationship between observed and expected frequencies, we confront a significant problem of inference. For example, if there is a positive relationship between religious conflict and intensity, then we should see that at the low/somewhat low intensity categories, the actual frequencies of religious conflict should be *lower* than the expected frequencies (and the actual frequencies of non-religious conflict should be *higher* than the expected frequencies). Likewise, at the higher levels of conflict intensity, the actual frequency of religious conflicts should be *higher* than the expected frequency (and the actual frequency of the non-religious conflict should be *lower* than the expected frequency). In some of the cells this is the case. However, as the bolded cells indicate, it is not so in the more extreme cases. And these may

Table 2.1. Intensity of religious and non-religious conflicts, 1946–2001 (Pearce 2006, 48)

Conflict Intensity	Non-religious	Religious	Total Row
Low Intensity	22	44	66
(Expected Frequency)	(15.91)	(50.09)	
Somewhat Low Intensity	14	53	67
(Expected Frequency)	(16.15)	(50.85)	
Moderate Intensity	15	72	87
(Expected Frequency)	(20.97)	(66.03)	
Somewhat High Intensity	10	34	44
	(10.60)	(33.40)	
High Intensity	6	8	14
	(3.37)	(10.63)	
Total Column	67	211	278

account for the chi-square statistic. In fact, using a statistic m_b that controls for the extent to which a given difference between actual and expected frequencies is consistent with the test hypothesis, we get a score of $m_b = 0.006$, which is not significantly different from zero.

As noted, the definition of a conflict as "religious" is fundamentally problematic. Related to Ellingsen's (2006) definition of a conflict as "religious," we have the work of Toft (2007; Toft, Philpott and Shah 2011, Ch. 6). Toft (2007, 97) defines a religious civil war as

> a war in which religious belief or practice is either a central or peripheral issue in the conflict. For religion to count as "central," combatants had to be fighting over whether the state or a region of the state would be ruled according to a specific religious tradition—as in the cases of Afghanistan, Chad, and Sudan. For religion to count as "peripheral," combatants had to identify with a specific religious tradition and group themselves accordingly, but the rule of a specific religious tradition could not be the object of contention. An example would be the conflict in the former Yugoslavia, which involved Bosnian Muslims (Islam), Croats (Catholicism), and Serbs (Orthodox Christianity).

Toft should be credited for being transparent about (a) the possible conflation of religious and ethnic issues and, more importantly, (b) the actual civil wars that she characterizes as religious (see Table 1, 2007, 114). In each of these cases one can judge whether religion played an important or "peripheral" role in the conflict. Several problems are evident in these definitions, however. First, it is possible that two different religious groups would fight each other but the conflict might not be religious. It might be over tangible goods: territory, resources, distribution of wealth, or taxes. Therefore, while the conflict may be between different religious groups, calling it a "religious" conflict may well be misleading. Second, a conflict may be highly religious even when the groups fighting each other have the same religious affiliation. Consider, for example, the conflict between fundamentalist Islamic groups such as Al Qaeda and ISIS and Saudi Arabia. Both the nonstate actors and the Saudi monarchy are staunch Sunni affiliates—even jointly Salafists. Still, the conflict centers heavily on religious interpretation and the policies suggested by them. Likewise, the conflict between the Muslim Brotherhood and the liberal opposition (ultimately decided by the Egyptian military in 2013) had a lot to do with the role of religious laws and practices in Egyptian politics. Calling some of these cases "religious" and others non-religious is potentially misleading.

While Toft (2007) is transparent about the list of "religious" civil wars, she is less transparent about the "non-religious" civil wars. Therefore, it is difficult to evaluate her hypothesis tests. Nevertheless, even without having an idea of the population of "non-religious" civil wars, the fundamental problems in Toft's analyses are the same as in Ellingsen's. The probability of the occurrence of a civil war that is "religious" compared to the probability of the occurrence of a civil war that is "non-religious" is left unspecified. Therefore we do not know if the chi-square tests reported in Toft's study (2007, 116) mean anything in the absence of a test for a priori opportunities for civil war outbreak.

Svensson's (2007, 2013) studies of religion and civil conflict offer an important perspective on the role of religion in conflict resolution. We discuss this work at greater length in chapter 7. Briefly, Svensson finds that civil conflicts that have religious claims are more difficult to resolve and less likely to end in a negotiated settlement. The reason for that is primarily that the issues at stake in such conflicts are perceived as indivisible. However, religious issues can be more or less central in a civil conflict; therefore, the degree to which the issues at stake are seen as religious is a function of the centrality of religious claims. The key to resolving religious conflicts lies in their "desacralisation," namely "a political or societal process of removing the religious status or significance from an armed conflict" (Svensson 2013, 5).

The key problem is not that it may be difficult to distinguish between a "religious" and a "non-religious" conflict—in fact, one may applaud efforts such as Toft's or Svensson's attempt to weigh the importance of religious issues in conflict. Rather, the problem involves biased sampling due to the truncation of data inherent in research designs that rely on conceptualizations and analyses of "religious wars." Focusing only on conflicts—interstate or intrastate—that *occurred* truncates the population of cases, because it does not account for "dogs that didn't bark," that is, for conflicts that could have occurred but did not. Specifically, to study any factor that may or may not impact conflict, one needs to account for the nonconflict instances, specifically for the opportunities for conflict to occur. We need to have some sense of the states, or the periods during which states "select" themselves into civil conflict. If it is indeed the case that states that are characterized by religious contentions (either interreligious tensions or tensions between religious and political institutions) are more likely to "select themselves" into civil conflict than states that do not have such tensions, then the results of studies such as Toft's or Svensson's, while potentially illuminating, may be systematically biased, resulting in Type 1 errors. However, if religious tensions are no more likely to cause conflicts than economic, political, or social tensions, then it is possible that religious tensions can be resolved without entering into civil conflict in the first place, but such cases are not accounted for in these types of research designs.

Without accounting for nonevents, we do not know the probability of two groups confronting each other in the first place. Nor can we tell what proportion of the interaction opportunities between groups of different religious affiliations was actually converted into conflict. Without accounting for conflict opportunities of religious and non-religious dyads, no meaningful inference on the relationship between religious conflict and intensity is possible. These are fundamental methodological issues. The arguments that "religious" conflicts are more severe than "non-religious" ones, or that the former are more likely to recur and less likely to be resolved than the latter, create an impression that religious violence is fundamentally different from other types of violence. However, we claim that without controlling for the opportunity of each type of violence to emerge in the first place, these results are potentially misleading. We will have more to say about these analyses in chapter 7.[6]

Methodological issues emerge even when the claims are based on descriptive evidence. First, consider the argument about religious resurgence that we reviewed above. In many cases, no evidence is provided to substantiate this far-reaching claim. In other cases, quantitative evidence is provided, but a close inspection reveals that it is quite misleading. For example, Jonathan Fox—one of the targets of the anti-quantification literature (e.g. Fitzgerald 2011)—has collected a valuable dataset on religion–state relations, and we use this dataset along with several others throughout this book. However, Fox (2015, 232) claims that "states have been heavily involved in religion, and this trend has been consistently increasing in strength between 1990 and 2008. The increasing ubiquity of government involvement in religion is perhaps the most obvious and incontrovertible result that emerges from this analysis." One of the figures he provides shows a consistent rise in the levels of religious discrimination, religious regulation, and religious legislation over this period. However, as Figure 2.1 shows, this trend is meaningful only if one does not control for the number of states in the international system.

Over the period 1990–2014, the number of states in the international system increased by 18.1 percent (from 166 to 196). Fox's data include 176 "valid" states (we exclude non-state entities such as Gaza, Kurdistan, West Bank, or Western Sahara). If we control for the number of states—and there is no telling what kind of religious policy occurred in the missing states—then patterns of religion-state relations are quite different from what Fox would have us believe. Using 2010 as the baseline and taking into account the variance across states in terms of religion-state relations the picture that emerges suggests significant stability over time. Specifically, neither the absolute nor the relative levels of religious legislation, regulation, or discrimination are significantly different in 2014 than in the baseline year. Fox's figure 9.1 (2015:232) shows only mean values of the religion-state indices but does not take into account variations across states, which yields biased inferences even for his own figure. So Fox's strong claim is clearly not supported by his own data.[7]

Another way of examining the question of religious resurgence in politics involves a study of religion-state relations as reflected in national constitutions. A dataset on national constitutions is based on a systematic content analysis of national constitutions that were legislated over the period

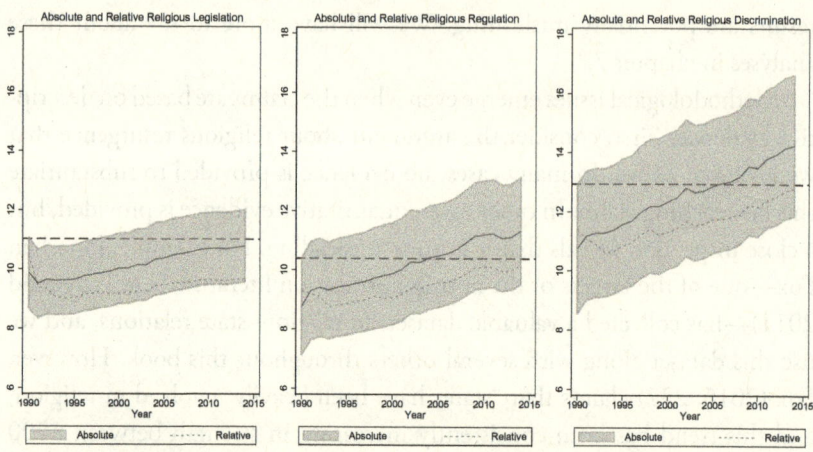

Fig. 2.1. Religious Policy 1990–2014. Solid lines are mean absolute values of religious policy indices; dotted lines are relative values (divided by the overall number of states). Shaded areas are 95% confidence intervals. Dashed lines indicate upper value of baseline year. A statistically significant change in the value of a given index exists if the lower bound of the shaded area is higher than the dashed baseline.

1789–2013. It contains data on whether the constitution identifies an official religion (or accords one or more religions a special status), as well on whether a given constitution contains an explicit stipulation about the freedom of religion. We focus on the post–World War II period. This dataset affords a much longer time span to analyze than the religion and state dataset. The downside of this dataset is that it covers only states that had or drafted and approved a constitution over this time span. It excludes states that did not have a constitution, which in some years accounts for more than 50 percent of the states in the system. Even when we control for the number of states whose constitutions contain clauses of religious freedom, separation of religion from state, noninclusion of an official religion, and civil laws as a proportion of all states in the system, we see a volatile period in the 1950s through the 1970s, but a clear upward trend of greater religious freedom after 1980 (see Figure 2.2). So, it is not clear what kind of evidence supports the notion of religious resurgence.

There is one area where religious factors and religious actors seem to have been on the rise: international terrorism (Toft, Philpott, and Shah 2011, Ch. 5; Saya and Scime 2015; Saiya 2016). This is an important topic, but one that we do not cover in this study. However, the data on the identity of perpetrators of terrorism and their religious nature are problematic. For example, the Global Terrorism Dataset (START 2017) lists marginal acts with no clear political motive as possible terrorist attacks. In addition, many actions by religiously motivated groups such as Al Qaeda, Hamas, or Hizballah against the United States in Iraq or Afghanistan and Israel in Lebanon and the occupied territories of the West Bank and Gaza can be classified as nationalist rather than "religious." The fact that religious groups have taken on nationalist causes is important, but it is not clear that the driving force is a religious belief system (which may be more visible in suicide bombings) or a nationalist ideology vis-à-vis a foreign power occupying one's land.

We do not deny that religious forces have influenced world politics during the last few decades. However, we should be more cautious about asserting the rising influence of religion on political processes. Specifically, religious factors have operated in world politics for a long time. Further, religious factors and religious actors interact with other political actors and processes. The nature of this interaction may provide

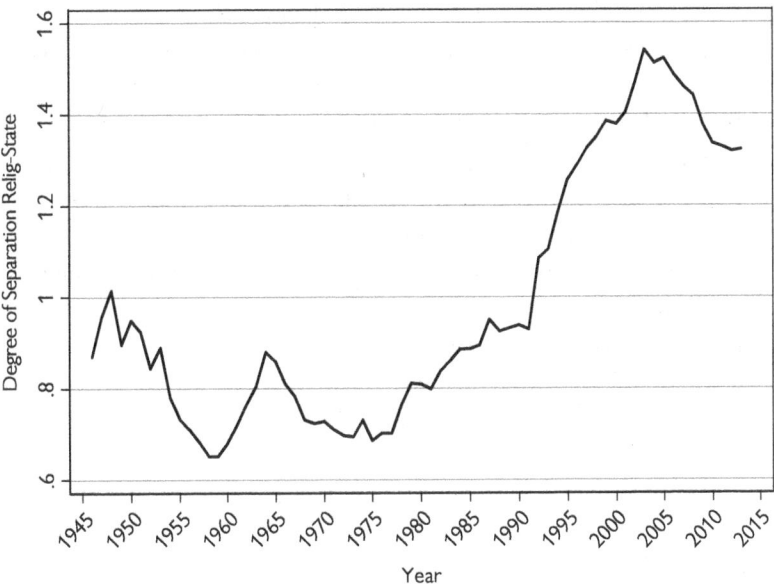

Fig. 2.2. Separation of religion and state in national constitutions, 1946–2013
Source: Zachary, Ginsburg, and Melton 2014. Measure discussed in chapter 4.

a more nuanced view of the role of religion and politics, rather than the exclusive emphasis on religion or the inflation of its significance relative to other factors.

5. Conclusion

We have not covered many polemical and descriptive accounts of religion and world politics in this chapter. We have also not discussed some foundational studies that will serve as the basis for the theoretical framework we present in the next chapter. Some of these were mentioned in passing, but we will provide a more coherent focus on these ideas in chapter 3. That said, however, this brief review is fairly representative of the burgeoning literature on religion and politics. Several common denominators underlie much of this literature.

1. *Polemical writings*. Almost any book or article on religion and politics starts with the argument that religion is an important force in world politics. Some argue this has always been the case, but the mainstream theories and paradigms—deliberately or due to sheer negligence—ignored this plain fact. This may be an important argument, but we view it more as an empirical question. To us, the puzzle concerns the role of religion—relative to other factors commonly associated with traditional theories of IR—in central phenomena such as international and internal conflict, international cooperation, and human security.

    Another characteristic of this literature is that most studies launch a sustained attack on straw men such as modernization and secularization theories or the more central paradigms of realism, liberalism, and even constructivism. Such attacks often come at the expense of original thinking about how to understand the role of religion in such processes. Prominent among these writings are debates regarding the possibility of quantification of religion or religious factors, or of the possibility of positivist theorizing about religion and politics. These debates, while intellectually interesting (and sometimes challenging), do not really add to our understanding of the topic. As is the case with the emergence of a new theoretical and empirical area of interest, these debates are unavoidable, especially in a discipline that is ideologically, theoretically, and methodologically diverse as is IR. At the same time, after nearly three decades that witnessed a significant surge of studies on religion and politics, it is high time we realized these debates do not advance knowledge. This is why we attempt to pose specific questions about the role of religion in politics, and to provide systematic answers to these questions—even if these answers may not be simply yes or no.

2. *Overemphasis on Religious Factors and Religious Actors.* A characteristic of the literature we have reviewed herein is that, in its effort to emphasize the role of religion in politics, it may well exaggerate the role of religious factors and religious actors in affecting major political outcomes, largely at the expense of other factors. Many of the reviewed studies acknowledge the interaction/competition between religious and secular or non-religious actors.[8] Where they fail is in recognizing that sometimes religious actors are manipulated by non-religious ones in ways that serve to advance the goals of the latter. Religion can, and sometimes is, a powerful motivating force of political action. However, because it is such a motivating force, it can be used for non-religious reasons by political actors. This aspect of the linkage between religion and politics is missing from most writings on the subject. It is one of the core arguments of our theory on religion and international relations.

3. *Critical Omission: Religion and International Cooperation.* One of the interesting aspects of our review concerns what is missing in the plethora of arguments and polemics. Specifically, a lot of ink has been spilled—quite understandably—on the relationship between religion and conflict, interstate and intrastate. However, just as Blainey (1988, 3) argued that "for every one thousand pages written on the causes of war, there is less than one page on the causes of peace," we note that a similar ratio exists in the writings on religion and international cooperation. The literature on religion and international cooperation is even more scant than the literature on religion and domestic order, democracy, and stability. Shah, Stephan, and Toft (2012) contains a collection of essays entitled *Rethinking Religion and World Affairs*. This collection contains chapters about religion and democracy, human rights, religion and

transnational justice, and religion and development, among others. Beyond the fact that many of these chapters are polemical and normative rather than analytical and descriptive, none discusses the relationship between religion and international cooperation. This is even more puzzling because the few studies that contain an analytical statement about the relationship between religion and world politics focus on the conflict-promoting aspect of religion, yet the very same causal mechanisms that they invoke may explain cooperation between or among religious actors and among states.

4. *Methodological Issues.* There exist some methodologically sophisticated works on religion and world politics, especially on the linkages between religion and international and intrastate conflict, as well as on the linkages between religion and human security. We review these in the relevant chapters. However, the sample of studies we reviewed herein suggests some major problems. Failure to recognize these problems may well lead to serious inferential biases even when the quantitative data are merely descriptive. We also discuss the fact that most empirical studies of religion and various aspects of world politics are limited in scope, focusing on specific elements and selective units of analysis. Therefore, the generalizability of these studies is quite limited. Our study seeks not only to fix some of the methodological issues of previous studies but also to provide a broader array of analyses than existing scholarship on religion and world politics.

5. *Disaggregated Empirical Evidence.* There is a general disconnect between the theoretical arguments about religion and world politics and the empirical examinations of these linkages. Theories of religion and politics tend to be general and provide concepts, arguments, and ideas that cover a general array of linkages between religion and various aspects of domestic and international relations. Most empirical studies that attempt to provide a more scientific perspective on the relations between religion and world politics focus on one limited aspect of these linkages. The typical empirical analysis focuses on a very limited argument. For example, as we point out in chapter 5, most empirical studies of religion and international conflict test the clash of civilizations thesis in one form or another. And as we

point out in chapter 7, so do most empirical studies of religion and intrastate conflict. Importantly, there is no general causal mechanism that seems to drive the empirical studies of conflict, and there is little empirical work on religion and international cooperation.

What is the sum total of the many studies on religion and international relations? There are several compelling arguments in the literature on religion and politics. One is the interesting dualism argument: *religion can be a force for conflict and a force for cooperation.* It depends on the circumstances and the specific groups involved. Another argument that we find meaningful as a basis for a theory of religion and world politics is the competition/collusion argument focusing on the relations between political actors and religious actors. On the whole, this literature is rich and diverse in terms of arguments, approaches, methodology, and scope.

Having said all that about the theoretical literature on religion and world politics, we find that much of it is not very useful in terms of usable knowledge. Despite the claim of some authors on the progress made in the understanding of the relationship between religion and politics, we argue that the theoretical foundations of these linkages are quite weak. There is some promising empirical work on the linkages between religion and international conflict, between religion and intrastate conflict, and between religion and human security. However, even in these areas, our knowledge of these linkages is weak, and the empirical field of these topics is fraught with debates, conflicting findings, and results of limited generalizability. This is where our study enters the picture.

CHAPTER 3

Religion and World Politics: An Integrated Theoretical Perspective

I. Introduction

This chapter offers an integrated theoretical framework of the role of religion in world politics. This framework builds upon, integrates, and expands existing theoretical perspectives that have addressed this topic. The approaches that we find most useful and relevant to the subject at hand—for example, primordialism, instrumentalism, and constructivism—do not focus exclusively (or even explicitly) on religion. However, they do highlight concepts and ideas that suggest relevant and compelling inferences about religion and world politics.

As we noted in the literature review, several theories link religion to various aspects of world politics. Some of these theories are complementary; some are competitive; and some are contradictory. Moreover, some theories are more compelling than others, primarily on logical grounds. We focus on the central and persistent ideas linking religion to politics in general, and to international politics in particular. We examine these major approaches and evaluate their internal logic, pointing out the strength and weaknesses of their key arguments. We then offer an integrated approach that builds on the salient arguments of each. We go on to present our own integrative theory of religion and world politics and explain the relationship between our theory and other leading theories on the subject. In order to facilitate a coherent discussion of and comparison among these theories, we focus on several questions, which also guide the fundamental logic of our integrative framework:

1. What is the role of religion in the social and political life of a state?
2. Is there a difference between religiously heterogeneous and religiously homogeneous societies in terms of the roles played by religion in social and political life?
3. How does religion affect the rise, survival, and downfall of political elites?
4. Under what circumstances can political elites utilize religious beliefs in order to advance their goals?
5. Under what circumstances are religious groups willing to mobilize politically in support of, or in opposition to, government policies?
6. Under what conditions does religion affect perceptions of affinity or enmity between and among societies across national borders?
7. Is there a link between specific religions and conflict? Is there a link between specific religion(s) and cooperation?

2. Primordialism

We discussed briefly the notion of religion as a communal institution in chapter 1. The primordialist perspective of religion offers a compelling explanation of the way in which religion has defined various communities in both ancient and modern times. It is also a potentially compelling explanation for the alleged resurgence of religious-based politics in the post–Cold War era. According to this conception, religion is a defining marker of individual and group identity. It contains a set of directives for moral behavior at the individual and communal levels. Many religions also involve collective rituals, such as prayers, sacred holidays, and pilgrimages to holy sites. Religions involve worshiping and idolizing individuals who are attributed with special—often superhuman—powers. Many religions assign to some places—shrines, graves, and even cities—a sacred status. Sacred sites attract pilgrims from distant places, but more importantly, they are controlled and managed by religious institutions. More generally, religion is a collective belief system, one that identifies virtuous behavior and distinguishes it from amoral behavior. Such belief systems also identify communities of believers and sharply distinguish these communities from communities of "infidels," "goyim," or "nonbelievers."

This distinction between members of a religious community and non-members is sometimes based on biological foundations, for example, the Jewish principle that a Jewish person is one who was born to a Jewish mother[1]; sometimes on an article of faith, for example, the requirement in Islam that a Muslim is a person who has stated the *shahada* that "there is no God but Allah and Muhammad is His Messenger"; and sometimes on a ritual, for example, the christening in Catholicism. In Buddhism, the criteria are to believe in the principles of Buddhism and to practice meditation. The primordialist conception of religion is that of a fundamental common denominator of a community based on shared beliefs. These include belief in one or more deities and the principles, rules, and rituals associated with the dictates of this/these diety/ies. This distinction between believers and nonbelievers is central to the primordialist approach.

Primordialism is often associated with superiority complexes. Believers—those who know the "true mind of God" (Juergensmeyer 2003)—often try to impose their religious beliefs and way of life on nonbelievers. This superiority complex induces perceptions of power and righteousness, which are often accompanied by discrimination against and repression of religious minorities in multicultural societies. In international contexts they are instrumental in processes of colonizing and subduing other peoples. The forced conversion of pagan communities into Islam during the Islamic expansion era (Cleveland and Bunton 2012) is a clear example of these conceptions of the superiority of Islam over paganism. Taking up the "White Man's Burden" was the rationalization for Christian Europe's colonization of African, Asian, and Native American lands (Abernethy 2000; Anievas, Manchanda, and Shilliam 2015; Du Bois 1915). At the same time, religion may affect perceptions of affinity and shared values among groups within a state, or between states, whose citizens share the same religion. This is evident in the role of the pope in moderating disputes among Catholics in Europe as well as the Americas. The Crusades of 1096–1291 represent a period of transnational "religious wars" mobilizing "believers" in the faith against "infidels."

The general idea of religion as a force in international politics is closely linked to the notion of communal identity markers. Simply put, the policies of states are affected by religion to the extent that religion becomes an important element in the definition of *national* identity. Thus, exploring the extent to which religion helps define national identity requires us to examine the circumstances under which a nation's identity is linked to the religious affiliation of its citizens. The answer to this question lies in the intersection of two factors: the relationship between political and religious institutions and the religious homogeneity/heterogeneity of the society.

As we noted in our literature review, one of the more compelling foci of existing theories linking religion to politics concerns the relationship between religious and political institutions. This relationship has an important effect on the ways in which religious factors affect domestic and international politics (Philpott 2007; Toft, Philpott, and Shah 2011; Fox and Sandler 2004; Gill 2007). The primordialist perspective accepts this argument. However, it interprets it in a different way than those discussed in the other theoretical perspectives.

In some societies, religious institutions and political institutions are one and the same. In other societies, they are closely linked. However, many modern societies separate religion from politics and from political institutions. In such states, religion—according to the primordialist perspective—has little impact on politics. Separation between the religious sphere and the political one suggests that factors other than religion define domestic or foreign policies. Such non-religious factors feature prominently in secular political theory: interests, power, rationality, or other aspects of civic nationalism based on political, ethnic, or linguistic rather than religious identity.

On the other hand, when religious and political institutions are closely allied, primordialism suggests a close relationship between religion and politics. In such countries, religion becomes integral to the state's political identity and of the national ethos, its history, and its vision of the future. It is a marker that defines the self-portrayed character of the state as well as the character other peoples and nations attribute to that state. This characterization affects the relations between the state and other actors in its external environment. It creates attachment to certain territories—holy places—or symbols that become a bone of contention between societies that belong to different religions.[2]

Religious homogeneity/heterogeneity reflects the distribution of religious beliefs and practices in a given society. Most societies lie somewhere on the religious homogeneity/heterogeneity continuum; only a few are fully homogeneous (all members practice the same religion) or fully heterogeneous (members are evenly split among several religious groups). In homogeneous societies, religion is more likely to become a visible marker of national identity. Religious adherence may be viewed as a principal determinant of individual loyalty to the community. It affects individual willingness to contribute to the public good and risk one's life in defense of, or for the purpose of spreading, the values of the dominant religion. In religiously heterogeneous societies, religion can be a powerful divisive force. Religious diversity creates loyalties to subgroups. There is potential friction among groups when religious loyalty supersedes other loyalties—even to the state. The prevalence of religious diversity makes these fissures particularly pronounced, threatening the cohesion of the larger community, that is, the state, as a whole. Leaders of religiously diverse states may find ways to overcome the primordial sources of tension among religious groups, for example, by separating the religious and political spheres and promoting religious freedom. However, where political and religious leaders in religiously diverse states are reluctant or otherwise unwilling to pursue policies that overcome such divisions, the likelihood of political and social strife increases substantially.

Those two factors—the degree of separation between religious and political affairs and the degree of religious homogeneity/heterogeneity—help determine the kind of political processes that affect the domestic and international politics of a given society. This conception is captured in Table 3.1 below. The top-left cell represents homogeneous societies that lack separation between religion and politics. For convenience, we label

Table 3.1 Social characteristics and primordial influences

Religious structure of society	Separation between Religion and State	
	No	Yes
Homogeneous	Primordial politics—Type I states (Iran, Saudi Arabia)	Informal primordialism—Type II states (Brazil, Ecuador)
Heterogeneous	Primordial politics, coupled with discriminatory practices—Type III states (Israel, Myanmar, Atheism in communist states)	Nationalism, rationalism—Type IV states (United States, United Kingdom, most Western European democracies)

those states as Type I states. The Islamic Republic of Iran and the Wahhabi Kingdom of Saudi Arabia are prime examples of this type. Religion plays a prominent role in the domestic and international politics of these societies. It affects leader selection: political leaders need to be acceptable to religious institutions and religious leaders. Even if—as in the case of Iran over the last three-plus decades—there are competitive elections for the office of president, candidates are screened by the supreme (religious) leader, and those who are not considered acceptable are prohibited from competing. Religious laws play a dominant role in the legal system. Loyalty to the state and loyalty to the prevailing religion are one and the same. Secularism is either disallowed or marginalized. Externally, international affinities and animosities—especially in security affairs, but also in other domains such as cultural and institutional interactions—are defined by religious similarity or differences. This affects both cooperation and conflict behavior.

The definition of religious homogeneity in these examples goes beyond the broad categories of religion and includes religious families within a given religion. Both Iran and Saudi Arabia are Muslim states. Sha'ria law is the foundation of the legal system of both states. In both states, religious and political institutions are closely aligned. However, both consider each other a potential enemy because Saudi Arabia is predominantly Sunni, whereas Iran is predominantly Shi'ite. This affects, for example, their conflicting interests in the civil wars in Syria and Yemen.

Examples of religiously homogeneous societies that have separated religion from state (Type II states) include states such as Brazil or Ecuador. These states practice a high separation between the Catholic Church (the dominant religion) and the state. Type II states tend to minimize the formal role of religion in politics via a constitution or a civil legal system. However, religious beliefs and practices of candidates for political office often play a (typically informal) role in their election or selection. Attitudes toward religious minorities are often mixed, if not outright suspicious, even though legally these societies practice constitutional religious freedom. Attitudes toward other states often correlate with religious similarity or dissimilarity. Religion is not formally invoked as a determinant of conflict or cooperation, but seems to lurk beneath the surface. An example of this is the attitude of the European Union toward Turkey. Whereas the European Union (EU) has admitted many of the Eastern European states that had democratized only recently, it has continued to reject Turkey's application.

The formal reasons provided by the EU are just feeble excuses; it is Turkey's Muslim identity that prevents its admittance to a predominantly Christian identified community.

Religiously heterogeneous societies that do not separate religion from state (Type III states) often reflect a situation wherein one religious group's rules, principles, and legal values dominate those of other groups. Religious discrimination is often coupled with economic, social, and political discrimination. These discriminatory practices are guided by a narrow sense of religious identity wherein one religious group imposes its values on other groups. Religious freedom may be etched as a formal legal or constitutional principle. However, such states practice political, economic, and social discrimination against religious groups that do not represent the "state's" religion. Leaders are selected exclusively from the religious group that dominates the political system; members of "outside" religions are excluded from positions of influence. Likewise, religious similarity between excluded religious groups and other states is often a source of both domestic and international tensions. Examples of this case include the imposition of atheism in communist societies, and the systematic discrimination against non-Jewish communities in Israel. In both cases, the formal legal system decreed freedom of religion. In practice, discriminatory policies are rampant and systematic.

The last quadrant consists of religiously heterogeneous societies in which the separation between religion and state is embedded in the constitution or the legal system (Type IV states). In such societies, national identity is formed around non-religious symbols and affinities. Type IV states may still reflect some tensions between different religious communities—as has been the case with respect to American attitudes toward Muslims in the United States since September 2001—but the role of religious factors in political discourses is minimal. Likewise, the degree of affinity or hostility such a state exhibits toward other actors in the international system is hardly influenced by religious affinities or dissimilarities. Interests or shared values in terms of secular ideological similarities define the foreign policies of such states. Most Western democracies offer examples of such states.

This framework illuminates how primordialism conceives the impact of religion on the domestic politics of states. It also suggests some general ideas about the international implications of a state's religious structure for its foreign policy orientations and possible behaviors. We interpret the principal operative factors in the primordialist perspective differently from the more traditional theories of religion and politics we have discussed in the previous chapter. We accept that the relationship between religious and political institutions is a key variable in determining the extent and manner in which religion affects politics. We argue, however, that the notion of "political theology," while important, is not an independent condition. Rather, it is a function of state-religion relations, and is typically determined by the ability and willingness of political institutions to allow religious beliefs to influence major political practices. A political theology, if one exists, can shape national politics only if it can unify society around it, and only if the political leadership is willing or capable to employ it as a unifying symbol.

What are the factors that define relations among states according to the primordialist perspective? As noted, the notion of religion as an identity marker shapes not only the perception of leaders and followers about who they are but also their perceptions of other political actors outside their borders. This applies in particular to the attitudes that leaders and followers develop toward neighbors or other actors that are relevant to the state's security and well-being. Much of the interaction in international relations—especially of the conflictual variety—takes place among contiguous states. Primordialism suggests that the religious similarity between a state and its neighbors has a powerful effect on the nature of this interaction. Here too, we can use the above scheme to explain how domestic structure and international politics affect each other.

Religiously similar states that border each other are likely to share values and identities. The political boundaries that separate one state from another may be formal and legally binding, but the people in these societies feel a strong affinity for each other. Consequently, ceteris paribus, the primordialist perspective expects little conflict between such states. The international relations of such states should be marked by various forms of cooperative interactions. Shared religious values serve as important trust-inducing mechanisms; they can cement contracts that form the foundation of international cooperation and international institutions.

On the other hand, religious differences between contiguous states may be a source of friction, both due to ideational divergence and potential religious conflict, and to competing claims for holy shrines, or the affinity of one state with a persecuted religious minority in another state. Religious differences imply differences in basic values, vocabulary, and priorities.

They are a source of miscommunication and misunderstandings, thereby impeding cooperative arrangements (Cohen 1997). Consequently, primordialism suggests that the degree of cooperation across cultures should be much lower than within cultures.

According to the primordialist perspective, religiously homogeneous states are less likely to experience internal strife. This is so because religion makes for a strong social bond. This is especially true in Type I states, because the leadership is seen as legitimated by God and supported by religious institutions. In Type II and Type IV states, the primordialist approach also expects relatively little internal strife. Whether or not the society is homogeneous—religious beliefs can be freely expressed, and religious practices are separate from political ones. Civil conflict, to the extent that it exists, may well be on issues that are more related to economic or social conditions than to religious freedoms. On the other hand, Type III states are expected to be highly prone to civil strife. The cohabitation of political and religious institutions tends to favor one religious group over others. This favoritism often causes grievances due to religious oppression. Such grievances often translate to violent opposition to the regime.

We are less likely to observe outside intervention in domestic politics of religiously homogeneous societies. Such societies build ideational walls to defend themselves against outside influence—ideological, economic, or political. By contrast, religiously diverse states are more prone to internal instability, often due to tensions among religious subgroups jockeying for position or patronage within the society. Affinity between religious minorities and neighbors of such states tends to increase the likelihood of external intervention in episodes of internal strife (Gartzke and Gleditsch 2006, San-Akca 2016).

In sum, the primordial perspective suggests several important themes about religion and world politics. First, religion can be—but is not always—an inherent marker of national identity. This depends on the religious homogeneity of the society and on the relationships between religious institutions and political institutions. Second, when religion becomes an important marker of identity, it affects the degree of internal political and social stability of states. It also affects the degree of conflict and cooperation between a given state and its external environment. Consequently, the interaction among these factors: the religious homogeneity of the state, the degree of separation between religion and politics, and the similarity/dissimilarity between the religious makeup of the state, its neighbors, and its more extensive international environment is what affects the patterns of conflict and cooperation in world politics.

The primordialist perspective is time invariant. That is, it does not tell us why religious factors increase or decrease in importance in a given society at different points in time. Accordingly, it has problems explaining when religious factors have a higher or lower effect on domestic and international politics. What it does tell us is which societies, which pairs of states, and which regions are more or less likely to exhibit internal strife, international conflict, or international cooperation. The lack of dynamics in this framework is a source of weakness because it cannot tell us of the changing importance of religion as a political force over time. Nevertheless, it does offer an important explanation of a more permanent connection between religion and political structures and processes.

3. Instrumentalism

Instrumentalism, a theory in the Machiavellian tradition, focuses on the uses of symbols, ideas, identities, or incentives as tools for political mobilization in the service of political elites. Political elites' interests may or may not be commensurate with those of ordinary citizens. However, this theory asserts that political elites are the principal drivers of political and social processes. The conception is that of trickle-down politics, but such politics requires resources and support. The question here is why, how, and when political elites would use religious ideas, symbols, and institutions, and what kind of interests such usages are supposed to serve.

Instrumentalism is rationalistic in nature. It assumes that political leaders have well-defined goals and pursue optimal strategies to accomplish those goals. The use of religious symbols, ideas, and institutions is seen in this context. It is helpful to explicate the general logic of this theory via one of its most important recent expositions in the work of Bueno de Mesquita, Smith, Siverson, and Morrow (1999, 2003), appropriately labeled the *political survival* theory.

Briefly stated, this theory relies on two fundamental assumptions. First, political elites seek to ascend into office and, once there, to retain their posts. Second, to accomplish their goals, they have to put together and sustain a "winning coalition," a group of people who support them and are capable of defeating any opposition that stands in their way. A strikingly simple but compelling theory follows from these assumptions. This theory applies to a wide spectrum of states, political leaders, and substantive issue areas—including international conflict, trade, and domestic political processes.

The political survival theory defines two central concepts or populations: the *selectorate* (S) is the population that is capable of seating or unseating political leaders. This population is generally the same across all states: it is typically the group of adults that has a stake in the domestic and foreign policies of the state. In democracies, this is a well-defined population—the eligible voters—who can decide the fate of political leadership via elections. In autocracies it may not be as well defined legally, but it is typically the population that can—via either legal or more commonly extralegal processes such as civil uprisings—potentially unseat an incumbent leadership.

The *winning coalition* (W) is the subset of the selectorate that is required to ensure the leadership's survival in office (or bring about a leadership change). This subset varies widely in size across different political regimes. In democracies, W typically accounts for 51 percent of the selectorate (given varying turnout rates and election rules, it may be smaller). In autocracies, this figure is considerably smaller; it is typically measured in qualitative terms (e.g., the size of the military and security apparatuses, the size of an aristocratic class, an economic elite, an ethnic group, etc.). At any rate, autocratic leaders need a small but highly capable group to fight and resist a potentially large section of the selectorate that might resist the autocrats' policies.

The key argument of the political survival theory is that the ratio of W to S—the ratio of the winning coalition to the selectorate—determines the kind of domestic and foreign policies political leaders pursue. In general terms, if the W-to-S ratio is relatively large, which is the case in most democracies, political leaders pursue policies designed to provide *public goods*, that is, goods that would serve a large number of people. This is so, because a leader's ability to stay in power requires that voters would be satisfied with her policies. So leaders who seek to retain their post must pursue policies that provide the kind of goods that would satisfy a large number of people.

By contrast, an autocrat's concern is with policies that provide *private goods*, that is, benefits that would satisfy and benefit a small group of people (the small W) who protect the regime. This is the fundamental institutional difference between democratic and autocratic politics. The implication is that political leaders seek different instruments that would keep them in office, given the constraints (the W-to-S ratio and the nature of the winning coalition) under which they operate. This is the fundamental idea of the instrumentalist perspective of religion: the conditions and the manner in which political leaders use religion as an instrument for retaining or acquiring political power.

There are two versions of the instrumentalist perspective as it applies to the relationship between religion and world politics. The first version, *collective instrumentalism*, does not distinguish between leaders and followers. It views religion as a collective good that benefits the entire body of believers, those who work for the survival, preservation, and expansion of this good. It is also supposed to make nonbelievers worse off for lacking a religion or for adhering to a different one, thereby affording a religiously cohesive community some evolutionary advantage over ones that lack this spiritual cohesiveness. The second version, *elite instrumentalism*, separates political elites from naive believers. For political leaders, religion is a political tool that can be used to further their goals. For followers, religion is a fundamental and all-encompassing guide to life and behavior. Elite instrumentalism builds on such elite-related policy manipulations as those posited by the political survival theory.

Collective instrumentalism is predicated on a utilitarian conception of religion as a collective good. Religion unites a community, creating a collective entity that is capable of providing its members with such benefits as common defense, laws that facilitate social order, and a set of institutions that are legitimized by religious beliefs. These institutions enforce laws and otherwise regulate behavior within the community. Clearly, religion is not the only community-forming and community-regulating philosophy. Secular philosophies based on rational logic of collective choice (such as social contract theories that emerged during the Enlightenment period) are ideological underpinnings of many modern societies.[3] Absolutist political doctrines such as Marxism and fascism serve a similar function. But in some places, and for some cultures, religion is the only encompassing logic that orients a community's survival and functioning. The principles that guide normative behavior in such communities are rooted in religious guidelines. They also define principles of dealing with other communities, depending on whether these other communities are religiously similar or different.

In some cases, and according to some interpretations of a specific religion, a community can thrive only if it (a) unites or cooperates with other communities that share the same religion, and (b) eliminates threats emanating from communities of nonbelievers or communities subscribing to other religions. Here too the definition of friends and foes is based on religious characteristics. However, in contrast to primordialist theories, collective instrumentalism is based on utilitarian principles of cost and benefit. The belief in collective virtue, or the threat of divine collective punishment, forges communal cohesion. Such beliefs, rooted in many religions, unite people through common feelings of righteousness or a common fear of collective punishment. These beliefs also tend to provide such communities a competitive advantage vis-à-vis communities that lack common religious bonds. This helps explain the rise of monotheistic Abrahamic religions and their ability to convert into imperial forces either locally (Judaism and the Israelites in antiquity) or globally (Christianity and Islam following the Council of Nicea, and the earliest caliphates, respectively).

The early histories of Judaism and Islam exemplify the ideas of collective instrumentalist conceptions of religion. In many ways both religions share similar histories. Both emerged in pagan tribal communities. Judaism, as related in the Old Testament (Kitchen 2003), emerged from a tribe that relocated from the Iraqi desert to Palestine. It did not really become a collective religion until this tribal community experienced demographic expansion in Egypt and then relocated to Palestine.[4] This process of "relocation" involved a historical occupation of major parts of Palestine from pagan communities, and the establishment of a set of religious and political institutions that have coexisted for several millennia. The modern nationalist version of the Jewish state of Israel also suggests that religion can be a powerful instrument of nation-building and social mobilization.[5]

Until the emergence of Islam, the various pagan communities in the Arabian Peninsula were weak, disparate, and engaged in frequent infighting and raiding. Mecca, the holy site of the Ka'ba, was a place of gathering of pagan groups, each worshiping a different God. The only meaningful central government in the Middle East—with very loose control over the Western parts of the Fertile Crescent (Palestine, parts of Egypt)—was the Byzantine Empire with its center in Anatolia and a regional capital in Damascus.

North Africa, most of Egypt, the Jordanian and Syrian deserts, and most of the Arabian Peninsula were the domain of different pagan tribes, mostly nomads living off their cattle, without any central organization or control. Cities like Mecca, Yathrib (later Medina), Cairo, Beirut, Amman, Acre, and Jerusalem were merely local trading posts, resting places for caravans going between Asia and Europe, or local residences of Byzantine aristocracy (Aslan 2011, 3–22). Muhammad, the founder of Islam, used religious rhetoric to unite several tribes, fend off attacks by pagans against Medina, occupy Mecca, and expand the rule of the Islamic protostate across much of the Arabian Peninsula. This new religion was instrumental in forging a new structure of centralized military and economic institutions, governed by Muhammad's charismatic personality. His successors defeated Byzantine rule in most of the Middle East, and within 100 years after Muhammad's death, the Islamic empire extended its rule to the entire Middle East, North Africa, and parts of Spain (Cleveland and Bunton 2012, 13–18, 33–35).

As these examples suggest, collective instrumentalism fails to explain why communities cling to their religious beliefs even when it is costly and even dangerous to do so. Jews adhered to their religion and maintained cohesive communities for nearly two millennia after the kingdom of Judea was destroyed by the Romans in the year 70 CE (and again in 136 CE). Unlike many other peoples in the Middle East and North Africa, Jews refused to convert to Islam during the Islamic expansion period, and again resisted conversion to Christianity during the Middle Ages. Large-scale expulsion of Jews on religious grounds took place in Spain (1492 CE), and the concentration of Jewish communities in restricted areas in Russia in the eighteenth and nineteenth centuries failed to dissolve these communities. If collective instrumentalism were at work, the fate of the Jewish religion would have been the same as the fate of pagan religions in the Middle East, North Africa, and Europe.[6] Likewise, the survival of substantial Islamic communities in Palestine during the Crusades also indicates the tendency of communities to cling to their religious beliefs even at great cost to themselves.

This qualification notwithstanding, collective instrumentalism views the principal utility of common religious and moral beliefs as community building and community preservation, especially in light of external threats to the community. Even when a religious community is persecuted or experiences rampant discrimination, religious beliefs and practices help it overcome hardships that may or may not be due to the distinct character of such communities.

The interpretation of the causal mechanism that connects people to a religion is somewhat different in the instrumentalist conception compared to the primordialist one. According to the primordialist conception, religion has an ideational role; it defines a relationship between people and a belief system, regardless of whether such a relationship serves a utilitarian function. Primordialism does not account for the collective nature of religion, nor does it explain why some religions establish highly hierarchical institutions, while others survive with very few or with a very loose institutional structure. On the other hand, the primordialist conception of religion as a system of belief that induces a collective identity is general and covers both institutionalized and less formal types of religions and religious groups.

The collective instrumentalist conception of religion views religion as an overarching mechanism that forges communal cohesion and creates individual commitment and loyalty to a group. As such, religion is designed, according to this conception, to provide evolutionary advantage to societies and other political organizations in a competitive system, be it a nonstate tribal system or a state system. The conception of religion as a political force does not attempt to account for all versions of religions; however, it does attempt to account for the more structured and institutionalized forms of religious organizations and communities. In the case of pagan religions and some of the nontheistic Asian religions (Buddhism, Jainism), the collective instrumentalist perspective does not offer a clear explanation of why they exist and how they affect politics. However, it does offer a relatively compelling explanation of the rise of monotheistic religions, especially those that have a well-established institutional structure and belief system.

For example, the Reformation and the rise of Protestantism represent not only a spiritual rebellion against the interpretation of Christianity by the Catholic Church and the papacy but also a way of organizing a rebellion against a political and economic empire that suppressed much of Europe during the Middle Ages. There was a need to form a collective culture that would mobilize both feudal aristocrats and vassals around a set of ideas that could combat Catholic orthodoxy and its political and economic supporters (Buck and Zophy 1972). As we discussed above, with regard to the rise of the Abrahamic religions, their growth and expansion vis-à-vis pagan societies characterized by diffuse religious belief systems (or in the case of Judaism, its survival despite persistent persecution and discrimination by other religions) suggests the adaptive power of religion in such communities.

Collective instrumentalism does not claim that religion can always serve as a mobilizing and community-sustaining force; it does suggest that religion may form a tool of social mobilization and communal functioning and survival. It also suggests that this tool can emerge as a grassroots movement or as an elite-driven instrument. Indeed, the origin of many religions, including Christianity, Islam, Buddhism, and Confucianism, reflect a grassroots process that was only later adopted by political elites. The abandonment of one (typically pagan) religion in favor of a monotheistic one reflects the community-building power of certain religious beliefs, sometimes led by charismatic "community organizers" such as Moses in Judaism, Jesus and Saint Paul in Christianity, Muhammad in Islam, or Siddhārtha Gautama (the Buddha) in Buddhism. Adoption of religions by political elites, however, is what gave a major push to these and other religions. And this adoption came typically when political leaders were convinced of the potential political power and legitimacy that such conversion would allow.

Elite instrumentalism makes a very simple statement. Political elites employ religious values, symbols, and manipulate religious institutions to advance their personal political goals and ambitions, which are often—as the political survival theory suggests—to retain power. These goals may have little or nothing to do with religious values. Religion is employed to motivate people into taking actions that are individually costly and dangerous. Elites require resources to accomplish their goals. Some of these resources are financial and require people to pay taxes. Other goals may require them to induce people to risk their lives for their country (or for the things that those elites wish to accomplish through violence). Both taxation and military mobilization are costly and risky endeavors. Political and social elites need either to coerce or induce citizens into giving away parts of their income or to risk their lives for their country or community.

In many cases, elites employ coercive mechanisms to induce compliance. However, coercion is both expensive and risky. Coercion requires deployment of military and security forces, which necessitate funding; these funds are typically extracted from the masses, which creates an even greater public opposition to elite policies. Moreover, security forces can be turned against their leaders. For that reason, elites opt for other, less coercive, means of inducing popular compliance such as persuasion through legislation, public opinion, or rational argumentation. But sometimes, and in some societies, such methods are not expected to work. In such cases, religious symbols and moral values dictated by religious beliefs can be effective instruments of mass mobilization. In certain societies, and with respect to certain issues, religion can be a powerful motivator of costly and risky collective action. It can be used as a tool for mitigating free riding—a common problem of costly collective action.

What makes elite instrumentalism different from collective instrumentalism is the idea that the goals of political elites may differ quite substantially from those of the masses. This divergence of goals creates a potential source of friction between what the elites and the masses want. A mass mobilization strategy is required when the goals of elites and masses diverge and the burden of accomplishing national goals is not shared equally. Religion can become an effective bridge between the goals of the elites and the willingness of the masses to pay the cost of accomplishing them. Elites' use of religion as a mobilization strategy can also be construed in terms of Marx's notion of an "opiate of the masses," where religion is used to divert attention from the failure of political elites to provide collective goods. In some cases, political elites actually share the values of their constituencies. Nevertheless, they consciously manipulate religious ideas to motivate people into costly action and overcome collective action problems.

There are numerous examples of how this theory has worked. The Crusades can be seen as a ploy by the Catholic Church to increase its power and control. By invoking the idea of Christian control of the holy places in Palestine, the religious establishment sought to strengthen allegiance to the Church and to dampen opposition to the Church's economic exploitation of poor European communities. It could also be viewed as a cynical attempt to weaken the various feudal lords who could challenge the Church's economic practices, by diverting their military resources to remote lands.

The modern call to jihad by political Islamic groups is also a case of instrumental mobilization of people to such extreme actions as suicide bombings through religious sanctioning. The use of fatwas (religious opinions) by ulema (Islamic scholars and religious authorities) sanctifying certain acts of violence, including against civilians, in the name of Islam is also a case of elite instrumentalism. Individual acts of terrorism—as large in scope as the September 11, 2001 attacks, let alone more limited ones such as the Boston Marathon bombing of April 2013—have no direct effect on the broader Islamic communities. In many cases such terrorist attacks actually worsen the conditions of the communities whose religious authorities endorse or encourage such actions. But this is precisely the idea of elite instrumentalism—the utility that the elites derive from the use of religious values to mobilize the masses is often different from (or even the inverse of) the utility that the masses derive from it.

When are political elites more likely to use religion to advance their goals? The simple answer is: when they feel they need to do so and if they believe they can. This implies several things. First, elites can effectively invoke religion to induce action when the level of religious belief in a society (or a significant group within society) is high. Second, religion is an effective instrument of mobilization when the society (or group) being mobilized is religiously cohesive. In a religiously diverse society, invoking religion to mobilize people for costly action may be much more difficult, because it requires elites to invoke several (sometimes contradictory) religious values simultaneously. Third, religion is often invoked to induce violence, and not so much to induce cooperation.

The religious economy model relies on similar ideas. As noted above, the focus of this model is on the relations between political elites, whose prime concern is political survival, and religious actors, who are also utility-maximizing entities (Gill 2007). Under certain social conditions—the degree of religious diversity—elites may be inclined to support religious freedom and allow for free competition among religious actors. Under such conditions, political elites focus on ensuring an open market for religion, which typically promotes economic development and political stability. On the other hand, a dominant religion—religious hegemony—is more likely to prompt political elites to form alliances with religious elites, largely through the regulation of religion, the restricting of religious competition, and discrimination against religious minorities. This is apt to invoke grievances, slow down economic and political development, and adversely affect political stability. As noted in chapter 2, these ideas are compelling as far as they touch upon the relations between political and religious institutions and some of the implications of these relations. However, we need to extrapolate from the foundations of this theory to the linkages between religious factors and international relations

In domestic settings, we can examine how and when leaders of different groups use religion to mobilize members to participate in political strife. In heterogeneous societies, religion can be, and is often used by leading figures to incite animosity and strife on the part of one group against other—religiously different—groups. In religiously homogeneous societies, religion is not an effective instrument to organize dissent against the regime or other political and social groups, because the latter are not religiously different.[7] In international settings, we can examine how national elites invoke religion to get people involved in international conflicts.

Linking domestic to international politics, elites of a faction within a society who wish to initiate action against other groups within that society are more likely to do so when they believe that they can rely on external support for such actions. If other states share a religious affinity with the focal group, it is more likely that leaders of that group will invoke religion as a central cause of conflict. In the absence of the prospect of outside help, especially when the balance of power between competing groups in a society is not favorable to the focal group, elites will try to downplay the role of religion, so as not to polarize the conflict even more.

These ideas highlight both the compelling aspects of the instrumentalist perspective as well as its limitations. Instrumentalism allows not only a way of distinguishing between societies in terms of when and under what structural social conditions religion is likely to be invoked as a tool of social mobilization. It also enables us to trace the dynamics of religious mobilization over time. Changes in social or international circumstances alter the conditions that enable elites to invoke religion to mobilize masses. Changes in the character of outsiders and their relation to the focal society affect elites' ability or willingness to use religion as a tool of social mobilization. Finally, changes in the goals of the elites, their perception of job security, or the religious affinity between the elites and masses may alter the instrumental use of religion within a society or between states.

The weakness of this approach is that it offers little insight into the religious sources of domestic and international cooperation. Inducing cooperation within a religiously homogeneous state that experiences political instability or social unrest by invoking religious values is likely to be difficult. If mobilizing for cooperation via religion were effective, such instability would not have emerged in the first place. Likewise, in a religiously diverse society, using religion is more likely to deepen existing differences, tensions, and suspicion among social groups. In international settings, religion can be used to help forge low-cost international cooperation such as forming and sustaining international cultural institutions. But it is not very effective as a tool of social mobilization for costly international cooperation such as trade agreements that open domestic markets to international competition.

Clearly, the instrumentalist perspective is a more dynamic theory of religion and politics than the primordialist perspective. Identity markers are fairly constant for a given society over time; if they change, this takes place over many years. By contrast, the conditions that allow, induce, or compel political elites to manipulate religious symbols fluctuate significantly, often from leader to leader within the same state. And even under the tenure of a specific leader or group, the conditions that affect their ability or willingness to use religion as an instrument of social mobilization might change significantly.

Primordialism suggests that there are significant differences between societies in the ways religion affects the choice of enemies or partners for cooperative ventures. However, there is little variation in the way religion affects the politics of a given society or state over time. This is so as long as the relations between religious and state institutions remain unchanged. By contrast, instrumentalism suggests a potential dynamic factor that affects the tendency of political leaders to manipulate religious factors as a tool of social mobilization over time. Specifically, the argument is that changes in the level of perceived job security of political leaders affect the tendency to use religion as an instrument of political mobilization and support. Political leaders at risk of losing their jobs are more likely to invoke religion as a tool of political mobilization than political leaders who feel secure in their posts. Several mechanisms account for this expectation. First, leaders may have an incentive to use religion in a diversionary context. When they feel that their winning coalition is crumbling, they may invoke religious symbols or issues to divert attention from their problems. If they rely on a religiously or ethnically cohesive coalition (for example, in autocracies that relied on the support of certain ethnoreligious groups such as in Saddam Hussein's Iraq or Bashar al-Assad's Syria), invoking religious symbols may become a powerful politically expedient strategy. Invoking real or imaginary threats to these values by an internal or external enemy that is religiously different can unite the winning coalition around the leader and divert the attention of those members who had considered defection to issues that unite them and compel them to support the leader.

Political instability that threatens the leadership's survival prospects can also emerge due to the rising power of the opposition relative to that of the winning coalition. In such cases, the leaders' goal is to divert the attention of broader elements of the selectorate—beyond the winning coalition—so as to relieve pressure on themselves. Here, too, when they can (that is, when the society is sufficiently cohesive), they may invoke religion so as to unite the selectorate against external or internal threats. Such threats are apt to be framed by the leadership as states, groups, or policies that place important religious values at risk (e.g., holy places, religious rituals, religious practices, dress codes, women's rights, etc.).

Second, it is possible that some of the threats to the leadership's survival or to the state's security emanate from groups or states that are religiously different from those of the focal state or of the leader's winning coalition. However, the issues at stake may have little or nothing to do with religion. These may be politico-economic issues or territorial issues. Nevertheless, the leader's need to mobilize human and material resources to face these material challenges may require her to invoke religious factors to ensure consent.

For example, many consider the Arab–Israeli or Palestinian–Israeli conflict as a religious conflict (e.g., Reuther and Reuther 2002, Fox and Sandler 2004, 137–62). There are certain religious aspects to this conflict; it is about control of holy places to Judaism and Islam; it is between two distinct religious groups. However, the conflict is also—and, from some perspectives, mostly—a conflict between competing national movements, and about territory, independence, and prestige (which also explains some of the less noticeable intra-Arab, intra-Palestinian, and intra-Jewish conflicts embedded within the larger contestation). Fox and Sandler (2004) provide a brief but insightful review of the Israeli–Palestinian conflict and show that (a) religious factors took prominence during some periods of the conflict, but were of secondary or even marginal importance during other periods of the conflict, and (b) the political leadership of both the Palestinian national movement and the Zionist movement found it expedient to promote religious factors during some periods of the conflict and to suppress such factors during other periods. They conclude their analysis by arguing that religion played an important but not dominant role in the evolution of the Israeli–Palestinian conflict, implicitly suggesting that its resolution may depend on reducing the religious (and ethnic) framing of the issues and elevating rational and secular factors that make the issues at stake divisible and thus subject to compromise.

Importantly, in such seemingly religious rivalries such as the Arab–Israeli, Indo–Pakistani, Greek–Turkish cases, or in domestic conflicts such as those branded as "religious civil wars" by Toft, Philpott, and Shah (2011, 160–71), religion can be seen as one, but not necessarily the dominant issue driving the conflict. It is, however, an important mobilizing instrument of national or quasi-national movements. For the instrumentalist approach, religion is a political weapon, part of the arsenal of political elites (and counterelites), that can be turned on or off based on political calculations regarding its utility and associated risks. The same leader, group, or regime may invoke religious symbols to mobilize support under one set of circumstances and avoid using such symbols under different circumstances, or with respect to different political challenges.

4. Constructivism

As noted above, constructivism does not assign an explicit role to religion in the ebb and flow of world politics. Snyder (2011, 2) points out that Wendt's field-defining book does not have a single index entry for religion. However, Snyder acknowledges—correctly—that there is ample implicit reference to religion as a fundamental ideational factor in the constructivist paradigm. Religion can play an important role in the constructivist paradigm's ideas about conflict and cooperation in world politics. Thus, we can derive propositions about the role of religious factors in world politics from constructivist ideas about the way politics function. In particular, these inferences rest upon the constructivist focus on the relationship among identity, ideas, and action. To derive such inferences, we start by outlining the fundamental assumptions that drive the constructivist paradigm.

1. *What I do depends on who I am (or who I believe I am)*. States (or social groups within states) operate on the basis of their subjective

understanding of their internal and external environment. This contrasts with the materialist conception of states' motives (e.g., power and interests).
2. *Subjective perceptions of reality are socially constructed.* The ways by which states define who they are and how they relate to their environment are "constructed" by a set of factors. Some of these factors are fairly constant; others are subject to change.
3. *States have corporate identities.* A corporate identity is "a property that generates motivational and behavioral dispositions" (Wendt 1999, 224). This assumption can be extended to social groups within states.
4. *National identity is defined largely by cultural factors.* The relatively stable factors that determine national identity are its cultural characteristics, such as the linguistic, religious, racial, gender, and ethnic composition of its population.
5. *States' experience in the international system defines the manner in which they construct their reality.* States' identities are not necessarily static. Rather, important aspects of the perceived identity of states are shaped by their interaction with their international environment and by their perception of the characteristics of this environment. Consequently, states may change and redefine their perception of the environment, and determine whom they perceive as friends and whom they perceive as foes. This, in turn, affects their behavior.

The first assumption about the effect of identity on behavior is perhaps the most important one in terms of a meaningful connection between religion and behavior according to this perspective. What it implies is that identity shapes behavior. It also implies that people, groups, and states, act and react not on the basis of some "objective" factors or stimuli; rather, they react to the way in which they understand these factors or stimuli ("anarchy is what states make of it," to use Wendt's [1992] famous title).

The fundamental idea in constructivism is that seemingly tangible factors, which appear to shape behavior in "materialist" paradigms of world politics (i.e., realism and liberalism)—interest, power, or international anarchy—are not exogenous. Rather, these are socially constructed concepts—ideas that people, organizations, or states accept as "given." These concepts can define the goals of units and help predict how they will act in certain circumstances as long as such units cling to these ideas. So, what we consider the central "objective" factors, are in fact an outgrowth of a set of common beliefs and ideas. When these ideas change, so does the world.

What constructivists mean by the social construction of ideas (or identities) is that a group of people comes to assign a common meaning to a certain concept. That common meaning serves as a foundation for communication and action within that group. The most obvious example of "social construction" is the concept of money. Money can have no value unless a lot of people believe that they can trade paper (or metal) for goods and services. Likewise, political power would have no meaning unless people who hold public office could command obedience from subordinates. Obedience would not take place unless subordinates believed that people in public office have the right to issue directives, or that they possess the ability to punish disobedience.

The notion that states (or specific groups within states) can have a corporate identity implies that being part of a collective entity and the responsibilities that follow from that association have a meaningful interpretation in international politics. This is particularly relevant here because religion may be one of the markers of this group or national identity. Given that corporate identity is indeed a property that generates "motivational or behavioral dispositions," then we can meaningfully incorporate religion into constructivist theories of national behavior and international structures.

One may deduce from constructivism a causal mechanism that connects religion to cooperation given the paradigm's focus on identity and ideational convergence. For example, constructivism maintains that a state's interests are a function of its identity, which is derived from its culture (Wendt 1992, Finnemore 1996). It follows that national identity and ideational convergence/divergence shape a state's international interactions, and that interactive experiences shape and alter national identities as well. In new states that lack interactive experience, identities are shaped by shared cultural attributes that bind their populations.

Two issues arise from these deductions, which connect the constructivist paradigm to primordialist or instrumentalist approaches (Lynch 2009, Fox and Sandler 2004, Hasenclever and Rittberger 2003). The primordialist element is that religion forms a natural common ground among people, causing them to share a set of common beliefs. Such beliefs encompass notions of right or wrong and shared commitments to collective values. This is what religion is all about. Moreover, political leaders who wish to establish a sense of loyalty to a new "state" concept, often manipulate religion as a unifying symbol. This symbol can define in-groups and out-groups within the state, between states, and between states and other actors in their external environment (e.g., alliances and intergovernmental organizations [IGOs]).

Religion helps shape not only the state's self-image but also its perception of its external environment. Religious similarity is presumed to foster an initial cooperative atmosphere between states. To the extent that such cooperation is not disrupted by other contentious issues, it reinforces shared ideational convergence due to interaction-related effects. Clearly, there are other determinants of the national identity of newly founded states. These may also affect perceptions of affinity or suspicion between states. A shared heritage of colonial domination may be one such factor. For example, shared colonial experience was the major means of socialization for the newly independent states in the post–World War II era. The socialization process took place on two levels, one reinforcing the other (Henderson 2015). On one level, there was the homogenizing effect of the international relations of the Cold War era, which Waltz (1979) largely describes. In this context, the former colonies in Africa, Asia, the Caribbean, and Oceania assumed the role of recognized independent states with clearly demarcated borders and the rights and responsibilities of sovereignty—although these were often violated by former colonial powers and the superpowers. Internationally, these postcolonial regimes competed with other states and, to a large degree, imitated practices that had proved successful in pursuing their political interests. These practices were evident with respect to the postcolonial states' international diplomacy, trade relations, membership in international organizations, and compliance with international law, as well as their economic development plans and pursuit of their national security. Most newly established states typically situated themselves within the respective blocs of the Cold War era. A few other new states pursued a "third way" through the Non-Aligned Movement. But in each of these initiatives they were conditioned and constrained by the homogenizing impact of the prevalent practices in that sphere of their international relations.

On another level, there was the homogenizing effect of the domestic relations of many of these postcolonial states, circumscribed as they were by the institutional apparatus established during the colonial era. For example, many of the postcolonial states retained the repressive military apparatus of the colonial state, which was more attuned to domestic repression than foreign war. Most new states kept intact, or with only marginal reforms, the colonial economy. Such economies focused less on internal industrial development and more on the often brutal extraction of resources and exploitation of labor. These economic policies maintained dependent relations in international trade by orienting their domestic markets for export to benefit the metropole and its domestic agents. In general, postcolonial states had their initial foreign and domestic policies constrained by the processes associated with European colonialism. As a result, their patterns of initial interactions and their relationship with other postcolonial states converged in several ways.[8]

Ethnic kinship or a history of racial persecution may also affect perceptions of affinity or suspicion between states; however, such factors may often play a less consistent role than shared religion because they offer a set of norms and behavioral directives that are fluid given the changing conceptions of ethnicity over time and the specious nature of race as a concept, which makes it amenable to redefinitions as well. By contrast, religious affinity implies shared beliefs in norms, institutions, and behavioral principles at the individual and communal level that are more time invariant.

Assumption 5 suggests that as the state matures and acquires experience in dealing with other actors in its external environment, interaction-based experience becomes increasingly important in defining both the self-image of the state and its attitude toward other states. This implies that we should expect a lowered impact of religious affinities on international interactions over time, as opposed to a growing impact of interaction-based experience, such as the effects of past cooperation and conflict on both national identity and on perception of the state's environment.

One result is that the more we focus on—and in our systematic analyses, control for—the conflict and cooperation histories of our cases, the less impact religious factors should evince in the outcomes of interest. This is not a "secularization" argument per se but a "socialization" one. It suggests that the socialization process of international relations conditions state and nonstate actors to draw from an array of political, economic, and social practices, institutions, and policies that do not strictly or predominantly privilege religious identities and interests.

There is another way to view the manner in which religious identity and interaction-based identities shape behavior according to the constructivist paradigm. According to the constructivist paradigm, identity affects perceptions of affinity and those, in turn, affect the initial interactions among states. This implies that initial interactions in dyads that have at least one "young" member are likely to be shaped by religious affinities or differences. However, these initial interactions may establish a pattern, which, in turn, shapes subsequent perceptions of identity such that religion may have an indirect impact on conflict and cooperation beyond the initial period of interaction between states.

Just like primordialism, constructivism views religion as an important identity marker. Therefore, we can apply the matrix describing the conditions under which religion affects domestic and foreign policies of states here as well (Table 3.1). Religiously homogeneous states that lack a clear separation between religion and politics (Type I states) are likely to define their identity in terms of religion (e.g., the Islamic Republic of Iran, or the Islamic Republic of Saudi Arabia). Domestic conflicts, especially ones with religious undertones, are less likely in these states. Likewise Type I states are likely to define their attitudes toward other states in terms of religious similarity or dissimilarity. Type II states are more likely to be politically stable than Type III states, but their relations with other states are also likely to be based on perceptions of religious similarity or dissimilarity.

Religiously diverse societies without clear separation between political and religious spheres (Type III states) are apt to be politically unstable. Internal instability in such states is likely characterized by religious conflicts. Their relations with other states are not as likely to be affected by religious similarity or dissimilarity as Types I or II states. However, one key issue that connects internal and external conflict in Type III states is the relationship between disadvantaged religious groups in these states and the dominant religious groups in neighboring states. Affinities between states whose dominant religious group shares an affinity with disadvantaged or persecuted religious groups in a Type III state increase the risk of external intervention in domestic conflicts in Type III states or the risk of external support for insurgent groups operating in Type III states (Gartzke and Gleditsch 2006, San-Akca 2016).

Both Type II—but even more so Type IV—states are apt to display the highest level of political stability domestically. These states are likely to define their identity in terms that are based on other shared values such as democracy, free trade, globalization, and so forth. These factors play a far more important role in the identification of partners for cooperation or potential rivals in the international system than religious similarity or dissimilarity.

In short, the ideas of the constructivist paradigm are quite similar to those of the primordialist perspective. The constructivist ideas provide, however, an important dynamism to the static primordialist perspective. Specifically, the importance of religion is not fixed over time; rather, religious elements of identity interact with other—experience-based—factors. These latter factors act to shape and reshape perceptions of self and of the environment along with the more basic and static cultural factors.

5. The Clash of Civilizations

Huntington (1993, 24) defines a civilization in terms of both objective elements such as "language, history, religion, customs, institutions," and subjective elements of self-identification. For Huntington (1996, 43), a civilization is "the highest cultural grouping of people and the broadest level of cultural identity people have short of that which distinguishes humans from other species." He maintains that a civilization "is a culture writ large" (p. 41), and that it is "the biggest 'we' within which we feel culturally at home as distinguished from all the other 'thems' out there" (p. 43). Civilizations are quite diverse in composition and may "involve a large number of people, such as Chinese civilization, or a very small number of people such as the Anglophone Caribbean" (p. 43). The "central defining characteristic" of a civilization is its religion (p. 47); hence, "the major civilizations in human history have been closely identified with the world's great religions" (p. 42). These civilizations include the Sinic, Japanese, Hindu, Islamic, Orthodox, Western, Latin American, (apparently) Buddhist, and "possibly African" civilizations (pp. 47–48). Since shared religion is the single most important indicator of a civilization, Huntington maintains that intercivilizational clashes are usually conflicts "between peoples of different religions" (p. 253). That religious difference should be the fulcrum on which the CoC thesis rests stems from Huntington's view that religion is "possibly the most profound difference that can exist between people." Therefore, he contends that warfare between states of different civilizations is "greatly enhanced by beliefs in different gods" (p. 254).

The argument of the CoC thesis is simple: the conflicts of the last several centuries—especially those that characterized world politics during the Cold War era—are likely to be replaced by conflicts between different civilizations in the post–Cold War era. Huntington (1993, 25–28; 1996) points out several reasons for this. First, civilizational divides are fundamental. They have always been there and are unlikely to disappear in the future. Second, growing contact between civilizations deepens the divide and increases mutual hostilities. This is in sharp contrast to liberal notions that contact increases interdependence and peace. Third, economic modernization reduces the state as a source of identity, and the vacuum left by declining nationalism is replaced by religion. Fourth, the growing power of the West leads to growing feelings of self-identification in terms of "roots" among non-Westerners. Fifth, cultural differences do not lend themselves to compromise and peaceful resolutions as do economic or political differences. The economic and political divides that characterized world politics during the Cold War era enabled the major powers and their allies to peacefully coexist and even display some degree of cooperation despite different ideologies. This is no longer the case in the post–Cold War era. Sixth, growing economic regionalism creates growing intracivilizational integration on the one hand, and a higher level of regional—and thus cultural—differentiation, on the other.

Inherent in the CoC thesis is that primordial currents were ever present in world politics. However, they have been modified and overshadowed by the politics of nationalism, in general, and Cold War politics, in particular. Now that nationalism is in decline and the Cold War is over, paradoxically, in this view, the economic dominance of the West is apt to invoke resentment from other civilizations. This resentment cannot be mitigated with politics of negotiation and compromise because the issues at stake are indivisible. So the result is a conflict among civilizations, but in particular, the West against "the Rest."

While the general prediction of the CoC thesis is similar to that of the constructivist paradigm, its logic is quite different. Constructivism views identity in general and national identity as evolving with experience. One of the key factors that affect change in the social construction of national identities—especially in relation to other states—is what Wendt (1999) calls "international cultures." An international culture consists of a set of commonly accepted principles of international conduct. Such international cultures may undergo long-term shifts as some norms arise and become widespread and other norms decline or disappear.

Wendt (2003), for example, claims that both micro- and macrolevel forces drive the international system toward a world state. At the microlevel, the drive of individuals and groups to recognize their "subjectivity," that is, their right to be different, leads to a process whereby individuals get to have their rights protected beyond a single state boundary. At the macrolevel, there are several forces that drive the system toward a unifying authority. These include the logic of anarchy, accompanied by the growing destructiveness of war. However, Wendt offers a long-term prediction, claiming that this process will take between 100 and 200 years. In contrast, for Huntington, cultural factors are permanent. However, they surface when globalization spreads and global hierarchies become increasingly steep. The end result is that the world—from the end of the Cold War and into the foreseeable future—is moving into a period where civilizations engage in violent clashes. As intercivilizational conflict increases, by implication, intracivilizational cooperation increases.

There are several issues with the CoC thesis. First, as noted above, it does not rest on a set of propositions deduced from well-defined assumptions about the world. It does not offer a clear causal mechanism that explains why there was no clash of civilization during the Cold War era or other nationalist periods beyond his assertion that the superpower standoff of the former kept a lid on such clashes. Nor does it provide a logical causal mechanism that explains why civilizations would clash rather than cooperate for the mutual benefit of all.

Second, Huntington assumes that civilizations are cohesive entities. In practice, civilizations may be far more diverse than what would be expected given his classification. This is particularly so when we take for granted his claim that religion is a central defining feature of a civilization. Islam, for example, is characterized by an often bitter animosity and mistrust between its two major religious families: Sunnism and Shi'ism. Less conspicuous, but no less severe, is the tension between these two religious families and other Islamic families, such as the Yazidis, Alawites, and Sufis. The wars of the Reformation within Christendom were not less violent and intense than the wars during the Crusades between Christians and Muslims. Huntington's argument implicitly suggests that the sense of common threat from other civilizations has a unifying power beyond the centrifugal forces within civilizations.

Third, the CoC thesis has at best a hazy conditional claim about why there is a high potential for conflict between some civilizations (e.g., between the Western civilization and the Islamic or the Asian—i.e., Confucian or Japanese), but not between others. This claim is rooted in a modified balance-of-power argument resting on whether the civilization has a core state to coordinate the activities of civilization members (e.g., the United States is the core state of the West) or does not (e.g., Islam lacks a core state, which contributes to its proclivity to violence, according to Huntington). Nor does it have a specific explanation of what these conflicts will be about—will they be about resources, territory, ideas?

Fourth, the CoC conception does not offer a clear classification of civilization. The characterization of the interaction among several characteristics that make up a "civilization" is vague and preoperational. Consequently, Huntington's classification of civilizations is quite idiosyncratic: it is a mix of religious, racial, ethnic, geographic, and political-economic attributes of societies. More importantly, Huntington wavers as to the role of religion in defining a civilization, most of the time focusing on it as the key determinant, and other times combining it with other factors. His classification of civilizations is also based on religion in some cases and on racial and geographical factors in others.

Nevertheless, the CoC thesis offers an interesting juxtaposition of cultural and political factors. It provides a clear and somber prediction about the structure of conflict in a post–Cold War world. Therefore it deserves serious treatment in any analysis of the relationship between religion and world politics.

6. Comparing the Different Perspectives

At the core, these perspectives have a great deal in common. First, they view religion as an independent—perhaps not unique but certainly important—factor in driving domestic and foreign policies. Consequently, all of these perspectives suggest a powerful connection between religion and politics. Second, at a general level, all of these perspectives have similar predictions about how religion affects domestic and international conflict and international cooperation. For example, they all expect to see more political tension in religiously diverse societies compared to homogeneous ones. Likewise, they expect some tension between religiously divergent states and some degree of amity between religiously similar states. Third, these perspectives are bottom-up approaches. Their focus is on the process by which individual and communal belief systems are converted into collective actions of groups and of states. Consequently, the aggregate—systemic—consequences of these processes are "emergent," that is, a complex and often unintended result of the convergence and divergence of beliefs and actions of multiple actors. This contrasts rather sharply with "top-down" perspectives of international relations, which emphasize the impact of external factors, principally the structure of the international system. The exception is the CoC thesis, which suggests an interaction between "bottom-up" forces, that is, cultural factors that drive human action, and top-down forces, that is, changes in the structure of the international system.

Both the primordialist and the instrumentalist perspectives assign a great deal of importance to the relations between religious and political institutions. Both approaches suggest that it is the interaction between religious diversity and the state-religion relations that produces the most marked effect on political processes. This interaction creates the context in which religion makes for a significant factor in a state's policies. It distinguishes between states whose domestic and foreign policies are strongly influenced by religion and those whose policies are influenced by other factors: power, prestige, political culture, and economics. By contrast, the constructivist approach and the CoC thesis do not accord a great deal of importance to the interaction between political and religious institutions; their key focus is on the religious structure of societies. The CoC thesis does not accord much significance to the religious diversity/homogeneity of societies; its focus is on broad definitions of civilizational divides and the manner in which they affect structural systemic processes.

There are, however, some marked differences in terms of when, how, and under what conditions religious factors influence political processes. These differences are due to the specific causal mechanisms that drive these relations between religion and politics. The primordialist perspective treats religion as an ever-present guide to individual and communal behavior. Religion matters more or less depending on the structure of specific communities—their level of religions cohesiveness or diversity and the degree to which religion and politics are separated or intermeshed. These variables are also important aspects of the instrumentalist perspective. However, for instrumentalists, the interaction between religion's cohesion and religion/state relations provides the context within which leaders may manipulate religious feelings for national or international goals. While primordialism treats the relations between political and religious institutions as relatively fixed, the instrumentalist approach suggests that political elites can manipulate state-religious ties to advance their goals, just as they can invoke religious values if these serve their prospects of political survival.

Both instrumentalism and constructivism suggest that the importance of religious factors as motivating political forces may change over time. In the former perspective, this variation is a function of elite priorities and goals, and especially their perception of job security. In the latter perspective, it is a function of the experiential evolution of a given community: as states mature, their national identity is increasingly shaped by their interactive experiences with other states or nonstate actors rather than by social and cultural factors.

What are the key expectations of these approaches with respect to the effect of religious factors on the domestic and foreign policies of states? Table 3.2 summarizes the key propositions deduced from these perspectives with respect to matters of international conflict, international cooperation, and internal political conflict and quality of life.

Some explanation of the contents of this table is in order. First, we pointed out some general expectations about domestic and foreign policy that are consistent with the logic of each of these perspectives. In some cases, these expectations are rather explicit (e.g., the CoC argument about intercivilizational conflict in the post–Cold War era). In other cases, they are implicit in the logic of the approach (e.g., the constructivist implication that cultural identity matters during the formative years of a state, but interaction-based identity matters more during later periods). In either case, the expectations listed in the table are logical consequences of the key claims of these perspectives. Second, we are careful to point out when a given perspective does not allow deduction of a clear answer to a question concerning the relationship between religious factors and a specific type of behavior.

Third, and very important, we derive some implications from these perspectives with respect to an issue that has not received sufficient attention in the literature on religion and politics: the relationship between religious factors and human security or quality of life in various states. These expectations are also implicit in these perspectives. We elaborate on each of these predictions in the relevant chapters. We now offer some of the key theoretical ideas that guide our analyses in the subsequent chapters.

7. An Integrative Theory of Religion and World Politics

Our theory does not attempt to reinvent the wheel. It builds on these theoretical perspectives as well as on the vast literature on religion and politics. What we attempt below is to integrate the key insights of the various perspectives, taking into account (a) the areas where their predictions overlap, (b) the relative strengths and weaknesses of each of these perspectives, and (c) areas that they do not cover explicitly. In the areas where the predictions of one of these perspectives differ from those of the other perspectives, we adjudicate and explain why we prefer one explanation to the others. Using Table 3.2 as a general guide, we offer an integrative theory of religion and political behavior.

Our theory rests on several key premises. First, there is a great deal of variation in terms of the relationship between states and societies. Some states are formed around homogeneous societal characteristics, encompassing a cohesive set of ethnic, religious, and linguistic groups. Other states are made up of patches of multiple ethnicities, religious groups, with people communicating via a multitude of languages. This is what Miller (2007) calls the *state-to-nation balance*. A high state-to-nation balance indicates a convergence of political sovereignty with social cohesion.[9] An imbalance exists when the political boundaries and institutions of a state do not match the social characteristics of the population within it. This variation, expressed not only—but quite often—in terms of religious homogeneity or diversity, plays an important role in shaping the state's domestic structure and its international outlook.

Table 3.2 Key expectations of theoretical perspectives regarding the relationship between religion and domestic and foreign policy

Domain	Question	Primordialism	Instrumentalism	Constructivism	Clash of Civilizations
Domestic Conflict	Which states are prone to civil conflict?	Religiously diverse societies where religious and political institutions are closely linked.	Religiously diverse societies where religious and political institutions are closely linked.	No specific prediction.	No specific prediction.
	When do religious factors affect civil conflict outbreak?	No specific prediction; general propensity prediction.	When economic, political, social conditions worsen.	No specific prediction.	No specific prediction.
International Conflict	Which states are conflict prone?	Religiously cohesive states where religious and political institutions are closely linked; low level of secularism.	Religiously cohesive states where religious and political institutions are closely linked; low levels of secularism.	Religiously cohesive; low levels of secularism.	Religiously cohesive (not clear); Muslim.
	When do religious factors affect states' conflict involvement?	No specific prediction.	During periods of political instability.	In early stages of political independence.	During the post–Cold War era.
	Who fights whom?	Religiously dissimilar states.	Religiously dissimilar states.	Religiously dissimilar states.	Religiously dissimilar states.
	When do religious factors affect dyadic conflict outbreak?	No specific prediction.	When either or both states experience political instability.	When one or both states are new states.	During post–Cold War era.

	Which regions are more likely to be conflict prone?	Religiously diverse regions.	Religiously diverse regions.	Religiously diverse regions.	Religiously diverse regions.
	When are religious factors more likely to affect regional conflict?	No specific prediction.	When multiple states experience political instability.	When multiple states emerge into the region.	During post–Cold War era.
International Cooperation	Who cooperates with whom?	Religiously similar states.	Religiously similar states.	Religiously similar states.	(Possibly) Religiously similar states.
	In what cooperative domains are religious factors more likely to play an important role?	Security, international organizations.	Security, international organizations.	All domains.	No specific prediction.
	When are religious factors more likely to foster cooperation?	No specific prediction.	When both states are politically stable.	When one or both states are new.	During post–Cold War era.
Quality of Life	What is the effect of religious factors on quality of life in societies?	Religious freedom and secularism are related to quality of life.	Religious freedom and secularism are related to quality of life.	No specific prediction.	No specific prediction.

Second, another source of variation in terms of domestic political structure and international outlook stems from the fact that we start our investigation at an admittedly important—but from a historical point of view quite arbitrary—time point: the end of World War II. At that particular time point, only a quarter of the contemporary international system consisted of sovereign and independent states (accounting for only two-thirds of the world's population). Most of these states had a fairly long political tradition, as well as substantial experience in international interactions—both cooperative and conflictual. However, over 140 new states formed since 1945. Most of these states emerged in territories that had been under colonial rule for many decades or centuries. As several authors (e.g., Maoz 1996, Robinson 2014, Henderson 2015) pointed out, these newly formed states' boundaries were charted out by representatives of colonial powers drawing lines on maps without regard to any ethnic, religious, linguistic, or communal ties between the people on both sides of the lines or within them. The lack of a tradition of political independence and the absence of a meaningful international experience of these newly established states compounded the typically diverse composition of their societies. These characteristics account for some fundamental differences between these new states and the pre-1945 states.

Our theory builds on the combined notions of religion as an identity marker and of religion as a political instrument. We also rely heavily on the political survival theory. In particular, we build on the idea that political leaders' main goal is to ensure their political survival. Accordingly, they are constantly engaged in figuring out how to build (if they are out of power) or sustain (if they are incumbents) a winning coalition. They design their domestic and foreign policies in a manner that would make an actual or potential winning coalition happy and thus supportive of their tenure.

Consequently, our theory combines the structural features of societies as a fundamental reality with the political preferences and strategies of leaders and of potential contenders to power. We also focus on the institutional structure of states—in particular on the relationship between political and religious institutions. In that sense, we adopt the categorization of the social and institutional structure of societies, presented in Table 3.1 above.

We do not diminish the role of religious actors, emphasized by such authors as Philpott (2007); Toft, Philpott, and Shah (2011); and Fox and Sandler (2004). However, we believe that the power of religious actors shifts from a spiritual to a political level when they are either employed by the state (as in most cases concerning foreign policy) or when they confront the state (which then becomes a key aspect of domestic politics). This shifts the center of attention to the manner in which political leaders can or are willing to use religious ideas, values, institutions, and principles.

Our theory separates the manner in which religious factors operate in foreign policy-related matters compared to the way in which religious factors affect domestic politics. The foreign policy of states is almost exclusively under the control of political leaders and the foreign policy and security establishments. Following the political survival theory, we argue that the selection of diplomatic, economic, or military instruments serves to provide public or private goods to the leaders' winning coalition. Accordingly, the manipulation of religious symbols, institutions, and rhetoric in order to mobilize resources for certain policies is also an instrument that the leadership can use if and when conditions are right. By contrast, domestic politics reflect a constant competition between the leader and her coalition against some counterelite (or several counterelites) that seeks to replace them. In that context, the use of religion may also be part of that competitive struggle. The leader may be able to use religion in some contexts, but the opposition may also be able to use religion to advance its claims.

Our theory focuses both on fairly stable characteristics of states and societies, on the international environment in which states operate, and on more dynamic factors that affect the propensity to apply religion to foreign and domestic affairs. In particular, we emphasize several key variables: (a) *social structure*—defined in terms of religious homogeneity or diversity; (b) *institutional structure*—defined in terms of the relations between political and religious institutions; (c) *the structure of the state's relevant external environment*—defined in terms of the degree of similarity between the religious composition of the state's society and that of its politically relevant international environment. These three variables are fairly structural and stable. They tend to exhibit limited change for a given state over time. By contrast, the fourth variable provides a more dynamic dimension to our theory. It is (d) *the circumstantial incentives to use religion*—defined primarily in terms of the degree of political stability of a given state. We discuss each of these variables in turn.

7.1 Social Structure

Political leaders come to power in a society whose social, religious, ethnic, racial and linguistic characteristics are established. Some leaders can attempt to fundamentally change some aspects of this structure. For example, they remove existing legal and institutional barriers limiting integration among social or religious groups, or impose new barriers on cross-community ties.[10] But many, if not most, leaders operate within the constraints imposed on them by that structure, because fundamental changes of this structure are either too difficult or too risky. At the same time, most political actors, as well as religious or spiritual leaders, work within the political order of the day. In many cases, they cooperate with the political and legal system enacted by political institutions. Here too, there are notable exceptions, whereby political actors become actively involved in political change. Our theory does not—at least not directly—attempt to account for the attempt of political leaders or religious actors to change existing social structures or the relationship between religious institutions and political ones. This is a topic better left to other studies. We are interested in the ways political leaders (and in the case of civil conflict—political opposition) use religion as a political instrument.

Two principal factors collectively determine the constraints on, or opportunities afforded to, political leaders' manipulation of religion in foreign affairs. First, we consider social structure in terms of the degree of religious homogeneity in a state. Clearly, there are quite a few other characteristics of social structure, for example, economic classes, racial and non-religious ethnic divisions, or ideological differences among individuals and groups. We attempt to control for those factors in the coming analyses. Our focus here, however, is on the religious structure of the society in terms of religious homogeneity or diversity.

Second, we examine, to the extent that our data permit, the structure of institutional and legal relations between politics and religion. The complexity of this relationship may well surpass the manner in which we operationalize state-religious relations. For example, we do not have a direct way to measure or estimate the degree of religiosity in society. Yet we do need to examine how the degree to which people take religion seriously—in both day-to-day matters and high-level political interactions among states—affects the outcomes of interest in our study. Therefore, we do not proxy religiosity directly; rather, we capture its obverse: the proportion of secularists in the society, which is measured as the percentage of people in the society who do not claim to practice any religion (or who are proclaimed atheists or agnostics). This is clearly not an ideal measure of secularism (as the opposite of religiosity), but this is the limit of what our data permit if we wish to examine long-term effects of religious factors on politics.[11]

In our view, secularism—as a contrast to "religiosity"—is part of the religious homogeneity/diversity of a society. We consider nonbelievers—atheists, agnostics, and general nonbelievers—to be part and parcel of the religious structure of a society. In many ways, these groups are not different from religious groups insofar as they often fight for or support certain values, practices, and norms—religious freedom, separation between religion and politics, economics, education, and social activities. Just as one religious group distinguishes itself from other religious groups by virtue of its unique characteristics, non-religious groups may have similar institutional, legal, and political characteristics.

These assumptions set the stage for the key ideas of our integrative theory of religion and politics. We start with a discussion of how religious factors may operate in foreign policy. Political leaders who contemplate mobilizing support for external conflict using religious symbols and values face two types of constraints: the social structure and the relationship between political and religious institutions. When a society is religiously diverse, it is much more difficult to use religion as a mobilization strategy than when society is religiously homogeneous. In a religiously diverse society it is especially dangerous to use religion as a mobilization strategy when some segments of the society are religiously similar to actual or potential enemies. Likewise, mobilizing support for cooperative ventures via religious commitments in a diverse society can backfire for the same reasons. By contrast, when a society is religiously homogeneous and when enemies are religiously dissimilar, political leaders feel more comfortable invoking the protection or acquisition of holy sites (in territorial disputes), treatment of religious minorities (in policy or regime-related disputes), or general ideas of fighting against infidels. In the same vein, costly cooperation with religiously similar states against potentially dissimilar common enemies becomes a more expedient and acceptable policy when a society is religiously homogeneous.

On the other hand, cooperative ventures that rely on more rational calculations and involve win-win benefit structures, such as international trade, are not as easily justified on religious grounds. Therefore, it is less likely that political elites would use religious ideas to justify trade agreements or more general trade policies. This is so even when certain religious principles impose constraints on the kind of deals (e.g., interest-based loans in Islam) or encourage them (e.g., "prosperity Gospel" among some Christians).

We expect that the religious structure of a society affects internal conflict in similar ways to those in which religious structure affects external conflict and/or cooperation. In religiously homogeneous societies, leaders may be reluctant to use religious mobilization strategies, especially if those are aimed at confronting a religiously similar opposition. Under such conditions, religious leaders may actually join the opposition, making it more difficult to eliminate or mollify it. By contrast, in religiously diverse societies, the use of religious mobilization by elites tends to be an expedient strategy. Opposition groups are likely to have a different religious affiliation than those of political elites. This may happen when opposition groups constitute the majority of the society and the political elites are affiliated with a minority religious group. Syria is a good example of this structure, with the Alawites, who constitute about 17 percent to 20 percent of the Syrian population, controlling the government and military, and fighting a primarily Sunni opposition. It may also happen when the political elite is affiliated with a religious group that constitutes a majority of the population, and the opposition group is a minority. This is the case, for example, in Israel where the Jewish majority controls the government and is in overt or covert conflict with both the Israeli–Palestinian citizens within Israel and with the Palestinian noncitizens in the occupied territories.

Therefore, we summarize our expectations about the effect of a religious social structure on foreign and domestic politics by the following propositions.

1. The religious homogeneity of a state increases the incentives and ability of political leaders to manipulate religious values and symbols as a mobilization strategy for
   a. conflictual ventures against religiously dissimilar enemies,

b. costly cooperative ventures such as security alliances with religiously similar states, and
   c. cultural cooperation with religiously similar states.

However, we do not expect the degree of religious homogeneity of a society to affect win-win cooperative ventures such as international trade or trade agreements.

In domestic politics, religious homogeneity is expected to have a positive effect on political stability. Internal conflicts, to the extent they occur, typically will be related to issues that are not immediately related to religion. However,

2. The religious diversity of a state increases
   a. the frequency, severity, and duration of internal conflicts, and
   b. the likelihood of political elites using a religious mobilization strategy.

7.2 Relations between Political and Religious Institutions

We now turn to a discussion of the second constraint that affects the use of religious factors as a political instrument by political elites. Before going into the analysis of this issue, we need to consider an important literature on religious freedom and religious repression that highlights the interplay between religious and political actors. We have already discussed the work of Gill in the context of economic theories of religion. However, the work of scholars like Gill (2007, 2013), Sarkissian (2015), and Grim and Finke (2011) offer important insights into the conditions under which political leaders use various techniques—some of them oppressive, others more cooperative—to deal with religious groups and religious actors. This research offers a window into the complex relations between political and religious actors. While Phillpot (2007) and Toft, Philpott, and Shah (2011) take this relationship to be exogenous to accounts of religious activity and political stability, Gill, Sarkissian, and Grim and Finke examine this variable as endogenous, and as a function of the calculations of both political elites and of religious actors.

Religious groups and organizations can be both potent allies and powerful enemies of political elites. Religious groups offer an organizational setting for large communities. The beliefs and values they nurture and disseminate may help overcome the collective action problem, that is, the reluctance of individuals to participate in risky behavior. Because of that, leaders may view some or all religious groups as potential allies under some circumstances, and as potential enemies—threatening their job security—under different circumstances. Sarkissian (2015) suggests the degree of religious repression in authoritarian states is a function of political competitiveness and the number of religious groups. He provides both quantitative evidence and a number of in-depth case studies to support this argument.

When the society is religiously diverse, the incentive of the regime to align with any single group declines, because it opens itself to criticism and opposition from other religious groups. When there exists a dominant religious group, the regime may form an alliance with this group, or directly emanate from this group (e.g., states like Iran or Saudi Arabia). Alternatively, it may engage in oppressive behavior against religious groups (e.g., Syria before the civil war of 2011; Myanmar versus the Rohinyga). If no dominant religious group exists, political elites do not, for the most part, see any single group either as an ominous threat or as a sole ally.

Given any type of social structure, political leaders need to consider the formal or informal constraints imposed on the use of religious values for political purposes by the structure of political-religious institutions. In a society that has formal restrictions on the relations between religion and politics, a strategy relying on religious symbols may cause more problems than it can resolve. It may mobilize groups that support this separation against the regime, and it may risk an existing balance that relies on this separation, especially in a religiously diverse society. Therefore, our general expectation is that, in foreign affairs, political elites of states that have a formal mechanism separating religious from political affairs would be less prone to use religious mobilization strategies than elites in states practicing a close formal relation between religious and political institutions. This seems to be most pervasive in the conflict behavior of states, and less pervasive in economic interactions.

By contrast, we do not expect to find any meaningful effect of state-religion relations on civil conflict. The relationship between political and religious institutions may serve both as an impetus of civil conflict and a check on political violence. Political, social, and religious groups may be on both sides of the fence in terms of their attitudes toward an existing formal or informal structure of the state-religion relations. This may be the case regardless of whether the state exercises freedom of religion and separation of religion from politics, or whether there is an institutionalized alliance between political and religious institutions. In the first case, groups and organizations that wish to impose religious restrictions and laws on political, social, and economic affairs would oppose the existing institutional freedom and separation between religious and political affairs. This may serve as a motivation for opposing the regime. Likewise, groups and communities that support such an arrangement would then support the regime's position on these matters. Freedom of religion and separation between religious and political affairs may also be a cause of political stability. Such an arrangement allows religious groups to operate freely in communal, educational, or social affairs, hence pacifying them. Such an arrangement may also please non-religious communities. So if civil conflict breaks out in such societies, it is more likely due to factors other than the institutionalized arrangements between politics and religion.

The same applies to states that practice an institutionalized alliance between religious and political affairs, embedded in legal and political structures. In such a case, the institutionalized state-religion alliance may favor a particular religion and discriminate against other religions. Even if such an alliance allows for religious freedom, this may still invoke opposition from groups that support separation of religion and state. By contrast, in societies where this institutionalized state-religion alliance pleases the dominant religious group, and allows some freedom of religious practice to other religious groups, such a reality may pacify an otherwise militant religious elite. The following propositions emerge

3. Political elites in states that practice a formal separation of religious from political affairs
    a. are less likely to use religious factors to mobilize support for international conflict involvement, especially against religiously dissimilar enemies;
    b. are less likely to use religious factors to mobilize support for costly cooperative ventures (e.g., security alliance), especially in support of religiously dissimilar states; and

c. are no more or less likely to use religious mobilization strategies in international economic affairs than states in which religious and political affairs are closely aligned.

4. State-religious relations do not have a meaningful effect on the outbreak, intensity, or duration of civil conflict.

7.3 The Effect of the International Environment

The social, political, and economic environment of states is composed of state and nonstate actors whose structure and behavior often affect these nations' external and internal affairs. The ability of political elites to mobilize support for their policies by using religious symbols and values can be effective under some conditions and counterproductive under different ones. We now include in these contingencies questions concerning the external targets of such manipulations.

When we focus on mobilization strategies used by political elites to support actions in foreign affairs, we need to ask about the targets of these actions. We discuss first the general structure of the state's environment, and then focus on particular targets of foreign policy behavior. First, and most important, we need to understand what constitutes a "politically relevant international environment." This concept was first developed by Maoz and Russett (1992, 1993). It was elaborated by Maoz (1996, 2010) and applied repeatedly, primarily in studies of conflict behavior (Lemke and Reed 2001, Bennett and Stam 2004, Benson 2005, Quackenbush 2006, Goertz 2006). Conceptually, the politically relevant international environment of a state (PRIE, Maoz 1996, 136–42) is defined as "the set of political units (state and nonstate units) whose structure, behavior, and policies have a direct impact on the focal state's political and strategic calculus. This is the environment upon which decision makers, intelligence agencies, the media and the public focus their attention on an almost daily basis. These units are deemed to deserve persistent and systematic attention . . . because developments in these units are perceived to have direct, immediate, and profound impact on one's own state" (Maoz 1996, 138). Operationally, the PRIE of a given state consists of

(i) states that are directly or indirectly (through colonial possessions) contiguous to the focal state;

(ii) regional powers with regional reach capacity, that is, a capacity of projecting force within the focal state's region; and
(iii) global powers with global reach capacity, that is, a capacity of force projection anywhere around the globe (Maoz 1996, 138–39).[12]

In our context, we focus on the religious characteristics of a state's PRIE—in particular, on the degree of similarity between the focal state and members of its PRIE. When a state's PRIE is composed of primarily religiously similar states, the ability of political elites to mobilize support against members of its PRIE is limited. If political leaders of a state contemplate conflict against a religiously similar member of their PRIE, they need to mobilize support via other mechanisms. For example, when Iraq became a target of members of the Arab League after its invasion of Kuwait in 1990, political elites in Egypt, Syria, Saudi Arabia, and the Gulf states faced public opposition when it came to joining the US-led coalition. They had to justify their involvement in the anti-Iraq coalition by invoking political norms (Arab League charter, universal nonaggression norms, etc.) rather than religious differences. Likewise, Saddam Hussein tried to incite resistance in the Arab world not as a struggle of Islam versus the infidels but rather as a struggle of Arab nationalism against neoimperialist ambitions (Freedman and Karsh 1995, Karsh and Rautsi 2007).

By contrast, a state situated in a religiously dissimilar environment can use religious factors as a powerful tool of social mobilization. Political elites can portray this environment as a constant security threat simply because of the religious differences between the state and its environment. They can thus justify investment of human and material resources in either reactive (defensive) measures or in proactive (offensive) initiatives. Moreover, a religiously dissimilar environment may constitute a real security threat that justifies mobilization of resources, because members of such an environment may view the focal state as a threat or a potential target, regardless of the actual intentions of the focal state. This adds a religious dimension to the security dilemma (Jervis 1978) under international anarchy.

This heightened security dilemma may push states toward security cooperation despite the risks associated with such cooperation (Maoz 2000, 2002; Morrow 2000). The choice of allies depends on an assessment of their reliability. A potential ally's reliability depends on the answer to two questions: (1) what are the chances that my ally will support me if I get into conflict with a third party? and (2) what are the chances that my ally will entrap me in wars that are not in my interest (Snyder 1991)? We suggest that the assessment of credibility may depend on the absence or presence of shared values and beliefs, as well as on shared interests (i.e., common enemies, Gowa 1995, Maoz et al. 2007, Maoz 2010).

These ideas translate into the selection of specific targets (or expected targets) of conflict and of specific candidates for security cooperation. If the political leaders of a given state view another state as a potential and/or actual enemy, the ability to use a religion-based strategy to mobilize domestic support for conflict against that enemy depends on the degree of religious similarity between the focal state and that enemy. By contrast, when a would-be ally is religiously similar to the focal state, political leaders can comfortably use common religious values as an indicator of mutual interests or reliability.

The religious structure of the focal state's PRIE also has an important effect on its level of internal conflict. When actual or potential opposition groups expect external support from members of the state's PRIE, they are more likely to resort to active opposition—using both violent and nonviolent strategies—against the incumbent government (San-Akca 2016; Jackson, San-Akca, and Maoz 2020). By contrast, if actual or potential resistance groups expect that the government will receive significant support from members of its PRIE, they are less likely to resort to active resistance strategies, even if they have significant grievances against their government. The incentives of opposition groups to rebel increase when their religious identity is similar to most members of the state's PRIE and when the religious identity of the government and its winning coalition is different from that of PRIE members.

This leads us to the following propositions regarding the effect of the religious structure of a state's environment on its foreign and domestic policies

6. The greater the religious similarity between the focal state and its PRIE,
    a. the less likely are political elites to mobilize support for conflict by invoking religious aspects of the state's identity, and
    b. the more likely are political elites to use religious factors as a mobilization strategy for security cooperation with religiously similar states.

7. The greater the religious similarity between actual or potential opposition groups and the states composing the focal state's PRIE,
   a. the more likely is civil conflict to break out;
   b. the more intensely violent are such civil conflicts;
   c. the higher the likelihood of external intervention in internal conflicts.

7.4 The Dynamics of Religious Influences on Foreign and Domestic Policy

Social structure, state-religion relations, and the religious structure of the state's international environment are relatively stable factors: they change very slowly over time. However, our theory emphasizes the idea that religion is an instrument of political control and is subject to manipulation by political and religious elites. In the previous sections, we focused on the structural conditions that make religion a more or less effective political weapon. Yet, religious factors are not always used as a political weapon even in homogeneous societies where there is a close collaboration between religious and political elites. And even in societies where there is a constitutional separation between religion and politics, some political leaders may find it expedient to invoke religious values to justify some foreign adventure or to advance a certain domestic policy. The key question, therefore, is when and under what circumstances political elites are more likely to use religion to advance their agendas?

We argue that the answer lies in the perception of job security by political elites. When political leaders feel secure in their job, their general tendency to use religious rhetoric and values to mobilize support is not particularly high. They can justify their policies and actions by rational concepts such as the expected utilities—due to the relative costs and benefits—associated with such policies. If they seek to acquire (or retain) territory by means of violent conflict with other countries, they can mobilize support by pointing out the intrinsic values of such territories (natural resources, strategic defense needs, etc.). They do not feel the need to invoke the religious beliefs of the enemies controlling or attempting to grab such territories. If the conflict of interests is over policies, leaders can obtain domestic support by pointing out the benefits associated with their country's policies and the risks associated with their opponent's policies. The same applies to cooperative international ventures. Forming an alliance with another state could be justified by explaining the relative benefits and risks associated with such an alliance in terms of strategic values. The religious identity of the would-be ally does not need to become a prime criterion in assessing the value of such an alliance.

Domestically, "safe" leaders do not need to invoke religion to pit one group against others; they can rely on either legitimate support or on oppressive power to secure their political survival. In this context, too, leaders can mobilize support for their policies by pointing out the utilities associated with such policies for the winning coalition.

Religious ideas and symbols become a political weapon when the leadership is at risk. In such cases, the tendency to use diversionary tactics in foreign affairs increases. Enemy selection becomes more based on the political value of a conflict in terms of a leader's survival, and less on the strategic benefits or costs associated with such conflicts. The enemy must be of a type that it invokes support to a degree that it diverts the opposition's attention from their domestic predicament to the foreign enemy. Religious differences become expedient political weapons in diversionary campaigns.

Likewise, in domestic politics, leaders at risk need to boost their winning coalition, prevent defections, or mobilize more supporters (or more "quality" supporters—that is, supporters with capacity to oppress the opposition) to secure their political survival. In such cases, rational defense of one's policies may not be seen as effective. Calls based on religious affinities or on religiously based animosities against domestic enemies may be seen as more effective. The framing of the struggle as one between religious groups enables the leader to use oppressive measures against the opposition. This, of course, is difficult if the opposition groups practice the same religion as the leader's coalition. However, in diverse societies, whether the leader represents the majority religious group or a minority one, framing this as an ideational struggle between religious groups may be perceived as an effective mobilization strategy.

The dynamic aspects of our theory of religion and politics suggest the following propositions:

8. The higher the actual or potential risk to political leaders' tenure of power, the more likely they are
    a. to initiate interstate conflict against religiously dissimilar states and
    b. to use religious values, symbols, and institutions to oppress political opposition.

All these propositions are quite general. We offer more precise discussions of each of the relevant domains that these propositions address in the specific chapters dealing with international conflict, international cooperation, domestic conflict, and quality of life.

The following figure provides a graphic representation of our integrative theory of religion and world politics.

It is instructive to represent our ideas in a dyadic context. These can be easily generalized into a more complex relationship between a focal state and its international environment. Consider two states. Each has a characteristic social structure. This structure may be defined by many attributes, but for our purposes, we focus on two variables—the degree of religious homogeneity or diversity of the society, and the nature of relations between religious and political institutions. We argue that in societies that are religiously homogeneous and in which there is a closely cooperative relationship between religious and political institutions, religious factors can be more readily mobilized to advance political goals. However, the conditions under which, and against or in support of which religion is used as a mobilization strategy depends on the degree of political stability. When political leaders feel that their tenure is guaranteed, they are less inclined to use religion as an instrument of national mobilization than when they feel that their job is at risk. Taken together, these structural and situational conditions define when and how religion may be used to advance national (or personal political) goals.

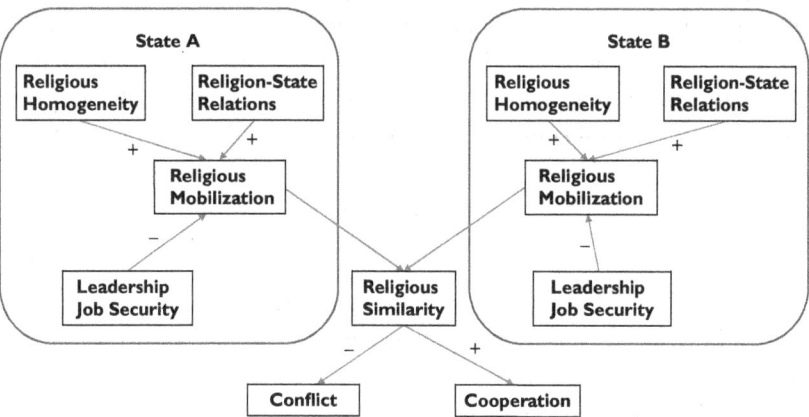

Fig. 3.1. The integrative theory of religion and world politics

Yet, the internal attributes of states are not sufficient to explain international interactions. We need to account for the ways in which states select targets for cooperative or conflictual interactions. What defines which state/s are selected for certain behaviors is the degree of similarity or dissimilarity between state A and state B. When the two states are similar, leaders in one state may find it difficult to mobilize support on religious grounds for conflictual policies against the other state. We can expect, however, that religion would be invoked in support of costly cooperative ventures, such as alliances against common enemies.

Internally, we expect that leaders at risk would invoke religious ideas to oppress potential foes in states that are relatively homogeneous, in which a dominant religious group exists that is also privileged economically and politically. In such societies, religion would be more likely to emerge as a mobilizing weapon against religious minorities to the extent that religious institutions and political institutions are closely aligned, but otherwise religion would not serve as a basis to address dissent in religiously homogeneous societies in which religious and political institutions are imbricated.

The integrative nature of our theory is therefore evident in this structure: it builds on both the primordialist perspective by emphasizing structural factors as underlying conditions that determine conflict and cooperation. It also builds on the instrumentalist perspective by using its ideas to define the conditions under which political leaders may invoke religious factors to mobilize support for foreign adventures.

Finally, this perspective offers a novel aspect that focuses on the structure of religious connections—defined by the degree of religious similarity—between and among states. This aspect explains target selection for both cooperative and conflictual ventures. It also suggests targets and conditions for domestic political conflict and cooperation.

8. Conclusion

In this chapter we explored several central perspectives that inform our theory of religion and world politics: primordialism, instrumentalism, constructivism, and the CoC thesis. Each of these perspectives has some compelling arguments about the types of linkages between religion and politics, and about the conditions under which religion becomes an important factor in shaping the foreign and domestic politics of states. Each of these perspectives also has some notable weaknesses that limit our ability to assess them empirically. They contain some ambiguous and incomplete testable propositions. These are not the only theories concerning religion and politics. However, in many ways, they encapsulate much of the knowledge we have on these matters. Taken together, these perspectives form the basic foundation of our theory, which builds on their logical and empirical strengths and attempts to overcome the weaknesses of each.

In brief, our theory suggests that to understand how, why, and when religious factors affect foreign and domestic politics, we must consider a combination of variables. These variables include structural constraints: social structure, relations between political and religious institutions, and the structure of the focal state's politically relevant international environment. They also include more dynamic political conditions: changes in the level of perceived job security of political leaders. The latter variables determine, given these structural constraints, when and how religion can and is manipulated by political elites.

Unlike other theories of religion and politics (e.g., Philpott 2007; Toft, Philpott, and Shah 2011), we do not accord a significant role to religious actors. This is not to suggest that such actors are unimportant. Rather, we believe that the role of such actors is captured in the structural constraints that affect the willingness and ability of political leaders to manipulate religious identity markers to advance their goals. Moreover, we believe that religious actors—spiritual leaders, religious institutions, informal religious communities and organizations—may be both a source of legitimacy to political leaders and a source of opposition. The theories that emphasize the role of religious actors in shaping political processes are extremely vague about when, where, why, and how these actors operate in concert with or opposition to non-religious political elites. It is difficult to derive generalizable and testable propositions from these theories with respect to the issues under study. We can learn, of course, about the type of role that religious actors take if we study individual cases of conflict or cooperation. This is a legitimate approach; however, it is not the one we follow in the coming pages. Our goal is to generate generalizable and reproducible knowledge about these issues. For that, we need a theory that provides testable propositions about the relationship(s) between religion and politics across substantive domains of international and domestic interactions. This is what our theory attempts to do.

In the following chapters, we subject the key ideas of our theory, as well as those of the various perspectives discussed in this chapter, to a set of rigorous empirical tests. In the last chapter we evaluate the theory and its components in light of these empirical results.

CHAPTER 4

The Religious Landscape of the World, 1945–2010[1]

1. Introduction

This chapter offers a systematic overview of the World Religion Project (WRP) that provides the informational baseline for the empirical study of religion and world politics. We discuss the underlying logic of coding data on religious adherence over a long period of time and across the globe. We explain how data were generated, the kind of problems we confronted in generating the dataset, and the solutions we devised. Finally, we offer a systematic description of religious adherence in the post–World War II era on a global scale. The purpose of a review of the WRP is to provide a transparent and replicable report on the dataset that we use for analyzing the role of religion in world politics. This will provide information about the advantages and shortcomings of our approach.

2. Measuring Religion: The General Logic of the World Religions Project

In this section, we provide a brief discussion of the general rationale of the WRP, and some details about the data collection and management process. A more detailed methodological exposition may be found in the appendix at the end of the chapter.

The empirical study of religion and various aspects of world politics has been based on a number of datasets that examine religion in specific domestic political contexts (e.g., Putnam and Campbell 2012) or in international contexts (Vanhanen 1999a b; Pearce 2005; Fox 2016). Other datasets offer a cross-national and longitudinal perspective on the distribution of religious adherents across time and space. These datasets formed the basis for many of the empirical studies discussed previously. The Correlates of War (COW) cultural dataset (Singer 1997) includes decennial observations on religious groups for states, but the observations end at 1990. The criteria for classifying and differentiating among major religions, religious families, and religious denominations are not clear in these datasets. Ellingsen (2000) provides annual estimates of the religious characteristics of states based on averaging values from three sources (i.e., *The CIA World Factbook*, *Britannica Book of the Year*, and the *Demographic Yearbook*) and interpolating missing years. These data go to 2000; they identify the largest and the second-largest religious groups in the country; and they have a straightforward list of nine major religions (Animism, Atheism, Buddhism, Hinduism, Islam, Judaism, Christianity, Shintoism, and Syncretism).

The WRP provides data at five-year intervals from 1945 to 2010 on the religious adherents of states coded for fourteen major religions, and also data on religious families within some of the major religions. It draws from multiple sources and also provides novel measures of the religious characteristics of states in terms of religious diversity and religious similarity. The WRP builds on existing datasets but improves on them in several important ways. We document these below. As such, it opens new and expanded opportunities for the study of the role of religion in world politics.

One of the distinguishing characteristics of the WRP is that our approach to the process of data collection was deductive in nature. Before collecting data on world religions, we had to come up with satisfactory answers to basic questions about the nature of religion and the classification of world religions. These answers were crucial in developing a "religion tree," that is, a systematic classification of major world religions and of religious families within each of these major religions. This, as we quickly noticed, was in stark contrast to the common practice in the scholarly disciplines that deal with these matters. These generally lack an explicit set of principles for deciding what constitutes a religion or for classifying religions and religious families.

The first step was to develop a definition of religion that is both consistent across disciplines and also is most relevant to the process of generating a world religions dataset. The definition of religion has been a focus of intense debate not only among theologians and religious studies scholars but also among sociologists, anthropologists, and philosophers. We had no pretension of developing yet another definition. Consequently, we conducted a comprehensive literature review designed to answer several questions that were essential to our enterprise.

1. What is a religion?
2. Can we find observable or tangible indicators that facilitate the systematic identification of religions?
3. Are there tangible indicators that allow us to distinguish among different religions, and among religious families/denominations within a given religion?
4. How can we validate our criteria for a religion and/or religious families within a given religion?

Without going into too much detail, our literature review covered multiple fields of scholarship that focus on the study of religion such as history, religious studies, anthropology, sociology, law, political science, and philosophy as well as specific regional studies.[2] The upshot of this review was that we could not find a consensus on any of the issues listed above. The definition of religion we adopted (Alston, 1967, 142) was one whose elements appeared most often in other definitions of religion, and which offered the clearest indications of tangible elements of religions.[3] This definition states that a religion is *a belief system held by an individual or a group that contains the following elements*:

- belief in supernatural being/s (god/s)
- a distinction between sacred and profane objects
- ritual acts focused on sacred objects
- a moral code believed to be sanctioned by the supernatural being/s (god/s)
- characteristically religious feelings (awe, sense of mystery, sense of guilt, obligation, duty, adoration), which tend to be aroused in the presence of sacred objects and during the practice of rituals, and which are connected in idea with the gods
- prayer and other forms of communication with gods
- a worldview or a general picture of the world as a whole and the place of the individual therein; this picture contains some

specification of an overall purpose or point of the world and an indication of how the individual fits into it
- a more or less total organization of one's life based on the worldview
- a social group bound together by the above

Clearly, this is a very general, but also quite vague, definition of religion. Other definitions are equally focused on beliefs, moral codes, and rituals. Empirically, one of the most important and commonly mentioned criteria for the classification of religions and religious families or denominations is self-identification. This, however, has limited application in the context of our project. Since we had to trace religions across time, surveys or census data were not available for most states and for most time points. Even when such data were available, the religious categories from which respondents had to select varied from one survey/census to another. In order to create a spatially and longitudinally stable definition of religion, we had to develop observable or tangible criteria that can guide data collection. This required heavy reliance on secondary data. Given this state of the literature, our next objective was to derive a set of fairly tangible criteria that define religions and religious families independent of subjective identification of people with a given belief system. The review yielded a definition of religion as *a belief system shared by a community of people that is identified by the following set of criteria.*

   a. *Scriptures.* A central text or a set of texts that—as a whole—encapsulate the general principles of the belief system of a given religion. The existence or type of scriptures is a key identifier of some but not all religions. Some religions do not have major scriptures; others incorporate scriptures from other religions with scriptures that are exclusive to a particular belief system. But the absence of central scriptures is also an important distinguishing feature of a religion, provided it possesses the other characteristics.
   b. *Institutions.* A set of formal or semiformal institutions that are responsible for interpreting the basic beliefs for adherents, modifying them or changing them over time, training and ordaining spiritual leaders of their communities—and determining who is a believer and who is not. The nature, size, and formality of institutions vary a great deal across religions. However, virtually every religion has a set of institutions or a group of individuals who interpret beliefs for adherents. In many cases, these institutions or

priests have primary responsibility for leading the practice of collective rituals. This set of institutions must be unique to that belief system and distinct from the institutions of other belief systems.

c. *Historical development.* It is possible to trace the origin, development, and diffusion of religions in terms of historical turning points and/or identifiable processes. At these turning points or processes, an individual or a group has formed the basic principles of a new religion. This individual or group is also responsible for forming certain institutions that guide religious practices, ordain spiritual leaders, and define principles for inclusion or exclusion of believers. This criterion is an important identifier not only of major religions but also of religious families and denominations. Since many religions developed in connection with other religions, the historical context in which religions were formed helps identify their origins.[4]

d. *A common class of beliefs, rituals, and practices.* This criterion allows identification of a broad set of religions that is characterized by polytheism. It also characterizes religions that contain identifiable rituals, which are followed without a clear set of institutions or historical evidence of how they were formed. Because such religions have developed or existed in areas that are geographically distinct and noncontiguous, they cover a wide variety of ritualistic elements. Yet there are some basic commonalities in the (rather weak) institutional structure of such religions and their rituals. These allow the grouping of such religions into a separate category. However, this criterion does not offer a simple way of dividing such religions into denominations and subdenominations.

These criteria provide a foundation for an operational definition of religion. A belief system with these four characteristics is clearly identified as a religion. As noted, there are religions that lack a major scripture. But the acceptance of a common scripture as a central guide of beliefs, rituals, and practices is almost a sufficient—though not necessary—identifier of a religion. The same applies to a set of institutions that defines the ethical and ritualistic codes for the community. Note that the key elements of Alston's definition do not apply to nontheistic religions or nontheistic versions of such religions as Buddhism, Hinduism, Jainism, and Confucianism. Nor does the last item in his definition tell us what that group or community is or what exactly binds such a community together.

The operational definition we offer allows us to identify religions empirically. Using these criteria we scanned the literature identifying major religions, religious families within major religions, and denominations within the religious families, which resulted in a three-level structure of the religion tree: major religions, religious families, and denominations. For example, Christianity contains several religious families such as Catholicism, Protestantism, Eastern Orthodox, and Anglicanism. Protestantism contains a number of denominations such as Presbyterian, Methodist, Mennonite, and so on. It became clear very quickly that it would be unlikely to obtain systematic, consistent, and reliable data going back in time on the denominational level. Therefore, our project contains data only on the first two levels of the religion tree: major religions and religious families.

Once the structure of the religion tree was set, we surveyed multiple classifications of religions, focusing in particular on those that were consistent with our observable criteria. This process was challenging due to the substantial variation in religious classifications in different sources and disciplines. Some classifications were fine-tuned, going down to the level of ethnically or "tribally" specific rituals unique to some regions (or within a given country). Other classifications were quite general, subsuming broad categories of religious groups. Given this state of affairs, we developed a "candidate" religion tree of the most plausible lists of religions/religious families in the literature.

Next, we formulated a questionnaire with several groups of questions. One group requested that experts assess the validity of the criteria for identifying religions and religious families. The other group asked about whether a given candidate religion qualifies as one of the major world religions. Likewise, for each candidate for a major world religion that was derived from the literature search, we asked whether respondents consider this to be a "proper" religious family. The survey also contained a set of open questions that asked respondents to specify additional criteria for identifying major religions or religious families, and for adding or deleting religions or religious families. We surveyed noted religion scholars from various disciplines as a way of validating or modifying our religion tree. Table A1 (in the appendix) provides a summary of the survey responses to the key questions.

The survey yielded a number of results. First, we received strong confirmation of four of the five criteria we had thought to use in identifying major religions and religious families. In the open questions asking whether we had omitted any important criteria, we found no significant responses that would cause us to reconsider these criteria. Second, two-thirds of the twenty-one candidates to the position of "major world religion" received a validity score of six or higher. With respect to the remaining candidates, answers to open questions suggested collapsing them with the "surviving" candidates. Respondents also mentioned a very low number of adherents as an alternative reason for entering a low validity rank for certain religions. Some of the candidate religions were collapsed into a broader group. For example, various animistic religions were collapsed into the animist group. Syncretic religions represent a wide array of belief systems, but they have some common underlying characteristics, so we decided to group them together. Also, the "other religions" category is a residual category that reflects either religions with relatively few adherents, religions that did not make it into the list, or a complement of a population that is known to practice some religion but there is no information about which religion/s they do practice (more below).

Third, with respect to religious families, we also found a substantial degree of agreement for most of the candidate families. In this case, low-validity religious families were grouped into "other" (e.g., "other Christians," "other Muslims," etc.). Fourth, we found no relationship between the degrees of agreement across different disciplines of respondents. Finally, the number of responses to some questions varied significantly (range = 30–67), because many of the respondents had expertise that covered a specific region or a specific religion. This made some respondents hesitant to respond to questions or items that were outside of their professional purview.

Table A4.1 in the appendix to this chapter presents the major world religions and religious families included in the dataset. It also includes information regarding the rate of agreement among experts in our expert poll regarding the validity of a given religion/religious family. The experts were asked to rate on a scale of 1–10 the degree to which they believe a given category constitutes a major religion or a religious family within a given religion. In general, we used a rule of thumb of an agreement rate of six or above for a given religion. The only exception was the non-religious category, which was rated lower. This category includes atheists, agnostics, and people who stated (or were estimated) as having no particular religion. The low ratings for this category were due to low response rates and (possibly) a confusing definition of this category in the questionnaire. Nevertheless, virtually every source we used provided data for this category. We also used a residual (other religions) category, but did not include this in the survey. This category includes adherents of religions that did not make it into the final religion tree as well as data reported by most sources under the same (other) label.

3. Trends in World Religions, 1945–2010[5]

Before presenting the data, some caveats about trends within nations and within religions over time are in order. First, our approach is state-reliant. We started our data collection of the distribution of religious adherents within a given territory when this territory became an independent state, following the COW definition of system membership. This means that the interpretation of the data presented below should reflect the changes in the size and character of the interstate system over the period 1945–2010. Second, the availability and reliability of data have improved considerably over time. We have more sources and fewer missing data for later years compared to previous periods.[6] Therefore, the figures provided below may reflect some temporal bias. Third, domestic political changes may have also affected reporting on religious affiliations. With these caveats in mind, we turn to a discussion of some major trends in religious adherence from 1945 to 2010.

3.1 Global Patterns

Figure 4.1 describes the distribution of adherents of some of the key religions over time. For convenience of presentation, the figure does not include all of the major world religions in the dataset. However, the discussion covers all of them. Several points are noteworthy. First, the proportion of religious adherents has increased over time from a low of about 63.5 percent of the world's population in 1945 to a high of about 88.9 percent in 2010. Non-religious percentages varied between 9 percent and 16 percent of the world's population over the same period, with the highest percent of non-religious people reported in 1975: 16.6 percent. This reflects two statistical artifacts rather than a major trend of increased religiosity. One concern, as noted above, is that a significant proportion (30 percent) of the world's population did not live in independent states in 1945. In contrast, by 2010, 99.9 percent of the world's population resided within independent states. Therefore, the increased trend in religiosity

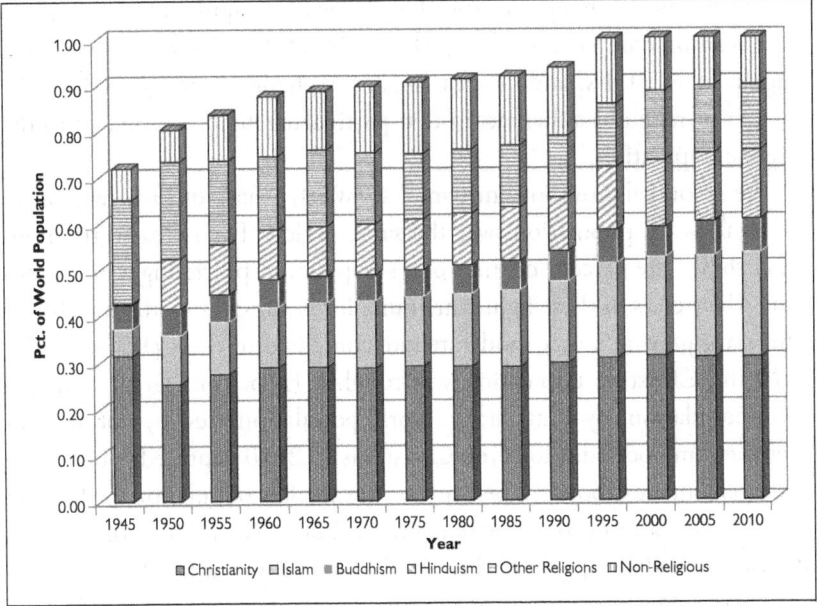

Fig. 4.1. The distribution of major world religions, 1945–2010

reflects the fact that many of the new states that emerged over the 1945–2010 period have an especially high proportion of religious adherents. Improved data quality over time may also affect these trends. One can argue, however, that since the mid-1970s, the changes in the size of the international system have been relatively marginal, and that these changes reflect a rearrangement of the system (secessions and partitions of multiethnic entities—e.g., the Soviet Union, Czechoslovakia, Ethiopia, Yugoslavia) into more ethnically homogeneous states. So at least some of the increase in religiosity reflects an actual trend rather than a combination of statistical artifacts. We leave this question open to future investigations.

Second, once we consider changes in the composition of the interstate system, Muslims are the only religious group that shows a consistent and significant upward trend relative to the world population. Hindus also have exhibited a growth trend, but this has been more modest. The other major religious groups capture a relatively stable proportion of the world's population (e.g., Christians, non-religious) or display a declining trend (e.g., Jews, animists, syncretics). Figure 4.2 provides two important items of information. The first (top panel) shows percent changes in the proportion of some of the major world religions over time. Each area in the left panel reflects changes in the share of world population practicing a given religion compared to the baseline share of the adherents of the same religion in 1950. Expanding areas suggest a change in the growth of the number of religious adherents of that particular religion compared to the baseline population.

The second figure (bottom panel) shows the share of each religion in the total world population over the same period. Each area in the right panel shows the percent of the world's population practicing a given religion. The trends in these figures are quite interesting. First, the number of Christians grew at a very moderate rate compared to their 1950 share: by 2010 the Christian population was roughly 13 percent larger than the 1950 population. By contrast, the world population grew by 268 percent over the same period. However, Christians in 2010 captured roughly the same percentage (about 30 percent) of the world's population as they did in 1950. The fastest expanding religion was Islam. The number of Muslims almost doubled compared to their 1950 share. This is also reflected in the right panel. Muslims accounted for roughly 10 percent of the world's population residing in independent states in 1950. In 2010, they accounted for over 23 percent of the world's population. The non-religious population underwent changes upward from the 1960s to the late 1980s, expanding to twice the size of the 1950 baseline. However, this trend was reversed in the 1990s and beyond, shrinking to slightly 150 percent of the 1950 baseline by 2010. The share of the non-religious group in the world's population in the right-hand panel shows a similar trend. The non-religious population accounted for roughly 7 percent of the world's total in 1945 and 1950, and increased to over 15 percent by 1985. However, this trend was reversed, and by 2010 the non-religious population accounted for slightly more than 11 percent of the world's total.

Two important reasons might account for these changes. First, changes in the political composition of the world—the growth of the world's population living in independent states—is a key factor. In 1945–50, only 67 percent of the world population lived in independent states. By 1970, all of the world's population was accounted for by independent states. Most of the newly added states during this period emerged in Asia, the Middle East, and Africa. Many of them had a substantial Muslim population; fewer of these states had Christian populations. Also, the share of animist and syncretic populations shrunk significantly, from about

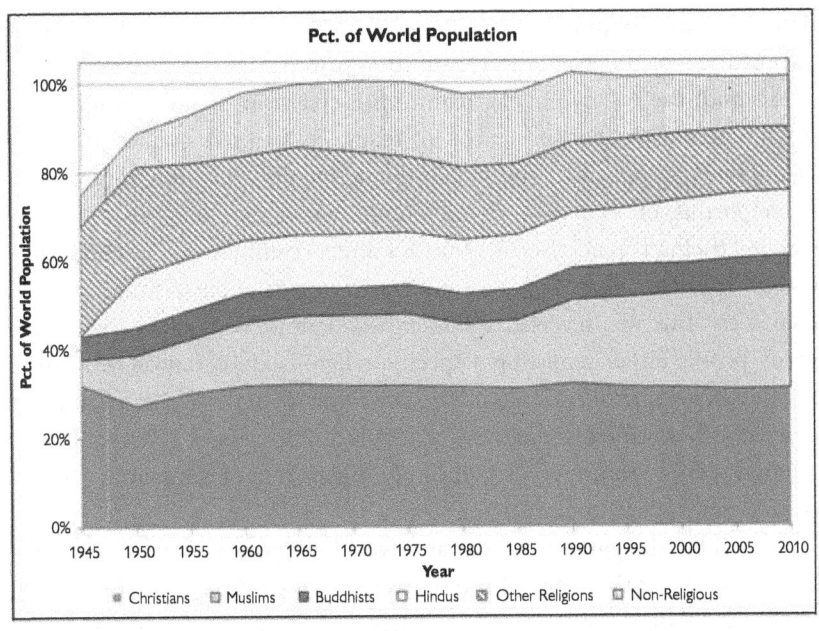

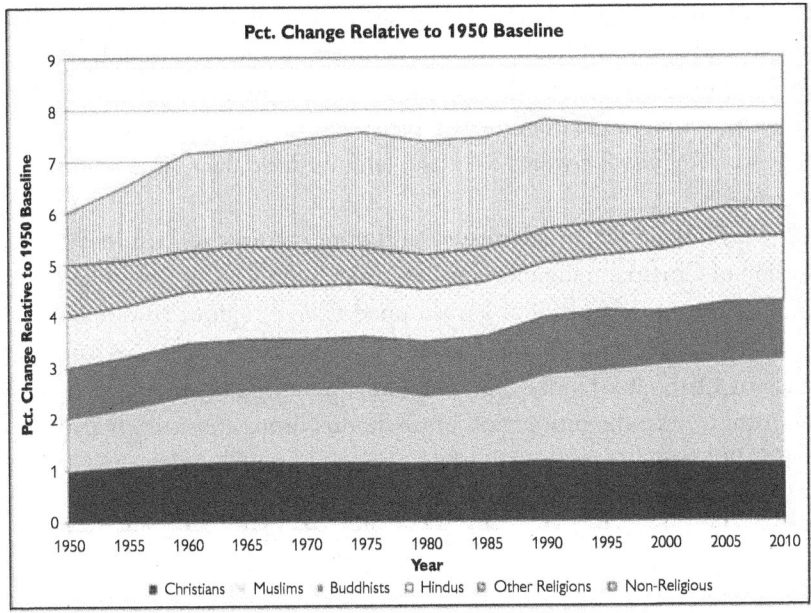

Fig. 4.2. Changes in relative share of world population

20 percent to less than 11 percent of the world's population. Since our data only cover populations residing in independent states, a substantial part of the world's population is omitted prior to the early 1970s.

Second, the collapse of the communist system in Eastern Europe and Russia created an artificial revival of religiosity in these countries. Much of the swelling in secularism during the period 1950–90 might be due to overreporting of secularism in the communist states. Many people proclaimed themselves atheists or agnostics under communism, or worse, official statistics reported high percentages of non-religious citizens in such countries. This was reversed following the demise of communism, with many people either reporting a specific religious affiliation or with more accurate reporting of religious adherence statistics in most postcommunist countries. Nevertheless, the trend of secularism is evident given that non-religious people captured a significantly higher share (as much as 50 percent more) in 2010 than in 1945.

The WRP disaggregates the major world religions into religious families. However, at this stage of the project we have a detailed and relatively reliable breakdown only for Christianity and somewhat less reliable data for the Islamic religious families. The data for the other major religions that are divided into identifiable religious families: Judaism and Buddhism lack for the most part a detailed breakdown into religious families. Currently, however, it is useful to examine the distribution of religious families within the two religions for which we have fairly reliable data. This is done in Figure 4.3.

With respect to Christianity, several things stand out. First, the distribution of Christian religious families is highly stable over time. However, the proportion of Catholics has dropped from a high of almost 58 percent of Christians in 1975 to a low of 49.7 percent in 2010. Second, the Eastern Orthodox family represents an interesting cycle due to global political trends: the proportion of Orthodox drops consistently over the 1945–90 period (from a high of 15 percent of all Christians in 1950 to a low of 8.7 percent in 1990). The collapse of communism in Eastern Europe and the collapse of the Soviet Union led to a steady rise in the percentage of Orthodox Christians up to about 12.7 percent in 2010.

This is a result of two factors. First, conducting fairly reliable censuses was one of the first things that most East European postcommunist states did after they democratized. In most of these countries questions about

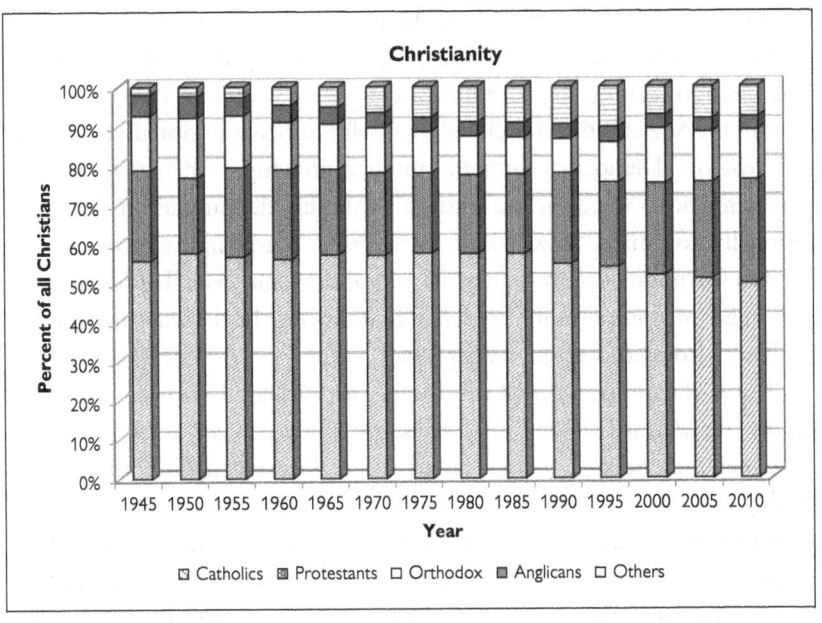
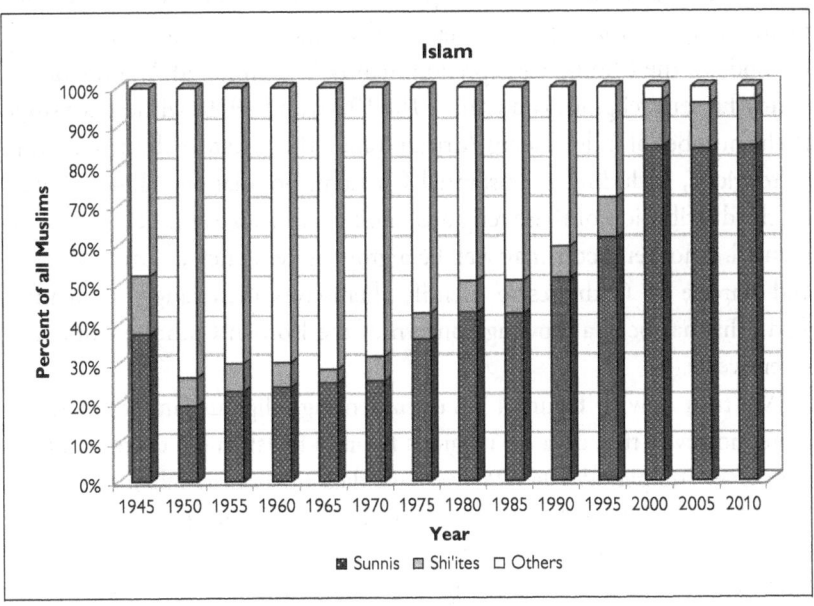

Fig. 4.3. Religious families in Christianity and Islam

religion were asked. So we have far better information about the religious adherence of roughly 500 million people following the end of the Cold War. Second, during the communist era, many people in those countries (and in the Soviet Union) declared themselves atheists or nonaffiliated with any religion. Democracy brought about a growing tendency to identify with a religion. Since various Eastern Orthodox denominations have traditionally dominated these countries, we have a surge in the proportion of Eastern Orthodox believers after the end of the Cold War. This is probably the single most important factor that accounts for the desecularization that we have witnessed over the same period.

Third, the proportion of Christians not affiliated with any religious family has increased from 2 percent to roughly 8 percent of all Christians. This seems to be due to two factors. One factor concerns information quality. Unlike the case of data on Eastern Orthodox Christians, which have improved markedly over time, data on other Christian families have improved sparingly and in some cases have become more problematic to acquire. In the 1950s, most independent countries were in the Western Hemisphere, Europe (predominantly Catholic, Protestant, and Eastern Orthodox), the Middle East (predominantly Muslim), and Asia (predominantly Eastern religions and Islam). The 1960s and 1970s witnessed a surge in the number of independent African states. Those states exhibit a mixture of religions, including a substantial Christian population. However, data on the distribution of these religious families are scarce and not well documented. Another factor may well be a growing tendency in Latin America and Europe by Catholics to identify themselves increasingly as unaffiliated. This has been a growing concern of the Roman Catholic Church in recent years.

We turn now to Figure 4.3.2 documenting religious families in Islam. Note, however, that data on religious families in Islam are quite problematic. Over the period 1945–95 we have data on Islamic religious families for only a fraction of the states with substantial Muslim populations. This is reflected in the proportion of the "others" category. The proportion of Shi'ites during these years also reflects a rough estimate. From 2000 on, we have fairly reliable estimates of the distribution of religious families in Islam, although this does not include all religious families. However, two things are evident. First, the ratio of Sunni to Shia believers is roughly 7:1. Second, the only other noticeable religious family in Islam on which we have data is the Alawite community that accounts for roughly 1 percent of all Muslims.

The "other Muslims" group is composed of people who have not identified themselves with any specific religious family, or is based on estimates of (or self-proclaimed) Muslims without a breakdown to the religious family level.

3.2 Regional Patterns

We turn next to a regional distribution of religious adherence. This is given in Figure 4.4. The data here are relatively self-explanatory. Christians constitute the vast majority of the population of the Western Hemisphere, averaging 87 percent of the region's population over the period 1945–2010. The dominant religious family was Catholicism, averaging 60 percent of the region's population. Christians were also by far the modal category in Europe, averaging 70 percent of the region's population over the same period. European Catholics were still the modal Christian category, but they accounted only for a third of the region's population. The other two categories: Protestants and Eastern Orthodox accounted jointly for a similar proportion of the region's population. The second-largest group in Europe is the non-religious group that reached over 27 percent

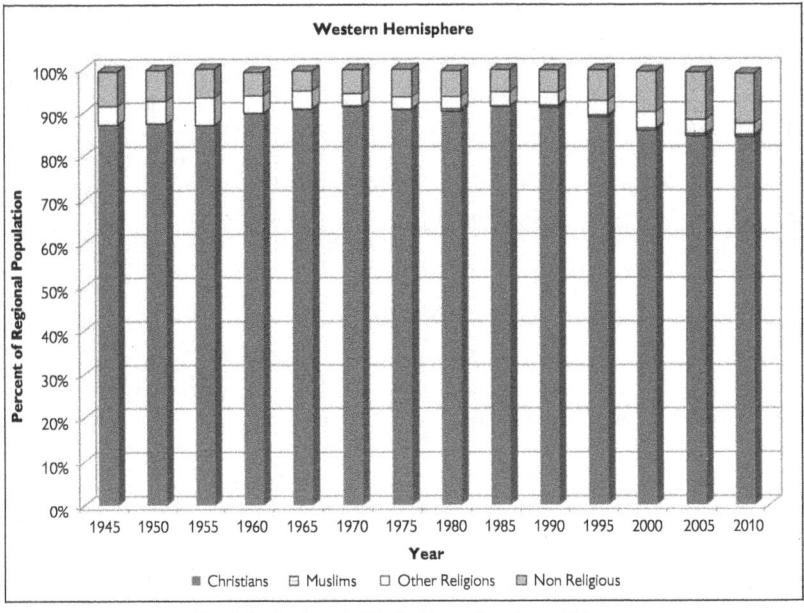

Fig. 4.4. Regional distribution of major religions

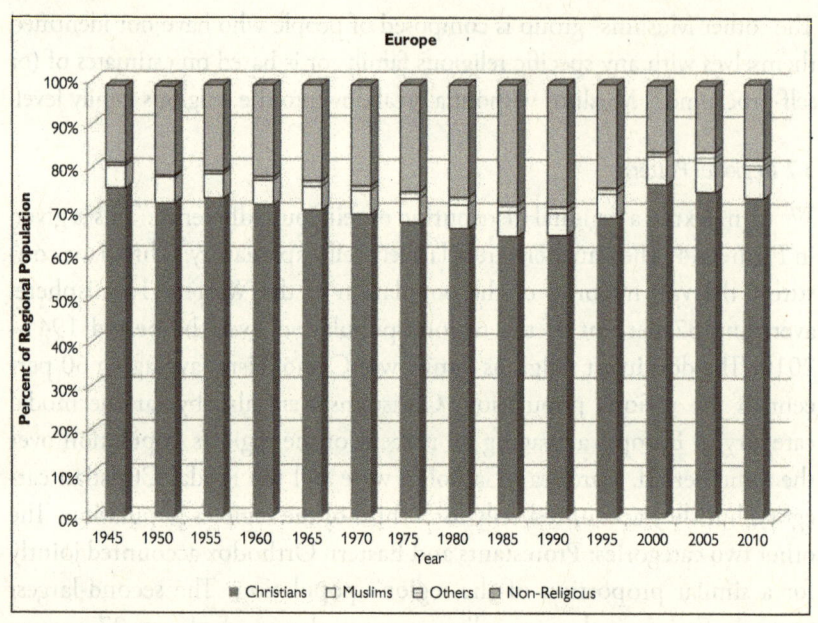
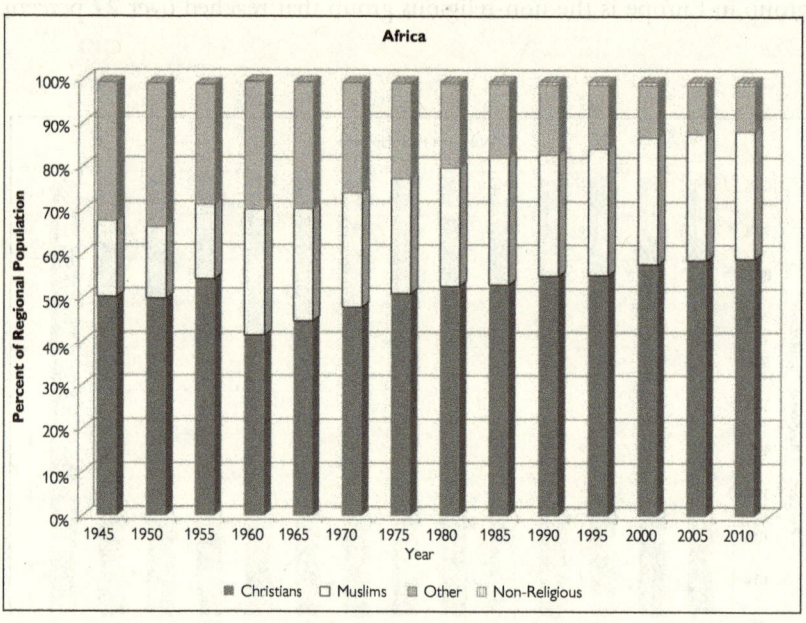

Fig. 4.4 *Continued*

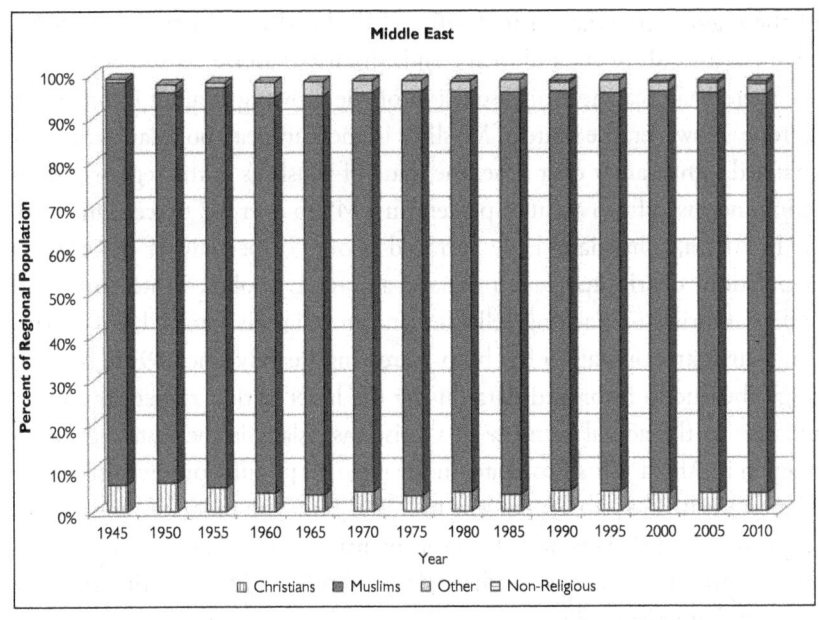

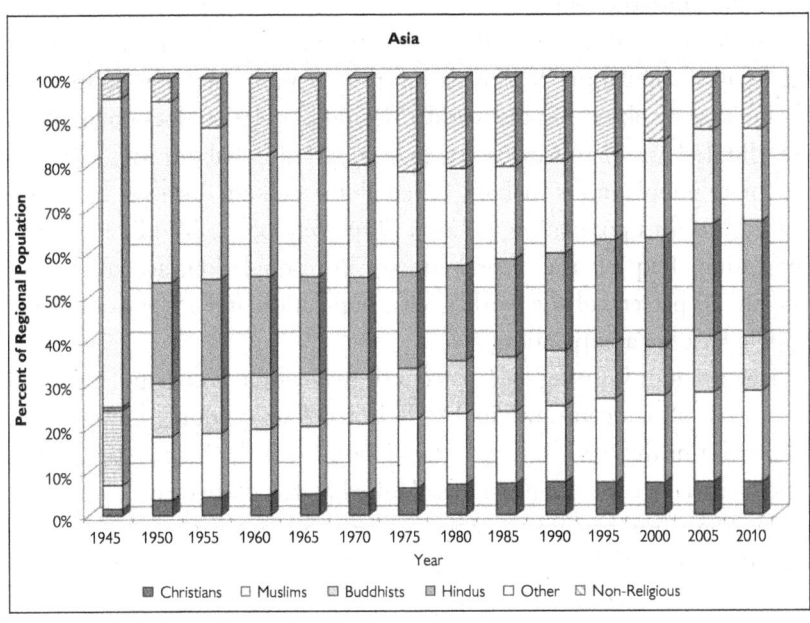

Fig. 4.4 *Continued*

of the region's population in 1990 and declined to 17 percent in 2010, again, as a result of the political trends discussed above.

There is a great deal of discussion of the growing Islamic influence in Europe. However, the share of Muslims in the European population has not changed significantly over time: the share of Muslims in the region's population increased from about 5 percent in 1945 to over 6.7 percent in 2010.

In Africa, Christians have averaged about 55 percent of the region's population, distributed rather equally among Catholics, Protestants, and "other" Christians (lacking reliable data on religious family breakdown). The Christian population has been increasing steadily since 1975, but this might be due to improved data during the latter period rather than to an increase in the actual number of Christians. Islam is the fastest-growing religion in Africa. Muslims' share in the regional population increased from 17 percent in 1945 to 29 percent in 2010. Both the moderate increase in the share of Christians and the steep increase in the share of Muslims in Africa came at the expense of sharp drops in other religions, primarily syncretic and animistic religions.

The Middle East is clearly dominated by Islam, with over 92 percent of the region's population. Within Islam, the 7:1 ratios between Sunnis and Shi'ites that we observe in the world's Muslim population does not apply to the Middle East. Here we observe an average ratio of about 3:1. The largest Shi'ite population is in Iran, which alone accounts for over a third of the world's Shi'a population and over 70 percent of the Middle East Shi'a population. Iraq has the second-largest Shi'a population, accounting for roughly 10 percent of the world's Shi'a population and 19 percent of the Middle East Shi'a population.

Jews account for roughly 1 percent of the Middle East population and are almost all concentrated in Israel. Israeli Jews account, however, for 40 percent of the world's Jewish population (with the highest percentage of Jews actually concentrated in the United States: 42 percent).[7]

In Asia, four categories capture nearly 80 percent of the population: these include Hindus (who account for an average of 22 percent of the region's population), Muslims (accounting for an average of 18 percent of the region's population), Buddhists (accounting for roughly 12 percent of the region's population), and others (mainly syncretic folk religions that account for about 20 percent of the region's population). If we ignore the distribution of religious groups in 1945—prior to the independence of India and several other East and South Asian states, where most of the

Buddhist and Hindu population resides—the only group that exhibited significant growth over time were the Asian Muslims who have increased their share in the region's population from 14 percent to 20 percent.

Interestingly, the trend of the non-religious Asian population is similar to that of European non-religionists: a marked increase between 1945 and 1990, and a significant decline in their share of the regional population since 1990. Here there was not as much retreat from communism as in Europe, so we cannot clearly explain this decline by some political shock. More research is required to explain the desecularization of Asian populations.

The final aspect of our global analysis focuses on the degree of religious diversity in the international system. We use the index of qualitative variation (IQV) to measure religious diversity. This index is given by:

$$IQV = \frac{k\left(1-\sum_{i=1}^{k}p_i^2\right)}{k-1}$$

where k indexes the number of religious groups and p_i is the percent of the state's population that practices a given religion. IQV varies from zero when a given state's population practices a single religion, to 1 when the population of a state is uniformly split among k religions such that the percentage of adherents of any given religion is exactly $1/k$. For example, consider three states: State A has three religious groups each accounting for 33 percent of the population. State B has five religious groups distributed as follows: Group I has 80 percent of the population, and each of the other groups has 4 percent of the population. State C involves two religious groups: one with 80 percent of the population and one with 20 percent. In the first state, we get an

$$IQV = \frac{3\left(1-3\times 0.333^2\right)}{2} = 1.00.$$

That means that the variation among groups is maximal; each group has exactly the same share of the population as every other group. In the second case, we get an

$$IQV = \frac{5\left[1-\left(0.8^2 + 4\times 0.04^2\right)\right]}{4} = 0.442.$$

This suggests that there is a significant concentration of religious adherents but this concentration is not perfect; there is some religious heterogeneity that emanates both from the number of religious groups and from their relative share in the population. In the third case, we get an

$$IQV = \frac{2\left[1-\left(0.8^2+0.2^2\right)\right]}{1} = 0.64.$$

Here, too, we have a 80/20 percent domination of one religion over the other. However, the fact that there are only two groups elevates the degree of variation in this society compared to the case exemplified by State B.[8]

We employ four versions of *IQV*. The first defines k ($k = 15$ for all states) as the number of all possible major religions. The second defines k ($k = 24$) both by major religions, for those religions that are not broken down into religious groups (e.g., Shintoism, Sikhism, etc.) and religious families, for those religions where we have family breakdowns (e.g., Christianity, Judaism, Islam, Buddhism). The two others apply a variable k, such that for each state k represents the number of religious groups that actually exist in that state. Figure 4.5 shows the *IQV* scores in the system over time. We use only the versions of religious diversity based on all possible religions. Patterns of religious diversity are virtually identical whether we focus on major religions or on religious families. Correlations

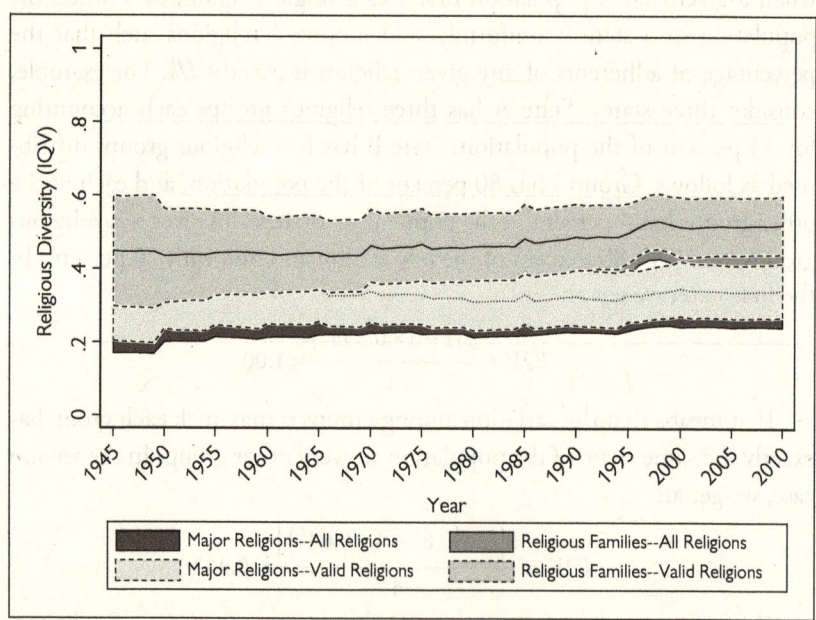

Fig. 4.5. Global religious diversity, 1945–2010

are in the 0.92–0.99 range (and this applies to the other two versions of the religious diversity indices based only on comparison of valid religions in each state).

We find two significant increases in global levels of religious diversity: between 1960 and 1970, and between 1995 and 2000. This is also where the gap between religious diversity based on only major religious groups, and religious diversity based on religious families is significant. We also find that religious diversity based on religious families—especially when the *IQV* is measured on the basis of valid religions and religious families in states—shows a marked upward trend over time. Much of this trend is accounted for by the growth in the size of the international system. But clearly religious diversity is affected also by migration patterns. This can be better seen when we examine regional patterns of religious similarity over time.

Figure 4.6 below shows regional levels of religious similarity over time.[9] Note that we use the cross-regional category as a baseline of religious similarity between states that belong to different regions. The first impression we have here is that of substantial cross-regional differences. The Western

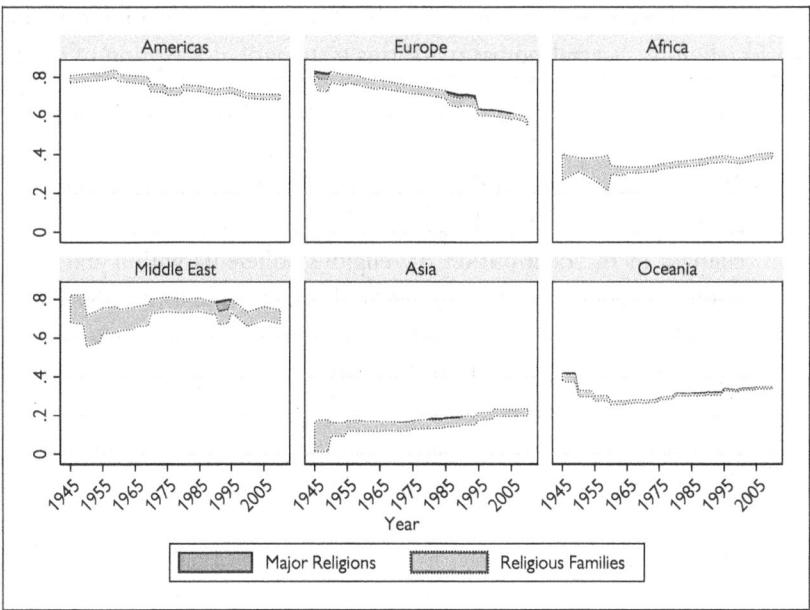

Fig. 4.6. Average religious similarity scores across regions, 1945–2010

Figures 4.5 and 4.6: Areas represent 95 percent confidence intervals. Lines represent means.

Hemisphere, Europe, and the Middle East show high levels of religious similarity among member states in these regions. On the other hand, Africa and Asia display very low levels of dyadic religious similarities. Second, we find a downward trend of religious similarity in the Western Hemisphere and in Europe, and an upward trend of religious similarity in Africa and Asia. The Middle East displays a fairly constant level of religious similarity between its members.

4. Conclusion

This chapter documents trends in national, regional, and global religious affiliations since the end of World War II, based on a new dataset on religion in the international system. The WRP dataset offers several innovations. First, it is based on a systematic classification of world religions and religious families. Second, we drew on a large number of sources to generate the dataset. Third, we used a number of methods to reconcile differences between sources and interpolated missing data. Fourth, the resultant dataset provides higher-resolution data, including data on the major world religions as well as on the religious families of the major world religions. Several points mark this systematic description of world religions:

1. The changes in the world's population over the period covered in this study have not, in general, been accompanied by major changes in the distribution of religious adherents within states. Some exceptions do exist, however. These include former Soviet republics (e.g., Kyrgyzstan, whose Muslim population increased by 37 percent between 1991 and 2010, and Kazakhstan, whose Muslim population increased by 42.5 percent over the same period).[10] Nor have these changes resulted in dramatic changes in the distribution of major religions across the international system as a whole.
2. The most dramatic changes in the distribution of religious adherents globally were due to two factors. First, the growth in the number of states in the international system. This reflects an artifact in our dataset—the focus on religion within independent

states—rather than a demographic trend or changes in the distribution of religious beliefs in the system. Second, political changes in states—primarily, the postcommunist transition in the 1990s—caused a large number of people in these states to reclaim religious affiliation instead of atheism.
3. Islam is the only major religion that has captured an increasingly larger share of the world's population over time. Other religions exhibited either significant fluctuations or a constant decline in terms of the relative share of their adherents from the world's population.
4. The impact of the growth of the Islamic population was noticeable primarily in Africa and Asia. In Europe, the migration from Islamic countries to primarily Christian countries has had an important effect on the religious diversity of European societies. In both Africa and Asia we see an upward trend in the number of Muslims, capturing an increasingly large proportion of those regions' population.
5. The proportion of the non-religious population has shown a modest increase over time on a global level. However, this group increased its size in Europe and Oceania, largely a reflection of the modernization and secularization trends in these regions.
6. Religious diversity increased in the two decades following World War II, largely due to the dramatic changes in the composition of the state system. Since the mid-1960s, the pace of growth in religious diversity has decelerated, and further changes in the size and composition of the state system have had only marginal effects on this diversity.

These trends mesh with other political, economic, and social changes that have taken place over the same period. This leads us directly into the substantive analysis of the role of religious factors in major facets of world politics.

Appendix to Chapter 4

This appendix discusses the methods and procedures we used to collect the data and to deal with several challenges of data collection and data management.

1. Detailed Questionnaire Responses

As mentioned in the chapter, we submitted the criteria for identifying major religions and religious families, as well as the candidate religions/religious families, to a panel of experts on global and regional religions. The results of the survey are given below (Table A4.1.)

Table A.4.2 provides the final religion tree used in the WRP.

2. Data Collection and Data Aggregation

We started the data collection project by forming a religion data bibliography.[11] These sources varied from census-based data to various estimates of religious groups, or sources that focused on a given religion in a longitudinal manner (either within a given country or for several countries). Some of the sources contained multiple data points on global or regional levels, but most contained scattered data on specific countries at discrete points in time.

Our coding manual reflected the kind of issues that we anticipated, given the literature review and a general review of source content and quality. The coding instructions presented several dilemmas. First, we had to ensure that denominational level data would be aggregated into the appropriate religious families. Second, in many cases or sources—even census data—mentioned only the number (or percent) of adherents of major religions but provided no reliable religion family data. In other cases, religion family data existed for only some of the families but not of others. The coding instructions were not always sufficiently specific to handle the diversity of categories provided by different sources; hence, we had to resolve multiple ambiguities in these sources.

Our initial strategy was to collect data from each source on a different record. We did that even if a given source listed only the number (or percent) of adherents for a single religion. Each data point (or a set of data points) was identified by the source from which it was taken, the date of the data, and the date these data were coded within the given source. We ran a number of tests on the data collected from each of the sources (such as consistency over time; source of the data coded in each source, e.g., census, secondary data, etc.; and comprehensiveness of coverage of different religions). We distributed a questionnaire among Association of Religion Data Archives (ARDA) members to solicit reliability estimates for each of the sources used. We then ranked sources according to an estimate of reliability.

Before aggregating the data, we had to deal with a number of problems:

1. *Adjusting source data to the categories of the religion tree.* In quite a few cases, the religious categories reported in a given source were not consistent with our religion tree. Here we had to make decisions about which specifically labeled religious group matched which of the religions or religious families in our religion tree. This proved to be a major challenge, especially within the Christian Protestant family. For example, some sources coded Anglicans as Protestants. Other included multiple Protestant denominations, sometimes under different labels. A related problem concerned aggregating the various Christian Orthodox denominations under the Eastern Orthodox family. Islamic denominations also presented a significant challenge.
2. *Eliminating the double counting of religious categories.* Several sources double counted religious groups. For example, some sources with data down to the denominational level counted Protestant adherents first by the number of Protestants and then by Protestant denomination. We had to make sure that the sum of the denominations matched the total number of Protestants. When discrepancies were observed, specific adjustments had to be made.
3. *Resolving categories such as "doubly affiliated" Christian groups (e.g., Protestants and Roman Catholics).* Since we view these religious families as mutually exclusive, we had to decide how to allocate doubly affiliated adherents into religious families.
4. *Addressing adherents of religions not under our religion tree categories.* We had to distinguish between religious groups that were labeled differently but in practice were within our religion tree, and those

Table A4.1 Survey of major world religions—validity scores N = 67

Question	Category	Response range	Response (SD)	Comments
Importance of criteria for identifying major world religions	Scriptures	1-6	5.13 (0.93)	Categories eliminated: Holidays
	Institutions	1-6	4.83 (1.12)	
	Historical Evolution	1-6	5.06 (0.91)	
	Beliefs, Practices, Rituals	1-6	5.06 (0.99)	
Importance of criteria for identifying religious families	Scriptures	1-6	4.95 (0.94)	
	Institutions	1-6	5.08 (0.86)	
	Historical Evolution	1-6	5.27 (1.02)	
	Beliefs, Practices, Rituals	1-6	5.10 (0.93)	
Rank order of criteria for identifying major world religions	Scriptures	1-8	2.91 (1.61)	1 = highest rank
	Institutions	1-8	3.40 (1.55)	5 = lowest rank
	Historical Evolution	1-8	3.55 (1.75)	
	Beliefs, Practices, Rituals	1-8	2.63 (1.80)	
Validity of Religion	Judaism	1-10	9.45 (1.79)	1 = completely disagree; 10 = completely agree. Validity scores below 6 were deleted or combined with other categories.
	Christianity	1-10	9.51 (1.82)	
	Islam	1-10	9.52 (1.82)	
	Bahá'i	1-10	7.34 (2.75)	
	Zoroastrianism	1-10	7.83 (2.82)	
	Hinduism	1-10	9.43 (1.95)	
	Buddhism	1-10	9.21 (2.26)	
	Sikhism	1-10	8.53 (1.87)	
	Shintoism	1-10	8.24 (2.26)	
	Taoism	1-10	8.71 (1.61)	
	Confucianism	1-10	8.27 (2.43)	
	Jainism	1-10	8.14 (2.14)	
	Syncretism Afro/Christian Religions of Latin America—Santeria	1-10	6.08 (3.02)	
	Animism	1-10	6.00 (3.60)	
	Non-religious[13]	1-10	4.68 (3.68)	
Validity of religious families	Judaism—Orthodox	1-10	8.93 (2.43)	Categories with validity rank below 7 were eliminated or grouped together as "other"
	Judaism—Conservative	1-10	8.93 (2.32)	
	Judaism—Reform	1-10	8.38 (2.37)	
	Christianity—Roman Catholic	1-10	8.95 (2.62)	
	Christianity—Orthodox	1-10	8.78 (2.70)	
	Christianity—Protestant	1-10	8.88 (2.38)	
	Christianity—Anglican	1-10	8.00 (3.02)	
	Islam—Sunni	1-10	9.56 (1.39)	
	Islam—Shi'a/Shiite	1-10	9.54 (1.39)	
	Islam—Ibadhi (Abāḍiyya)	1-10	7.91 (2.56)	
	Islam—Nation of Islam	1-10	7.24 (2.97)	
	Islam—Alawites (Nusayris)	1-10	7.00 (3.09)	
	Islam—Ahmadiyya	1-10	7.31 (2.93)	
	Buddhism—Mahayana	1-10	9.08 (2.16)	

Question	Category	Response range	Response (SD)	Comments
	Buddhism—Theravada	1-10	9.20 (2.07)	
Discipline of	Humanities		77.6 percent	
respondent[14]	Social Sciences		40.3	
	Physical Sciences		1.5	
	Biological Sciences		1.5	
	Other Academic		14.9	
	Non-academic Religion		19.4	
	Non-academic Other		7.46	
World Religions Scholar?		1-5	1.92 (1.15)	1= definitely; 5 = not at all

religions that had been candidate religions but that we had deliberately grouped into other categories (e.g., a variety of animist or syncretic religions).

5. *Dealing with religious practice of noncitizens.* In several nations, a large number of noncitizens exist who might be adherents of different religions than the citizens of the state, for example, the population of noncitizens in some of the Persian Gulf states (e.g., the population of the United Arab Emirates consists of 20 percent citizens and 80 percent noncitizens). In some cases, especially when using secondary sources, there is no distinction between citizens and noncitizens. In general, we attempted to collect data only for citizens and, if available, for permanent residents. However, this was not always possible. In such cases we downgraded the estimate of data quality.

This required us to review multiple sources and specific data points, and make decisions about how to deal with these problems. We documented our decisions in the raw data files, with specific comments. These are available upon request.

Reconciling data points from multiple sources. We sorted the data by state, year, and source. There were two types of cases in which data existed in two or more sources for the same state and year. One was a case where two or more sources contained complete or near-complete data for all major religions or religious groups within the state. The second consisted of cases where one source provided partial data on some of the religions and another source provided partial data that covered other religions, which were not documented in the previous source.

Table A4.2 Major world religions and religious families in the WRP

Major Religion	Religious Family	Pct. Agreement in Expert Poll (Std. Dev.)	Comments
Christianity		9.51 (1.82)	
	Protestants	8.88 (2.38)	
	Roman Catholics	8.95 (2.62)	
	Orthodox	8.78 (2.70)	This includes all the Orthodox families (Greek, Russian, etc.)
	Anglican	8.00 (3.02)	
	Other Christians		Residual category
Judaism		9.45 (1.79)	
	Orthodox	8.93 (2.43)	
	Conservative	8.93 (2.32)	
	Reform	8.38 (2.37)	
	Other		Residual category
Islam		9.52 (1.82)	
	Sunni	9.56 (1.39)	
	Shi'a	9.54 (1.39)	
	Ibadhi	7.91 (2.56)	
	Nation of Islam	7.24 (2.97)	
	Alawite	7.00 (3.09)	
	Ahmadiyya	7.31 (2.93)	
	Other Muslims		Residual category
Buddhism		9.21 (2.26)	
	Mahayana	9.08 (2.16)	
	Theravada	9.20 (2.07)	
	Other Buddhists		Residual category
Zoroastrianism		7.83 (2.82)	
Hinduism		9.43 (1.95)	
Bahá'i		7.34 (2.75)	
Sikhism		8.53 (1.87)	
Shintoism		8.24 (2.26)	
Taoism		8.71 (1.61)	
Confucianisn		8.27 (2.43)	
Jainism		8.14 (2.14)	
Syncretism		6.08 (3.02)	Afro/Christian Religions of Latin America—Santeria
Animism		6.00 (3.60)	
Non-religious		4.68 (3.68)	

When two sources provided relatively comprehensive coverage of all or most religions and these data were very similar or identical, this did not present a major problem. The problem emerged when there were substantial differences across sources in terms of the number (or percentages) of adherents of certain religions. The strategy we applied for reconciliation was threefold. First, we checked for within-source consistency over time. The assumption here is that—unless a dramatic political or natural event occurred between two time points (e.g., a major population transfer, a genocide that eliminated a significant proportion of a religious group)—the percentage of a state's population that practiced a given religion did not change dramatically within a given five-year interval. If a given source indicated dramatic shifts in the distribution of religious adherents without evidence of an event that would have caused such a shift, we concluded that there was a reliability problem. Second, if we had information about the source for this specific data point (e.g., census, survey, estimate), we assigned a specific reliability score to this data point. This enabled us to make aggregation decisions later on.

When a given source contained only partial data on one or more religious groups, we compared these data to data on those religious groups from other sources. We checked for consistency over time as well as the origin of the data for this source. Source reliability information is given in the dataset.

The general strategy for all cases that were covered by multiple sources was to generate single records of religious groups via a reliability-weighted mean of all sources.

Interpolating missing data. Missing data were a more serious and more common problem. We confronted four types of missing data issues:

1. missing data on the first data point[12]
2. missing data on a specific five-year point, but with data existing for adjacent years (e.g., no data on 1955 but existing data on 1956 and 1957)
3. missing data on a specific five-year point but with data existing for previous and subsequent five-year points (e.g., no data for 1955 but data available for 1950 and 1960)
4. missing data for 2010

In the case of missing data on the first or last time point, we applied trend interpolation. We calculated a moving average rate of change coefficient for the series of that particular state and applied it to the first or last data point. In the case of missing data with adjacent data points available, we applied a two-step process. First, if we had data for more than one adjacent year before or after the data point for which data were missing, we calculated an expected distribution of religious groups based on the trend for these two or more years for which data were available. Second, we calculated an expected trend between the two time points for which data were available before and after the date for which we needed data. Third, we calculated the average between the expected distribution of religious groups and the trend distribution. For cases included in #3, we interpolated a yearly distribution from the two time points in which data were available, and applied it to the year where data were needed.

In order to ensure that users know how we obtained the data for a specific record, we created a variable labeled "DATA TYPE" that specifies whether the data for that country-year are from a single source or multiple sources, and whether they are interpolated or trend based.

Dual Religions. In general, religious adherence forms mutually exclusive groups. People typically practice one type of religion or do not practice any religion at all. This means that when summing across all religious groups in a given state (including "non-religious" and "other religion" categories), the total should equal the state's population—and the percentages of religious groups should sum up to 100 percent. There are, however, a few states in which dual religion is a common practice. In such cases, the sum of religious adherents exceeds the population, sometime by a wide margin. We therefore introduced a code for dual religions.

Final Cleaning of Data. We applied two additional tests in the process of final data cleaning: population adjustment and trend adjustment.

The first test was meant to ensure that—with the exception of states with dual religions—the sum of the religious groups equaled the state's population. We used the COW (2008) total population data as the benchmark. There were, however, a few cases where population adjustments had to be made. In some cases, the sources we used included data on total population that were dramatically different from those of COW (e.g., one of the sources, Barrett et al. 2011, lists Afghanistan's population in 2005 at 27 million, whereas COW's total population for Afghanistan is only 24.86 million). In that case, we adjusted the number of religious adherents in that state to fit COW's total population, by first calculating the percentage adherents for each group based on the original source's population, and then remultiplying the percentages by the COW total population to get the adjusted raw figures of adherents for each religious group.

Third, there were a few cases where the COW population figures reflected some break points over time. Specifically, there were some cases of significant dips in population figures for the same state over a single year period (for example, COW's data indicate that Jordan's population dipped by over 33 percent—from 6.669 million in 2000 to 4.978 million in 2001). Some of these cases are due to political changes. For example, the dissolution of Yugoslavia between 1991 and 1999, or of Pakistan in 1971 explains dramatic declines in population. Thus, for each case of population decline, we investigated first whether any political shifts explain this trend. If we could not find such an explanation, we informed the COW data host of these changes and adjusted religion groups accordingly, while maintaining consistency with the COW data. These caused some breaks in the distribution of religious groups over time within a given country, as is evident in the significant downward trend in the Bulgarian population since 1991 and its effect on the distribution of Christians in the country.

The trend adjustment was designed to ensure that—barring major events that caused dramatic population changes in a given state—the rates of change in the relative size of any given religious group in a state would not exhibit dramatic changes from one five-year point to another. This proved to be difficult to ensure, as data for specific five-year points were derived from different sources. However, whenever necessary, we applied an adjustment rule to ensure that rates of change in the relative sizes of various religious groups are fairly smooth. This was the case especially if the data for a given five-year time point exhibited a dramatic difference between a preceding set of five-year points and a subsequent set of five-year points. However, in quite a few cases, such a smoothing operation was not possible because we lacked sufficient information enabling us to carry out a smoothing operation. In particular, this was the case when the data for that specific time point were drawn from a high-reliability source. This implies that in several cases, there are significant changes in percent adherents of a given religious group's across five-year time points. This is the case in particular with respect to two groups: "non-religious" and "other religion." Both of these groups represent residual categories in many of the sources. We used the latter as an adjustment category to ensure that the total number of adherents matched that of the total population.

CHAPTER 5

Religion and International Conflict

1. Introduction

Chapter 2 reviewed some of the writings on religion and conflict. We argued that the attempt to use religious factors to explain "religious conflict" is both logically tautological and empirically misleading. Consequently, our focus in this chapter is on general forms of international conflict, regardless of precipitating issue(s). The questions we pose do not concern when a conflict becomes "religious" but rather what kind of factors affect the propensity of states to engage in conflict with other states, what kind of factors increase or decrease the propensity of states to fight each other, and what factors increase or decrease the level of regional conflicts.

Specifically, this chapter addresses the following questions:

1. Which particular characteristics of states determine their propensity to engage in international conflicts? Specifically, how do the religious characteristics of states and their environment affect the scope, timing, and nature of their involvement in international conflicts?
2. How do the religious characteristics of states determine whom they fight? Specifically, which religious characteristics of states determine how they select enemies?
3. How do the religious characteristics of regions affect the conflict levels in them?
4. Do religious factors affect the characteristics of conflict, such as their duration, the likelihood of escalation, and their outcomes?

In chapter 3 we discussed in rather general terms the ways in which various theories address the relationship between religious factors and international conflict. In this chapter we provide a more in-depth theoretical and empirical focus on this linkage. Empirical research on the relationship between religion and international conflict was minimal for many years. The emergence of the CoC thesis, and even more so the terrorist attacks on September 11, 2001, stimulated a significant number of empirical studies on these issues. Results, however, have been mixed, at best, reflecting substantial disagreement on whether and to what extent religious factors affect the outbreak and characteristics of international conflicts.

We believe that such disagreements are due to weaknesses of the case-study and quantitative literatures on the subject. Accordingly, we employ several alternative approaches and data that help us provide a clearer picture of this linkage. We also build on recent empirical research on the relationship between religious factors and international conflict. We aim to innovate in several important respects.

First, we draw upon a broader range of perspectives and ideas than previous studies. Much of the empirical literature on the linkages between religious factors and international conflict focused on the arguments of the CoC thesis. Our approach relies on more nuanced ideas concerning the possible effects that religion may exert on international conflict. Some of the propositions we derive from the theories articulated in chapter 3 are different from, and broader than those that have been examined in previous studies. Tests of these hypotheses enable us to provide a more nuanced and balanced assessment of various theories linking religion to international conflict.

Second, we base our analyses on far more comprehensive and nuanced data than previous studies on both the factors that affect international conflict and on the characteristics of such conflicts. Our data contain high-resolution information on religion, international conflict, and a set of control variables related to our theory. On religion, the WRP dataset enables us to develop sophisticated measures of the religious characteristics of states, dyads, and entire regions. It allows us to quantify the degree of religious similarity and diversity within societies and between societies with a wide range of measures, some of them of very high resolution, and some of them more generic and coarse. These data that measure the religious demography of states, dyads, and regions are supplemented by additional data on the relationship between political institutions and states, and by data concerning the political stability of regimes, adapted from other data sources. These data lead to a wide range of analyses assessing the empirical support for various hypotheses that are derived from our theory, as well as from the other perspectives we discussed in chapter 3. On the conflict side of the equation, we build on a newly expanded, cleaned, and updated dataset on militarized interstate disputes (MIDs) (Maoz et al. 2018) that allows a set of systematic analyses covering more states, dyads, and regions than most previous empirical forays into the relationship between religion and international conflict.

Third, the scope of the current study is significantly wider and the probing of the possible religion-conflict linkages is significantly deeper than previous forays into this subject. We examine multiple units of analysis, including the state-year, the state-history, the dyad-year, the dyad-history, and the regional level. At each level we examine different aspects of religion-conflict relations. As we show below, the theoretical perspectives we discussed in chapter 3 have different predictions about which specific aspects of the religious characteristics of states, dyads, or regions affect which types of conflict behavior. These multilevel analyses of the religion-conflict nexus enable a more nuanced assessment of the relative validity of the different theoretical perspectives with respect to the effect of religion on international conflict.

Fourth, we offer several methodological innovations that help overcome biases, problems, and errors that pervaded many of the previous studies on the subject. Here, too, we believe that our results enable more credible inferences regarding the questions under study. Taken together, these analyses move the empirical study of religion and international conflict well beyond what was done and known in the past.

This chapter is organized as follows. In the next section we review the empirical literature that addresses the effect of religious factors on international conflict. We provide a critical appraisal of this literature and identify some of the theoretical and methodological difficulties associated with it. In the third section, we outline the hypotheses derived from the various perspectives discussed in chapter 3 with respect to the religion-conflict linkages. Section 4 discusses the research design in general and nontechnical terms. A more detailed methodological exposition of the research design is provided in the appendix at the end of the chapter. Section 5 discusses the results of the empirical analyses. In section 6 we provide a general assessment of the linkages between religion and conflict across levels of analysis.

2. Religion and International Conflict: A Review of the Empirical Literature

Much of the empirical study of religion and international conflict was revived in the post–Cold War era, and much of it was due to the CoC thesis. While there were a few studies of the religion-international conflict linkage in the preceding periods—and we discuss them below—not surprisingly, many recent empirical analyses have focused on testing the CoC thesis. Since we have reviewed the more general theoretical (and polemical) studies of religion and politics in previous chapters, this review focuses on empirical studies of religion and international conflict.

Perhaps the first systematic treatment of this subject was a set of studies by Lewis F. Richardson during the 1920s and 1930s. These studies were published posthumously in 1960. Analyzing more than 300 wars and disputes from 1820 to 1929, Richardson (1960) found that, in general, common religion did not have a dampening effect on the incidence of war. There appeared to be a relationship between religious dissimilarity and conflict in the case of Christianity versus Islam (p. 245), but Christians were also very likely to fight each other (pp. 235–39). The problem with the Richardson study has to do with its truncation of the population of cases. Like other studies of religion and conflict—discussed in chapter 2—Richardson ignored the opportunities for conflict, that is, those cases in which conflict did not occur.

Building on Richardson's work, Henderson (1997, 1998) studied the relationship between religious, linguistic, and ethnic similarity for all state dyads and their involvement in international war from 1820 to 1989. Utilizing the Cultural Composition of Interstate System Members dataset from COW (Singer 1997),[1] he found, inter alia, that religiously similar states were less likely to fight interstate wars against each other than religiously dissimilar states. These studies supported the view that "religion matters" in international conflict—and over a long period of time extending back to the early post-Napoleonic era. But given that the religious characteristics of states are similar to but not synonymous with Huntington's civilizations, then they could go no further in either supporting or refuting

Huntington's claims.[2] Moreover, these studies showed that while religious similarity exerted a conflict-dampening impact on international war, ethnic and linguistic similarity was found to increase the likelihood of war. Therefore, with respect to international war, the impact of religion was opposite that of ethnicity and language, demonstrating that they did not operate as part of the cultural monolith suggested by Huntington's terminology of "civilizations."

Gartzke and Gleditsch (2006) provided an extensive analysis of the relationship between religion and international conflict for the period 1950–2001. Their analysis drew on a different dataset (Ellingsen 2000) and examined a broader range of international conflicts, including MIDs, MIDs incurring battle deaths, and international wars. Their results replicated Henderson's main findings regarding the role of religious similarity in international conflicts. They also found that religious similarity exhibits opposite directional effects on international conflict compared to ethnic and linguistic similarity. Finally, Gartzke and Gleditsch also found that dyads in which a religious majority in one state shared religious identity with a minority in another state were more likely to experience MIDs. Like the previous studies, these findings converged with Huntington's claims that religion was an important factor in world politics, but diverged from them by showing that this impact transcended the post–Cold War era.

In a study of the impact of religion on international war over the broadest spatial temporal domain yet examined systematically (i.e., the period 1816–2001), Maoz (2006) found that religious polarization had a significant impact on systemic conflict, although the direction of its impact was not consistent across time and with respect to different measures of conflict. Religious polarization was positively and significantly associated with MIDs in both the nineteenth and the twentieth century. Yet, it was positively associated with wars during the nineteenth century but negatively associated with wars during the twentieth century. Religious polarization also had a positive effect on the duration of international conflict during the nineteenth century, but was negatively associated with it in the twentieth. In his findings of a two-century impact of religion on international conflict, Maoz's (2006) findings, like those of Richardson, Henderson, and Gartzke and Gleditsch, revealed that religion matters in world politics—and that it has for at least the last two centuries and into the present, but not in the way Huntington envisions it.

Additional studies that empirically test the CoC thesis on international conflicts include Russett et al.'s (2000) study of MIDs from 1950 to 1992, and Henderson and Tucker's (2001) analysis of international wars over the 1816–1992 period. Both studies found little if any support for the main claims of the CoC thesis. Similar disconfirming results emerged from subsequent systematic analyses of the CoC thesis (e.g., Chiozza 2002, Bolks and Stoll 2003), although there were a few exceptions (e.g. Tusicisny 2004, Charron 2010).[3] Thus, while IR scholars have demonstrated an empirical relationship between religion and international war, the main empirical claims of the CoC thesis—which these studies attempted to test—have not been consistently supported.

A somewhat different approach is used by Johns and Davies (2012). These authors employ an experimental design to test the—seemingly competing—claims of the democratic peace and the CoC theses. They examine the attitudes of subjects toward hypothetical conflict situations involving enemies that represent different regime types and different religious affinities. They find that British respondents are more likely to support the use of force against a dictatorship compared to a democracy, and that they are more likely to support the use of force against an Islamic enemy than against a Christian one. By contrast, American respondents' attitude is driven entirely by Christianity. Non-religious and non-Christian American respondents are no more likely to endorse the use of force against Islamic enemies than against Christian ones. This offers an interesting, albeit limited, take on the CoC thesis in that two largely similar publics in terms of religion and political culture show significantly different propensities toward conflict with religiously dissimilar enemies. However, the generalizability of an experimental study of this sort to real-world decision-making settings, or to broader cross-national settings is extremely limited.

Neumayer and Plümper (2009) test CoC-related hypotheses on international terrorism. They argue that the CoC thesis suggests a greater propensity for terrorism by Islamic perpetrators against non-Islamic targets. An alternative explanation for Islamic terrorism is that target selection is based on the strategic value of Western states, in particular, their support of the home regimes of terrorists (or of groups within those home countries). They find that the strategic model of international terrorism provides a better explanation of terrorists' choice of targets than the CoC thesis. However, they do find some support for the argument that the Islam versus the West hypothesis is better supported in the post–Cold War era than during the Cold War period.

The record of empirical investigations testing the CoC thesis is decidedly mixed. On the one hand, the results suggesting that conflict between religiously dissimilar states (Henderson 1997, 1998; Gartzke and Gleditsch 2006) may be seen as supportive evidence of this thesis. On the other hand, more direct analyses of the CoC thesis (Russett et al. 2000, Henderson and Tucker 2001, Chiozza 2002, Henderson 2005) suggest that there is not much evidence to support this thesis. Studies such as Neumayer and Plümper (2009) and Johns and Davies (2012) show that there is some overlap between hypotheses deduced from the CoC argument and alternative explanations for target selection by terrorists, or public support for the use of force against religiously dissimilar states. Consequently, we have yet to establish with a sufficient degree of reliability whether the world has gone from a Cold War superpower ideological standoff to a post–Cold War clash of civilizations. It may be that the answer to this question is neither definite nor simple. However, another possibility is that the empirical research on the religion-conflict nexus is marred by some significant theoretical and methodological problems. In fact, several issues with the empirical research of the CoC thesis stand out.

First, religious similarity is largely a function of how we measure religion and of the level of aggregation at which this concept is measured. For example, European states would be coded as religiously similar if similarity is measured in terms of major religions, such as Christianity; however, differentiating among Christian religious families (e.g., Catholic, Protestant, Anglican, or Orthodox) reveals much greater religious diversity. The same applies to conflict between various religious families in Islam.

Second, the studies we reviewed do not provide a consistent categorization scheme to determine the variability within and similarity across the worlds' major religions. For example, Richardson's (1960) analysis included thirteen religious groups. The COW data (Singer 1997) included sixty religious groups, ranging from major religions to minor denominations. Gartzke and Gleditsch's (2006) study focused on six of the nine religious groups in Ellingsen's (2000) data. The range of empirical results suggests that we need a standard and systematic classification of religious groupings.

Third, most studies focus on the dyadic level of aggregation. At this level of analysis we can provide answers to the question who fights whom, when, and (perhaps) why (Singer 1971: 63-4, Bremer 1992). This is an important level, but it is not clear that this level captures the various theoretical perspectives that claim a relationship between religious factors and international conflict. Important arguments on the relationship between religious adherence, religious diversity, and religious identity, respectively, and the conflict behavior of states, have rarely been systematically examined. For example, are religiously homogeneous states more or less conflict prone than religiously heterogeneous states? Are states in which there is significant religious discrimination more conflict prone than states that practice formal freedom of religion and separation between religious and political institutions? Are states wherein the vast majority of the population practices a given religion (e.g., Christianity, Islam, Hinduism) more conflict prone than states of other religious majorities?

Importantly, the CoC thesis's focus is on changes in the pattern of major armed conflicts during and after the Cold War. It is not evident that the dyadic level of analysis captures the logical import of this thesis. While dyadic analyses answer the question of who fights whom and when, it focuses on the trees rather than on the forest, and the CoC thesis is about forests not just pairs of trees.

Fourth, the research design of most previous studies on the subject is marred by significant methodological problems. These may lead to biased inferences. Several issues are apparent. One, the religious characteristics of states and dyads are stable over time.[4] This suggests that most studies that focus on a time-series cross-sectional (TSCS) design suffer from stationarity bias because the religious characteristics of states and dyads typically vary little over time.[5] By repeatedly analyzing the same dyads over time, analyses stack time invariant covariates on highly fluctuating outcome variables. This is likely to bias the resulting estimates and pose a major threat to inference. Another problem concerns the size of the population analyzed. With a very large number of cases, even a moderate or weak relationship becomes statistically significant. Even when some studies have used theoretical filters to reduce sample size,[6] the resulting samples are in the tens of thousands of observations. Finally, the dependent variables (the outbreak or occurrence of conflicts and wars) are extremely skewed: a small group of states or dyads are responsible for the vast majority of conflict, and many states/dyads have experienced no conflict involvement. This is also a source of bias in the results. We discuss these methodological issues at greater length in the appendix to this chapter. The general point, however, is that we need to find a way to fix these methodological problems in order to derive more reliable inferences regarding the relationship between religion and international conflict. And we need multiple robustness checks in order to have greater trust in our findings and assessments of them.

Importantly, the focus of this literature on religion and international conflict is quite narrow. Most of the empirical studies use the CoC thesis either as a source of their argument or as a foil. This often results in a lack of or rather superficial specification of the causal mechanisms that link religious factors to international conflict. In this context, Henne's (2012) study offers a major advance. Henne argues that the relationship between religion and state has an important effect on the state's behavior. Specifically, close ties between religious and state institutions suggest that the state can use or is inclined to use religious ideas, values, and symbols when it confronts a "secular" enemy. His analysis of MIDs over the period 1990–2000 suggests that, while religious-secular dyads do not exhibit a higher risk of conflict, these MIDs tend to be more severe than MIDs between secular-secular or religious-religious dyads. His analysis offers a window into more refined arguments that are related to the major theoretical perspectives discussed in chapter 3.

As noted above, with few exceptions, the theoretical (and in several cases, the empirical) focus of these studies is rather limited. The central question underlying these analyses is rather simplistic: are religiously similar states less likely to fight each other than religiously dissimilar ones? The "why" issue is asserted, explicitly or implicitly, in the CoC thesis. Huntington's argument is certainly no more sophisticated than the underlying ideas behind these analyses: it is fundamentally primordialist. However, Huntington's (2000) response to the critical empirical tests of the thesis is simply: the CoC is a child of the post–Cold War era that was born out of the decline of the bipolar Cold War system. The collapse of the bipolar system brought to the fore underlying intercivilizational divides that had been overshadowed by the struggle between the communist and capitalist blocs. This, too, is not a sophisticated theory of religion (or culture) and conflict. It does not answer the question of why the superpower rivalry suppressed the intercivilizational tensions prior to the end of the Cold War. Nor does it provide a clear explanation of why civilizational factors rather than national, territorial, economic, or technological issues emerged as the defining characteristic of post–Cold War conflicts.

The poor specification of causal mechanisms underlying religious factors as potential determinants of international conflict is perhaps the most glaring problem with the empirical analyses reviewed above. This goes beyond the narrow focus on CoC-related investigations. Accordingly, we need a broader perspective that addresses the key questions motivating this inquiry. Before explaining how our approach addresses these questions, however, we turn to a more detailed specification of the causal mechanisms that connect religion to conflict according to the various perspectives we reviewed in chapter 3. This is the focus of the next section.

3. Theory: Religion and International Conflict

We discuss below how each of the theoretical perspectives discussed in chapter 3 envisions the relationship between religion and conflict across levels of aggregation. We then compare these predictions. This comparison guides and may help us interpret the empirical results.

3.1 *Primordialist Propositions on Religion and International Conflict*

The primordialist perspective views religion as a permanent political force. This force is not equally powerful in all societies, however. It depends on two principal variables: the religious homogeneity/diversity of the society and the degree of separation between religious and political institutions. We also noted that this interaction between religious homogeneity and state-religious relations offers a way of distinguishing between and among societies in terms of the effects of religious variables on their external and internal behavior. It does not offer, however, a way of assessing variations in the foreign policy behavior of a given society over time. The prediction of this perspective with respect to the effects of religious factors on the conflict behavior of a given state can be summarized by the following propositions. We number these hypotheses as P# (where P represents Primordialism).

P1. The effect of religious factors on the conflict behavior of states is a function of the interaction between the religious homogeneity of the society and the embeddedness of religion in the political institutions of the state (i.e. the degree of state-religion separation): the more religiously homogeneous the society and the more intwined its religious and political institutions the greater its level of conflict involvement.

P2. Religious similarity between a focal state and its politically relevant international environment (PRIE) has a negative impact on the state's conflict proneness: the more similar the focal state to members of its strategic reference group, the lower its level of conflict involvement.

The first proposition follows from the classification of religious homogeneity and state-religion relations specified in Table 3.1 (chapter 3). Specifically, religiously homogeneous states that have a close association between religious and political institutions (Type I states) are significantly more likely to engage in conflict than religiously diverse states that have a clear separation between religion and state. The former types of states are more likely to use identity factors to motivate their external relations. Religious leaders are more likely to be in concert with political leaders when it comes to identifying national interests, delineating friends and foes, and deciding on the conditions that justify using force. By contrast, religiously diverse states that practice separation between religion and politics (Type IV states) are more likely to define their national interests and treat their environment in political and strategic terms. Thus, to the extent that they engage in conflict, the underlying motivations are not likely to be couched in religious logic or imperatives.

To clarify the causal mechanism behind P2, we reiterate the significance of the concept of politically relevant international environment (PRIE, Maoz 1996). Recall that we discussed in chapter 3 that each state has an environment it considers highly relevant for its national security. This environment is composed of a set of neighboring states and of states that have the capacity to project a significant number of troops and military equipment across distances. The focal state considers the actions and behavior of, or processes taking place within, the states in that environment to have an immediate and profound impact on its own national security. It has been shown (Maoz and Russett 1993, Lemke and Reed 2001, Maoz et al. 2018) that if we examine only dyads that are in each other's PRIE, this accounts for over 84 percent of the militarized interstate disputes over the period 1816–2010.

P2 offers a dynamic dimension of the primordialist perspective. The degree of religious homogeneity of a society is unlikely to change dramatically over time, at least not over short time spans.[7] However, the size and composition of the group of actors making up a state's relevant environment might change considerably from one point in time to another. For example, the size of the interstate system changed from 64 states in 1945 to 194 in 2010. Consequently, a state's neighborhood may change significantly over time as new states are added, other states secede from previous states (e.g., the secession of Slovakia from the former Czechoslovakia), and other multinational states collapse into smaller national units (the breakup of the Soviet Union, the breakup of Yugoslavia). Global and regional powers rise, fall, or move up the status ladder.[8] The second proposition suggests that a state's tendency to fight depends on the degree to which the focal state is religiously similar to or different from its actual or potential enemies. Because the primordialist perspective asserts that states' identities are strongly influenced by their religion, their attitude toward other states in their environment is predicated on comparing such identities. A state surrounded by religiously different neighbors, therefore, is likely to view its PRIE as hostile, while a state surrounded by religiously similar enemies is less likely to attribute to them hostile intentions. The behavioral implications specified in P2 logically follow this perceptual structure.

These ideas can be extended to the dyadic level. At this level we attempt to determine enemy selection, that is, to answer the question of who fights whom and when. Specifically, the likelihood of conflict according to the primordial perspective is determined by the religious identity of societies and by the degree of separation between religion and politics. Specifically,

P3. The higher the religious similarity between two states, the lower the probability of conflict between them.
    P3.1. The probability of conflict between two states is significantly lower when the two states share the same major religious group than when they share different modal religious groups.

P3.2. The probability of conflict between two states increases when the largest religious group in one state is the same as the largest minority religious group in another.

P.3.3. The emergence of a strategic rivalry between religiously dissimilar states is significantly higher than between religiously similar states.

P.3.4. Strategic rivalries between religiously dissimilar states last significantly longer than between religiously similar states.

P4. Conflicts between religiously similar states are likely to be (a) shorter, (b) less violent, and (c) more likely to end in an agreement than conflicts between religiously dissimilar states.

P5. The higher the degree of religious homogeneity of one or both societies—controlling for religious dissimilarity—the more likely is conflict to break out between them.

P6. The probability of conflict between two states increases with the degree to which one or both of them is/are characterized by lack of separation between religion and politics—controlling for religious dissimilarity.

Proposition P3 is predicated on the assumption that religion is an ever-present factor in the politics of states. Therefore, ceteris paribus, religious similarities between states are said to attract (see next chapter), and religious differences are a fundamental source of suspicion, mistrust, and animosity. Hence, the likelihood of conflict increases with the level of religious dissimilarity, and the likelihood of conflict diminishes with the level of religious similarity between dyad members. The subpropositions P3.1 and P3.2 follow from the general logic spelled out in P3.

Proposition P3.1 captures a coarser notion of religion similarity based on the identity of the dominant religious groups in both societies. This proposition assumes that majority religious groups in religiously diverse societies typically drive the identity of these societies. Therefore when two states—each of which is composed of a number of religious groups—share the same majority groups, they would be less likely to fight than if they shared different majority groups. Likewise, P3.2 suggests that there is a natural tension in dyads composed of members wherein the majority religious group in one state is the same as the largest minority religious group in the other state. In these cases, the likelihood of conflict increases because the majority group in the first state shares a spiritual affinity with the minority group in the other state. When the latter group suffers from discrimination or otherwise has grievances toward the ruling elites, the likelihood of its seeking (and getting) military help from the former group increases. This serves as a frequent cause of conflict between states.

It is worth spending some time on propositions P3.3 and P3.4 given their focus on the concept of strategic rivalries and its association with similar terms used in the literature, such as protracted conflicts, or enduring rivalries (Diehl and Goertz, 2000, Thompson 2001, Maoz and Mor 2002, Colaresi, Thompson, and Rasler 2008). Strategic rivalry describes a long-term disputatious relationship between two states, characterized by repeated conflicts that extend over a long time. Most of these repeated conflicts involve the same issues. Even when conflict is not actively taking place, these states view each other as competitors or enemies. The relationship between strategic rivals is laden with suspicion and mistrust. Nonconflict periods are often used to prepare for future conflict by their arming against each other, using propaganda within their own societies that stigmatizes the rival, and attempting to form alliances or other measures to presumably contain the rival and prevent it from accomplishing its goals (Senese and Vasquez 2008). Prominent strategic rivalries in the post–World War II era include the US–Soviet rivalry, the Indo–Pakistani rivalry, and the various dyads of the Arab–Israeli conflict (Egypt–Israel, Syria–Israel, Jordan–Israel). In the post–Cold War era some of the previous rivalries have continued, some have disappeared, and some new ones (e.g., Israel–Iran, China–Japan) have reemerged.

Propositions P3.3 and P3.4 suggest that a protracted state of conflict is more likely to arise between religiously dissimilar and homogeneous states than between religiously similar or diverse states. Moreover, Proposition P4 suggests that the characteristics of both isolated conflicts and long-term strategic rivalries between religiously dissimilar states have fundamentally different characteristics compared to conflicts or rivalries between religiously similar states. Specifically, conflicts between religiously dissimilar states are expected to be more violent, last longer, and end in some form of stalemate or one-sided victory (rather than in a negotiated settlement) than those involving religiously similar states. The underlying reasons should be obvious and are stated numerous times in the relevant literature: conflicts involving religious differences are more likely to be over indivisible issues and values. Religious differences may induce value conflict that can form an independent reason for conflict, but more often, religious differences exacerbate or become superimposed on other factors such as territory, natural resources, or political ideology that often serve as more direct causes of disputes.

Religious factors may not only ignite sporadic fights between states but also contribute to entrenchment when such conflicts arise. An added aspect in several such religious divides involves conflict over holy places (Hassner 2009). Such conflicts add an element of indivisibility to other factors that fuel the conflict and render it zero-sum in nature, making them more violent, durable, and less susceptible to negotiated settlements.

Proposition P5 is predicated on the notion that religion can serve as an increasingly important cause of conflict when a society is religiously homogeneous. Consequently, when dyad members are both religiously homogeneous and religiously dissimilar, they are more likely to fight each other. Proposition P6 presents a similar idea, except that here the leading factor is the comingling of religious and political institutions. In such cases religion can be more prominent as an identity marker. Thus, two dissimilar states that do not separate religion from politics are more likely to fight each other than states that establish a clear separation between religion and politics.

Finally, on a regional level, primordialism suggests that we should expect fewer conflicts in religiously homogeneous regions than in religiously diverse ones. This is reflected in P7.

> P7. The likelihood and severity of conflict in a given region is negatively related to the degree of religious homogeneity in the region.

P7. is a natural extension of the monadic and dyadic hypotheses to the regional level. Because most of the conflicts are between geographically contiguous states, this directly follows. When regions are religiously homogeneous (e.g., Catholicism in Latin America, Catholicism and Protestantism in Europe, or Islam in the Middle East), religious bases of conflict are less likely to prevail.

3.2 Instrumentalist Propositions about Religion and International Conflict

As noted in chapter 3, the instrumentalist perspective shares many ideas with the primordialist approach. In particular, instrumentalists agree that religion can become an attractive tool of social mobilization for foreign policy adventures when the society is religiously homogeneous and when religious and political institutions are closely related. Consequently, instrumentalism concurs with most of the propositions derived from primordialism. For example, political elites can more reliably mobilize religious symbols to secure the support of their constituents for foreign adventures against religiously different societies. By contrast, leaders may find it difficult to depict the opponent as infidels or as posing a threat to one's basic religious values if the opponent practices the same religion. In such cases other identity issues need to be invoked in lieu of religious symbols to justify risking people's lives for their country.

What is unique to the instrumentalist approach, however, is the focus on the specific circumstances in which elites are likely to employ religious symbols as a mobilizing tool. Specifically, instrumentalists view both the reliance on religious symbols and the resort to external conflict as tools in the arsenal of political elites. Political elites may invoke either of these tools or both depending on the specific goals they have and depending on the circumstances. One of the most popular theories of conflict suggests that political elites often use international conflict as a diversionary tool (Levy 1989). Specifically, political elites often resort to conflict as a diversionary tactic when they face internal problems and their political tenure is at risk. Under such circumstances political leaders seek to rally the population around the flag, thereby having constituents forget or push aside their domestic grievances and concerns. This connects nicely with the instrumentalist use of religion. Political leaders—especially when religion and politics cohabitate—can manipulate threats to religious values or holy places as a cause of conflict. Such ideas often serve as tools of mass mobilization. Given the "right" enemy and the "right" causes, religious fervor can be a powerful motivator for people to risk their lives and properties.

By contrast, religious values are not useful when trying to mobilize the society against an enemy that shares religious beliefs. In that case, elites need to resort to other ideas to mobilize support. Such ideas tend to be more tangible, for example, national security, territory, political values, and so on.

Accordingly, the following propositions address the effect of religious variables on national conflict behavior. (The I# labels are for Instrumentalism.)

I1. Religious factors are more likely to affect the conflict behavior of politically unstable states than politically stable ones.
I2. Politically unstable states are more likely than politically stable states to engage in conflict against religiously dissimilar states.
I3. Religious variables are more likely to affect conflict levels in politically unstable than politically stable regions.

The causal mechanisms driving these hypotheses are straightforward. Political leaders whose political survival is at risk are more likely to use conflict as a diversionary tool in order to fend off their internal opposition. Under such circumstances leaders tend to manipulate threats to basic values, or lay meaningful claims to assets held by other states. In other words, political elites must motivate people so as to make them forget their daily problems and risk their lives for their country. Religious values can serve as a powerful mobilizer under such circumstances. However, the enemy must be the "right" enemy. Therefore, proposition I2 follows, implying diversion. Given that religion is the mobilizing instrument, the enemy must be depicted as threatening or challenging religious values, which is more convincing when the enemy is religiously different.

The regional implication also follows. When most countries in the region are politically unstable, diversionary conflicts based on religious differences between states are likely to be more prevalent. In stable regions, although conflict may be frequent, the effect of religious variables—such as the degree of religious similarity in the region—on conflict is expected to be marginal or insignificant.

3.3 Constructivist Propositions about Religion and International Conflict

The constructivist contribution to theorizing the religious-conflict nexus is straightforward as well. Constructivists—as we have seen in chapter 3—concur with the primordialist notion that religion is an important identity marker. They also view religion as particularly prominent in homogeneous societies that lack separation between religion and state. However, constructivists suggest that there is variation over time in terms of the impact of religion as a central identity marker. Religion—as well as other cultural characteristics such as language, race and ethnicity—competes with the state's interactive experience. Constructivists suggest that identity is shaped both by constant (e.g., cultural) factors and by experiential factors, which change as a function of the interaction between the focal state and its external environment. Experiential elements of national identity are also a function of socially constructed ideas on the international level such as democracy, interdependence, or anarchy. Thus, as states accumulate more interactive experience, the significance of religion as a predominant identity marker diminishes. This implies the following propositions:

C1. Religious factors are more likely to affect the conflict behavior of states at their early stages of national independence than at latter stages.
C2. Religiously similar states are less likely to engage in conflict if one or both states are newly formed than if both have been independent for a long time.
C3. Religious factors are more likely to affect conflict levels in newly formed regions than in regions in which most states have been independent for a long time.

Again, the intuition here is straightforward. Consider C1. State formation has typically taken one of two forms: the nation-state model and the state-nation model. The nation-state model is largely predicated on social contract theories. This process involves, first, the presence of a community within a defined territory, whose members share cultural or civic characteristics, historical experience, and a common vision of the future. Second, this community forges political institutions that are designed to safeguard individuals' basic rights and protect the community from outside predators. In the nation-state model, the nation precedes the state, and the state is defined in terms of an existing set of identity markers that bind members of this community together.

The state-nation model is one where a community (that might be more or less diverse culturally) is governed by an outside colonial power. That colonial power chooses to pull out from that territory (or is forced to do so by indigenous resistance) and transfers power to a local elite. The key task of elites in the newly established state is to forge—often from scratch—a national identity. In most cases, postcolonial communities did not have prior experience of self-governance as an integrated political unit. The primary loyalty of individuals may be to tribes, clans, nations preceding the colonial era, or other traditional institutions other than the post-colonial state. In such cases, to the extent that common religion dominates other cultural, ethnic, racial or ideological characteristics as a common denominator of a sufficiently large portion of the new state's population, religion can become a key element of national identity.

Thus, the nation-state model emphasizes religion as a primordial aspect of the community's identity. By contrast, the state-nation model suggests that religion may be used instrumentally by the elites of the new states as a way of forging national identity where none exists. In either case, religion is a key determinant of identity and citizenship in new states. Once such states acquire interactional experience, however, they affect the religious aspects of identity. In some cases such interactive experience may in fact boost the importance of religion as a prism through which elites and masses in states identify friends and foes. In other cases, however, elements of national identity change as a function of the interaction between the state and other states in the system so that religion plays a less prominent role in the identification of friends and foes or the definition of interests. These ideas extend to the dyadic and regional level as well, and this is expressed in hypotheses C.2 and C.3, which expands the vision of the constructivist paradigm to larger levels of analysis. C3 also accounts for the historical formation of regions and the evolution of dyadic relations over time.

3.4 The Clash of Civilizations and International Conflict

The CoC thesis suggests a different breakdown of the linkages between religion and conflict. As we have seen in chapter 3, the key argument of the CoC thesis is that intercivilizational conflict has been simmering below the surface for a long time, but during the Cold War era it was overshadowed by the struggle between the superpowers and their satellite states. Importantly, as the Cold War ended, these underlying intercivilizational tensions resurfaced. Currently, these tensions define the key divides in world politics. Accordingly, we deduce the following proposition:

CoC1. The likelihood of conflict between religiously dissimilar states increased during the post–Cold War era compared to the Cold War era.

CoC1.1. This difference can be seen across levels of analysis.

3.5 The Integrative Theory of Religion and International Conflict

We pointed out in chapter 3 that these perspectives share some features in common, but also differ in some important respects. Our theory builds on the strengths of the various arguments. We agree with the primordialist perspective that religion is an important identity marker and helps define not only the nation's character but also some fundamental attitudes of the state's leaders and general population toward their environment. We also agree that religion becomes a more important political instrument when religious institutions and political institutions are closely aligned than when they are formally or informally separated. We agree as well with the instrumentalist perspective that political leaders are more likely to invoke religious mobilization strategies when they feel that their political survival is at risk than when they feel a high degree of job security.

However, our theory structures these arguments within a more coherent framework. We distinguish between the structural constraints under which political leaders operate, and the needs/opportunities they have to build or consolidate their winning coalition so as to ensure their political survival. We adopt therefore the structural arguments of the primordialist perspective about the interaction between (a) the religious homogeneity of the state's population and (b) the relations between political and religious institutions. We also consider the structure of the state's PRIE to impose constraints (or incentives) on the use of religious factors to motivate conflict. At the same time, our theory supports the more dynamic aspect of the instrumentalist perspective suggesting that the use of religious factors as motivators of conflict mobilization increases as the leadership's job security is at risk. With respect to international conflict involvement this implies the following:

IT1. A state is likely to engage in conflict when its leader's job security is at risk and it is
 a. religiously homogeneous,

b. characterized by close relations between political and religious institutions, and
  c. surrounded by religiously dissimilar states in its PRIE.
IT2. The probability of conflict between two states increases with the degree of instability in one or both states when
  a. they are religiously dissimilar,
  b. the major religious group in one state is the same as the second-largest religious group in the other state, and
  c. one or both maintain close relations between religious and political institutions.
IT3. Conflicts between states characterized by the aforementioned structural and situational conditions tend to be (a) more violent, (b) last longer, (c) less likely to end in a negotiated settlement, and (d) evolve into strategic rivalries than those that lack some or all of these conditions.

In short, the integrative theory posits that religious homogeneity, religion-state relations, and the religious structure of the state's PRIE by themselves do not account for national or dyadic conflict. Rather, it is the interaction between leaders' job security, the religious structure of the society and the state, and the structure of the state's PRIE that combine to account for such behavior.

4. Research Design

This section provides a general and intuitive discussion of the methodology we employ in this chapter. A detailed explication of the data, measures, and methods we use in our analyses is given in the appendix to this chapter. Readers who are not well versed (or interested) in technical details about the research design can skip the appendix without much loss.

4.1 *Units of Analysis: Who and What Are We Studying?*

Our analyses progress along several levels of analysis (or levels of aggregation): national, dyadic, and regional. We discuss briefly the type of analyses we conduct at each level. A level of analysis contextualizes the key unit that is the focus of research. Typically, it identifies a type of actor or set of actors that we wish to study, such as an individual, a group of people, an institution, or, in our case, states or groups of states. It also identifies an interval of time during which we observe that unit, such as a day, a month, a year, or a number of years. Here we use several levels of analysis (aggregation) to examine the linkages between religion and conflict.

At the national level of analysis we focus on the behavior of all states in the international system over the period 1945–2010. For a more restricted period (1990–2010), we examine whether the relationship between political and religious institutions within a state affects its propensity to engage in conflict (this is due to data limitations on the key variable of interest). In this set of analyses, we control for other factors that are known to affect a state's conflict behavior.

At the national level of analysis, we focus on two types of observations: the nation-year and the nation-history. The nation-year unit relies on observations consisting of each state's behavior for each year during which it existed as an independent system member. The nation-history level allows us to examine general tendencies of states over their entire history (within the period 1945–2010). As we explain in the appendix, this unit of analysis, which is not commonly used in studies of international conflict and cooperation, offers another layer of understanding of the relationship between national attributes—including religious characteristics of societies—and national behavior.

At the dyadic level we focus on all politically relevant dyads over the period 1945–2010. A politically relevant dyad (Maoz and Russet 1993) is a pair of states that satisfies one of the following three conditions: (a) it is contiguous through direct land or maritime border, or through colonial possessions of one of the states, (b) one of them is a major power, or (c) one is a regional power and the other is any state within the same region. We focus only on politically relevant dyads because these are theoretically and empirically the most likely dyads to engage in conflict. At the dyadic level we conduct additional analyses that test propositions P4 and IT3. These analyses include all possible dyads due to some methodological considerations, which we discuss below.

Here, too, we examine a dyad-year unit of observation, meaning that we observe each dyad during each year of its existence. We also study the dyad history by aggregating all relationships over the entire period of the dyad's existence. This allows us again to investigate general propensities of dyadic conflicts rather than specific fluctuations over time. As was the case for the national level of analysis, we examine differences between "new" and "old" dyads, between "stable" and "unstable" dyads, and between the Cold War and post–Cold War periods in terms of the effect of religious variables on dyadic conflict.

Finally, at the regional level, our unit of analysis is the region-year, using the COW project's regional classification. We examine patterns within given regions and between regions in terms of the effects of regional characteristics—including the degree of religious cohesion within the region as a whole, or the average religious similarity of region members—on levels of regional conflict.

4.2 Key Measures

Dependent variables.

MID occurrence. Using the dyadic militarized interstate dispute (DYMID, Maoz et al. 2018), we define the following occurrence variables. First, at the nation-year level, a MID occurrence variable is assigned a value of one if the focal state was involved in at least one dyadic MID during the given year, and zero otherwise. Likewise, at the dyad-year level, we assign a value of one to the MID occurrence if the states fought at least one MID against each other during that year, and zero otherwise.

War occurrence. This variable is defined the same way as the MID occurrence variable if the MID involvement of the state or if the MID between dyad members reached the level of war (as defined in Maoz et al. 2018), and zero otherwise.

Hostility score. Using Maoz's (1982) hostility scale, we sum the level of hostility across all dyadic MIDs in which a state was involved in a given year. This measure takes into account both the number of MID dyads of a given state and the level of hostility of each.

Escalation. This analysis focuses only on MIDs that actually occurred. Escalation receives a score of one if a given MID escalated to an interstate war, and zero otherwise.

Agreement. Maoz et al. (2018) coded the outcome and settlement of each dyadic conflict. There are several categories of MID settlement. We assign a value of one to a MID that ended in a negotiated settlement, and zero otherwise.

Duration. Duration of MID in days.

Strategic rivalry. We use the strategic rivalry dataset (Thompson and Dreyer 2011). A strategic rivalry receives a score of one in its first year of outbreak, and zero otherwise. We consider each year of a rivalry as missing for the analysis of rivalry outbreak.

Rivalry duration. Number of years during which rivalry was underway.

Independent Variables

The hypotheses discussed above involve several independent variables. We discuss them briefly by level of analysis.

Level of religious homogeneity. The data for religious homogeneity, as well as for percentages of specific religious groups within states are all drawn from the WRP dataset (Maoz and Henderson 2013). We use several measures of religious homogeneity. These are discussed in greater detail in the appendix to this chapter. The one we employ in the presentation of the results in the next section is the level of religious homogeneity. Recall the Index of Qualitative Variation (IQV) we discussed in the previous chapter. This index varies between zero, if the entire state's population practices a single religion (or belongs to a single religious family within that religion), and one, if there are two or more religious groups (say k religious groups), and each of these religious groups accounts for $1/k$ of the state's population. In other words, religious diversity is maximal if the state's population is distributed equally among several religious groups. For convenience, we break down this index into three levels so that high homogeneity (i.e. low diversity) accounts for IQV values of 0.25 or lower, moderate homogeneity (i.e. moderate diversity) accounts for IQV values of above 0.25 and below 0.66, and low homogeneity (i.e. high diversity) accounts for IQV values 0.66 and above. We show analyses based on actual IQV values in the book's website (Table A5.1).

Religion-State relations. We use two separate datasets to generate this index; both were mentioned in previous chapters. The first is the religion and state (RS) dataset (Fox 2016). As noted, this dataset covers most states during the period 1988–2008, and it contains significant information about various forms of religious discrimination, religious regulation, and religious legislation. The shortcoming of this dataset is that, while it is spatially general—including most states during that period—it covers only a limited time span compared to the longer period we are interested in. This is particularly problematic if we wish to get a sense of the effect of religion-state relations during the Cold War era.

Second, we use the comparative constitution (CCS) dataset (Elkins, Ginsburg, and Melton 2014). The advantage of this dataset is that it covers a long temporal span. The downside of this dataset is that it covers only states that have constitutional documentation. Nevertheless, this dataset allows us to examine two variables that gauge the relations between religion and state. First, does the constitution contain a freedom of religion clause? If it does, this provides evidence of relative religious freedom, which suggests some degree of potential or actual separation between religious and political institutions. Second, the dataset contains information about the status of religious law in the constitution. In some cases, religious law is deemed superior to non-religious law. That is, laws contrary to religious laws are deemed void. In other cases, religious law is a basis for general law. And in still other cases, religious law has no special standing in the constitution.

We use a combination of the religion and state variables on religious discrimination, religious legislation, and religious regulation, as well as the religious freedom and religious legislation variables from the CCS dataset to generate a three-level variable of religion-state relations. This variable gets a value of 1 = separate, when either or both the RS and the CCS suggest that the state practices a relative independence of religious and state institutions. It assumes a value of 2 = some relationship, if there is indication of some level of religious discrimination, regulation, or legislation in either the RS and the CCS dataset or both. Finally, the religion and state variable assumes a value of 3 = cohabitation, if the state's constitution or its laws and practices indicate high levels of religion legislation, discrimination, and/or regulation. We discuss the generation of this variable in greater detail in the chapter's appendix.[9]

Religious similarity state-PRIE. The data for this variable are drawn from (a) the WRP dataset, and (b) the definition of PRIE adapted from Maoz (1996, 2010). We expand on this measure in the appendix, along with several examples. Here, however, we describe the intuition for this measure. As noted, the PRIE of a state consists of (a) its immediate neighbors, (b) all the states in the focal state's region designated as regional powers (states in the region that are capable of projecting force in the region), and (c) all global powers (states that are capable of projecting power across the globe). We code the degree of religious similarity between the focal state and each state in its PRIE separately. The degree of religious similarity between two states is based on the degree to which the distribution of the religious adherents in one state is similar to or different from the distribution of religious adherence of the other.

For example, two states that have both a Christian–Catholic majority of 0.8 and a Muslim–Sunni minority of 0.2 will receive a religious similarity score of 1; their populations are exactly alike in terms of religious adherence. By contrast when we compare a state that has a Christian–Catholic majority of 0.8 and a Muslim–Sunni minority of 0.2 with a state that has a Muslim–Sunni majority of 0.8 and a Christian–Catholic minority of 0.2, we get a religious similarity score of 0.32. These two states have the same religious groups, but the distribution of adherents in these groups is dramatically different. In general, the religious similarity score varies between zero, if the two states have dramatically different religious groups (for example, one state has all of its population practicing Sunni Islam and the other state has its entire population practicing Protestant-Christianity), and 1, if the states have the same religious groups and the distribution of adherents over these groups is the same in both states.

Once we calculate the dyadic religious similarity between a focal state and each of the states that constitutes a member of its PRIE, we average the religious similarity score over the PRIE membership. Thus, a high similarity value means that the state's PRIE is composed of states that are religiously similar to itself; a low similarity value suggests a significant religious difference between the focal state's population and its PRIE membership.

Percent adherents. In some of the analyses we examine whether states dominated or populated by specific religious groups are more or less conflict prone than states dominated or populated by other religious groups. Accordingly, we use the percent adherents of certain religions in a given state. For example, we use the percent Christians, Muslims, Buddhists, and Secular (atheists, agnostics, or people with no religious affiliation) as a possible predictor of conflict proneness.

Coup risk. To measure the degree of political leaders' job security—a central variable in the integrated theory—we use the coup risk measure developed by Sudduth (2017). This variable relies on the Powell and Thyne (2011) coup dataset that lists all instances of irregular and extralegal government and political changes or attempted changes over the period 1945–2010.

Sudduth developed a Bayesian method of calculating the potential risk of a coup in a given state at a given time point. This method combines the history of coups in that state, per-capita GDP, democracy score, and whether the current regime is a military regime. Using a logit model, he calculates the expected probability of a coup in a given state. Replicating his analysis allows us to generate a similar index (which in our case ranges from three hundredth of 1 percent to about 20 percent). We partition this variable into two levels: the low-risk level has a coup risk of 5 percent or lower and the high-risk level has a coup risk of above 5 percent.[10]

Control variables.

We use a number of control variables commonly employed in empirical studies of international conflict, including regime score (or democracy/nondemocracy variable), national capabilities, reputational status (minor power, regional power, major power), number of allies, log trade (imports and exports), number of IGO memberships, and the past conflict experience of the focal state. We discuss these variables in more detail in the appendix. For the nation-history level of analysis, we average the dependent, independent, and control variables over the state's history. Again, we demonstrate this in the appendix. The dyad-year level of analysis involves largely the same variables, but their measurement is based on dyadic values.

In terms of independent variables, we employ the following measures.

Religious homogeneity. We use the individual religious homogeneity variables of dyad members to generate a combined religious homogeneity index. Specifically, this index has a value of low homogeneity if both dyad members have low individual homogeneity scores (both are religiously diverse), and it has a value of high religious homogeneity if both dyad members have a high religious homogeneity (i.e. both have low diversity scores) scores. Medium levels of religious homogeneity are mixes of low and medium religious homogeneity scores of individual members.

Religion and state. We use a similar strategy as in the case of religious homogeneity to generate a dyadic religion-state classification given individual religion-state classifications. Specifically dyads composed of states that have a separation of religion and state are designated as "separate" dyads; dyads composed of members both of which exhibit a strong association between religion and state are designated as "cohabitation" dyads; other dyads are in the "some relation" category.

Coup risk. We combine the coup-risk measures of both states in the following way:

$$couprisk_{ij} = \begin{cases} 0 \text{ if } couprisk_i = 0 \text{ and } couprisk_j = 0 \\ 1 \text{ if } couprisk_i = 1 \text{ or } couprisk_j = 1 \\ 2 \text{ if } couprisk_i = 1 \text{ and } couprisk_j = 1 \end{cases}$$

Control variables are the same as in most dyadic analyses of interstate conflict and include joint democracy, alliance, reputational status, distance, trade dependence, IGO comembership, and past conflict/enmity relations. These are discussed in the appendix.

The dyad-history level of analysis is also based on averaging dyad-year figures over the common history of dyad members. At the region-year level of analysis, we average both dependent, independent, and control variables over all states in a given region for a given year. A more detailed explanation is provided in the appendix.

4.3 Estimation Methods

Several issues are covered here. A more detailed discussion underlying the modeling decisions is given in the appendix. First, our analyses are based on methods that have been employed in many previous studies of international conflict. However, we also make some methodological modifications in order to mitigate some inferential problems associated with the more traditional methods. These methodological modifications help shed a more reliable light on the complex relationship between religion and conflict. In particular, we note that the values of the religious variables do not change much over time for a given state, dyad, or even region. This applies as well to other control variables that are used in the more traditional analyses. Therefore, analyses that are based on the entire population of cases are subject to what is commonly referred to as "stationarity bias." What that means, in laymen's terms, is that while the level of conflict a state experiences may fluctuate quite considerably from one year to another, its religious composition changes very slowly—if at all—over short time spans. Therefore, inferences drawn from analyses where each state appears repeatedly at each year, are apt to be biased.

In order to overcome this bias as well as other biases inherent in the data, we use a repeated sampling process known as "bootstrapping." Bootstrapping involves drawing a random sample from the population of cases, running a specific analysis on this sample, and repeating this process a large number of times. The cumulative results of these repeated analyses are then evaluated statistically, to remove any biases that may characterize results drawn directly from the entire population (e.g., effects of outliers on the results). Our inferences are based both on this strategy and on the more conventional strategy of analyzing all observations. We consider as meaningful only those results that are consistent across strategies of data analyses.

Second, in order to enable a meaningful test of the integrative theory, we need to focus on the interaction between the anticipated level of regime/leadership insecurity—as measured by the coup-risk variable—and the probability of conflict between the focal state and religiously dissimilar states. Specifically, the theory anticipates that political leaders at risk are likely to use religious values and symbols to mobilize support for the initiation or escalation of conflict. Such a strategy can be effective if the "enemy" is different, if it threatens or violates important religious values held by the focal state's population. Hence, we would expect to find a significant interaction between coup risk and conflict against religiously dissimilar states. So, the key to testing our theory is not only in finding a relationship between the more static elements of religious similarity or religion-state relations and conflict propensity. It is also this dynamic interaction between the leadership's job security and its willingness and ability to use religion as a mobilization weapon that forms the core of the theory.

Third, when analyzing the characteristics of conflicts (duration, propensity for escalation, outcomes), we need to take into account the possibility that states select themselves into MIDs in a nonrandom fashion. Specifically, the factors that affect states' decisions about initiating a MID, or responding forcefully to a challenge by an opponent, may have an impact on the characteristics and outcomes of these MIDs. Consequently, we need to control for "selection bias." Accordingly, in the analysis of MID and rivalry characteristics, we use Heckman selection models (Heckman 1976, Newey 2009), which first use MID outbreak as the selection variable and then use the specific MID characteristic as the dependent variable. For example, when we test whether a dyadic MID escalated to war, we use dyadic MID outbreak as a selection variable. The key independent variables that we believe affect states' selection into MIDs include PRIE membership and joint democracy. We then use the selection equation as a basis for estimating those MIDs that escalated to war, given that a MID broke out.

5. Results

We provide herein a summary of the multiple empirical analyses we have conducted. The book's website contains a detailed outline of the results. Also, in order to enable readers who are not versed in the intricacies of complex statistical analyses to understand the results we focus on graphical presentation and intuitive interpretation of the results. As noted, the appendix provides detailed information about the things contained "under the hood" of these inferences, and the mechanics of the various analyses.

5.1 *National Level of Analysis*

Table 5.1 provides the summary results of this set of analyses. We focus our discussion on the religious characteristics of states and of their PRIE. The most robust result concerns the effect of the similarity between the focal state and its PRIE on the probability and magnitude of the state's conflict involvement. As the degree of similarity between the religious makeup of the focal state and that of its PRIE increases, its level of conflict involvement declines. The degree of the focal state's religious homogeneity has a positive effect on the probability of MID outbreak and on the hostility score the state applies during these MIDs. However, religious homogeneity does not significantly raise the risk of escalation.

Secularism increases the risk of MID outbreak, but it reduces the level of hostility of such MIDs. Secularism does not seem to affect the probability of dispute escalation to war. The relations between religious and political institutions in states do not seem to affect conflict involvement, regardless of the measure of conflict used.

However, the focus of our theory is not on the independent effects of these factors on conflict propensity. Rather, we explore the conditions under which religious factors are apt to be used by political elites as tools for mobilization—in this case for conflict-related mobilization. Our expectation was that leaders in politically unstable systems—those perceiving a high level of job insecurity—are more likely to invoke religious issues

Table 5.1 The effects of religious characteristics of states on conflict behavior, 1945–2010: nation-year unit of analysis

	MIDs	Escalation	Hostility
Religious Homogeneity	0.098*	0.06	18.537**
	(0.048)	(0.112)	(4.728)
Pct. Nonreligious	1.157**	0.21	-430.58**
	(0.257)	(0.513)	(45.37)
Religious Similarity State-PRIE	-2.34**	-5.803**	-84.094*
	(0.673)	(1.438)	(36.253)
Religion-State Relations	0.12	-0.22	4.29
	(0.113)	(0.247)	(6.955)
Rel. Sim. State-PRIE#Coup Risk	-1.456**	1.94⁺	-61.827*
	(0.481)	(1.049)	(25.984)
Rel. Sim. State-PRIE#Relig.-State Relations	1.598**	2.718*	6.64
	(0.528)	(1.256)	(28.932)
Cohabitation	2.414*	0.29	136.18*
	(0.947)	(2.842)	(54.574)
Coup Risk Level	0.983**	-0.19	22.346**
	(0.129)	(0.272)	(7.924)
Constant	-1.167**	-0.57	58.597**
	(0.259)	(0.514)	(20.615)
N	6,707	2,311	6,707
Chi-Square/F-statistic	701.144	107.410	15.967
Pseudo R-Squared	0.1645	0.061	

Notes: Numbers in parentheses are robust standard errors. Control variables are omitted to conserve space. Full results are given in the book's appendix
\# Indicates an interaction term
* $p < 0.05$ ** $p < 0.01$

as pretexts to launch diversionary conflicts. This is more likely to happen when the environment can be seen as "religiously hostile," that is, when there is a sharp difference between the religious makeup of the focal state and that of states in its environment. Likewise, when there is a close relationship between religious and political institutions, political leaders are more likely to invoke religion as a cause of the rift between themselves and the environment.

To assist the interpretation of the numerical results, we show graphically how the interaction between the focal state's political situation and the structure of its environment affects the focal state's propensity for conflict. This is given in Figure 5.1.

The top-left panel of this figure (5.1.1) shows that the probability of conflict involvement of a state declines as the degree of religious similarity between itself and its PRIE increases. This is true for both low coup-risk states and high coup-risk states. However, the probability of MID involvement of high-coup risk states is nearly twice that of low-coup risk states when the religious makeup of the focal state is markedly different from that of its PRIE. This difference between the conflict propensity of low and high coup-risk states diminishes as such states' religious makeup is similar to their PRIE. In such cases, political leaders in trouble, and political leaders who feel "safe," behave in pretty much the same manner.

The top-right panel (Fig. 5.1.2) suggests the probability of conflict involvement of states decreases as a function of religious similarity between the focal state and its PRIE. However, the decline seems to be marginally sharper for states that practice separation of religion from politics compared to states that maintain a close relation between religious and political institutions.

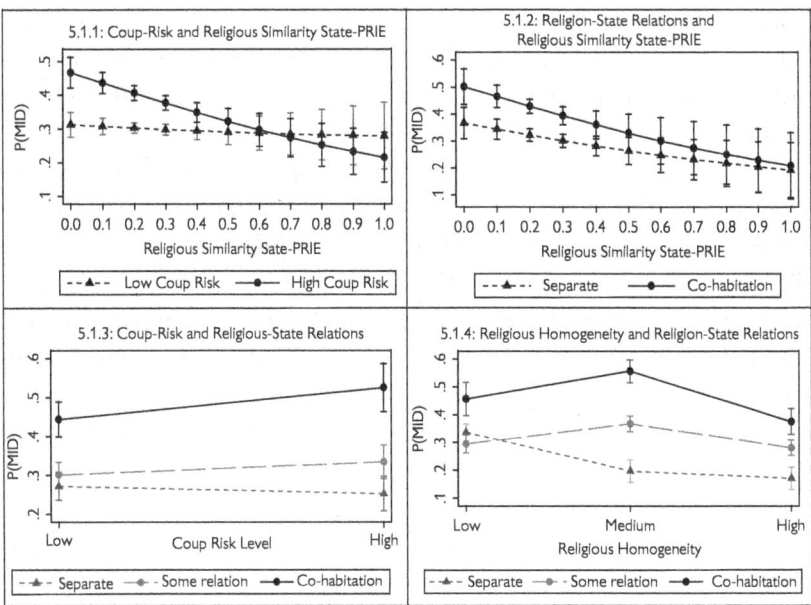

Fig. 5.1. Religious factors interaction with political instability and their effects on the conflict propensity of nations
Note: vertical lines are 95% confidence intervals.

Fig. 5.1.3 suggests stark differences between states that practice separation of religious and political institutions and those that have close religion-state relations. The conflict propensity of states that practice religion-politics separation is not affected by coup risk. By contrast, the combined effect of coup-risk and religion-state relations is significant for states that have a moderate or close relationship between religion and politics. These results lend support to our argument that it is not only the degree of dissimilarity between the focal state and its environment that makes the state more prone to fight but also the combination of specific political conditions within the state and the structure of its environment that interact to produce a higher or lower propensity to fight other states.

Figure 5.1.4 addresses the interaction between religious homogeneity and state-religion relations and its effect on conflict behavior. The most important result in this figure is the difference between states that practice separation of religion and state and those that have a moderate or close relationship between these institutions. States practicing religion-state separation tend to reduce their involvement in interstate conflict when their societies are increasingly homogeneous in terms of religion. By contrast, states that have a moderate or close association between religious and political institutions tend to increase their conflict involvement as their societies are increasingly homogeneous in terms of religion. This provides support for P1.

We find no consistent statistical relationship between any specific religion and conflict proneness (see appendix). The notion that a specific religion (e.g., "Islam has bloody borders," Huntington, 1996, 35) is more likely associated with conflict behavior does not appear to hold. However, several results in the table above seem to indicate some support for CoC claims. In particular, the negative effect of state-PRIE religious similarity on conflict suggests that states are more likely to fight with religiously different enemies than with religiously similar ones. We will return to this point when we explore dyadic-level conflict propensities.

The most important prediction of the CoC thesis, however, is given in proposition CoC1 above, which suggests that the effect of religious variables on conflict has become more pronounced since the end of the Cold War. To test this proposition, we examine how different religious factors affect national conflict involvement patterns during the Cold War era compared to the post–Cold War era. The results of these analyses are shown in Figure 5.2.

The results reported in Figure 5.2.1 uniformly and conclusively contrast the expectations of the CoC thesis: the effect of religious factors on interstate conflict was significantly more pronounced during the Cold War era compared to the post–Cold War era. First, the negative relationship between religious similarity state-to-PRIE and conflict that characterized the Cold War era is reversed during the post–Cold War era. Specifically, during the post–Cold War era, states are more likely to get involved in conflict when they face a similar politically relevant environment than when they face a dissimilar environment (Fig. 5.2.1). Second, we also find a reversal of the relationship when we examine the effect of religious homogeneity on conflict over time. During the Cold War era, religiously homogeneous states were more likely to engage in conflict than religiously heterogeneous states, but during the post–Cold War era, the inverse is happening: religiously heterogeneous states are more likely to engage in conflict than religiously homogeneous ones (Figure 5.2.2).

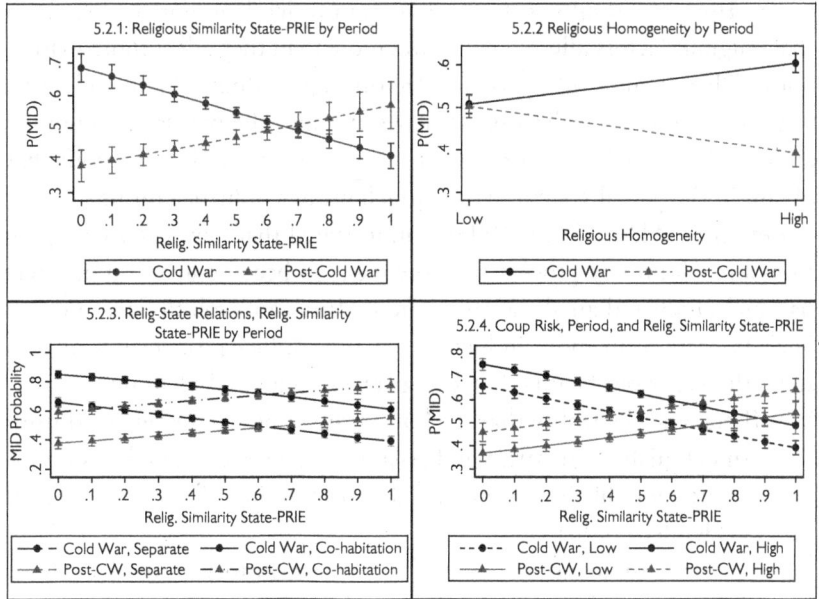

Fig. 5.2. Testing the CoC thesis on monadic conflict—differences between Cold War and post–Cold War patterns
Note: vertical lines are 95% confidence intervals.

When we test more complex interactions that follow from our integrative theory, we find interesting temporal differences. In general, states that practice a close relationship between religious and political institutions (Type I or Type III states in Table 3.1) are generally more likely to engage in conflict than states that separate religion from politics (Type II or Type IV states). This is true for both the Cold War and the post–Cold War era. However, once we take into account the religious similarity between the focal state and its PRIE, we find again a relationship reversal. During the Cold War era, the likelihood of conflict involvement declined as a function of religious similarity between the focal state and its PRIE, whereas in the post–Cold War era, this relationship became positive and significant (Figure 5.2.3). We find a similar pattern when we take into account the effect of coup risk and religious similarity state-PRIE on national conflict involvement (Figure 5.2.4).

With regard to the propositions deduced from constructivism we find—in the results reported in the appendix—that the effect of religious factors on the conflict behavior of "new" states is not significantly different from the effects of these factors on the conflict behavior of more mature states. Thus, our results so far do not seem to lend support to the claim that religious factors affect "new" states more than they affect more mature ones. What is more likely is that factors superseding religious identity, but central to the socialization of new states into the political, economic, and social—as well as cultural—status quo practices and institutions that obtain in the global system, have a much greater influence on new states. For example, Maoz (1989, 1996) demonstrated that new states emerging from a revolutionary process are more likely to become involved in international conflict than those that emerge from an evolutionary process. Such impacts seem more influential on the conflict propensities of new states than religious factors. Further, given our temporal focus on the post-WWII era, and the reality that the lion's share of new states emerged from Western colonialism in Africa and Asia, then processes related to decolonization are more likely to influence the socialization of the new states of the era (Henderson 2015).

We now turn to an analysis of the nation-history unit of analysis. Table 5.2 provides the results of these analyses. The results of the nation-history analysis largely confirm those of the nation-year analyses. The degree of religious similarity between the focal state and its PRIE is the only religious characteristic that consistently dampens national conflict proneness.

In addition, states that practice a close association between religious institutions and political institutions tend to have more MIDs and display a higher average level of hostility than states that are characterized by a separation of religion and state. However, the former types of states have been no more war prone than the latter type of states. In contrast to the expectations of the primordialist perspective, religious homogeneity does not have a significant effect on conflict proneness. Finally, in this case too, we do not find support for arguments linking any particular religion to higher or lower levels of conflict involvement over national histories. It does not appear that states with a majority practicing a specific religion tend to be more or less conflict prone than states with other religious characteristics.

The national history level offers a good test regarding the effects of the more permanent characteristics of states—those that exhibit little variation over states' history, such as religious homogeneity. At the same time, this type of analysis does not permit meaningful tests of interaction effects that emphasize dynamic aspects of religion. This prevents testing the hypotheses linking regime stability to the tendency to invoke religious factors as a mobilization tool for conflict.

Table 5.2 Effect of religious factors on conflict history of nations

	MIDs	Hostility	War
Religious Homogeneity	0.01	2.78	-0.28
	(0.035)	(8.855)	(0.321)
Secularism	-0.09	11.05	1.911*
	(0.14)	(38.717)	(0.831)
Religious Similarity State-PRIE	-0.23*	-33.15*	-1.915*
	(0.098)	(15.966)	(0.898)
Religion-State Relations	0.351**	64.95*	1.20
	(0.103)	(28.354)	(0.611)
Coup Risk	0.05	5.00	-0.01
	(0.029)	(6.724)	(0.29)
State-Rel Relations # Relig. Sim- State-PRIE	-0.41*	-64.44	-1.25
	(0.166)	(47.633)	(1.157)
Constant	0.18	43.118**	1.474*
	(0.1)	(16.684)	(0.587)
N	185	185	185
F/Chi-Squared	23.616	121.637	143.579
R-Squared	0.482	0.606	0.402

Notes: Control variables omitted to conserve space. Full results are reported in the book's website.
* $p < 0.05$; ** $p < 0.01$

5.2 Dyadic Level of Analysis

Table 5.3 provides the key results of the relationships between the religious characteristics of dyads and the probability/severity of conflict between their members. Figure 5.4.1 shows the effects of religious similarity on dyadic conflict, controlling for the intervening variables of regime instability, dyad years, and Cold War/post–Cold War periods.

As was the case with the nation-level analysis, religious similarity has a robust negative effect on the probability and magnitude of dyadic conflict. When we measure religious similarity in coarser terms—that is, whether dyad members share the same majority religion—we find a similar result. Dyads that share the same largest religious group are significantly less likely to fight than dyads that do not share the same major religious group (results

Table 5.3 Religion and dyadic conflict—Dyad-year unit bootstrapping results (except for Escalation)

Independent Variable	MIDs	Escalation	Hostility	Strategic Rivals
Religious Similarity	-1.07**	-0.66	-1.602**	-0.381**
	(0.308)	(0.743)	(0.61)	(0.107)
Religious Homogeneity				
Medium	0.066	0.191	0.638*	-0.234
	(0.116)	(0.231)	(0.251)	(0.132)
High	0.041	0.151	0.506	0.587**
	(0.208)	(0.472)	(0.44)	(0.216)
Religion-State Relations				
Some Relation	0.301**	0.984**	0.665**	0.742**
	(0.117)	(0.229)	(0.183)	(0.138)
Cohabitation	0.087	-0.151	0.342	0.813**
	(0.146)	(0.359)	(0.233)	(0.163)
Coup Risk#Religious Similarity	1.181**	-1.188	0.106	1.363**
	(0.349)	(0.76)	(0.451)	(0.359)
Coup Risk	-0.162	1.437**	-0.033	-0.087
	(0.165)	(0.317)	(0.231)	(0.181)
N	56,150	56,150	56,150	504,551
Chi-Square	624.966	545.486	2694.257	2719.056
R-Squared	0.196	0.297	0.078	0.939

Notes:
1. Results are based on 300 bootstrapped samples (with replacement) of size 15,000 each. Escalation analyses based on entire dataset.
2. Control variables omitted to conserve space; full results are shown on the book's website

reported on book website). The effect of religious homogeneity on dyadic conflict is positive, as expected, but this effect is less robust than the religious similarity variable.

As was the case with the nation-level analyses, we did not find any religious combination to be more conflict prone than another. In particular, we did not find a West versus Rest effect, nor did we find that dyads composed of one member who is predominantly Christian and another member predominantly Muslim were more conflict prone than any other dyad combination. However, we did find that the likelihood of conflict between Christian states is significantly lower than expected by chance. We also found that Muslim dyads are less likely to be involved in conflicts than what we would expect by chance alone. (These results are also reported in the book website.)

A more demanding test of our own theory focuses on the relationship between political instability and the tendency to invoke religious factors as instruments of social mobilization for diversionary purposes. Specifically, we examine the interaction between dyadic instability and religious similarity and the way it affects MID outbreak and MID escalation to war. The results are reported in Figure 5.3.

Figure 5.3.1 shows that both low-coup-risk states and high-coup-risk states are more likely to fight religiously dissimilar enemies. A similar result is given in Figure 5.3.2 that focuses on the probability that a MID between two states would escalate into all-out war. However, the tendency of high-risk states to fight dissimilar enemies, or to escalate conflict with dissimilar enemies to an all-out war, is significantly higher than that of low-coup-risk states.

Related to this are the results reported in Figures 5.3.3 and 5.3.4, respectively. Figure 5.3.3 shows that states that separate religious institutions from political institutions are significantly less likely to fight when facing either low or high coup risk than states in which religious and political institutions are closely linked. Likewise, in Figure 5.3.4 we find that religiously homogeneous states are more likely to fight each other when they face high levels of political instability (high coup risk). Taken together, these results provide additional support for our argument that the interaction of political instability and religious factors influence dyadic conflict outbreak and escalation.

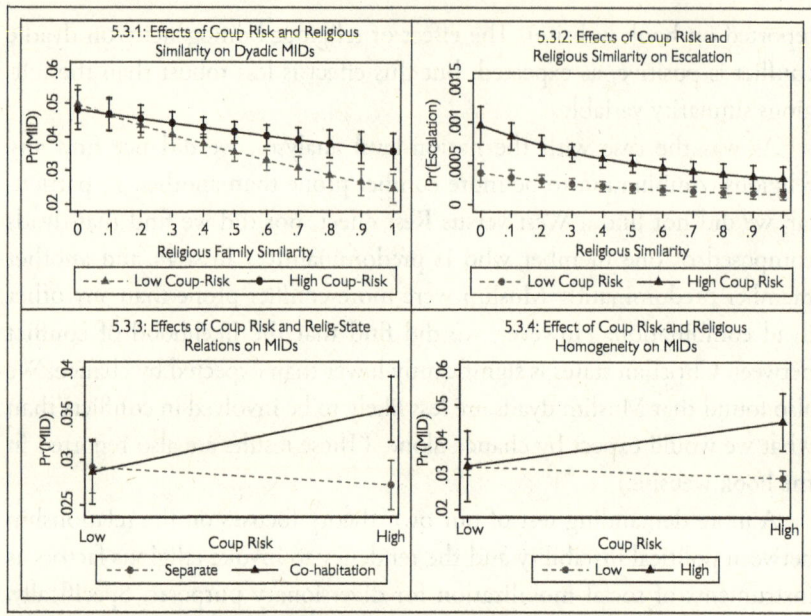

Fig. 5.3. Effect of religious similarity on dyadic conflict: intervening variables
Note: Lines are marginal effects of religious similarity (horizontal axis) on the probability of dyadic MID outbreak (vertical axis). Separate lines indicate effects by level of intervening variable (e.g., religious homogeneity, religion-state relations, era). Error bars are 95% confidence intervals. The effect of religious similarity on conflict at one level of the intervening variable is significantly different from the effect of religious similarity on conflict at another level of the dependent variable if the confidence intervals associated with these two lines do not overlap.

Figure 5.4 reflects tests of the CoC thesis that religious conflict has become more prominent since the end of the Cold War, and of the constructivist claim that the importance of religious factors is greater for new dyads than for established ones. As we can see in Figure 5.4.1, the CoC expectation that the post–Cold War era would exhibit higher levels of conflict between religiously dissimilar states is refuted by our data. In fact, just the opposite is the case: religiously dissimilar states were significantly more likely to clash with each other during the Cold War era than after the end of the Cold War.

The constructivist expectation that religious identity would be more instrumental as a predictor of conflict in dyads involving one or more "new" states than between "mature" dyads is also soundly refuted. In fact, conflict between religiously similar "new" dyads is more likely, while "mature" dyads

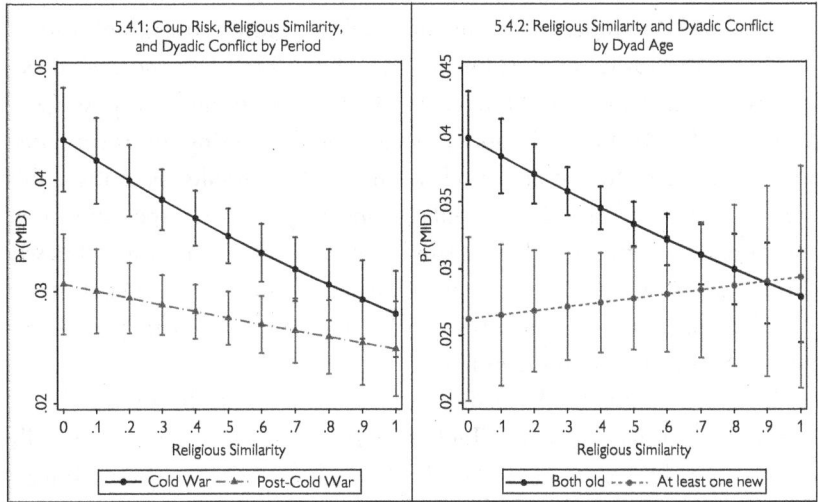

Fig. 5.4. Period, dyad age, and dyadic conflict

match the general expectation that religious similarity reduces the probability of dyadic conflict.

There are several key takeaways from these analyses. The first is that religious similarity does tend to dampen conflict within dyads; states with similar types of religious adherents are significantly less likely to fight each other than those with different types of religious adherents. This also applies to dyads that share the same major religious groups. However, this does not imply that specific religious combinations induce a higher propensity to fight than other religious combinations. Our results clearly refute such claims.

Second, the probability of conflict between religiously dissimilar states increases with the level of domestic instability in one or both. Political instability also increases the risk of conflict involving dyads composed of religiously homogeneous states (probably of different religions). Likewise, dyads made up of members that have close links between religious and political institutions are significantly more likely to experience conflict when one or both members are politically unstable than either dyads of states that practice separation of religion from politics, and/or stable dyads.

Finally, the argument that religious similarity reduces the risk of conflict may seem to provide support for the CoC thesis. However, the CoC thesis makes a clear distinction between the Cold War era and the post–Cold War era. The clash of civilizations, according to Huntington, is supposed to be evident in the latter period, primarily. Our results disconfirm this argument. Our results also disconfirm the constructivist expectation that the dampening effect of religious similarity on conflict is a feature of newly formed dyads. In fact, newly formed dyads are more likely to clash when they are composed of religiously *similar* states than when they are composed of religiously *dissimilar* ones.

Do these results hold when we examine the entire history of dyads? The answer to that is given in Table 5.4. The results in Table 5.4 generally corroborate the results of the dyad-year analyses. First, religious similarity has a dampening effect on the dyadic propensity for conflict. Second, regime instability and state-religion cohabitation also affect the history of dyadic conflict. Concomitantly, the conclusion that there is no significant relationship between specific religious combinations and dyadic conflict is also retained. We also do not find support for the assertion of a propensity for conflict between Western Christendom and the rest of the world's

Table 5.4 Effect of religious variables on conflict—dyad history unit of analysis (politically relevant dyads only)

Variable	No. MIDs	No Wars	Escalation	Hostility
Religious Homogeneity	-0.001	-0.001*	-0.002**	0.07
	(0.002)	(0.000)	(0.001)	(0.14)
Avg. Religious Similarity	-0.021**	-0.005**	-0.007**	-1.612**
	(0.007)	(0.001)	(0.002)	(0.551)
Avg. Rel-State Relations	0.003	0.001*	0.002*	0.185
	(0.002)	(0.000)	(0.001)	(0.183)
Avg. Coup Risk	0.112*	0.009	-0.009	8.095*
	(0.048)	(0.008)	(0.009)	(3.612)
Constant	0.337**	0.045**	0.065**	25.461**
	(0.048)	(0.014)	(0.014)	(3.75)
N	4074	4074	4074	4074
F	20.405	7.102	11.323	18.440
r2	0.095	0.039	0.078	0.088

Note: ** $p < 0.01$; * $p < 0.05$.
Control variables are omitted to conserve space. Full results are presented in the book's website.

civilizations as Huntington opines. However, the significant relationship between religious homogeneity and conflict we observed at the dyad-year unit of analysis is not retained at the general dyad-history level.

Figure 5.5.1 examines the key hypothesis of our integrative theory on the dyad-history unit of analysis. Here, too, the results support our expectation: dyads made up of unstable states are significantly more likely to invoke religious factors against dissimilar enemies than dyads that are made up of stable member states. Likewise, in Figure 5.5.2, we find that the greater degree of conflict between religiously similar states is a key feature of the post–Cold War era, in direct contradiction of what the CoC thesis would have us expect.

Turning to the regional analysis, the results are given in Table 5.5 and suggest clearly that the average level of religious similarity in a region has a consistent dampening impact on conflict across the different outcomes. These results are consistent with the results at the other units of analysis. Religious homogeneity has a significant positive impact on the number of MIDs and their level of hostility, but does not significantly impact either the number of wars or the probability of escalation in various regions. Likewise, the

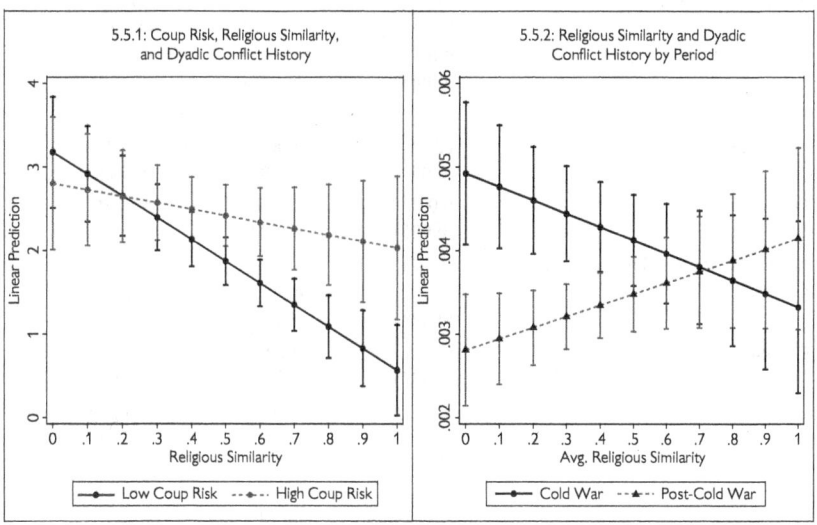

Fig. 5.5. Effects of religious similarity and period on dyad history

average regional level of institutionalized relations between religious and political structures has a positive impact on the number of MIDs and their levels of hostility. However, this relationship does not affect the number of wars or the probability of escalation of regional conflicts.

All in all, we find that the degree of religious similarity—measured in more precise terms as the similarity in the distribution of specific religious groups between one society and another (or relevant other societies)—reduces the probability of conflict, the severity of conflict, and the duration of conflict. This result is consistent across levels of analysis and across units of analysis within a given level. Other religious characteristics also tend to affect conflict indicators, but the results there are less robust.

In Figure 5.6, we examine some of the interactions between regional religious similarity and various intervening variables and their impact on MID outbreak across regions.

Table 5.5 Determinants of international conflict—region-year unit of analysis

	MIDs	Escalation	Hostility
Religious Similarity	-0.107**	-0.02**	-7.963**
	(0.018)	(0.005)	(1.357)
Avg. Coup Risk	0.05	0.124**	8.252
	(0.083)	(0.025)	(6.308)
Religious Homogeneity			
Moderate	0.035**	0.003	2.742**
	(0.007)	(0.002)	(0.532)
High	0.055**	0.003	4.169**
	(0.007)	(0.002)	(0.547)
Religion-State Relations			
Some Relations	0.005	0.001	0.37
	(0.004)	(0.001)	(0.315)
Cohabitation	0.02**	-0.002	1.348**
	(0.007)	(0.002)	(0.509)
Constant	3.59	0.86	351.848
	(6.365)	(1.913)	(484.393)
N	297	297	297
Chi-Square	238.807	75.498	237.151
R-Squared	0.458	0.211	0.456

Key: ** $p < 0.01$; * $p < 0.05$
Control variables are omitted to conserve space. Full results are presented in the book's website

This figure suggests that regions composed of religiously homogeneous dyads experience a greater level of conflict across levels of religious similarity than religiously diverse regions. Likewise, regions that are characterized by a high proportion of states that have close ties between religious and political institutions are more likely to exhibit conflict—primarily between religiously dissimilar dyads. By contrast, regions composed of states that practice separation between religion and state are typically less conflict prone. Moreover, the level of conflict in the region is not affected by the degree of regional religious similarity.

We did not find supporting evidence that religious dissimilarity had more pronounced effects on conflict in the post–Cold War era compared to the Cold War era, as Huntington's thesis would have us expect. In fact, the effect of religious dissimilarity on conflict was *more pronounced* during the Cold War era than during the post–Cold War era, again, in contradiction of the CoC's expectation.

We also did not find significant differences between the conflict behavior of new dyads and that of established dyads. This result challenges the

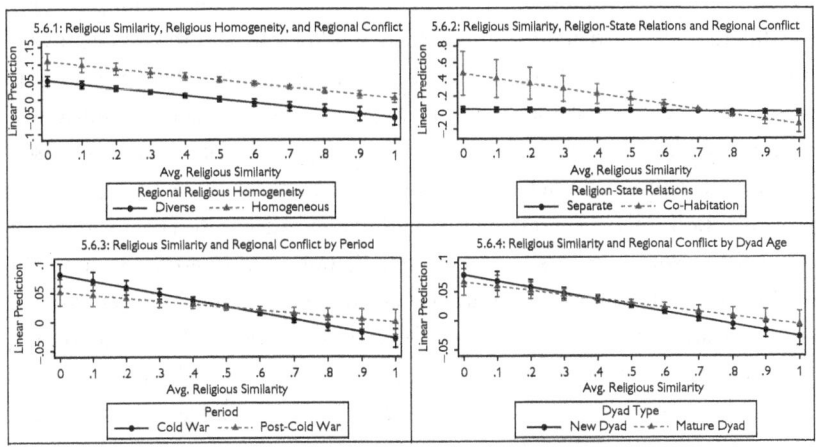

Fig. 5.6. Interaction of regional religious similarity and intervening variables and its effect on MID outbreak: region-year level of analysis

constructivist proposition focusing on the presumed heightened impact of cultural factors on behavior at early stages of states' independence and the reduced (but still significant) impact of religious factors on behavior at more advanced stages of states' involvement in the international system.

6. Conclusion

This chapter is the most comprehensive analysis to date of the relationship between religious factors and international conflict in the post–World War II era. It offers several key contributions with respect to (a) the range of measures of religious adherence, religious diversity and religious similarity employed; (b) the different levels of aggregation examined; (c) the datasets analyzed; and especially (d) the robustness checks we introduced.

Conflict is a risky venture. The best-laid plans in starting a conflict can result in a catastrophe. Consider the German detailed plan to invade the Soviet Union in June 1941 or Japan's attack on Pearl Harbor in December of the same year. Because conflict is risky, it requires leaders to mobilize resources from their societies, including troops for warfare and materials for supporting and supplying the military machine. Political leaders contemplating conflict use different tactics to get their followers to risk their lives in those violent ventures. They also need to have those citizens who do not directly engage in warfare to provide material and political support for the conduct of conflict. We find that religion and religious factors play an important role in such processes. However, the ways such religious factors relate to these processes depends on particular political circumstances within the state and specific characteristics of the society. Not all leaders can mobilize religious ideas to attract support for conflict. Even those leaders who live in societies wherein religious elements are an important part of the national identity, need to choose the "right" timing and the "right" enemies if they wish to use religion as a mobilization tool.

Our analyses suggest several key ideas about the linkage between religion and international conflict.

1. *Religious similarity decreases conflict propensity, while religious dissimilarity increases it.* This result is robust across different measures of conflict and different levels of analysis. Note the significance of these results: they are consistent with three of the four perspectives that connect religion to international conflict. On the latter point, while

the dampening effect of religious similarity on conflict may suggest support for the CoC thesis, the results actually disconfirm it. In contrast to what the CoC thesis would have us expect (Huntington 2000), we find that intercivilizational conflicts were far more prevalent during the Cold War era than during the post–Cold War era.
2. *Religious similarity dampens conflict at the level of major religions and at the level of religious families.* Religious similarity has a dampening impact on conflict whether we use coarse measures of similarity based only on major religions (or on the similarity between the largest religious group in a given state/dyad/region), or whether we use higher-resolution measures of religious similarity (that is, if we break up Christianity, Judaism, Islam, and Buddhism into religious families). These results are shown on the book's website.
3. *Unstable regimes are significantly more likely to fight against religiously dissimilar states.* It is not only that similarities assuage and dissimilarities aggravate international relations but also that the combination of religious dissimilarities and political instability makes for a fatal brew. Religious differences and religious values are more likely to be invoked by unstable leaders—those who face a high probability of losing their seats of power—and used as a tool to mobilize support for conflict. This result holds across levels of analysis and across different measures of conflict.
4. *Religious homogeneity generally increases the probability and severity of conflict.* This result holds at the nation-year unit and the region-year unit. However, the relationship between religious homogeneity is less robust at the nation-history, dyad-year, and dyad-history levels of analysis.
5. *The interaction between political instability and religion-state relations seems to affect conflict propensities across levels of analysis.* Note that the temporal span of the data concerning the relations between religious and political institutions in the religion-state dataset (Fox 2016) is quite short (about twenty years as opposed to sixty-six years for most other variables). The addition of observations from the Comparative Constitution Project is also incomplete, as it covers only about 45 percent of the states with constitutions or constitution-like legislation. This restricts to some extent the generalizability of these results. Nevertheless, we do find fairly consistent

effects across levels of analysis. Generally speaking, states, dyads, or regions that have a higher degree of cohabitation between political and religious institutions tend to experience higher levels of international conflict than actors that separate the religious from the political spheres. This is even more pronounced if the former types of units are politically unstable than if they are politically stable. This result also corroborates one of the key arguments of our integrative theory of religion and politics.

6. *Secularism is not a significant factor.* States with a high proportion of secular populations are neither more nor less likely to fight, nor are they more or less likely to fight each other than less secular states.

7. *We do not find robust support for the constructivist argument that religious factors have a stronger effect on the conflict behavior of new states as opposed to more mature states.* The behavior of new states or new dyads is not significantly different from that of established states and dyads in terms of the effect of religious factors on their behavior.

8. *CoC conflicts are not more prevalent in the post–Cold War era*, again in contradiction of the expectations of the CoC thesis. The evidence for this point is overwhelming. We find that, in fact, wars between religiously similar states were more common in the post–Cold War era than during the Cold War period (see Tables A5.6 and A5.7 in the appendix).

9. *There is no evidence that specific religions are more conflict prone than others.* Our results clearly refute the notion that states that are dominated by a specific religion are more or less conflict prone than those of another religion. The notion of "Islam having bloody borders" (Huntington 1996) is not supported in our results. Conflict between specific religious combinations is not more likely (or more severe) than conflict between other religious combinations. In fact, we find that the likelihood of conflicts between Christian and Muslim states is significantly less likely than what would be expected by chance alone. We also find consistent lack of support for the argument that the West versus Rest conflicts are more likely either during the Cold War or in the post–Cold War era.[11]

10. *Implications: there is a need for caution when making claims about the relationship between religious factors and international conflict.* The results connecting religion to international conflict are consistent,

with a range of often contrasting theses, and this advises caution in asserting a singular role for religion in international affairs. To be sure, religion has and continues to have a clear impact on international conflict. Yet, in contrast to prominent notions of the post–Cold War "clashes of civilizations" or "God's Century" (Toft, Philpott, and Shah 2011), this relationship is neither new, all-encompassing, or simple. Religious factors have a significant effect on conflict, but this effect is most pronounced when considered in conjunction with the political conditions—specifically, with the level of political stability—in states or in various regions.

What is the evidence for or against the various theoretical arguments about religion and international conflict put forth in this chapter? Generally speaking, the fact that we find religious similarity to have a consistently dampening effect on conflict suggests support for both primordialist and instrumentalist perspectives. The same applies to the—less robust but nonetheless visible—aggravating effect of religious homogeneity on conflict. At the same time, the similarity between the predictions that may be deduced from both of these perspectives prevent us from reliably assessing which one is more closely tied to the results. We do find, however, consistent evidence of the more dynamic aspects of religion-regime instability-conflict that are associated with our integrative theory of religion and politics. This supports the notion that political elites elevate the religious "causes" of conflict when they feel that their regime is under risk. Using religion as a tactic to mobilize support for foreign adventures appears to be particularly attractive under such circumstances.

The general takeaway from this chapter is that religion plays an important role in international conflict, but not in the simpleminded manner we may think about religious conflict. Religious factors interact with other ideational and material factors in ways that are rather complex. At the national level, religious similarity serves to dampen animosities that are based on territorial and other material claims. States that have enmities grounded in or amplified by religious differences are more likely to use force to resolve their claims than states that have religiously similar adversaries. At the dyadic level, religious similarities consistently reduce the risk of conflict. It remains to be seen if religious factors play a role in the practice of peaceful cooperation. This is what we explore in the next chapter.

Appendix to Chapter 5: Religion and International Conflict

1. Introduction

This appendix provides a detailed discussion of the research design used in chapter 5. It covers discussion of data sources, provides operational definitions of all the variables used, and details the methods used to estimate the models analyzed. Because this appendix covers many issues that are common to several chapters in the book, it is quite detailed. Subsequent chapter appendices rely on the information provided herein.

2. Datasets

Table A5.1 provides a detailed review of the datasets used in the various analyses of chapter 5.

3. Units of Analysis

We first distinguish between a *level of analysis* and a *unit of analysis*. A level of analysis is defined by the identity of the actor or actors that is the focus of the investigation. A unit of analysis combines the level of analysis and the time-related aggregation used to define individual observations/cases. In addition, a unit of analysis may impose some spatial or conceptual restriction on the actors selected for analysis at each level. We demonstrate this distinction below.

National level of analysis. At this level, the actors selected for analysis are all states in the international system that existed at any given time point during the period 1945–2010. We focus here on two units of analysis: the state-year unit and the state-history unit.

>   a. *State-year unit of analysis.* Each observation in this set of analyses consists of a given state at a given year. Each state is observed for each year during which it existed as a member of the interstate system. Thus, the United States, which existed during the entire period, appears in sixty-six observations. On the other hand, Kosovo, which gained independence in 2008, appears in only

Table A5.1 Datasets

Dataset Name	Years Covered	Variables Used	Source	Comments
World Religion Project (WRP)	1945–2010	Secularism; Religious diversity; Religious similarity with PRIE; Dyadic religious similarity; Major and Minor religions; Major religions/religious families	Maoz and Henderson (2013)	Original data measured in 5-year intervals; interpolated to yearly observations for purpose of analyses
Religion and State Dataset (RSD)	1990–2010	Religious discrimination; Religious regulation; Religious legislation	Fox (2010)	Combined with CCP (below) to generate a religion and state variable
Comparative Constitutions Project (CCP)	1800–2010	Official Religion, Clause on religious freedom	Elkins, Ginsburg, and Melton (2014)	Combined with RSD to generate a religion and state variable
Coup attempts	1950–2010	Attempted and successful coups	Powell and Thyne (2011)	Used to calculate coup-risk
Dyadic MID dataset (MID)	1945–2010	MIDs, Wars, Hostility Levels (monadic, dyadic, regional levels)	Maoz et al. (2018)	
Alliance Treaties and Obligations Provisions (ATOP)	1945–2003	No. of Allies; Dyadic Alliance; Regional Alliances	Leeds (2005)	
Alliance Dataset (COWALLY)	1945–2010	Same as above	Gibler (2007)	ATOP data expanded to 2010 using COWALLY
Trade Datasets	1945–2010	No. trading partners; total trade; dyadic trade; regional trade	Gleditsch (2002); Barbieri, Keshk, and Pollins (2009)	Both datasets are combined to cover missing cases
IGO data	1945–2004	No. of IGO memberships; joint IGO membership (dyad); No. regional IGOs	Nordstrom, Pevehouse, and Wrenke (2004)	
National Capabilities	1945–2007	National capability score; dyadic capability ratio; Regional power concentration	Singer (1990); COW (2016)	

(Continued)

Table A5.1 (Continued)

Dataset Name	Years Covered	Variables Used	Source	Comments
Polity IV Dataset	1945–2010	Regime attributes and regime change information	Marshall (2010)	
Coup Data	1945–2010	All instances of coups and coup attempts	Powell and Thyne 2011	Used to code coup risk
Strategic Rivalries	1945–2010	Strategic Rivalries	Thompson and Dreyer (2011)	

three observations. At any given year, the number of observations consist of the number of independent states during this period. So in 1945 there are 44 observations, whereas in 2010, there are 194 observations. The entire dataset used for this unit of analysis has a time-series-cross-sectional (TSCS) structure. However, for reasons discussed below, we use both the entire data and repeated samples thereof.

b. *State-history unit of analysis.* There are several good reasons to aggregate the behavior of each state over the entire period during which it was independent. First, the likelihood of a state getting involved in an international conflict is highly uneven: a few (about 20 percent) of all states account for about 80 percent of all militarized conflicts during this period (Maoz 2004, 2009a). Given this extreme inequality in the conflict proneness of nations, on the one hand, and the fairly stationary structure of the religious variables, on the other, it is fair to examine the extent to which the religious characteristics of states relate to their general conflict proneness over their entire history. Second, since several of the theoretical arguments linking religion to national behavior are fairly fixed—that is, indicate a general propensity of a state—it makes sense to see if certain types of states (e.g., religiously homogeneous, with a high religion-state cohabitation structure, with high state-PRIE religious differences) indicate greater or lesser proneness to engage in conflict throughout their history than others.

For this level of analysis we aggregate the characteristics of states and analyze the relationship between religion and conflict propensity. Each state is observed once over the entire period during which it was independent.

This means that states that were independent in 1945 have a total "history" of sixty-six years, while states that emerged at a later point during this period are observed from the year in which they gained independence to the final year in our sample. For example, Chad attained independence in 1960, so it is observed over a period of fifty-one years, while Slovakia, which became independent after it seceded from Czechoslovakia in 1993, is observed over a period of eighteen years. Each observation in this set of analysis is a single state. The variables used for this set of analyses consist of aggregated (or averaged) figures for the focal state across its entire history over the period 1945–2010. We illustrate this in the next section.

Dyadic level of analysis. The dyadic level of analysis has been the focus of much of the research on international conflict in the last thirty years. A dyad reflects a pair of states, and the most popular unit of analysis has been the dyad-year. However, the literature on international conflict is sharply divided on which dyads to include and which dyads to exclude. Some (e.g., Bremer 1992) have focused on the entire population of dyads since the Congress of Vienna; every possible pair of states that existed at a given point in time afterward was included in the sample under analysis. Others (e.g., Maoz and Russett 1993) argued that this practice inflates the sample size with multiple cases that are ex ante unlikely to have any conflict. Conflict between Costa Rica and Thailand is highly unlikely due to the distance between these states, their inability to project power over that distance, and the lack of contentious issues that might give rise to conflict. Instead, Maoz and Russett argued that dyadic analyses of conflict should focus on the population of *politically relevant dyads*. A politically relevant dyad is a dyad that meets one of the following conditions:

1. It is geographically contiguous—that is, it shares a land border or separated by a body of water with a distance of 150 nautical miles between the shores of these countries.
2. At least one of the members of the dyad is a major power with global reach capacity or a regional power with a regional reach capacity. By reach capacity we mean an ability to project force—to transfer a large number of troops and materiel—over distance.[12]

Maoz and Russett (1993), Lemke and Reed (2001), Bennett and Stam (2004), and Maoz et al. (2018) among others showed that (a) the politically relevant dyads sample captures over 83 percent of all dyadic MIDs over the period 1816–2010; (b) most of the dyadic MIDs not captured by this sample consist of states joining MIDs between politically relevant dyads; and (c) this selection does not cause significant biases in results. These results suggest that it is more sensible to focus on politically relevant dyads than on the entire population of dyads. However, as a robustness check, we examine both this limited sample and the more general population of all dyads.

In this case too, we focus on two units of analysis: the dyad-year and the dyad-history.

1. *Dyad-year unit of analysis.* The observation here is a (politically relevant) dyad at a given year. Thus the US–Canada dyad makes for sixty-six observations over the period 1945–2010, whereas the US–Dominica dyad makes for only thirty-three observations because Dominica became independent only in 1978. The entire population of dyads over this period totals 696,075 observations of undirected dyads, whereas the population of politically relevant dyads consists of 65,364 undirected dyads. Both samples have a TSCS structure

2. *Dyad-history unit of analysis.* As in the case of the aggregate nation level, the distribution of conflicts over different dyads suggests extreme levels of inequality. Over 75 percent of all politically relevant dyads did not have a single conflict during their history and an additional 8 percent had only one conflict. Likewise, over 96 percent of all politically relevant dyads did not fight a single war during the period under analysis. Consequently, we aggregate dyads to examine whether religion increases the propensity of a dyad to fight repeatedly over its common history. Here, too, we start observing a dyad when the "youngest" state of the dyad enters the international system. Again, for reasons explained below, it makes sense to examine dyadic histories as a whole. As in the case of the national level of analysis, we include dyads that had a common history of at least twenty years, so that they would have a sufficient "chance" to fight. Thus, the entire population of dyads that satisfy the twenty-year rule consists of 12,571 dyads. In contrast, the population of politically relevant dyads that satisfy

the same rule consists only of 1,677 dyads. Here too, this unit of analysis has a cross-sectional structure.

The use of the state-history and of the dyad-history units of analysis is uncommon in conflict research. Therefore an explanation is required. As noted above, a number of studies of interstate conflict (e.g., Bremer 1980, Gochman and Maoz 1984, Maoz 2004, 2009a) pointed out that the distribution of conflicts across nations or dyads is highly uneven; a small proportion of dyads accounts for most dyadic conflicts. The same dyads seem to repeatedly fight each other, whereas other dyads never engage in conflict. Consequently, if religious factors play a role in increasing or decreasing the probability of national conflict involvement of individual states, or the probability of conflict between pairs of states, then we need to take this uneven distribution of conflict participation into account. This is especially pertinent if we wish to test hypotheses derived from primordialist theories of religion and politics.

Regional level of analysis. The Correlates of War classification of regions divides the world into five geographic regions and one residual (extraregional) category. These regions are (a) the Western Hemisphere consisting of North and South America; (b) Europe; (c) sub-Saharan Africa; (d) the Middle East including North African states, Fertile Crescent states, and Persian Gulf states; (e) Asia; and (f) extraregional, covering conflicts between states that belong to different regions.

Note that some states can be members of two regions. For example, the Soviet Union/Russia is in both Europe and Asia. Thus, conflicts between the Soviet Union and Czechoslovakia are European conflicts. In contrast, conflicts between the Soviet Union and China are Asian conflicts. Likewise, Turkey is a member of both Europe and the Middle East. Thus, conflicts between Turkey and Greece are European conflicts; whereas, conflicts between Turkey and Syria are Middle Eastern conflicts. Here our dataset consists of a single unit of analysis: the region-year unit. Each region aggregates or averages the variables under analysis over all states in the region for each year during the period 1945–2010. In principle, this dataset should have consisted of $6 \times 66 = 396$ observations. However, since some of the regions (e.g., Africa) were not meaningfully comprised of sovereign units until the early 1960s, we use differential periods for different regions. In the Western Hemisphere, Europe, Asia, and the extraregional category, we have sixty-six years for each region. In the Middle East, we start observations in 1947 and in Africa we start observations in 1960. This makes for a total of 378 region-year observations.

4. Variables and Measures

We discuss the measures of the various variables at each unit of analysis.

4.1. Explaining the Measurement of the Religious Independent Variables

At the nation-year unit of analysis we employ several independent variables that characterize the religious structure of the state and the relations between religion and state.

Religious diversity. As noted in the text, religious diversity is the variance of religious groups in the state. It is measured by the IQV. We demonstrate this below. Following the common practice in network analysis (Maoz 2010: Ch. 2), we consider each year as a religious affiliation matrix of order $n \times k$, where the n rows represent the states that existed at that point in time, and k reflects the number of religious groups (plus the religious families of some of these religions as mentioned above). Denote the religious affiliation matrix for year t as RA_t. Each entry in this matrix ra_{irt} represents the proportion of state i's population that practices religion r on year t. For demonstration purposes, Table A5.3. lists the religious distributions in a number of selected states for the year 2010.

As noted in the appendix to Chapter 3, we measure religious diversity as the variance of the distribution of religious groups in society. This is given by

$$IQV = \frac{k\left(1 - \sum_{i=1}^{k} p_i^2\right)}{k-1},$$

where k indexes the number of religious groups that actually exist in a society and p_i is the proportion of the state's population that practices religion i. We calculate two versions of the IQV: one that considers only major religions (with the maximum k being 15), and one that considers religious families for some of the religions (with the maximum k being 28). Note that religious diversity should vary between zero and one. When a given state has k religious groups, each of which accounts for $1/k$ percent of the population, $IQV = 1$, this state is maximally diverse. When the state has all of its population in a single religious group, the IQV will be indeterminate because the denominator of the formula is zero. In this case we set the IQV arbitrarily to zero. Such cases represent absolutely no religious diversity.

A few interesting points can be made about the religious diversity of states as indicated by the data in the table. First, Haiti is highlighted because it is one of the few states (Japan is another example) where people practice dual religions. This causes the sum of religious group percentages to exceed one. It follows that religious diversity for these states would also exceed one. In order to avoid this problem, we normalize the religious proportions of the various groups in these states so that their sum will be one. This has little to no effect on the overall results.

Both Haiti and Trinidad provide good examples of states with high religious diversity. Their populations are relatively evenly split among several religious groups. In contrast, Mexico and Saudi Arabia are examples of states with very low religious diversity, with the former having a vast majority of its population practicing Christianity (predominantly Catholics), and the latter having a vast majority of its population practicing (Sunni) Islam.

Religious homogeneity. Religious homogeneity is the complement of religious diversity, that is, $H = 1 - IQV$. In order to provide a more intuitive interpretation of homogeneity, we use an ordinal version of this measure by breaking it up into three levels: 1 = low homogeneity (the upper third of the diversity measure), 2 = medium homogeneity (the middle third of the diversity measure), and 3 = high homogeneity (the lower third of the diversity measure).

Religious similarity with the PRIE. This is the degree to which a state's religious composition is similar to the states that make up its strategic reference group. This measure is developed in two stages. First, we calculate a set of dyadic religious similarity scores that reflect the extent to which the distribution of religious adherents in two states—i and j—are similar to or different from each other. We discuss the development of the dyadic religious similarity below. Second, we average the dyadic religious similarity score between the focal state and the members of its PRIE.

For example, in 1948, the PRIE of Egypt was made up of three neighboring states: Jordan, Saudi Arabia, and Israel. The religious similarity between Egypt, on the one hand, and Jordan and Saudi Arabia, on the

Table A5.2 Measures of variables

Status of Variable	Variable	Measure	Source of measure	Data Source
	Nation-Year Unit of Analysis			
Dependent Variables	Dichotomized MID	Coded as 1 if a state was involved in a MID during the year and zero otherwise		Dyadic MID dataset
	Dichotomized War	Coded as 1 if a state was involved in a war during the year and zero otherwise		Dyadic MID dataset
	Escalation	Coded as 1 if a state was involved in a war during the year, zero if it was involved in a MID but not a war, and missing if it was not involved in a MID		Dyadic MID dataset
	Hostility Initiated	Sum of hostility scores of the MIDs initiated by the state during the year	Maoz (1982)	Dyadic MID Dataset
Independent Variables	Coup risk level	Coup-risk statistic derived from the Sudduth (2017) algorithm; assigned a level of zero (low coup risk) if the coup-risk level is below 5% and 1 if it is higher than 5%	Powell and Thyne (2011); Chiebub, Ghandi, and Veerland (2010); Barbieri and Keshk (2014)	Coup attempts Regime Types GDP
	Religious Homogeneity	Degree to which the state is homogeneous in terms of religious adherence of its population $$RH = 1 - IQV = 1 - \frac{k(1 - \sum_{i=1}^{k} p_i^2)}{k-1}$$ Coded as Low if RH≤p(33), Medium if p(33)≤ RH ≤ p(67), and High if RH >p(67) (where $p(33) = 33^{rd}$ percentile, etc.)	p_i = percent of the state's population practicing religion i, k = number of religious groups within the state.	Maoz and Henderson (2013)

	Percent Nonreligious	Percent of state's population without a religious affiliation (atheists, agnostics, nonidentified)	Maoz and Henderson (2013)
	State-Religion Relations	Relations between religious and political institutions $SR = reldiscrim + relregulat + relegislat$ Coded as separate if $SR < 9$, Some relation if $9 \leq SR < 22$, and Cohabitation if $SR \geq 22$	Fox (2008) $Reldiscrim = religious\ discrimination$, $Relregulat = religious\ regulation$, $Relegislat = religious\ legislation$
	Religious similarity state-PRIE	Average religious similarity between focal state and its politically relevant environment $$RSPRIE_i = \frac{1}{PRIE} \sum_{j|PRIE=1} religsimsoc_{ij}$$	Maoz (1996, 2010) Maoz and Henderson (2013) For religious similarity ($religsimsoc_{ij}$) see below
Control Variables	Pct. Christians, Muslims, Hindus, Buddhists	Percent of the state's population practicing Christianity, Islam, Hinduism, Buddhism, etc.	Maoz and Henderson (2013)
	Regime Score	Maoz-Russett regime score	Maoz and Russett (1993), Maoz (1996, 1998)
	Democracy	$REGIME = (DEMOC - AUTOC) \times CONCEN$ $DEM = 1$ if $REGIME \geq 30$	
	No. States in PRIE	Number of states in the focal state's politically relevant international environment (PRIE)	Maoz (2010)
	National Capabilities	Combined Index of National Capabilities (CINC)	Singer 1991
			Dyadic MID, ATOP, Strategic Rivals, COW 2008

(Continued)

Table A5.2 (Continued)

Status of Variable	Variable	Measure	Source of measure	Data Source
	Number of Allies	Number of states with whom the focal state has a formal alliance treaty	Maoz (2010)	ATOP dataset
	Reputational Status	0 = Minor power, 1 = Regional Power, 2 = Major Power	Maoz (2010)	Maoz (2010)
	Log Trade	Log of total exports and Imports of state during the year		Barbieri and Keshk (2009)
	Avg. MIDs as Target	3-year moving average of the number of MIDs in which the state is the principal target	Maoz (2010)	Dyadic MID dataset
Nation-History Unit of Analysis				
Dependent Variables	Number of MIDs	Average number of MID involvements of the state over the 1945–2010 period		Dyadic MID dataset
	Number of Wars	Average number of war involvements of the state over the 1945–2010 period		Dyadic MID dataset
	Strategic Rivals	Average number of strategic rivals of the focal state over the 1945–2010 period		Thompson and Dyer (2011)
	Hostility initiated	Average hostility score of MIDs initiated by the focal state over the 1945–2010 period		Dyadic MID dataset
Independent Variables	Years politically unstable	Proportion of state years during which coup risk = 1		POLITY IV

	Religious Homogeneity	Mean of religious homogeneity over state's years of independence recoded as above	Maoz and Henderson (2013)
	Religious-State Relations	Mean of religion-state relations recoded as above	Fox (2009)
	Secularism	Average proportion of non-religious population	Maoz and Henderson (2013)
	Religious Similarity with PRIE	Average religious similarity state-PRIE	
	Pct. Christians, Muslims, Hindus, Buddhists	Avg. percent of Christians (Muslims, Hindus, Buddhists) in population over state's years of independence	Maoz and Henderson (2013)
Control Variables	National Capabilities	Average CINC score	Maoz (2004, 2009) COW (2008)
	Number of Allies	Average Number of Allies	Maoz (2004, 2009) ATOP (2005)
	Years as Major Power	Proportion of years of independence during which state was designated as a major power	Maoz (2004, 2009) Maoz (2010)
	Years as Regional Power	Proportion of years of independence during which state was designated as a regional power	Maoz (2004, 2009) Maoz (2010)
	Log Trade	Average logged trade (imports+exports) of the state during its years of independence	Barbieri and Keshk (2009)
Dyad-Year			
Dependent Variables	MID Occurrence	1 = one or more MIDs underway between dyad members, 0 = no MID	Dyadic MID dataset

(Continued)

Table A5.2 (*Continued*)

Status of Variable	Variable	Measure	Source of measure	Data Source
	War	1 = War underway between dyad member; 0 = no war		Dyadic MID dataset
	Hostility	Sum of hostility scores of MIDs between dyad members for year	Maoz (1982)	Dyadic MID dataset
	Escalation	1 = MID between dyad members escalated into war, 0 = MID but no war, missing = no MID		Dyadic MID dataset
	Strategic Rivalry Start	1 = first year of rivalry, 0 = no rivalry year, missing = rivalry years after first year		Thompson and Dyer (2011)
	Strategic Rivalry End	1 = Last year of rivalry, 0 = year of rivalry before last, missing = no rivalry year.		Thompson and Dyer (2011)
Independent Variables	Religious Similarity	Degree of covariance between the distribution of religious adherents by religious family across dyad members (see operationalization below)	Maoz (2006, 2010)	Maoz and Henderson (2013) (See below for *religsimsoc$_{ij}$*)
	Major-Major Religious Match	1 = the largest religious group in state A is the same as the largest religious group in state B, 0 = otherwise		Maoz and Henderson (2013)
	Major-Minor Religious Match	1 = the largest religious group in one state is the same as the second-largest religious group in the other state, 0 = otherwise		Maoz and Henderson (2013)
	Christian Majority	1 = The largest religious group in the dyad is Christian		Maoz and Henderson (2013)
	Muslim Majority	1 = The largest religious group in the dyad is Muslim		Maoz and Henderson (2013)

Christian-Muslim Dyad	1 = the largest religious group in one state is Christian, and the largest religious group in the other state is Muslim, 0 = otherwise	Maoz and Henderson (2013)
New Regime	0 = Both stable regime, 1 = One state is unstable, 2 = Both are unstable	POLITY IV
Religious Homogeneity	Minimum level of religious homogeneity in dyad: 1 = Low, 2 = Medium, 3 = High	Maoz and Henderson (2013)
Religion and State	Combined religion and state score of both states: 1 = Both practice separation of religion and state, 2 = some relationship between religious and political institutions, 3 = religion-state cohabitation (close ties between religious and political institutions)	Fox (2016)
Joint Democracy	1 = if both states democracies, 0 otherwise	
Log Distance	Log distance between capitals	Gleditsch and Ward (2001)
PRIE Members	1 if states are in each other's PRIE, 0 otherwise	Maoz (2010)
Capability Ratio	$$CAPRAT = \frac{CINC_i}{CINC_i + CINC_j},$$ where CINC is the combined index of national capabilities	COW (2008) Singer 1991
Allies	1 = States have a formal alliance, 0 otherwise	Leeds et al. (2002)

(Continued)

Table A5.2 (*Continued*)

Status of Variable	Variable	Measure	Source of measure	Data Source
	Log Trade	Log of total trade between states		Barbieri et al. (2009); Gleditsch (2002)
	Relative IGO Membership	Ratio of joint IGO membership to state *i*'s total IGO membership	Maoz 2010	Pevehouse et al. (2004)
Dyad-History				
Dependent Variables	No. MIDs	Average number of MIDs per year of shared dyadic history $$NOMIDS = \frac{\sum_{t=1}^{T} NOMID_{ijt}}{T},$$ where T is the number of years of common system membership of dyad members	Maoz (2004, 2009)	Maoz et al. (2018)
	Avg. hostility	Average hostility score over the years of common system membership of dyad members	Maoz (1982, 2004, 2009)	Maoz (2005); Maoz et al. (2016)
	Duration	Average number of days during which dyad members were in a MID over the years of common system membership	Maoz (2004, 2009)	Maoz (2005); Maoz et al. (2016)
	Strategic Rivals	Average number of years during which dyad members were strategic rivals over the years of common system membership		Thompson and Dyer (2011)

Independent Variables	Religious similarity	Average religious similarity (religious family similarity) over the years of common system membership of dyad members	Maoz and Henderson (2013)
	Regime stability score	Average number of years during which at least one dyad member was politically unstable	POLITY IV (Marshall and Gurr 2010)
	Religious homogeneity	Average religious homogeneity score over the period of common system membership	Maoz and Henderson (2013)
	State-Religion Relations		See above for religious homogeneity	Fox (2011)
	Prop. Years Christian Dyad	Proportion of years of common system membership in which both dyad members had Christianity as the largest religion group	Maoz and Henderson (2013)
	Prop. Years Muslim Dyad	Proportion of years of common system membership in which both dyad members had Islam as the largest religion group	Maoz and Henderson (2013)
	Prop. years Christian–Muslim Dyad	Proportion of years of common system membership in which one member had a Christian modal group and the other had a Muslim modal group	Maoz and Henderson (2013)
	Joint Democracy	Proportion of years of common system membership in which both members were democratic	Marshall and Gurr (2010)

(Continued)

Table A5.2 (*Continued*)

Status of Variable	Variable	Measure	Source of measure	Data Source
	Avg. Log Distance	Average log distance between capitals over the period of common system membership		Gleditsch and Ward (2001)
	Avg. Capability ratio	Average of the focal state's capabilities by the sum of dyadic capabilities (see above)		COW 2008
	Prop. years allies	Proportion of years of common system membership during which states were allies		Leeds et al. (2002)
	Avg. Log trade	Average logged trade volume between dyad members		Barbieri et al. (2009)
	Avg. joint IGO membership	Average joint IGO membership over dyad's common history		Pevehouse et al. (2004)
Region-Year				
Dependent Variables	MIDs	Average number of MIDs between dyad members within region		Maoz et al. (2016)
	Hostility	Average hostility score of MIDs between dyad members in region	Maoz (1982)	Maoz et al. (2016)
	Duration	Average duration of MIDs within region		Maoz et al. (2016)
Independent Variables	Avg. religious similarity	Average religious similarity between dyads in region	See below	Maoz and Henderson (2013)
	Religious homogeneity	Average religious homogeneity of states within region		Maoz and Henderson (2013)

State-Religion relations	Average score of state-religion relations of states within region	Fox (2011)
Pct. Christians	Percent of regional population practicing Christianity	Maoz and Henderson (2013)
Pct. Muslims	Percent of regional population practicing Islam	Maoz and Henderson (2013)
Pct. Non-religious	Percent of regional population claiming Atheism, Agnosticism, or non-religious affiliation	Maoz and Henderson (2013)
Democratic Dyads	Pct. dyads in region that are jointly democratic	Marshall and Gurr (2010)
Avg. Log Distance	Average log distance between capitals in region	Gleditsch and Ward (2001)
Avg. National Capability	Average CINC score of states in region	COW (2008)
Prop. Dyads in PRIE	Proportion of regional dyads that are in each other's PRIE	Maoz (2010)
Prop. Allies	Proportion of regional dyads that have alliances	Leeds et al. (2002)
Prop. Major/Regional Powers	Proportion of states in region that are major or regional powers	Maoz (2010)
Avg. Log Trade	Average log trade between dyad members in region	Barbieri et al. (2009)
Avg. Joint IGO membership	Average joint IGO membership score of dyads in region	Pevehouse et al. (2004)
Pct. Unstable States	Percent states with unstable regimes	Marshall and Gurr (2010)

Table A5.3 Religious affiliation matrix, 2010—selected states

State	Chrst	Jud	Islm	Bud	Zoro	Hindu	Sikh	Shint	Bahai	Tao	Conf	Jain	Sync	Anm	Norel	Othr	IQV
USA	0.745	0.019	0.009	0.011	0.005	0.006	0.001	0.001	0.002	0.000	0.000	0.000	0.003	0.006	0.190	0.003	0.437
CAN	0.766	0.010	0.019	0.019	0.000	0.008	0.008	0.000	0.001	0.000	0.000	0.000	0.001	0.002	0.164	0.001	0.413
BAH	0.966	0.001	0.000	0.000	0.000	0.000	0.000	0.000	0.001	0.000	0.000	0.000	0.000	0.003	0.029	0.001	0.079
CUB	0.509	0.000	0.001	0.000	0.000	0.002	0.000	0.000	0.000	0.000	0.000	0.000	0.387	0.000	0.102	0.000	0.697
HAI	0.820	0.000	0.000	0.000	0.000	0.000	0.000	0.000	0.001	0.000	0.000	0.000	0.450	0.000	0.100	0.000	0.662
DOM	0.870	0.000	0.000	0.000	0.000	0.000	0.000	0.000	0.000	0.000	0.000	0.000	0.000	0.000	0.120	0.010	0.343
JAM	0.688	0.000	0.001	0.000	0.000	0.006	0.000	0.000	0.000	0.000	0.000	0.000	0.000	0.000	0.199	0.106	0.543
TRI	0.559	0.000	0.050	0.000	0.000	0.184	0.000	0.000	0.000	0.000	0.000	0.000	0.000	0.000	0.135	0.072	0.785
BAR	0.643	0.000	0.008	0.000	0.000	0.004	0.000	0.000	0.000	0.000	0.000	0.000	0.000	0.000	0.205	0.139	0.612
DMA	0.920	0.000	0.000	0.000	0.000	0.000	0.000	0.000	0.000	0.000	0.000	0.000	0.000	0.000	0.060	0.020	0.224
GRA	0.870	0.000	0.005	0.000	0.000	0.002	0.000	0.000	0.001	0.000	0.000	0.000	0.000	0.000	0.048	0.073	0.283
SLU	0.922	0.000	0.001	0.000	0.000	0.003	0.000	0.000	0.000	0.000	0.000	0.000	0.000	0.000	0.059	0.015	0.183
SVG	0.899	0.000	0.001	0.000	0.000	0.003	0.000	0.000	0.002	0.000	0.000	0.000	0.000	0.000	0.019	0.076	0.223
AAB	0.914	0.000	0.000	0.000	0.000	0.000	0.000	0.000	0.000	0.000	0.000	0.000	0.000	0.000	0.059	0.027	0.241
SKN	0.898	0.000	0.003	0.000	0.000	0.010	0.000	0.000	0.000	0.000	0.000	0.000	0.000	0.000	0.089	0.001	0.232
MEX	0.969	0.001	0.000	0.000	0.000	0.000	0.000	0.000	0.000	0.000	0.000	0.000	0.000	0.000	0.027	0.003	0.073
....																	
SAU	0.030	0.000	0.938	0.000	0.000	0.010	0.000	0.000	0.000	0.000	0.000	0.000	0.000	0.000	0.020	0.002	0.148

Key to Table A5.3
Chrst = Christians; Jud = Jews; Islm = Muslims; Bud = Buddhists; Zoro = Zoroastrians; Hindu = Hindus; Sikh = Sikhs; Shint = Shintoists; Baha'i = Bahá'ís; Tao = Taoists; Conf = Confucianists; Jain = Jains; Sync = Syncretic Religions; Anm = Animist Religions; Norel = Non-religious (atheists, agnostics, nonbelievers); Othr = Believers in other religions; IQV = Index of qualitative variation

other, was quite high (0.78 and 0.81, respectively). The religious similarity with Israel was low (0.09). Egypt was also connected to the United Kingdom via indirect contiguity (the United Kingdom was still in colonial possession of Sudan—similarity score 0.15), and we add to it the major of that time, the United States and the Soviet Union, with relatively low similarity (0.12 and 0.17, respectively). Thus, on average, Egypt had a religious similarity score of 0.35 with its PRIE, a medium-low level of religious similarity.

In 1962, Argentina had a total of eight states in its PRIE—five neighbors (Brazil, Bolivia, Paraguay, Chile, and Uruguay), and four major powers—the United States, the United Kingdom, the Soviet Union, and China. Its religious similarity score with all of its PRIE members—except the Soviet Union (similarity score of 0.31)—was quite high (between 0.76 and 0.93). Thus, its overall similarity score with the PRIE for that year was also very high (0.796).

Dyadic religious similarity. As noted, this is a measure of the extent to which the religious distributions of two states are similar to or different from each other. To do that, we use the religious affiliation matrix for each year and convert it to a religious similarity matrix. We use two different methods to convert this matrix into a religious similarity matrix of order n, each producing a slightly different measure of religious similarity.

The first measure is based on the standard method of affiliation-to-adjacency matrix conversion in network analysis (Wasserman and Faust 1994, Maoz 2010, Chapter 2). The adjacency matrix **RS** is given by $\mathbf{RS}_t = \mathbf{RA}_t \times \mathbf{RA}_t'$ and has the following structure:

(1) $$rs_{iit} = \sum_k ra_{irt}^2 = \sum_k p_{it}^2,$$

which means that diagonal entries reflect the degree of religious homogeneity in a given state (that vary between $1/m$ when the state's population is evenly distributed over $2 \leq m \leq k$ religious groups, and 1 when the entire population of the state practices a single religion);

(2) $$rs_{ijt} = \sum_{r=1}^{k} ra_{irt} ra_{jrt},$$

that is, the off-diagonal elements are the degree of covariance between the distribution of religious affiliation in state i and the parallel distribution of state j (entries vary from one when the two populations are perfectly aligned in terms of religious groups to zero when any religious group that exists in state i does not exist in state j and vice versa);

(3) symmetry: that is, $rs_{ijt} = rs_{jit} \forall i, j \in \mathbf{RS}$. This means that the religious similarity between state i and state j is the same as between state j and state i.

The second method is based on a correlation between any two rows of the religious affiliation matrix. Thus, $rs_{ijt} = corr(ra_{it}, ra_{jt})$. Obviously, the diagonal elements of **RS** are all ones. Here too, **RS** is symmetrical, and $-1 \leq rs_{ijt} \leq 1 \ \forall \ rs_{ijt} \in \mathbf{RS}$.

Both methods produce highly similar results. The correlations between the religious similarity scores obtained across methods is $r = 0.958$. Thus, while we ran tests for religious similarity based on both methods, we present the results for religious similarity employing the standard conversion.

Table A5.4 displays the conversion of the religious affiliation matrix to an adjacency matrix. Entries in the matrix reflect religious similarity scores. Let us consider some of the cases discussed above. First, examine some of the diagonal entries. We highlight the entries for Trinidad, the Dominican Republic, Mexico, and Saudi Arabia. Given the religious diversity of the former, the homogeneity score of Trinidad is quite low. On the other hand, the latter states are quite homogeneous in terms of religious composition. Second, we highlighted the column corresponding to Mexico and the row corresponding to Saudi Arabia. As we can see, the religious similarity scores between Mexico and the other states in the table—with the exception of Saudi Arabia—are quite high. This is so because all the other states have a substantial proportion of their population who are Christian (and many of them predominantly Catholic). By contrast, the religious similarity scores between Saudi Arabia and all other states are very low given the predominantly (Sunni) Muslim population of Saudi Arabia.

In Table A5.5, we show religious similarity scores based on correlating the religious distributions of each pair of states in the sample we used for illustration. This correlation is based on the distribution of religious families (as opposed to religious similarity measured in terms of major religions only in Table A5.3). The results are similar to the results in Table A5.3, but a number of things need to be pointed out. First, some of the correlations—especially between states whose population is overwhelmingly Catholic—are extremely high. On the other hand, the correlations between states with

Table A5.4 Religious similarity matrix 2010—selected states

	USA	CAN	BAH	CUB	HAI	DOM	JAM	TRI	BAR	DMA	GRA	SLU	SVG	AAB	SKN	MEX	...	SAU
USA	**0.719**	0.719	0.737	0.735	0.762	0.829	0.691	0.545	0.600	0.759	0.733	0.755	0.742	0.697	0.772	0.781	...	**0.040**
CAN	0.719	**0.722**	0.744	0.745	0.770	0.838	0.689	0.550	0.596	0.764	0.738	0.761	0.747	0.702	0.781	0.788	...	**0.053**
BAH	0.737	0.744	**0.775**	0.779	0.795	0.867	0.706	0.563	0.615	0.790	0.766	0.790	0.769	0.733	0.813	0.816	...	**0.036**
CUB	0.735	0.745	0.779	**0.785**	0.798	0.870	0.704	0.563	0.614	0.792	0.769	0.793	0.770	0.736	0.818	0.819	...	**0.036**
HAI	0.762	0.770	0.795	0.798	**0.557**	0.900	0.728	0.583	0.624	0.815	0.788	0.813	0.798	0.748	0.837	0.843	...	**0.037**
DOM	0.829	0.838	0.867	0.870	0.900	**0.980**	0.791	0.635	0.678	0.888	0.858	0.886	0.868	0.815	0.913	**0.919**	...	**0.040**
JAM	0.691	0.689	0.706	0.704	0.728	0.791	**0.667**	0.523	0.584	0.728	0.703	0.724	0.711	0.670	0.738	0.747	...	**0.034**
TRI	0.545	0.550	0.563	0.563	0.583	0.635	0.523	**0.466**	0.451	0.578	0.560	0.576	0.574	0.531	0.591	0.596	...	**0.098**
BAR	0.600	0.596	0.615	0.614	0.624	0.678	0.584	0.451	**0.522**	0.631	0.611	0.628	0.612	0.588	0.639	0.645	...	**0.031**
DMA	0.759	0.764	0.790	0.792	0.815	0.888	0.728	0.578	0.631	**0.809**	0.783	0.807	0.790	0.746	0.829	0.835	...	**0.037**
GRA	0.733	0.738	0.766	0.769	0.788	0.858	0.703	0.560	0.611	0.783	**0.758**	0.781	0.763	0.724	0.803	0.808	...	**0.039**
SLU	0.755	0.761	0.790	0.793	0.813	0.886	0.724	0.576	0.628	0.807	0.781	**0.806**	0.787	0.746	0.829	0.833	...	**0.037**
SVG	0.742	0.747	0.769	0.770	0.798	0.868	0.711	0.574	0.612	0.790	0.763	0.787	**0.774**	0.725	0.808	0.815	...	**0.049**
AAB	0.697	0.702	0.733	0.736	0.748	0.815	0.670	0.531	0.588	0.746	0.724	0.746	0.725	**0.694**	0.767	0.770	...	**0.035**
SKN	0.772	0.781	0.813	0.818	0.837	0.913	0.738	0.591	0.639	0.829	0.803	0.829	0.808	0.767	**0.855**	0.858	...	**0.038**
MEX	0.781	0.788	0.816	0.819	0.843	0.919	0.747	0.596	0.645	0.835	0.808	0.833	0.815	0.770	0.858	**0.863**	...	**0.038**
...	...	...	...	...	...	...	...	...	...	...	...	...	...	...	...	...	...	...
SAU	**0.040**	**0.053**	**0.036**	**0.036**	**0.037**	**0.040**	**0.034**	**0.098**	**0.031**	**0.037**	**0.039**	**0.037**	**0.049**	**0.035**	**0.038**	**0.038**	...	0.867

a substantial Protestant population (e.g., the United States and Canada) and predominantly Catholic states are substantially lower. Second, the correlation between states that are highly homogeneous (e.g., Dominican Republic, Mexico) and states that are more religiously diverse (e.g., Trinidad, Barbados) is still positive, but low. Third, the correlation between predominantly Christian states and Saudi Arabia is low and slightly negative.

4.2 Estimation

We use a number of methods to estimate the relationships between religious factors and various measures of international conflict across levels of analysis. The relevant method for each analysis is defined by the measurement scale of the dependent variable. For the nation-year and dyad-year units of analysis we use logit models when estimating the probability of MID or escalation. For these analyses we also use years without conflict and cubic splines to control for temporal dependence.

For the nation-year and dyad-year, we use fixed effect time-series cross-sectional regressions when the dependent variables are continuous hostility scores. For the region-year, we use region fixed effect models to estimate regional conflict (since all measures of conflict at this level are continuous). Finally, for the nation-history and the dyad-history we use ordinary least squares (OLS) models.

In contrast to most other analyses of conflict at the national and the dyadic level, we rely both on conventional as well as alternative estimation methods. These alternative methods are due to issues that affect the data structures we employ and raise threats to inference. Unfortunately, these issues are also present in other studies of religion and conflict. Some of these problems are present as well in other analyses of international conflict that do not incorporate religious variables. Several problems are significant in this context.

Stationarity. As noted above, methods used in previous studies of monadic or dyadic conflict, and in particular, of religion-related determinants of conflict, suffer from stationarity bias. Specifically, the variation of several key covariates in such models is limited or even fixed within time series. Variables such as distance and/or reputational status exhibit little or no change over time for a given state or dyad. Other covariates—such as democracy/joint democracy, alliance relations, and in our case the religion variables—are typically time invariant: they exhibit little fluctuation over time within a given state or dyad. The average changes in percentages of major religions within states, as well as religious diversity within states, are about one-tenth of 1 percent within five-year intervals. When interpolated into annual scores, annual rates of change averaged five-hundredth of 1 percent. This suggests that several independent and control variables are stationary within series. Some variables such as distance are dropped in fixed-effect models due to their stationary nature. Other highly stationary—but not fixed—variables (e.g., alliance with average duration of seven years, or joint democracy with average duration of twelve years) are retained in such models, but their interpretation is problematic.

Number of cases. In some of the analyses, the size of the population under analysis is huge (in the hundreds of thousands of observations). Even if we impose sampling filters on the population of dyads—and we do impose the politically relevant dyad filter—the number of cases under analysis is still very large. For example, even with the politically relevant dyads filter and using undirected dyads, the N for the dyadic analyses hovers around 68,000 cases. Given this population size, even a very small effect is likely to be statistically significant, and in many of the dependent variables (war, in particular) it creates a huge rare event bias.

Significance levels in entire populations. The meaning of significance tests when examining an entire (or close to an entire) population of cases is not clear. Significance tests are based on the probability of obtaining a given result in a sample that is drawn randomly from the population. When analyzing the entire population of cases, even a minuscule relationship is significant. So the distinction between a meaningful effect and a negligible one in terms of statistical significance is not clear.

To address these problems, we employ bootstrapping techniques to supplement the standard analyses on the entire population of state years and dyad years. Bootstrapping involves a process of repeated sampling with replacement in which the estimated coefficients and standard errors are recalculated across samples and bootstrapped standard errors are corrected for bias (Mooney and Duval 1993). This technique draws a random sample of size k (in our case k ranges between 15 and 20 percent) from the entire population of cases, and runs the analysis on each sample. The statistics we wish to estimate in the sample are then saved, and the process iterates for a

Table A5.5 Religious similarity based on religious families

	USA	CAN	BAH	CUB	HAI	DOM	JAM	TRI	BAR	DMA	GRA	SLU	SVG	AAB	SKN	MEX	....	SAU
USA	1	0.866	0.841	0.434	0.503	0.674	0.842	0.848	0.71	0.639	0.74	0.783	0.753	0.781	0.428	0.61		-0.037
CAN	0.866	1	0.603	0.667	0.75	0.932	0.503	0.798	0.529	0.91	0.947	0.956	0.932	0.59	0.6	0.892		-0.005
BAH	0.841	0.603	1	0.153	0.225	0.351	0.915	0.738	0.797	0.341	0.565	0.541	0.541	0.96	0.473	0.321		-0.049
CUB	0.434	0.667	0.153	1	0.987	0.753	0.056	0.404	0.074	0.749	0.667	0.705	0.692	0.121	0.301	0.748		-0.035
HAI	0.503	0.75	0.225	0.987	1	0.84	0.099	0.474	0.104	0.84	0.763	0.803	0.793	0.185	0.347	0.84		-0.031
DOM	0.674	0.932	0.351	0.753	0.84	1	0.218	0.643	0.222	0.996	0.933	0.973	0.962	0.307	0.448	0.991		-0.015
JAM	0.842	0.503	0.915	0.056	0.099	0.218	1	0.724	0.837	0.185	0.39	0.392	0.389	0.861	0.269	0.148		-0.052
TRI	0.848	0.798	0.738	0.404	0.474	0.643	0.724	1	0.692	0.619	0.741	0.731	0.728	0.71	0.483	0.592		-0.063
BAR	0.71	0.529	0.797	0.074	0.104	0.222	0.837	0.692	1	0.185	0.483	0.347	0.35	0.89	0.671	0.147		-0.066
DMA	0.639	0.91	0.341	0.749	0.84	0.996	0.185	0.619	0.185	1	0.935	0.974	0.968	0.294	0.44	0.999		-0.013
GRA	0.74	0.947	0.565	0.667	0.763	0.933	0.39	0.741	0.483	0.935	1	0.963	0.968	0.572	0.675	0.927		-0.036
SLU	0.783	0.956	0.541	0.705	0.803	0.973	0.392	0.731	0.347	0.974	0.963	1	0.993	0.483	0.482	0.967		-0.025
SVG	0.753	0.932	0.541	0.692	0.793	0.962	0.389	0.728	0.35	0.968	0.968	0.993	1	0.483	0.472	0.962		-0.025
AAB	0.781	0.59	0.96	0.121	0.185	0.307	0.861	0.71	0.89	0.294	0.572	0.483	0.483	1	0.654	0.273		-0.061
SKN	0.428	0.6	0.473	0.301	0.347	0.448	0.269	0.483	0.671	0.44	0.675	0.482	0.472	0.654	1	0.433		-0.05
MEX	0.61	0.892	0.321	0.748	0.84	0.991	0.148	0.592	0.147	0.999	0.927	0.967	0.962	0.273	0.433	1		-0.011
....																		
SAU	-0.037	-0.005	-0.049	-0.035	-0.031	-0.015	-0.052	-0.063	-0.066	-0.013	-0.036	-0.025	-0.025	-0.061	-0.05	-0.011	....	1

Table A5.6 Religious similarity of dyads in interstate wars, 1945–2007

War No.	War Name	State A	State B	Year	Relig. Sim. Score	Level
139	World War II	Brazil	Germany	1945	0.952	High
139	World War II	Canada	Germany	1945	0.880	High
139	World War II	Canada	Japan	1945	0.016	Low
139	World War II	China	Japan	1945	0.060	Low
139	World War II	France	Germany	1945	0.902	High
139	World War II	France	Germany	1945	0.902	High
139	World War II	Germany	Australia	1945	0.920	High
139	World War II	Germany	Bulgaria	1945	0.823	High
139	World War II	Germany	Bulgaria	1945	0.823	High
139	World War II	Germany	New Zealand	1945	0.934	High
139	World War II	Germany	Romania	1945	0.913	High
139	World War II	Germany	Romania	1945	0.913	High
139	World War II	Germany	South Africa	1945	0.545	Med
139	World War II	Germany	USSR	1945	0.332	Med
139	World War II	Hungary	USSR	1945	0.341	Med
139	World War II	Japan	Australia	1945	0.010	Low
139	World War II	Japan	New Zealand	1945	0.010	Low
139	World War II	Mongolia	Japan	1945	0.066	Low
139	World War II	South Africa	Japan	1945	0.006	Low
139	World War II	United Kingdom	Germany	1945	0.908	High
139	World War II	United Kingdom	Hungary	1945	0.853	High
139	World War II	United Kingdom	Japan	1945	0.010	Low
139	World War II	United States	Germany	1945	0.760	High
139	World War II	United States	Japan	1945	0.017	Low
139	World War II	USSR	Japan	1945	0.010	Low
147	First Kashmir	India	Pakistan	1947	0.171	Low
148	Arab-Israeli	Egypt	Israel	1948	0.088	Low
148	Arab-Israeli	Iraq	Israel	1948	0.111	Low
148	Arab-Israeli	Jordan	Israel	1948	0.094	Low
148	Arab-Israeli	Lebanon	Israel	1948	0.054	Low
148	Arab-Israeli	Syria	Israel	1948	0.088	Low
151	Korean	Belgium	China	1951	0.005	Low
151	Korean	Belgium	North Korea	1951	0.026	Low
151	Korean	Canada	China	1950	0.004	Low
151	Korean	Canada	North Korea	1950	0.024	Low
151	Korean	China	Australia	1950	0.007	Low
151	Korean	China	Philippines	1950	0.006	Low
151	Korean	China	South Korea	1950	0.042	Low
151	Korean	China	Thailand	1951	0.105	Low
151	Korean	Colombia	China	1951	0.003	Low
151	Korean	Colombia	North Korea	1951	0.019	Low
151	Korean	Ethiopia	China	1951	0.019	Low
151	Korean	Ethiopia	North Korea	1951	0.160	Low
151	Korean	France	China	1951	0.011	Low
151	Korean	France	North Korea	1951	0.044	Low
151	Korean	Greece	China	1951	0.003	Low
151	Korean	Greece	North Korea	1951	0.020	Low
151	Korean	Netherlands	China	1951	0.011	Low

(Continued)

Table A5.6 (Continued)

War No.	War Name	State A	State B	Year	Relig. Sim. Score	Level
151	Korean	Netherlands	North Korea	1951	0.042	Low
151	Korean	North Korea	Australia	1950	0.033	Low
151	Korean	North Korea	Philippines	1950	0.033	Low
151	Korean*	North Korea	South Korea	1950	0.359	Med
151	Korean	North Korea	Thailand	1951	0.051	Low
151	Korean	Turkey	China	1950	0.018	Low
151	Korean	Turkey	North Korea	1950	0.000	Low
151	Korean	United Kingdom	China	1950	0.007	Low
151	Korean	United Kingdom	North Korea	1950	0.039	Low
151	Korean	United States	China	1950	0.018	Low
151	Korean	United States	North Korea	1950	0.074	Low
153	Offshore Islands*	China	Taiwan	1954	0.387	Med
155	Sinai War	Egypt	Israel	1956	0.105	Low
155	Sinai War	France	Egypt	1956	0.111	Low
155	Sinai War	United Kingdom	Egypt	1956	0.114	Low
156	Soviet Invasion of Hungary*	Hungary	USSR	1956	0.346	Med
158	Ifni War	France	Morocco	1958	0.043	Low
158	Ifni War	Spain	Morocco	1957	0.048	Low
159	Taiwan Straits*	China (PRC)	Taiwan (ROC)	1958	0.321	Med
160	Assam	China (PRC)	India	1962	0.006	Low
163	Vietnam War*	Cambodia	Vietnam	1970	0.126	Low
163	Vietnam War	South Korea	Vietnam	1965	0.078	Low
163	Vietnam War	United States	Vietnam	1965	0.114	Low
163	Vietnam War	Vietnam	Australia	1965	0.081	Low
163	Vietnam War	Vietnam	Philippines	1966	0.050	Low
163	Vietnam War*	Vietnam	South Vietnam	1965	0.187	Low
166	Second Kashmir	India	Pakistan	1965	0.144	Low
169	Six Day War	Egypt	Israel	1967	0.085	Low
169	Six Day War	Jordan	Israel	1967	0.087	Low
169	Six Day War	Syria	Israel	1967	0.085	Low
170	Second Laotian, Phase* 2	Laos	Vietnam	1968	0.130	Low
170	Second Laotian*	Thailand	Vietnam	1970	0.113	Low
170	Second Laotian	United States	Vietnam	1968	0.112	Low
172	War of Attrition	Egypt	Israel	1969	0.094	Low
175	Football War	Honduras	El Salvador	1969	0.926	High
176	Communist Coalition	Cambodia	Vietnam	1970	0.126	Low
176	Communist Coalition	United States	Vietnam	1970	0.112	Low
176	Communist Coalition*	Vietnam	South Vietnam	1970	0.185	Low
178	Bangladesh	India	Pakistan	1971	0.124	Low
181	Yom Kippur War	Egypt	Israel	1973	0.100	Low
181	Yom Kippur War	Iraq	Israel	1973	0.104	Low
181	Yom Kippur War	Israel	Saudi Arabia	1973	0.106	Low
181	Yom Kippur War	Jordan	Israel	1973	0.101	Low
181	Yom Kippur War	Syria	Israel	1973	0.098	Low
184	TurcoCypriot	Cyprus	Turkey	1974	0.191	Low
186	War over Angola	Angola	South Africa	1975	0.686	High

Table A5.6 (Continued)

War No.	War Name	State A	State B	Year	Relig. Sim. Score	Level
186	War over Angola	Cuba	Dem. Republic of the Congo	1975	0.692	High
186	War over Angola	Cuba	South Africa	1975	0.590	Med
186	War over Angola	Dem Repub of Congo	Angola	1975	0.793	High
187	Second Ogaden War,	Cuba	Somalia	1977	0.001	Low
187	Second Ogaden War	Somalia	Ethiopia	1977	0.298	Med
189	Vietnamese Cambodian	Cambodia	Vietnam	1977	0.122	Low
190	Ugandan–Tanzanian*	Tanzania	Libya	1979	0.313	Med
190	Ugandan-Tanzanian	Uganda	Tanzania	1978	0.364	Med
193	Sino-Vietnamese*	China	Vietnam	1979	0.339	Med
199	Iran–Iraq	Iran	Iraq	1980	0.902	High
202	Falkland Islands	Argentina	United Kingdom	1982	0.807	High
205	War over Lebanon	Syria	Israel	1982	0.114	Low
207	War over the Aouzou Strip	Chad	Libya	1986	0.441	Med
208	Sino Vietnamese Border War*	China	Vietnam	1987	0.313	Med
211	Gulf War	Canada	Iraq	1991	0.028	Low
211	Gulf War	France	Iraq	1991	0.050	Low
211	Gulf War	Iraq	Egypt	1991	0.821	High
211	Gulf War	Iraq	Kuwait	1990	0.862	High
211	Gulf War	Iraq	Oman	1991	0.831	High
211	Gulf War	Iraq	Qatar	1991	0.839	High
211	Gulf War	Iraq	Saudi Arabia	1991	0.919	High
211	Gulf War	Iraq	Syria	1991	0.876	High
211	Gulf War	Iraq	United Arab Emirates	1991	0.905	High
211	Gulf War	Italy	Iraq	1991	0.028	Low
211	Gulf War	Morocco	Iraq	1991	0.944	High
211	Gulf War	United Kingdom	Iraq	1991	0.037	Low
211	Gulf War	United States	Iraq	1991	0.034	Low
215	Bosnian Independence	Croatia	Yugoslavia	1992	0.679	High
215	Bosnian Independence	Yugoslavia	Bosnia	1992	0.461	Med
216	Azeri–Armenian	Armenia	Azerbaijan	1993	0.043	Low
217	Cenepa Valley	Ecuador	Peru	1995	0.953	High
219	Badme Border	Ethiopia	Eritrea	1998	0.451	Med
221	War for Kosovo	France	Yugoslavia	1999	0.577	Med
221	War for Kosovo	Germany	Yugoslavia	1999	0.579	Med
221	War for Kosovo	Italy	Yugoslavia	1999	0.635	High
221	War for Kosovo	Netherlands	Yugoslavia	1999	0.543	Med
221	War for Kosovo	United Kingdom	Yugoslavia	1999	0.634	High
221	War for Kosovo	United States	Yugoslavia	1999	0.631	High
221	War for Kosovo	Yugoslavia	Turkey	1999	0.190	Low
223	Kargil War	India	Pakistan	1999	0.138	Low

(Continued)

Table A5.6 (Continued)

War No.	War Name	State A	State B	Year	Relig. Sim. Score	Level
225	Invasion of Afghanistan	Afghanistan	Australia	2001	0.018	Low
225	Invasion of Afghanistan	Canada	Afghanistan	2001	0.021	Low
225	Invasion of Afghanistan	France	Afghanistan	2001	0.062	Low
225	Invasion of Afghanistan	United Kingdom	Afghanistan	2001	0.031	Low
225	Invasion of Afghanistan	United States	Afghanistan	2001	0.015	Low
227	Invasion of Iraq	Iraq	Australia	2003	0.034	Low
227	Invasion of Iraq	United Kingdom	Iraq	2003	0.048	Low
227	Invasion of Iraq	United States	Iraq	2003	0.033	Low
228	Second Lebanon	Israel	Lebanon	2006	0.108	Low

Sources: Sarkees and Wayman (2010); Maoz et al (2018).

* A case can be made that this dyad is in fact characterized by high religious similarity; one member of the dyad was a communist state with a high self-reported percent non-religious. Given the changes in self-reporting of religious affiliation in the postcommunist countries of Eastern Europe, there is a good reason to assume that religious affiliations are similar to those of the other dyad member.

large number of replications (r) specified by the user. The ultimate calculation of the standard errors is given by:

$$\widehat{SE} = \frac{1}{r-1} \sqrt{\sum_{i=1}^{r} \left(\check{\theta}_i - \overline{\theta} \right)^2}, \quad [1]$$

where θ_i is the test statistic (coefficient) of the ith sample and r is the number of replications (Hall and Wilson 1991). This reduces drastically the probability that two adjacent observations in a given national or dyadic series will emerge in the sample, thus removing the stationarity bias. In addition, since the samples are only a fraction of the entire population, the effects of the independent variables on the outcomes need to be much stronger to survive statistical significance.

Our inferential rule is that a given relationship is statistically significant if and only if it holds for both the entire population model and for the bootstrapping analyses. This is a more demanding but also less biased rule of inference compared to previous works examining these relationships.

Network effects. Another threat to inference is spatial dependence between observations at the nation-year and dyad-year level of analysis. Since conflicts evolve in relational networks, there is a strong possibility that individual observations are not independent and identically

Table A5.7 Distribution of religious similarity across warring dyads

Religious Similarity Level	Cold War		Post–Cold War
	Raw Pct.	Modified Pct.[1]	
Low	0.643	0.601	0.486
Medium	0.133	0.105	0.143
High	0.224	0.301	0.371

1 Modified to change asterisked cells in Table A10 (online appendix) to the High category.

distributed (iid) random variables. This has been shown to be the case in a number of networks, including conflict (Cranmer, Desmarais, and Meninga 2012; Desmarais and Cranmer 2011; Ward et al. 2013). In other words, the relationship between two states is apt to be affected by the relations between each of them with third parties. We call this type of dependence a network effect. In order to control for network effects, we use a number of network statistics that measure different types of network dependence. These are measured at the dyad-year unit of analysis, and are then transformed in a way that can capture network effects on national behavior. These measures include two stars, three stars, and expected values. For a given dyad ij, the number of two-stars is calculated by:

$$S2_{ij} = \sum_{j \neq i} MID_{ji} + \sum_{i \neq j} MID_{ij} - 2 * MID_{ij}. \quad [2]$$

And the number of three-stars is calculated by:

$$S3_{ij} = \sum_{j \neq i} MID_{ji} \sum_{i \neq j} MID_{ij} - 3 MIN \left(\sum_{(j \neq i)} MID_{ji}, \sum_{i \neq j} MID_{ij} \right). \quad [3]$$

Triangles are calculated as

$$T_{ij} = \sum_{k \neq j} MID_{ij} MID_{jk}. \quad [4]$$

For the nation-year we average the two stars, three stars, and EVs over all of a given state's neighbors—that is, the states with which the focal state had conflict.

CHAPTER 6

Religion and International Cooperation

1. Introduction

In the previous chapter we examined the possible linkages between religious factors and conflict behavior. This chapter centers on the relationship between religion and international cooperation. We examine when, why, under what conditions, and in what ways religion can foster or inhibit cooperation among states. The theoretical discussion and empirical results presented here go well beyond what has been previously written on the relationship between religion and international cooperation. In particular, we innovate in several key areas.

1. *We provide a focused theoretical framework on religion and cooperation.* While the literature on international cooperation and its various aspects (security, economic, institutional) forms a cottage industry in the academic scholarship on international relations, relatively little has been written on the underlying causal mechanisms that connect religious factors to various forms of cooperation. We offer a focused theory of the linkages between religious characteristics of states, dyads, and regions and different areas of international cooperation.
2. *We provide a multidimensional analysis of cooperation.* The typical study of cooperation focuses on a specific cooperative domain. Studies of security cooperation tend to ignore economic or institutional cooperation. Studies of economic cooperation tend to ignore security and institutional cooperation and so forth.

There are a few studies that examine linkages between different cooperative domains. For example, there has been a relatively vigorous debate on the relationship between alliances and trade (Mansfield and Bronson 1997; Gowa 1995; Gowa and Mansfield 1993, 2004; Morrow, Siverson, and Tabares 1998; Fordham 2010; Vijayaraghavan et al. 2015). However, this literature is the exception rather than the rule. More importantly, religion does not come into play in studies focusing on such linkages. By contrast, this chapter covers multiple issue areas where cooperation takes place, and our theory offers differential insights on the role religion plays in different cooperative domains. Likewise, the empirical analyses in this chapter allow a general assessment of the linkages between religious factors and multiple cooperative domains. Finally, we offer both an integrative measure of cooperation and results on the effect of religious factors on integrative cooperative ties.

3. *We provide a multilevel analysis of international cooperation.* As in the previous chapter, we offer a multilevel analysis of the linkages between religion and international cooperation. We examine national cooperative patterns, dyadic cooperative relations, and regional levels of cooperation. Here, too, our analyses go well beyond the common practice in studies of cooperation, which focus primarily on one level of analysis. Importantly, we study emergent properties of cooperative relations—cooperative communities. Our analysis of cooperative international communities adds novel insights into the emergent properties of religious factors in ways that have never before been demonstrated.

4. *We provide several methodological innovations.* We add several additional layers to the key methodological innovations discussed in the previous chapter—high-resolution measures of religious similarity and religious characteristics, more appropriate estimation techniques, and multiple robustness checks. Some of these innovations are related to the estimation of cohesive communities and their political and religious characteristics. We employ network analytic techniques, which enable us to estimate unobserved effects of cooperative structures and the role of religion in these structures. The methodology of community detection and the estimation of community cohesion allows us to estimate whether

cooperative communities are organized around religious lines, and whether religion is a determining factor in their emergence and persistence over time.

All these innovative features combine to provide new insights into and assessment of the conditions under which religious factors affect cooperative international relations. To begin a discussion of the linkages between religion and cooperative behavior, we need to provide a definition of international cooperation.

Following Keohane (1984), we define international cooperation as *coordinated behavior between or among states that is designed to benefit them more than unilateral behavior.* This definition has several elements. The first is the notion of coordinated behavior. What we mean by coordination is that two or more actors behave in a manner that is consistent with the expectations of all parties involved in this coordination. These expectations can be established by some formal agreement that stipulates the expected behavior under a prespecified set of circumstances. They can also emerge due to some informal or tacit adjustment of expectations by the actors without a formal agreement or even without communication among them. Schelling (1963, 1978) provides multiple examples of coordination without communication. Axelrod's (1984) study of cooperation among egoists provides both a formal foundation and a number of intriguing examples of how coordinated behavior can take place without communication betweeen actors who are out to maximize their gains, sometimes even at the expense of others.

The second element of the definition has to do with the underlying reasons for such coordinated behavior. The general idea here is that actors coordinate their behavior because each of them believes it can benefit more from—explicitly or tacitly—coordinating behavior with others than by trying to realize one's goals without coordination. This may sound like a rationalization of cooperative behavior. However, the benefit that actors expect to receive from such coordination need not be material; it could entail emotional, spiritual, or psychological fulfillment. The point is that such coordination is deliberate and conscious, and it occurs for a reason.

There is a third element that is absent from the definition, but it features prominently in general theories of cooperation, and has led to a number of important discoveries about social behavior across a number of disciplines.

Coordinated behavior that arises from individual expectations of gains does not necessarily yield social outcomes that maximize the society's benefits. Most social dilemmas or collective goods problems that have been analyzed by game theorists address situations where cooperation yields socially optimal outcomes, but individual incentives yield egoistic behaviors that result in suboptimal individual and social outcomes.[1] However, the opposite is also possible, as Schelling (1978) shows: coordinated behavior due to common expectations may result in social disasters. Runs on banks due to expectations of bank collapse, stock market crashes, major traffic jams due to drivers slowing down to observe minor car accidents, the spread of unsubstantiated rumors (e.g., false allegations of crimes committed by black Americans as precipitant to white mob violence and lynchings in the US) are examples of coordinated behavior resulting in social disasters. However, these cases reflect collective outcomes driven by common expectations that unilateral behavior may minimize risk or maximize gain. Therefore, this mob behavior is not what we typically mean by cooperation.

Our focus is on cooperation among states. Such cooperation can take a number of different forms. States may cooperate in one issue area and avoid cooperation in another. In fact, states may cooperate in one issue area and fight in another. This happens more often than one might think possible. For example, over the period 1945–2010, 47 percent of all dyads that had a MID also traded with one another to a significant degree.[2] Over 19 percent of all warring dyads had substantial trade between them. More commonly, over 50 percent of all warring dyads had substantial overlap in their IGO membership.[3] More than two-thirds of the dyads that were involved in a MID over that period had substantial overlap in IGO membership. Therefore, when discussing international cooperation, it is important to understand that cooperation and conflict are two sides of the same coin. Also, it is important to emphasize that, while there is some association across different issue areas of cooperation, these relationships are not very strong.[4]

There are many areas within and across which states can and do cooperate, and while we cannot cover them all, we nevertheless focus on some of the most important and visible areas of international cooperation, which include the following:

1. *Security cooperation*. Formal security alliances are formal treaties between or among states stipulating different forms of coordinated

behavior under prespecified circumstances. Such agreements can cover cases of common defense against enemies of one of the allies; common offensive treaties that coordinate attacks against common enemies; nonaggression or neutrality pacts that stipulate nonviolence against members of the treaty; or even consultation pacts (i.e., ententes), which stipulate consultation, coordination, or information sharing during crises. Some of these treaties involve extremely costly commitments because they require states to sacrifice the lives of their citizens and to commit large amounts of material resources to help another state if the latter is attacked. Other security treaties may impose on signatories an enormous amount of restraint because compliance requires them to refrain from violent action, even if they have major claims or grievances toward each other. For reasons that we discuss below, states rarely enter into alliances lightly. Therefore, such treaties represent one of the most exacting forms of international cooperation.

2. *Economic cooperation*. We analyze two forms of economic cooperation: total trade and preferential trade agreements. The process of trading goods and resources is one of the most common forms of international cooperation. International trade very often involves limited political intervention; much of it is a firm-to-firm or even citizen-to-citizen enterprise. Governments may have some control over exports and imports via taxes, tariffs, or various export and import regulations. However, governments have very little control over citizens' demand for foreign goods and services, or their willingness and ability to sell goods and services internationally. Preferential trade agreements (PTAs), on the other hand, are government-to-government agreements that stipulate special terms of exchange of goods and services between or among states (Saggi 2006). These agreements may entail both benefits and costs, as they improve the competitive edge of goods that one country exports to another. At the same time, such agreements might make local producers worse off because they need to compete with more attractive import goods in terms of quality and price.

3. *Institutional cooperation*. Here we examine the cooperation of countries within multilateral institutional contexts, defined by

their membership in different types of IGOs. A formal definition of an IGO (Pevehouse, Nordstrom, and Wranke 2004, Wallace and Singer 1970) views it as an institution that meets four conditions: (1) it involves members of three or more states; (2) it has a plenary that meets at least once a decade; (3) it has a secretariat or an equivalent executive body that meets at least once a year; and (4) individual state representatives are appointees of their respective governments. When a state joins an IGO it pledges to comply with the IGO's mission. The extent to which IGOs actually constrain unilateral state behavior is a central topic of debate in international relations theory (Mearsheimer 1994/5, Keohane and Martin 1995, Koremenos, Lipson, and Snidal 2001). However, for the purpose of this chapter we assume that states do not join IGOs lightly. Likewise, IGOs do not admit states if they do not expect member states to use the IGO's facilities and institutions for cooperative purposes. We focus on IGOs that perform different functions, including security, economic, administrative, and more general (e.g., human rights, environment) functions. Note that institutional cooperation often overlaps with economic or security cooperation. For example, NATO is both a collective security organization that can be translated into a series of bilateral alliance treaties among its members, as well as a security IGO. Multilateral PTAs also meet the definitional conditions of an IGO, and some PTAs have embedded within them security alliances (Powers 2004, Henderson 2015). However, many IGOs cover administrative or symbolic issue areas that do not fall into the security or economic categories. So the overlap between security cooperation or economic cooperation, on the one hand, and IGO membership, on the other, is far from complete.

4. *General cooperation.* We also develop a general cooperation concept that encompasses the three areas of cooperation discussed above. General cooperation distinguishes between states that cooperate with each other in one issue area (e.g., security) and states whose cooperative ventures encompass multiple issue areas. This enables us to examine how religious factors affect multiple areas of cooperation.

The study of religion and international cooperation is a relatively new topic. In contrast to the multitude of studies on the role of religion in international conflict, the study of religion and cooperation is not well developed. Thus, the theoretical foundations of these linkages are rather weak, and empirical research is almost nonexistent. To a large extent, this chapter represents an initial foray into uncharted waters. As such, the present chapter provides a number of important contributions to our understanding of the role of religion in world politics.

1. It offers a set of theoretical ideas—derived from the various perspectives we discussed in chapter 2—about the role that religion might play in fostering international cooperation.
2. These ideas center on the presence or absence of linkages between religious factors and different forms of cooperative ventures among states. We put forth a nuanced theory of religion and international cooperation whose central point is that religion may play an important role in fostering some forms of cooperation but not others. A key objective of the theory is explaining which particular areas of cooperation are influenced by religious factors and which are not.
3. In keeping with the practice of previous chapters, we study the linkages between religion and cooperation at multiple levels of analysis. In contrast to other chapters, however, we highlight a new unit of analysis—endogenous cooperative communities (ECCs). Such communities emerge as dense clusters of cooperative states. Members in any one ECC tend to cooperate with each other much more often and more intensely than with members of other ECCs. Consequently, the level of cooperation *within* ECCs is much higher than *between* ECCs (Maoz 2017). We offer the first analysis of the role that religion plays in the emergence and persistence of ECCs.

2. International Cooperation—State of the Art

We do not purport to provide a comprehensive review of the literature on international cooperation; others have done that (e.g., Gilligan and Johns 2012, Oneill, Balsiger, and VanDeveer 2004, Milner 1992). Our review centers on key ideas regarding different forms of international cooperation, the factors that foster or inhibit cooperative behavior, and, in particular, the role of religion in international cooperation. One of the issues that make such a review somewhat complex is that none of the major paradigms of world politics offers a unified framework of international cooperation that cuts across issue domains. This is so, despite that all major paradigms discuss the possibility, causes, and implications of international cooperation in rather general terms. Our review covers, first, the general ideas about international cooperation of each of the three paradigms.[5] We then review the key issues that separate these paradigms from each other as well as some aspects of common ground.

The definition of cooperation discussed above outlines a utilitarian drive for cooperation. If two actors can do better by coordinating their behavior than by acting alone, then they have an incentive to cooperate. This is what we describe as a potential "win-win" situation. In such situations, the anticipated benefit from cooperation may have implications that go beyond the individual gains. For example, cooperation may generate public goods that improve the conditions of others beyond those actors who pay the costs of obtaining/sustaining these goods.

Yet, as some of the key theories of social interaction suggest, cooperation is not guaranteed even if it offers higher rewards to all units involved and to each of them separately. Two models of social interaction illustrate this point: the Prisoner's Dilemma and the Stag Hunt Game (Axelrod 1984, Jervis 1978). In both models the cooperative outcome provides each player a higher payoff than the payoff of unilateral action. In both models, the cooperative outcome is also Pareto superior; that is, it maximizes the social utility. In both models, however, the mutual defection outcome—where each player fails to cooperate—is either the only equilibrium (Prisoner's Dilemma) or one of the two equilibria (Stag Hunt) in the game. This means that, once players choose not to cooperate, no one has an incentive to move toward cooperative behavior. This dilemma of cooperation lies in the fact that individual rationality dictates defection. Each actor expects other actors to defect. Even if an actor would have liked to cooperate in order to maximize its payoff, it cannot rely on the others to do the same. In that case, defection is the best (or the least-worse) choice.

Many real-life problems of this sort (contributing to collective goods, creating environmental pollution, supporting allies under attack, maintaining production quotas in cartels) involve repeated interactions. In other words, the problem reemerges every time actors have to make a decision about cooperation, and typically with the same partners. This helps mitigate the dilemma to some extent. The trade-off becomes one between short-term gains and long-term losses. Building on the concept of the "shadow of the future," Axelrod (1984) showed that some fairly simple strategies for playing a repeated Prisoner's Dilemma game induce cooperation. Moreover, such simple strategies tend to "invade" more exploitative ones and survive better in an environment made of egoistic strategies seeking to exploit other actors' weaknesses.

Cooperation may be difficult to sustain if actors are rational because there are short-term incentives to defect. There are also good reasons not to trust other actors' cooperative gestures. Even if cooperation is spelled out in formal contracts, in the absence of an authority that can sanction violations, there are rational incentives to renege on commitments. If actors expect others to violate these contracts, there is no rational reason to sign them in the first place.

However, even in an anarchic setting that lacks mechanisms of enforcement, cooperation can and does happen frequently. Evidence of the magnitude of international cooperation abounds. First, the degree of trade cooperation increased from less than 20 percent of dyads in 1870 to nearly 80 percent of dyads in 2009. Second, the degree to which security alliances are reliable varies among studies, with some (e.g., Leeds 2003) arguing that alliances are reliable in over 75 percent of the cases where states are called to help their allies in war. Others (e.g., Maoz 2015) argue that the reliability rates are much lower (and depend on both alliance type and the specific circumstances in which commitments are invoked). Yet even so, allied states are at least four times more likely to help their allies against third parties than they are likely to fight those third parties when no alliance commitments are invoked.

Third, the average state was a member of 0.2 IGOs in 1816, of seven IGOs in 1900, of twenty-seven IGOs in 1945, and of over seventy IGOs in 2004 (Pevehouse, Nordstrom, and Wranke 2004). The number of IGOs increased from one in 1816 to 27 in 1900, to 101 in 1945, and to 352 in 2004. Fourth, data on PTAs start in 1950, but the density of state membership in PTAs increased from 1.7 percent of the dyads having a PTA in 1950 to 38.7 percent of all dyads having one or more PTAs in 2006.[6] Other types of defense cooperation agreements covering such issues as intelligence sharing, joint exercises, bases, and the like have also increased exponentially over the same period (Kinne 2014).

These data clearly suggest that states cooperate with each other across a wide array of issues. And the density of international cooperation is significantly higher than the density of international conflict. Moreover, the degree and scope of cooperative activities have increased significantly over time. So any serious attempt to understand modern international relations must address how and why cooperation expands and increases in spite of continued anarchy.

2.1 Realism and International Cooperation

There are two versions of the realist (or neorealist) paradigm: offensive realism and defensive realism. Both differ primarily with respect to the kind of goals they attribute to states. Both rely on the idea that international anarchy—the absence of an institution or actor that is capable of enforcing order and guaranteeing contractual compliance by states—is the fundamental characteristic of international relations. However, defensive realists assume that the key actors—states—are driven primarily by the desire to ensure their security. Thus, they are *absolute gain* maximizers: each state wishes to maximize its payoffs regardless of whether or not other states gain or lose. By contrast, offensive realists assume that states are power seekers. Since power is relative, they are driven by a desire to maximize their power relative to, and at the expense of, others. This makes them *relative gain* maximizers. This is a crucial difference in terms of what drives (or compels) states to cooperate.

If states are absolute gain maximizers, then international interactions are mixed-motive games. States compete with each other in general, but there are certain outcomes that represent collective gains. These outcomes may drive states to cooperate. There are also outcomes that offer mutual losses. Such outcomes—for example, nuclear war—also drive states to coordinate behavior to minimize the likelihood of collective disaster. The mixed-motive nature of international interactions suggests that states cooperate when cooperative outcomes maximize individual gains as well as mutual gains. Likewise, states cooperate when they are driven by a desire to avoid individual—as well as collective—disasters. However, even if most international games are mixed-motive games, actual cooperation is not assured, and in fact—as in the case of games like the Prisoner's Dilemma, the Stag Hunt, or Chicken—disaster may strike nevertheless.

These mixed motives apply to various forms of interaction. States form security institutions, such as alliances or collective security organizations, to protect themselves against common threats. Such security structures offer capability pools that can deter common enemies from attacking. However, alliances also entail risks. First, states lose a measure of autonomy because decisions on war and peace may be made for them by their allies or by the enemies of their allies (Smith 1995, Morrow 1994, Maoz 2000). States wish to enter into alliances to get their allies' support when they get into trouble. They may also wish to enter into alliances to avoid trouble in the first place, hoping that the added capability that the alliance entails will deter their adversaries (Smith 1995). The benefits of alliance for a given state, however, are often severely discounted or even offset by the prospect that it will have to help its ally when the latter gets into trouble. In many cases, a state may form an alliance precisely so it can draw its ally into war with a third party, one that its ally had no prior reason to fight. This is what Maoz (1990b) called the "ally's paradox."[7]

Defensive realists suggest that states enter into security cooperation reluctantly; they form alliances only when they cannot confront their security challenges via their own resources. This is what we call the "need" factor of alliance formation. A state defines its security challenges in terms of the size and capabilities of its strategic reference group. A state that faces a large and powerful group of enemies (or would-be enemies), whose capabilities far outweigh the focal state's capabilities, is badly in need of allies. By contrast, a state that has few enemies, or a state whose capabilities outweigh those of its enemies, has no strategic incentive to form alliances.

The problem of cooperation is exacerbated if one accepts the offensive realist notion of states as relative gain maximizers. The underlying implication of relative gain maximization is that international interactions reflect constant- (or even zero-)sum games. In such games, players have no interest in cooperation because one player's gains come at the expense of (or are equal to) another player's losses. Cooperation is fleeting, yet it may occur, and for the same reasons that defensive realists suggest: the pooling of resources against common enemies (Mearsheimer, 1994/5).

Given that a state has determined that it needs allies, who are the "best" candidates for alliance? For realists, the answer to this question is fairly straightforward: the best candidates for alliance are states that share common interests. Common interests in realism translate to common enemies (Farber and Gowa 1995, Gowa 1999). Other affinities—cultural, ideological, or political—between states matter very little.

With respect to trade, however, both offensive and defensive realists agree that states are out to maximize absolute gains. Because trade is based on the theory of comparative advantage, pursuing relative gains in trade would greatly damage the benefits of trade. If a state defines its benefits from trade as a function of its revenues relative to its trading partner, then trade cannot be an equilibrium outcome. This is so because the state that "loses" in terms of relative gains would be better off without it. Trade is a means of increasing a state's national power—via access to resources and raw materials. These are used to boost a nation's economy and its military. Trade also generates revenues and foreign currencies from exports. Cooperation via exchange of goods and services is also possible if both sides feel that they can benefit more from such exchange than from a self-contained economy—which might be both inefficient and perpetuate some structural scarcities.

Institutional cooperation is also seen by realists as a necessary evil. Institutions enable states to coordinate behavior that serves their interests. However, realists believe that states design international institutions in a manner that reflects the distribution of power in the international system. Institutions are built so that they will not be able to override state interests. One of the important aspects of such designs is the lack of meaningful enforcement mechanisms of most international institutions. When they attempt to enforce institutional norms, they cease to function effectively (Mearsheimer 1994/5). The manner in which the major powers designed the UN Security Council reflects this point more than anything else. However, the realist claim extends to other international organizations as well (Koremenos, Lipson, and Snidal 2001).

In short, the driving forces behind international cooperation, according to the realist paradigm, are fundamental national interests. If states could safeguard or advance their national interests without relying on other states, they would avoid cooperation altogether. But the reality is that—in most cases—they cannot. Thus, cooperation is a necessary evil; it starts when it converges with states' mutual interests, and ends when it does not. Lord

Palmerston's famous statement epitomizes this position: "We [Great Britain] have not eternal allies and we have not perpetual enemies. Our interests are eternal and perpetual and those interests it is our duty to follow."

This discussion suggests that realists see little room for any kind of ideational attachments, such as those that are based on religious affinity. Such factors are not taken to have a causal impact on the propensity, duration, or type of cooperation. Realists accept the fact that some areas of international cooperation may reflect cultural affinities. For example, institutional cooperation in areas that do not directly impinge on national security—for instance, administrative matters or cultural affairs—may reflect a significant degree of cultural affinity. However, security cooperation, both via collective security organizations and formal alliances, is based on hard interests that have very little to do with religion. The same applies to economic cooperation, an area where interests play a critical role.

It is instructive to summarize the realist theory of cooperation with a number of key headlines that emerge from the realist view of world politics.

- Cooperation is born of necessity; it happens when a state cannot meet the external challenges it faces with its own resources.
- Thus, cooperation is motivated by need—the difference between what a state wants to accomplish and what it can accomplish by its own resources.
- Partners for cooperative ventures are states that share common interests; ideational or cultural affinities have little impact on cooperation
- Institutions are designed to reflect the balance of power in the international system. They are convenient mechanisms for coordination and function as long as their activity does not challenge states' national interests. When it does, states follow their interests first.

2.2 Liberalism and International Cooperation

As in the realist paradigm, liberal scholars assume that states are driven by interests. However, liberal scholars argue that states pursue a broader range of interests than the power-centered (or survival-centered) types of interests on which realists focus. This wide range of interests is predicated on the assumption that the domestic makeup of states matters. Political leaders attempt not only to maximize national interests but also work to maximize their political survival, that is, their chances of staying in office (Bueno de Mesquita et al. 2003). The goal of political survival requires political leaders to provide for their "winning coalition," those who helped bring them to power and sustain them there. In autocracies, leaders need to provide private goods to the members of their winning coalition: the military, aristocracy, economic elites, or some ethnic group. In democracies, political leaders must provide public goods so that a majority of the voters will reelect them.

The liberal paradigm suggests that domestic politics and international politics interact. Domestic needs and pressures affect the ways states behave in the international system, just as events in the international system might affect domestic political processes. The raison d'état is not independent of leaders' personal goals and aspirations, or of social needs and structures.

Liberals also assume that states seek absolute gains. As such, they are aware that many areas of interaction—economic, cultural, or scientific—offer multiple win-win opportunities. However, the actual realization of cooperative ventures may be hampered by short-term incentives to exploit others. These issues extend and become more complicated when we move from a two-person (or two-state) interaction to multilateral interactions. In such areas, the problem of cooperation becomes essentially a public-good problem, or in professional jargon a "tragedy of the commons" problem. To sustain public goods such as parks or a sustainable environment, a minimum number of actors have to contribute to the maintenance of such goods. However, since such public goods are nonexclusionary—the benefits they provide are general, not restricted to those who contributed toward their existence—there is a strong incentive to "free ride," to enjoy the public good without contributing to its sustainability.

States' remedy to the free-riding or defection problem, according to liberal scholars, is the design and establishment of international institutions (Keohane 1984, Keohane and Martin 1995, Axelrod and Keohane 1985). International institutions serve a number of purposes: first they increase transparency, so that defection and free riding can be more easily detected. Second, they create a longer horizon for states, so leaders can perceive the long-term benefits of cooperation. Once they understand that long-term benefits trump the short-term benefits of free riding, states might be willing to accept the short-term costs of cooperation so that they can reap the long-term benefits. Third, international institutions gradually develop norms that induce compliance. Even though most international institutions lack any enforcement capacity, they are capable of "naming and shaming" violators. As such, they force states to think twice before violating these agreements.

Unger (2013) examined processes of joining and complying with human rights treaties. She shows that when a state depends on joiners and compliers, its tendency to join and comply with the provisions of such treaties increases. By contrast, if the state depends politically or economically on nonjoiners or noncompliers of such treaties, it is less likely to join human rights treaties. And if it does join, it is less likely to comply with such treaties.

There are three fundamental issues that separate liberal explanations of international cooperation from realist ones. First, the nature, extent, and persistence of cooperation among states—across issue areas—is a function of domestic factors as well as of common interests or mutual gains. Specifically, joint democracy is not only an important factor in reducing the probability of conflict among states but also an important facilitator of cooperation (Russett and Oneal 2001; Mansfield and Milner 2000, 2012; Mansfield and Pevehouse 2003). Second, institutions increase the magnitude of cooperation (Pevehouse and Russett 2006, Keohane and Martin 1995). Third, even in the security realm where realists expect little cooperation, there is evidence that institutional cooperation is prevalent and stable.

An important aspect of liberal thinking about cooperation concerns spillover effects. States that engage in a successful cooperative venture in one realm are likely to expand such cooperation to other realms. A longstanding debate in the liberal literature concerns the direction of spillover—especially spillover between security and economic cooperation. Classical liberal theorists (e.g., Kant, Auguste Comte) suggested that the spillover process goes from trade to security. That is, states that share successful trade relations are likely to increase their cooperation in the security realm. Most empirical evidence suggests, however, that the causal path goes the other way—at least in the post–World War II era. Specifically, when two states form security cooperation ties, they are likely to increase their economic cooperation, but not vice versa (Mansfield and Bronson 1997, Gowa 1995, Gowa and Mansfield 2004, Maoz 2010, Vijayaraghavan et al. 2015).[8] The general point, however, is that cooperation may spill across issue areas.

Several key points about cooperation can be deduced from the liberal paradigm.

- Cooperation emerges from the pursuit of absolute gains; most international interactions are best represented by mixed-motive games. Therefore, states cooperate when they view an exchange as generating win-win opportunities or opportunities to avoid lose-lose situations.
- Even when cooperation is threatened by social dilemmas such as the collective good problem, there are strategies that can mitigate the tendency to defect from cooperative ventures. These strategies include institutional design, transparency, and reciprocity. Conditional cooperative strategies (e.g., tit for tat) may induce cooperation even in environments that contain a relatively large number of exploitative strategies.
- Importantly, international institutions create cooperative norms even when they lack enforcement mechanisms and when they cannot directly sanction violators. These norms create a "shadow of the future" for potential violators—an awareness that short-term gains due to defection may be offset by long-term losses. Such norms reduce the tendency to violate cooperative agreements.
- Domestic politics—in particular democratization—plays an important role in increased cooperation across different issue-areas.
- Cooperation in one realm increases the probability and magnitude of cooperation in other realms (i.e. spillover effects).

2.3 The Constructivist Paradigm

The principal criticism leveled by constructivists against the other paradigms is the assumption of the latter that interests are (a) exogenous, (b) fixed, and (c) primarily material. Constructivists argue that we cannot treat interests as independent variables, as both realists and liberals do. The key questions that constructivists ask include the following: (a) Where do interests come from? (b) Which factors affect interest formation? (c) When, how, and under what conditions do interests change? The origins of interests are a central area of inquiry in constructivism. Constructivists also dispute the notion that interests are fixed. Whereas realists assume that states—regardless of time and space—pursue either power or security, and liberals assume that political leaders aim to maximize their political survival, constructivists assume that interests change over time and differ from one state to another.

Both realists and liberals argue that states' interests are material—that is, they can be measured by such things as military capability, economic wealth, or domestic stability. Constructivists claim that material indicators of interests are derivative of ideational factors such as national identity. The latter point is the core idea of constructivism. As we noted in chapter 3, constructivists claim that identity shapes perceptions. Perceptions shape leaders' (and therefore states') worldviews, their characterization of friends and foes, and, to a large extent, their interests. Such identities are based in part on fixed elements—cultural, social, and political attributes—and in part on experiential learning due to their interaction with the environment.

This idea shapes the way constructivists view cooperative incentives. The less "radical" constructivists (e.g., Alexander Wendt, Michael Barnett, Emanuel Adler) do not dismiss completely the material basis of interests. States need resources to survive and prosper; they need allies to deter or defend against common enemies; and they require institutions to administer the international commons such as the environment. Nor do constructivists challenge the fact that political leaders can seek both domestic and foreign benefits from cooperation. Yet, their arguments center on two questions: (1) why cooperate, and (2) with whom?

Part of the constructivist answer to the first question is similar to that of the realist and liberal paradigms: states cooperate because they need to or because they can benefit more by cooperation than by going it alone. However, constructivists add to these incentives two other ones. First, states cooperate if and when such action conforms to their identity conception. This identity conception is not only dependent on the domestic attributes of the state but also on the ideational relations between the focal state and its external environment. This affects the answer to the second question. The other factor that influences states' incentives to cooperate is the prevailing "international culture" (Wendt 1999). Specifically, a prevailing Lockean culture restricts cooperation to the minimum necessary to ensure survival.[9] By contrast, within a prevailing "Kantian" culture, states see themselves as part of a corporate identity, shared values, and inherent interdependence. This renders states' identities commensurate with a collective international identity. Under these circumstances, states are driven to high levels of cooperation across issue areas.

International cultures may not be universal, however. They can be limited to certain regions, or to a certain type or group of states. So the question of "with whom to cooperate" is still germane even when the prevailing international culture is "Kantian."[10] As noted, realists identify friends as states with common interests. This often translates to states with shared enemies. Liberals identify potential cooperators as states that share a similar political culture—in particular, joint democracy. Constructivists' answer to this question is: cooperation is between states that have common identities or between states that share values. States define friends and foes not only on the basis of what they do but also on the basis of who they are. We saw this argument in the constructivist claims about the origins of conflict. This applies to cooperation as well. Trust is based on shared values and shared ideas. Since cooperation requires trust, the likelihood of cooperation between states increases with the degree of ideational convergence.

Both identities and interests may change over time. The argument about states' age can be extended to cooperative activities. When states are young, their identities are shaped primarily by cultural characteristics. Their definition of friends and trustworthy partners for cooperative ventures is based primarily on shared cultural attributes. Consequently, at the early stages of states' interaction with their environment, they appear to seek partners for cooperative ventures among states with which they share cultural identities. As states grow "older," their identity is increasingly shaped by interactive experience. When states' cooperation with other states creates net benefits, they begin to share a corporate identity and growing sense of a community. Once such a corporate identity is consolidated, cooperation not only increases within the issue area where such benefits are manifest but also begins to spill over to other interactive realms. The choice of partners to cooperation is shaped less by common cultural traits and increasingly by shared experiential identities. The following ideas emerge.

- Shared ideas/identities affect international cooperation as much as common interests.
- At the early stages of a state's international activity, it tends to cooperate with actors that share common cultural traits. At later stages of a state's life cycle, however, it is increasingly more likely

to cooperate on the basis of shared cooperative experience than on the basis of cultural traits.
- The level of cooperation increases as the international culture shifts from a Lockean culture to a Kantian one.

3. Religion and Theories of International Cooperation

In order to examine how religious factors influence international cooperation, we need to provide some principles that characterize a general theory of cooperation that covers several questions:

1. Why do states need to cooperate?
2. How do states select partners for cooperation?
3. What are the emergent implications of international cooperation?

A general theory of international cooperation contains four principal elements: *need, attraction, prevention, and trust* (NAPT). The first element addresses the first question. The other three elements answer the second question. The answer to the third question is a logical consequence of the answers to the first two. We discuss each element in turn.

Need. The need factor defines why some states choose to cooperate more than others. It also explains why some states have more cooperative partners than others. As we have seen in the various theories of cooperation, cooperation may entail risks and problems. Therefore, a state chooses to cooperate due to one of two reasons. The first reason is that it feels that it cannot accomplish its goals by using its own resources. Alternatively, a state cooperates—as the original definition suggests—because it can gain more from cooperation than by going it alone. The need factor describes a gap between what a state can accomplish via cooperation and what it can accomplish by following a unilateralist strategy. The wider the gap between what states can accomplish via cooperation and what they can accomplish on their own, the greater the need to cooperate, and consequently, the more partners they require.

In practice, the need for cooperation differs by issue area. In security affairs, the need for cooperation is a function of the gap between the capabilities of the focal state's strategic reference group and the capabilities of the focal state. A state's threat perception is a function of the size and characteristics of its actual or potential enemies. This is what Maoz (2010) called the focal state's strategic reference group (SRG). The SRG of a given state consists of its past enemies and the allies of these enemies. A state's enemies include (a) states with which the focal state had a MID over the past five years, or (b) a war over the past decade, and (c) its strategic rivals. When a state cannot meet the challenges posed by its SRG, it needs to pool resources with other states to ensure its survival. The size of the SRG was found to be a strong motivator of alliance formation (Maoz 2010, Ch. 5).

The need for trade cooperation (or the need to form PTAs) is a function of two principal factors: scarcity of some resources that are required for economic development and growth, and surplus production. A state may require resources for its economy such as raw materials, food, or certain technologies and cannot extract these resources internally. Thus, it needs to import these commodities from other providers outside its own borders. Second, specialization leads to efficient production. In such cases, the goods or services that a certain sector produces exceed the internal needs for such goods and services. Hence, producers need to sell these goods and services to other states. This creates an export-oriented economy. The import-related needs and the export-related needs are often embodied in the same economy. Thus, the greater the need for certain imported goods and services and the greater the surplus production of other goods, the stronger the need to trade.

The need for coordination is what drives institutional cooperation. Security institutions such as multilateral alliances require coordination among members, including common planning, joint maneuvers, and shared resources such as intelligence. These drive the formation of institutions that manage these coordinative activities. Likewise, multilateral trade agreements require mechanisms for the resolution of conflicts and disagreements and monitoring. Here too, institutional solutions are often the way of dealing with such needs. In security, economic, or institutional settings, increased interdependence creates a higher need for cooperation.

Attraction. The attraction element defines how states select partners for cooperation. Once a state has determined it cannot accomplish its goals on its own (or it cannot do so in an optimal manner), it enters a large market of potential partners. How does it choose its partners in this market?

A would-be partner is attractive to the extent that it can provide the focal state with what it needs from such cooperative ventures. Attraction is both a function of the domain in which cooperation is sought and of the theory we use to explain cooperation. In security affairs, attraction is defined in terms of common interests, that is, shared enemies (Gowa and Farber 1994, Mearsheimer 2001, Maoz 2010). Liberal scholars acknowledge that shared interests are an important component of mutual attraction. However, the overriding factor that determines attraction is similar political systems, in particular, joint democracy and economic compatibility (i.e., similar economic systems).

Constructivists consider attraction to be a function of convergent identity conception and a common value system. These traits may even create a need for cooperation when no material need is present. Shared values or identities between two societies determine how they view themselves, each other, and third parties. In this sense, constructivist conceptions of attraction encompass both realist and liberal conceptions of the same concept. Joint democracy or compatible economies may help define national identities. Consider the two overriding themes in US national rhetoric: democracy and capitalism. These themes shape the attitudes of Americans toward other nations. The same applies to many other states.

Prevention. This factor plays an important role in the calculus of security cooperation and, to a lesser degree, in economic cooperation processes. It has little or no impact on institutional cooperation. Prevention is an important factor in realist theories of cooperation, but it does not feature prominently in liberal and constructivist theories. The basic idea is that states choose to cooperate not only because they need each other or find each other attractive but also out of fear. For example, state A may choose to cooperate with state B because it fears that if it does not cooperate, B might forge cooperative ties with C, A's enemy. This is the underlying logic of neutrality pacts or nonaggression treaties. Such forms of cooperation reduce the probability that the would-be partner may join one's enemies if a conflict breaks out.

Prevention may also be a motive for some forms of trade cooperation. The evidence on alliance to trade spillover suggests that "trade follows the flag" (Keshk, Reuveny, and Pollins 2004, Vijayaraghavan et al. 2015). This means that given that the prevention motive is a powerful driver for security cooperation, it may also spill over into economic cooperation. The latter type of cooperation is used as an incentive to stay out of the relations between one's partner and its enemies. This kind of incentive may have been an important factor driving PTAs between the major powers and "third world" countries during the Cold War era.

Trust. As we have seen from the outset of this chapter, a key question for anyone considering a partner for cooperation is, "Can I trust that partner?" Trust derives from an assessment of the probability that the potential partner will honor the agreement underlying the cooperative venture. Trust is different from attraction. Attraction addresses the question "Can the partner give me what I need (or does the partner possess the qualities that can give me what I need)?" By contrast, trust addresses the question "*Will* the partner give me what I need when I need it?" The ability to trust a potential partner is a function of the partner's reliability. Reliability may be related to the partner's reputation of honoring agreements, the costs associated with the partner's compliance, and the partner's value system. The latter factor is an important aspect of assessment of the partner's reliability. Carrying out promises implies incurring some cost. In many instances promises—or even pledges cemented in formal treaties—may be cheap talk, especially if the pledging actor does not expect to be called upon to fulfill the promises.

In the movie *The Godfather*, there is a scene where a baker (Nazorine) requests a favor from Don Corleone (the Godfather) on behalf of his would-be son in-law Enzo. The Don promises to fulfill this request and tells Nazorine that sometime in the future he might request a return favor from the baker. It turns out that when Enzo returns the favor, the cost is potentially very high: he is to pretend to be a bodyguard confronting the Don's would-be assassins.

Taken together, these factors determine the onset, duration, and effectiveness of cooperation. Actors cooperate when they expect the benefits from cooperation to exceed those from unilateral pursuits. They choose partners for cooperation among those who are capable and willing to contribute to the collective good, and those who are trustworthy. Actors are also willing to select partners for cooperation even if such partners are not really attractive. This is done for preventive purposes, to derail the prospect of such partners cooperating with third parties, thereby preventing the focal actor from accomplishing its own goals. Finally, partner selection is strongly dependent on an assessment of the partner's reliability.

How does religion enter this picture? Religion plays a role in determining both the attractiveness of a potential partner for cooperation and the trust one can place in such a partner. We discuss the drivers of cooperation as these are seen by the key theories addressed in the present study.

3.1 Primordialist Cooperation

Religion serves as a normative guide to behavior; it contains a set of dos, don'ts, and values that cover a wide array of interpersonal interactions. As a social institution, virtually all religions provide fundamental principles that regulate social exchanges. Some religions, such as Islam, impose strict restrictions on economic transactions. The Sharia prohibits Muslims from providing loans that carry interest. For a long time, a similar custom was in place in Catholicism, especially in the Middle Ages. In many cases, religious adherence implies identification with an all-encompassing value system.

Cooperation requires trust, especially when no mechanisms or sanctions exist to enforce compliance. Under such circumstances, people are more likely to cooperate when they share the same values. In disputes over the interpretation of agreements, religious institutions, which are held in high esteem by the disputants, often serve as facilitators and arbitrators. The primordialist conception of religion and politics considers religious dissimilarity to be a source of suspicion, mistrust, and even outright animosity. By contrast, religious similarity engenders affinity. Such affinity becomes a source of attraction beyond the trust instilled by shared normative values. When people look for potential partners for cooperative ventures, religious affinities become an important source of attraction.

Both trust and affinity are crucial in areas of *costly cooperation*, such as international security, especially if the benefits from cooperation are not immediately attached to the costs paid to sustain it. This is the case in alliance politics. When a state signs an alliance, it may be forced to help its ally who is attacked by a third party. If it honors its alliance commitment, it pays sometimes a high cost for doing so. The benefit it derives from the alliance may come only if at some later date one's ally comes to one's aid when one is attacked. This conditionality—costs first, benefits (perhaps) later—is not unlike the Godfather's reliance on return favors. However, in the case of alliance politics, the threat of retribution that may secure compliance in Mafia politics is not very meaningful. Therefore, the element of trust is crucial.

Affinity due to shared religion tends to drive institutional cooperation in cultural and social affairs. Both the tangible costs of, and the tangible benefits from, such institutions are not very high, so the reason for their emergence and persistence is that they cement such affinities in symbolic contractual arrangements and associations. In contrast, the need for trust and the significance of value-based affinities are not principal determinants of economic cooperation. This is an area of mutual gains in which violation can be reciprocated. Both costs and benefits are tangible and in most cases can be reaped immediately. More important, in economic affairs differences, rather than similarities, may attract. Trade is more likely to take place between economies producing complementary products. Economies producing similar products are more likely to compete over the same markets.

3.2 Instrumentalism and Cooperation

According to primordialism, religious similarities attract because they entail shared identities and shared value systems. This applies to the perception of both leaders and publics. Instrumentalism, on the other hand, suggests that leaders use religious values selectively when they want to cooperate. The goal of leaders' invoking religious values and religious identity is to mobilize public support for cooperative ventures. This can happen only when societies are religiously homogeneous and when leaders can co-opt the religious leadership in support of their cooperative visions. Here, too, leaders are more likely to invoke religious factors when the costs of cooperation are high and when the benefits of cooperation are not immediately visible—as in the case of alliance ties. The need to manipulate religious values or symbols in order to ensure cooperation is less prevalent in economic transactions.

The instrumentalist perspective also suggests that leaders are more likely to manipulate religious values to garner support for cooperative ventures when they feel that their hold on power is tenuous, that is, under conditions of political instability, than when they are fairly confident of their political survival. Cooperative ventures like alliances are not only designed to increase national security but also may be designed to help maintain leaders in power. In such cases, the need to mobilize support for such ventures requires leaders to invoke religious symbols of shared values and shared belief systems. This is done not only to create an image that their country can trust its would-be ally but also as a diversionary tactic, drawing attention away from domestic difficulties and toward some foreign policy objective that can be obtained with the help of allies.

3.3 *The CoC Thesis and Cooperation*

The CoC thesis focuses mainly on intercultural conflict; nevertheless, Huntington (1993, 34) contends that states are more likely to "cooperate with and ally themselves with states with similar or common culture and are more often in conflict with countries of different culture." Although Huntington argues that the primary characteristic of a civilization is its religion, he portrays civilizations in rather broad brushstrokes; therefore, it is hardly a straightforward task to draw explicit inferences about the religion-cooperation linkage from the CoC thesis, itself. For a civilization to form, and for it to harvest some fundamental grievances toward another civilization to the point that it is willing to confront its enemy by force, its elements need to cooperate with each other. Intracivilizational alliances must form; trade deals among sectors of a given civilization must be struck so that resources would be available for such a fight; and institutions must be established to ensure coordination. The latter is consistent with Huntington's claim that increased economic regionalization has emerged from and been reinforced by heightened civilization consciousness

The upshot is that from the perspective of the CoC thesis, we need to expect high intracivilizational cooperation across issue areas, and low intercivilizational cooperation, also across the board. Here, too, the expectation of the CoC thesis is that such intracivilizational cooperation is primarily a post–Cold War phenomenon.

3.4 *The Integrative Theory of Religion and World Politics*

As we pointed out in chapter 3, our theory emphasizes the conditions under which political elites find themselves as the mechanisms by which religious factors may be invoked to motivate international action. Political elites can turn on or off the "religion switch" to mobilize support for their policies, their ability to do so depends on the structure of the society and the relationship among those actors toward which a given action is contemplated. We discuss the implications of this idea as it relates to international cooperation.

Leaders in states characterized by high levels of political stability may seek strategies to reduce the risk of being removed from office. As we have seen in the previous chapter, one approach is to apply diversionary tactics by finding external scapegoats. The goal of diversionary policies is to direct the attention and energy of the coalition that sustains them in power to an external enemy. However, there are other strategies that leaders may use to increase their chances of political survival. Some of them involve finding cooperative ventures. These ventures may provide benefits that improve the standard of living of the general population, allowing them to reshuffle the winning coalition.

Chow and Kono (2017) argue that authoritarian leaders who ascend to power via extralegal methods (that is, via a coup or revolution) are politically vulnerable and have a tendency to placate their constituencies by reducing tariffs on food products, thus increasing food imports. Baccini and Chow (2018) show that authoritarian leaders who face a high coup risk are more likely to sign PTAs than political leaders who acquire their position via legal means. These ideas cover economic policy.

Political leaders who are at risk of losing their job can employ cooperative security strategies to increase external support for their tenure. Seeking allies who can extend support for the focal leader in conflictual ventures is directly related to the diversionary approach we discussed in the previous chapter. Political leaders who use conflict as a diversionary strategy need to succeed in such risky ventures. If they engage in conflict and end up on the losing side, their job insecurity is bound to increase even more (Bueno de Mesquita et al. 1992). One way of increasing the chance of success in external adventures involves getting outside help in the form of alliances. However, as we noted, alliances are a risky and potentially costly form of cooperation. One's ally may drag a state into an unwanted war before the focal state drags the ally into a war of its own making. Therefore, trust is an important factor that determines which allies to seek. Moreover, mobilizing public support for alliance formation suggests that the leader must find allies that are "attractive" and "trustworthy." This suggests that states would seek religiously similar allies, because this similarity helps mobilize public support for the alliance and increases the probability that the ally will fulfill its obligations when necessary.

The relations between religious and political institutions also come into play in such cases. Religious leaders and/or religious institutions may or may not enter this equation. When religious and political institutions are closely aligned, political leaders may use religious organizations and religious leaders to mobilize support for their venture. For example, when Iran negotiated a nuclear deal with six powers (including the "hated" United States), there was a great deal of internal opposition from conservative circles associated with the Revolutionary Guard (as well as conservative circles in the United States). Once the deal was reached, President Hassan Rouhani turned to the supreme leader and Muslim cleric Ali Khamenei for his support. Khamenei's support of the nuclear deal allowed this agreement to be signed and implemented (Tabatabai 2017).

This leads to the following hypotheses regarding religion and international cooperation:

H1. Religious similarity increases the probability of security cooperation.
H2. Religious similarity increases the probability and magnitude of institutional cooperation.
H3. Religious similarity does not have a significant effect on economic cooperation.

A more refined expectation covers the interaction between political stability and religious similarity and its effect on international cooperation, specifically:

H4. Political instability increases the effect of religious similarity on international cooperation.
H5. States that have close ties between religious and political institutions are more likely to cooperate with religiously similar states.

These hypotheses cover the expectations of the primordialist, institutionalist, and integrative perspectives on religion and cooperation. To address the expectations of the CoC thesis, we hypothesize the following:

H6. The relationship between religious similarity and international cooperation is higher during the post–Cold War era than during the Cold War era.

The following hypothesis addresses the expectations derived from the constructivist perspective.

H7. New states are more likely to cooperate with religiously similar states than mature states.

3.5 Religion and Cooperative International Communities

International cooperation has emergent properties. Cooperative interactions are not strictly dyadic; they cumulate and transform into multilateral cooperative structures. We call these structures cooperative communities. Since religious similarity is expected to affect the behavior of individual states, dyads, and to determine levels of regional cooperation, we suggest that religious factors have similar emergent effects. Specifically, religious factors are expected to affect the structure of cooperative security and institutional communities, but not the structure of economic communities.

Before we discuss why this is the case, we need to explain the concept of cooperative communities. Cooperative communities are clusters of states that are characterized by high levels of cooperative ties among members. These groups may emerge due to a formal agreement among members, such as a collective security treaty (e.g., NATO, the Warsaw Pact, or the Arab League). More often, however, they emerge endogenously—due to the density of cooperative ties among members but without a formal agreement. All the major paradigms discuss cooperative endogenous groups. The realist paradigm, overwhemingly, focuses on cooperative security structures. The central concepts that offer a close equivalence to the notion of endogenous cooperative groups in the liberal paradigm are the concepts of international regimes and international institutions. The concept of international regimes is also part of the realist vocabulary, but it is restricted to security cooperation (Krasner 1982, Jervis 1982). According to liberal scholars, international regimes and international institutions cover both formal arrangements and implicit ones. These emergent structures apply to security affairs, economic affairs, and other domains, for example, administration, environment, culture, and so forth. In the constructivist paradigm, the central concept is that of communities (Wendt 1999,

Adler and Barnett 1998). This concept has several versions (including "epistemic" communities; Adler and Hass 1992, Adler 2005), but it broadly refers to a collection of units (states in our case)[11] that assign some shared meaning to each other and to out-groups. Members of such communities also have a set of common norms and engage in high levels of cooperative behavior within the community compared to cross-community cooperation. In sum, the factors that define the emergence of endogenous cooperative groups differ across paradigms. Each paradigm identifies one or more key factors that affect the formation of such groups. Table 6.1 lists the causal mechanisms that drive the formation and persistence of cooperative communities.

We suggest that religious similarity of societies helps cement trust and creates natural attraction tendencies among states in such issue areas where the risk of fulfilling obligations in a multilateral context is high. This implies that we can extend the monadic and dyadic arguments about religion and cooperation to the community level. Specifically,

> H9. Security cooperation communities and institutional communities tend to be religiously cohesive; in contrast, economic communities tend to be religiously diverse.

What we mean by religious cohesion is that the religious similarity between members of a given community is significantly higher than the religious similarity between members of that community and nonmembers. Likewise, religious diversity of a given community implies that the degree of within-community religious similarity is little different than the degree of religious similarity between community members and nonmembers.

4. Research Design

In this chapter, too, we provide an intuitive and nontechnical description of our research strategy. Much of this strategy resembles the design of the research in the previous chapter. Therefore, we focus on the novel aspects of the current chapter. A more detailed technical discussion of the key issues in the research design appears in the appendix that accompanies this chapter.

Table 6.1 Paradigms' explanations of the emergence of endogenous cooperative groups

Paradigm	Variable	Causal Mechanism	Outcome
Realism	Shared common enemies	Balancing against common threats	Collective security communities, security regimes
Liberalism	Joint democracy	Common contractual norms induce trust	Collective security communities, trading blocks, collective PTAs, Institutional communities, international regimes
	Spillover effects	Beneficial experience in one cooperative domain generates shared interests, interdependence, and mutual trust	
Constructivism	Common culture	Shared identities induce shared values and norms	Collective security communities, trading blocks, collective PTAs, institutional communities
	Spillover effects	Beneficial experience generates shared interests and ideational convergence	
	Epistemic communities	Cross-national expert groups that share ideas and norms induce policy cooperation	

4.1 Units of Analysis

We follow the same levels of analysis as in the chapter on religion and international conflict: specifically, the nation-year and nation-history, the dyad-year and dyad-history, and the region-year levels. For brevity, we report the results of the nation-year, dyad-year, and region-year analyses. The more extensive results (including nation-history and dyad-history levels of analysis) are reported on the book's website. The discussion of the results covers those latter analyses as well. However, a key innovation of this chapter is the examination of a new level of analysis: cooperative communities. The concept of "communities" is derived from network analysis. All of the cooperative structures we examine here can be studied with the tools of network analysis.

A brief definition of a network is instructive at this point. A network is a set of units—states in our case—and a rule that defines the presence, the direction, and/or the magnitude of a tie between any pair of units (Maoz 2010: 11). Thus, for alliance networks a tie exists between two states if they have any alliance (in some cases we restrict ties to defense pacts only). For trade networks, we recognize a tie between states if the level of trade between these states exceeds 0.1 percent of their respective GDPs. The presence of a PTA between two states indicates a tie in the PTA network. In the IGO network we observe a tie between states when the proportion of overlapping IGO membership between these states exceeds the average proportion of IGO membership overlaps for all states at a given year.[12]

A cooperative network reflects the strength of cooperative ties between two states across the three cooperative dimensions: security, economics, and institutions. Once these networks are defined, we can identify communities. The general concept of "community" in network analysis refers to a subset of the units that (a) have a high density of ties among them and (b) a low number of ties between members of a community and nonmembers. There are a number of methods that enable community detection—the partition of the network into a set of groups, based on the ties between members. The community detection algorithms seek to maximize a statistic called the modularity coefficient (Newman and Girvan 2004), which measures the degree to which communities have the following characteristics:

1. Maximal density of ties between states belonging to the same community: states that share community membership are likely to have direct ties (or tend to be connected via short paths) with each other.
2. Minimal density of ties between states belonging to different communities: states that belong to different communities are unlikely to have direct ties (or tend to be connected by long paths) with each other.
3. Maximal difference between the actual community structure and chance.

Substantively, cooperative communities are emergent structures of highly dense cooperative interaction between state members, and highly sparse interactions between states belonging to different communities. Here we analyze the structure of such communities.

4.2 Measures of Key Variables

In the previous chapter, we offered definitions for many of the independent and control variables used in the empirical analyses. We do not repeat those here. Instead we focus on (a) the definition of the key cooperation variables, and (b) additional variables not discussed before.

Security cooperation. In the previous chapter we defined security cooperation in terms of the number of alliances of a given state (at the monadic level), the presence or absence of an alliance (at the dyadic level), and the average number of alliance commitments per state (at the regional level). Here we add a new variable that incorporates both the number of alliance commitments of a state/dyad and the level of these commitments. The *relative commitment* variable (Maoz 2010, 42) is a ratio of the weighted alliance commitment score between two states to the largest possible level of commitment of any two states. The appendix provides a more detailed discussion of this variable. At the region-year level, we define this as the number of within-region alliances divided by the number of within-region dyads.

Economic cooperation. We define economic cooperation by two variables: *relative trade* and *number of trading partners*. Relative trade is defined as the total amount of trade (imports + exports) divided by the state's GDP. The number of trading partners is the number of states with which the focal state trades more than one-tenth of 1 percent of its GDP. At the dyadic level, this variable is defined as *log trade*: the (logged) total amount of goods and services exchanged between two countries. At the regional level, we define this as the average level of *relative trade* of states in a given region. At the region-year level, economic cooperation is defined as the average dollar amount of trade between regional dyads.

Preferential trade agreements. At the nation level, we use a count of the number of PTAs involving the focal state. At the dyadic level, we use a binary variable assigned a score of one if dyad members had at least one PTA between them, and zero otherwise. At the regional level, we average the number of PTAs per state member. We again define this as the ratio of within-region PTA dyads to the number of regional dyads.

Institutional cooperation. At the nation level, we measure institutional cooperation as the number of IGO memberships of the focal state. At the dyadic level, we employ Maoz's (2010) index of relative IGO membership score defined as a ratio of the number of shared IGO memberships between dyad members to the number of IGO memberships of the focal state. At the regional level, institutional cooperation is the average number of IGO memberships of states in the region.

Combined cooperation. We combine the security, economic, and institutional cooperation variables as follows. At the national level, we first generate a rank order for each of the cooperation variables for every year, such that the most cooperative state (e.g., the state with the most allies, the state with the largest share of trade to GDP) gets the highest number and the least-cooperative state (e.g., the state with the fewest allies, the state with the least trade per GDP) gets the lowest rank.[13] Second, we generate a relative rank by dividing the state's rank by the number of states in the global system for that year. This gives us a relative rank score on each of the cooperative dimensions (e.g., a state gets a security cooperation rank score, an economic cooperation rank score, etc.). It allows us to generate a cooperative ranking of states that takes into account changes in the number of states in the system over time. Third, we average the cooperation rank scores for each state across all the cooperative variables. This gives us a *combined cooperation score*.

At the dyadic level, we assign each dyad a score of one for alliances if it had an alliance. We assign it a score of one if its level of trade (measured by log trade dollars of exports and imports exchanged by the members of the dyad) exceeded the average dyad trade score for this year. We assign the dyad a score of one if it had a PTA in a given year. Finally, we assign the dyad a score of one if its level of shared IGO membership exceeded the mean level of shared IGO membership for that year. We then average across the four binary cooperation scores. Thus, a dyad that had a high level of alliance commitment, a high degree of trade, a PTA, and a high level of joint IGO membership receives a score of one, and so forth. Note that we did not assign weights to different areas of cooperation, although it would make sense to assign to alliance and/or trade levels a higher weight than joint IGO membership. When we do that, results do not change substantially. At the region-year level, we average across the combined cooperative scores of the states making up a given region.

Religious Cohesion of Cooperative Communities. The appendix provides a detailed methodological discussion of the community detection algorithm and the derivation of the cohesion score. Here we discuss the general intuition of this method. First, for each cooperation variable, we use a known algorithm (Leicht and Newman 2008) to detect communities. We improve on this algorithm by allowing states to overlap over multiple communities. This method is discussed in Maoz (2017, Appendix). We then partition the original adjacency matrix (for example, the one that indicates whether states have an alliance), into a community-overlap matrix. In this matrix, communities are aligned along the main diagonal of the matrix, and off-diagonal blocs represent between-community membership. We insert into the community overlap matrix the religious similarity scores. So each cell in that matrix reflects the degree of religious similarity between the row state and the column state.

At this point, we calculate the cohesion coefficient. This coefficient reflects the degree to which the within-community religious similarity is different (higher or lower) than the between-community religious similarity. Specifically, we measure the average within-community religious similarity and subtract from it the between-community religious similarity. The cohesion coefficient varies between 1 (when the religious similarity of all dyads within a given community is 1, and the religious similarity between community members and nonmembers is zero) to -1 (when the opposite holds—that is, when the religious similarity between dyads within communities is zero and the religious similarity between members of one community and noncommunity members is 1). We then run a significance test based on the within- and between-community variances. This test allows us to assess the probability of getting a specific cohesion coefficient by chance alone. Again, a detailed discussion of this procedure is given in the appendix and in Maoz (2017).

4.3. Estimation

As in the previous chapter, we run bootstrapped estimations of the nation-year and dyad-year models, in order to (a) account for stationarity biases in measures of religion (as well as stationarity biases in long-term cooperative ties), (b) reduce the sample size to ensure that inferences are not biased by excessively large N's,[14] and (c) test for the robustness of the results. For the nation history and dyad history, we run simple OLS models. Finally, for the region year we run binary or continuous (fixed-effects) time series cross-sectional regressions. Note that for the nation year and dyad year we include spatial controls (e.g., two stars and three stars) as discussed in the previous chapter.

5. Results

5.1 Nation-Level Analyses

We begin our discussion of the results with the nation-year analyses (Table 6.2). We focus on the effect of religious factors on cooperative

Table 6.2 Effects of determinants of monadic (nation-year) international cooperation, 1945–2010

	No. Allies	Log Trade	No. PTAs	IGOs	Combined Cooperation
Religious Similarity State-PRIE	0.222**	0.022	-0.361**	0.029	0.363**
	(0.018)	(0.38)	(0.123)	(0.028)	(0.044)
Religious Homogeneity					
Medium	0.023**	-0.12*	-0.189*	-0.034	0.01
	(0.005)	(0.054)	(0.089)	(0.024)	(0.013)
High	0.043**	-0.185**	-0.309**	0.048	0.08**
	(0.005)	(0.052)	(0.084)	(0.024)	(0.011)
Religion-State Relations					
Some relation	0.01	0.217**	-0.295**	-0.064**	0.029**
	(0.005)	(0.055)	(0.084)	(0.022)	(0.011)
Cohabitation	0.002	0.63**	-0.038	-0.046	0.047**
	(0.007)	(0.074)	(0.113)	(0.035)	(0.013)
Pct. Non-religious	-0.046**	1.753**	0.546**	0.638**	0.171**
	(0.019)	(0.169)	(0.212)	(0.082)	(0.028)
Coup Risk	0.015	-0.372*	0.089	0.024	-0.009
	(0.009)	(0.152)	(-0.309)	(0.048)	(0.02)
Religious Similarity State-PRIE#Coup Risk	-0.012	0.147	-1.391*	0.031	-0.032
	(0.027)	(0.38)	(0.566)	(0.163)	(0.056)
Constant	-0.074**	1.685**	0.793**	2.797**	0.298**
	(0.009)	(0.177)	(0.185)	(0.101)	(0.017)
N	7,444	7,444	7,443	7,456	7,479
F			385.99	1,385.13	
Chi-Square	877.13	3,247.14			655.74
R-Squared	0.374	0.652	0.029	0.092	0.338

Notes: All analyses are bootstrapped models based on a sample of $n = 1,500$ out of roughly 10,000 nation-year observations and 300 replications.
Control variables omitted to preserve space. Full tabular results are provided in the book's website.
* $p < 0.05$; ** $p < 0.01$

behavior. The first important takeaway from these analyses is that the effect of religious characteristics of states on cooperation is domain specific. As noted above, most analyses of the relationship between religion and international cooperation have not differentiated among separate domains of cooperation. We find that religious homogeneity has a positive effect on security, institutional, and combined cooperation. However, it has a negative effect on trade and on PTA membership. Second, we find that high levels of religious similarity between the focal state and its PRIE increase the number of alliances and the level of commitment these alliances entail.

Religious similarity of state-PRIE also affects the combined cooperative status of states. However, religious similarity between the focal state and its PRIE has little or no effect on its trade ties and reduces the number of its PTAs. Third, as the percentage of Christians and/or Muslims in a country increases, its number of alliances, and its overall cooperative rank, also increases. By contrast, we do not find significant cooperative tendencies in countries dominated by other religious groups.

Finally, secularism—measured by the size of the non-religious population in states—has a negative impact on security cooperation; however, it positively affects states' level of economic and institutional cooperation. Secularism also has a positive effect on the overall cooperative rank of a state. It appears that while secularism may encourage a range of international cooperation, it does not supersede the impact of religious similarity when it comes to the important domain of security cooperation.

In the previous chapter we found that regime instability mediated between religious factors and international conflict. By contrast, we find that regime stability or instability does not have a meaningful effect on international cooperation at the national level of analysis. Figure 6.1 highlights some of the results on the interaction effect between political stability or religious homogeneity, on the one hand, and religious similarity, on the other, on various measures of cooperation. First, there is no significant interaction effect between political instability—measured as coup risk—and religious similarity state-PRIE on cooperation. In general, religious similarity between the focal state and its PRIE has a positive effect on security cooperation and overall cooperation. However, this effect is not different for politically unstable states compared to stable ones (Figures 6.1.1 and 6.1.4). By contrast, politically stable states tend to reduce their degree of trade as the level of religious similarity between the focal state and its PRIE increases (Figures 6.1.3). Second, we do find that highly religiously homogeneous states facing high risk of regime transition tend to form more security alliances than stable or low-risk states (Figure 6.1.2).[15]

Figure 6.2 assesses the hypotheses derived from the CoC thesis and from the constructivist approach with respect to national cooperation. Figure 6.2.1 clearly illustrates that the relationship between religious similarity between the focal state and its PRIE and cooperation was significantly more pronounced during the Cold War era than during the post–Cold War era. This casts doubt on the CoC's argument. The same applies to the

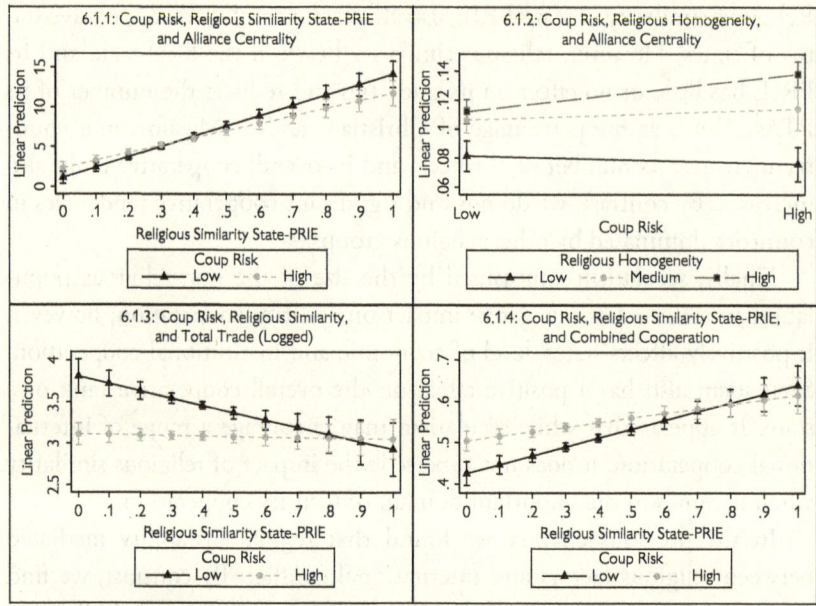

Fig. 6.1. Interaction effects on measures of cooperation, nation-year unit of analysis
Note: Solid lines indicate statistically significant relations; nonsignificant relations are marked by dashed lines. Bars in the figure are 95 percent confidence intervals.

Significant differences between the effects of different values of the intervening variable (e.g., state age) exist when the confidence intervals associated with one level (e.g., mature) do not overlap with the confidence intervals associated with another level (e.g., new).

constructivist expectation that religious similarity will have a stronger effect on cooperation when states are "young" than when they are more mature. Figure 6.2.2 suggests that the opposite is, in fact, the case: religious similarity has a greater effect on the combined cooperative rank of more mature states than on that of new states.

The results of the nation-history level of analysis (reported in the book's website) largely mirror those of the nation-year level. Specifically, religious similarity between the focal state and its PRIE affected the tendency of the former to form and maintain allies, but not its level of trade or IGO membership. Religious homogeneity and religion-state relations do not have a significant effect on any of the issue areas of cooperation examined herein. The interaction between coup risk and religious similarity state-PRIE also did not have a meaningful effect on different areas of international

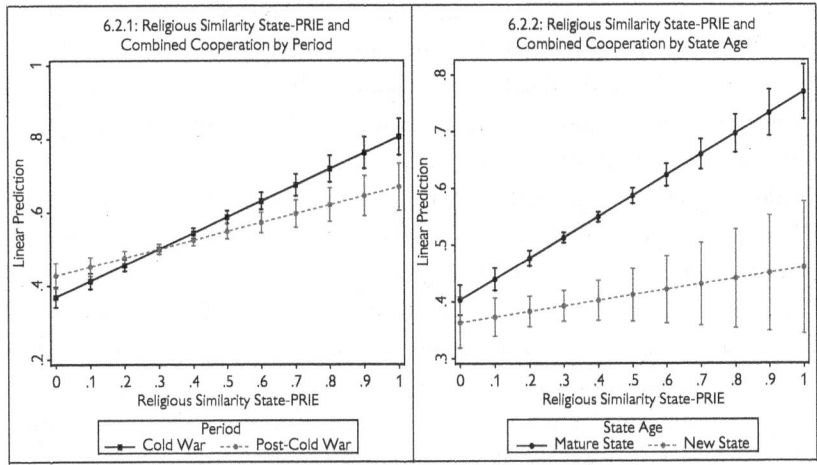

Fig. 6.2. Effects of political instability, religious similarity state-PRIE by period and state age

cooperation. By contrast, secularism appears to have significant impact on the state's history of cooperation. This applies to all cooperative dimensions except alliances, as well as to the average cooperative rank of the state over its history. This leads us to the dyadic analyses.

5.2 Dyadic Analyses

The dyad-year analyses are given in Table 6.3. There are several key results in these analyses. First, dyadic religious similarity has a strong effect on security cooperation, PTAs, joint IGO membership, and combined cooperation. This effect is consistent and robust across issue areas. However, religious similarity has a negative impact on the degree of dyadic trade. These results again provide support to H1 and H2 above. Specifically, dyads that are composed of religiously similar states are more likely to form alliances, share IGO membership, and have a generally higher cooperative profile than dyads made up of religiously different states.

Second, religious homogeneity has a negative effect on trade ties, PTA relations, and IGO membership, and a mixed effect on combined cooperation levels. This means that if both members of the dyad are made up of highly homogeneous states, they are less likely to trade than if one or both members of the dyads were religiously diverse. Likewise, the effects of religion-state relations are inconsistent across indices of dyadic cooperation. Generally speaking, dyads made up of members who have a moderate or high degree of religion-state coordination tend to trade less, have fewer PTAs, and are generally less likely to cooperate than dyads whose members practice separation of religion from politics.

Third, we find that secularism in the dyad—that is, dyads composed of states with a higher level of non-religious people—has a consistent effect on dyadic cooperation. Relatively secular dyads are more likely to form alliances, trade, and have a higher probability of forming and maintaining PTAs; however, they are less likely to share IGO membership. Nevertheless, such dyads are more likely to have a higher cooperative profile.

We present the results of the interaction effects, as well as tests of the hypotheses derived from the CoC thesis and the constructivist perspective in Figure 6.3. The results of these analyses suggest that religious similarity has a strong effect on dyads made up of states facing a low level of political instability as well as on dyads composed of states facing high levels of political instability. However, dyads composed of the latter type of states—those facing high coup risks—are more inclined to cooperate the more religiously similar they are.

As was the case with the nation-level analyses, we find that the effect of religious similarity on cooperation was more pronounced during the Cold War era than during the post–Cold War era. This provides additional evidence contradicting the expectation of the CoC thesis. Likewise, we find that the level of cooperation of dyads composed of "mature" states is more strongly affected by religious similarity than dyads composed of one or both "new" member states. This too runs against the expectation of the constructivist perspective. Common identity seems to run deep even after states become more experienced members of the club of nations. In fact, the latter is more consistent with an early argument (Maoz 1989) that the behavior of newer states as they join the "club of nations" is more a function of their provenance as "revolutionary" or "evolutionary" states, and that regardless of either process, their international behavior is likely to regress to the mean of that of more mature states. Thus, given the general relationship between religious similarity and international cooperation, in general, it is

Table 6.3 Effects of religions factors on national cooperation—dyadic analysis

	Alliance	Trade	PTA	IGO	Combined Cooperation
Religious Similarity	2.353**	-0.167**	0.831**	0.037**	0.103**
	(0.096)	(0.053)	(0.105)	(0.005)	(0.006)
Religious Homogeneity					
Medium	-0.045	-0.08**	-0.629**	-0.017**	-0.024**
	(0.051)	(0.025)	(0.051)	(0.003)	(0.003)
High	0.082	-0.203**	-0.712**	0.031**	-0.018**
	(0.051)	(0.023)	(0.056)	(0.003)	(0.003)
Religion-State Relations					
Some Relation	-0.052	-0.056*	-0.602**	0.011**	-0.028**
	(0.045)	(0.025)	(0.046)	(0.002)	(0.003)
Cohabitation	-0.067	0.274**	-0.103	-0.092**	0.012**
	(0.056)	(0.032)	(0.054)	(0.003)	(0.004)
Secularism in Dyad	4.498**	9.164**	0.538*	-0.147**	0.591**
	(0.182)	(0.160)	(0.248)	(0.022)	(0.044)
Coup Risk	0.299**	-0.61**	0.63**	0.061**	-0.024**
	(0.078)	(0.032)	(0.08)	(0.003)	(0.002)
Coup risk#Religious Similarity	0.132	0.051	-0.643**	0.006	
	(0.116)	(0.066)	(0.128)	(0.007)	
Relig-State Relations#Religious Similarity					
Some Relation					0.088**
					(0.008)
Co-Habitation					0.094**
					(0.01)
Constant	-7.755**	2.211**	-3.144**	0.137**	0.534**
	(0.213)	(0.105)	(0.15)	(0.01)	(0.01)
N	533.393	539.420	445.442	539,420	508,816
chi2/F-Statistic	7,628.01	12,195.18	5,575.79	57,543.62	8,867.89
r2	0.464	0.259	0.272	0.250	0.143

Note: All analyses are bootstrapped models with sample size of 15,000 observations and 300 replications.

less surprising—though contradictory to a constructivist argument—that mature states reflect this status quo bias more than newer states.

Another way of viewing the latter finding is that according to constructivism, the newly independent state should start off relying on cultural factors more than on material factors in determining their partners for international

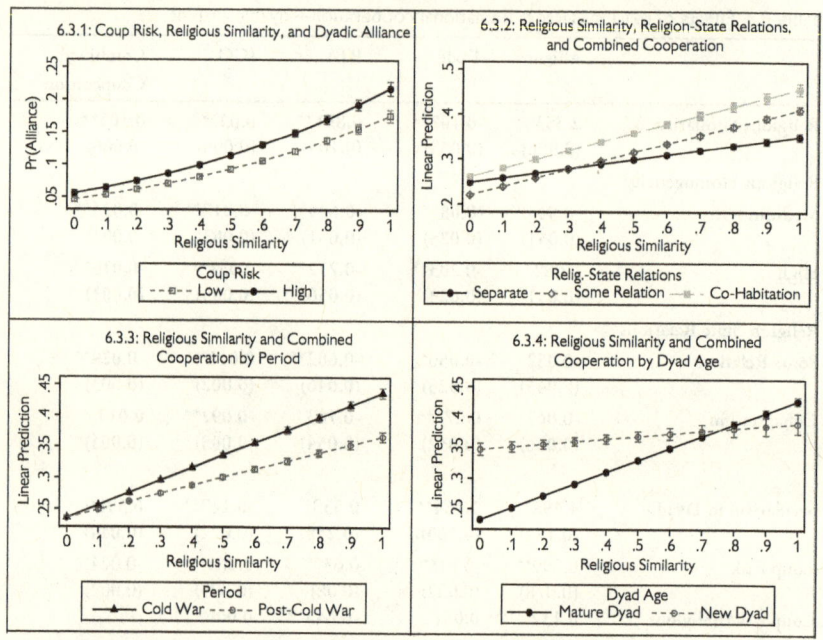

Fig. 6.3. Interaction effects of intervening variables and dyadic cooperation

cooperation; but actually since most of the world's states emerged from colonialism into the bipolar ideological standoff of the Cold War, there was a historical and contemporary bias toward either supporting the former colonial power or opposing it.[16] To a large extent, this was captured in Maoz's (1996) evolutionary versus revolutionary framework, but one can add to this another layer concerning the international orientation of the newly formed states. States that emerged through an evolutionary process usually were accommodating to the metropolitan power, which in this context was either a direct member of, or allied with, the international status quo powers (i.e., the United Kingdom, France, or NATO allies Portugal, Belgium). If, however, these new states emerged following a revolutionary anticolonial struggle, they tended to establish a politico-military leaning toward the major power opponents of their colonial masters, namely, the USSR and China (and their satellites).

The implications for the study of religion and conflict/cooperation is that given that the Western states were more oriented toward Christianity and the Eastern states toward atheism, maturation, in this scenario, would be from identities influenced by the relatively weaker newly independent state's politico-military alignments toward more cultural ones as the states matured and became stronger and began to articulate and promote their more self-determined orientations in the global system as they advanced from the conditions of their birth (i.e., their early independence). Thus, maturation in this postcolonial process is more likely to be away from initial politico-military orientations in considering international cooperation partners and toward more cultural ones as the state matures: the opposite of what constructivists would expect from extant states (i.e., those that had been independent for some time prior to the postwar era), but consistent with our findings that more mature states that are religiously similar are more likely to cooperate.

5.3 Regional Analyses

Our final set of "conventional" analyses centers on the region-year level. Table 6.4 displays the results of the analyses at that level.

The regional results resemble the dyadic and monadic results. Regional religious similarity increases regional security cooperation and combined cooperation, but it does not affect regional trade or regional institutional cooperation. We also find a similar effect of regional secularism on cooperation. Specifically, regions composed of states with a higher proportion of atheists, agnostics, or non-religious populations tend to have a higher level of security cooperation and overall cooperation than regions composed of highly religious member states.

Regional religious homogeneity seems to have unstable and contradictory effects on different areas of cooperation. The same can be said for the average structure of relations between religious and political institutions within regions. However, this variable seems to have a positive effect on security cooperation and on combined cooperation, but it has a negative impact on institutional cooperation. Figure 6.4 shows some of the interactions that are suggested by various hypotheses in a regional context.

Figure 6.4 suggests that regional religious similarity has positive effects on regional cooperation and this applies both to low-coup-risk regions and high-coup-risk regions. Interestingly, the effect of religious similarity on regional security cooperation is significantly higher in regions marked by close ties between religious and political institutions (e.g., the Middle East, Asia), suggesting that the co-habitation of religion and politics domestically in these states finds its corollary in the security sphere as religious similarity

Table 6.4 Effects of religious characteristics on regional cooperation

	Alliance	Trade	PTA	IGO	Combined Cooperation
Avg. Religious Similarity	0.706**	-2.253	55.824**	-0.11	0.629**
	(0.172)	(1.528)	(14.517)	(0.374)	(0.099)
Religious Homogeneity					
Moderate	0.055**	-0.019	-2.422	-0.208**	-0.008
	(0.02)	(0.172)	(1.628)	(0.04)	(0.011)
High	0.029	-0.522*	-4.758*	-0.258**	-0.048**
	(0.024)	(0.209)	(1.996)	(0.049)	(0.013)
Religion-State Relations					
Some Relations	0.053**	-0.117	1.81	-0.094**	0.013
	(0.014)	(0.121)	(1.149)	(0.029)	(0.008)
Cohabitation	0.078**	0.055	2.878	-0.152**	0.028**
	(0.019)	(0.166)	(1.574)	(0.04)	(0.011)
Coup Risk	0.132**	-0.712**	-2.42	-0.122	-0.019
	(0.029)	(0.257)	(2.466)	(0.063)	(0.017)
Coup Risk#Religious Similarity	-0.17**	0.112	-0.868	0.136	-0.05
	(0.044)	(0.393)	(3.723)	(0.096)	(0.026)
Secularism	1.970**	6.543	1.645	1.360	1.880**
	(0.601)	(4.821)	(0.932)	(1.288)	(0.296)
Constant	-1.244**	3.544*	69.702**	0.446	0.954**
	(0.171)	(1.6)	(15.278)	(0.393)	(0.098)
N	315	315	315	315	315
F-Statistic	17.901	30.652	30.524	34.458	21.927
R-Squared	0.419	0.552	0.572	0.581	0.422

Notes: Control variables omitted to conserve space. Full results are given in the book's appendix.
* $p < 0.05$ ** $p < 0.01$

breeds regional security cooperation; however, this does not extend to the effects of religious similarity on economic and institutional cooperation.

Examining the CoC expectation that regional cooperation within religiously similar regions would be higher in the post–Cold War than in the Cold War era, we find that just the opposite holds. The effect of religious similarity on cooperation was significantly higher during the Cold War era than in the post–Cold War era. Likewise, the hypothesis derived from the constructivist perspective suggesting that regions composed of "new" states (e.g., Africa, the Middle East, Asia) would engender more cooperation than regions composed of mature states (e.g., the Western Hemisphere, Europe) is also not supported. The effect of religious similarity on cooperation is higher in more established regions than in the newer regions.

5.4 Cooperative International Communities

The final and most original aspect of our analysis of the effect of religion on international cooperation centers on cooperative international communities. As noted in the research design, cooperative international communities are emergent structures that reflect clusters of states marked by high density of within-community cooperation and sparse cooperative ties between states belonging to different communities. Rather than characterize security communities such as NATO or the Association of Southeast Asian Nations (ASEAN) by some exogenously defined agreement, we allow the network of relations to determine the community structure of cooperative networks. Figure 6.5 shows the religious cohesion levels of various cooperative communities. Religious cohesion is defined as the difference between the average religious similarity within communities and the average religious similarity between communities.

The results of the community-cohesion analyses provide evidence that security community structure is significantly affected by the religious composition of members. Note that the modularity coefficient—an index of the "quality" of the partition of the security cooperation network into

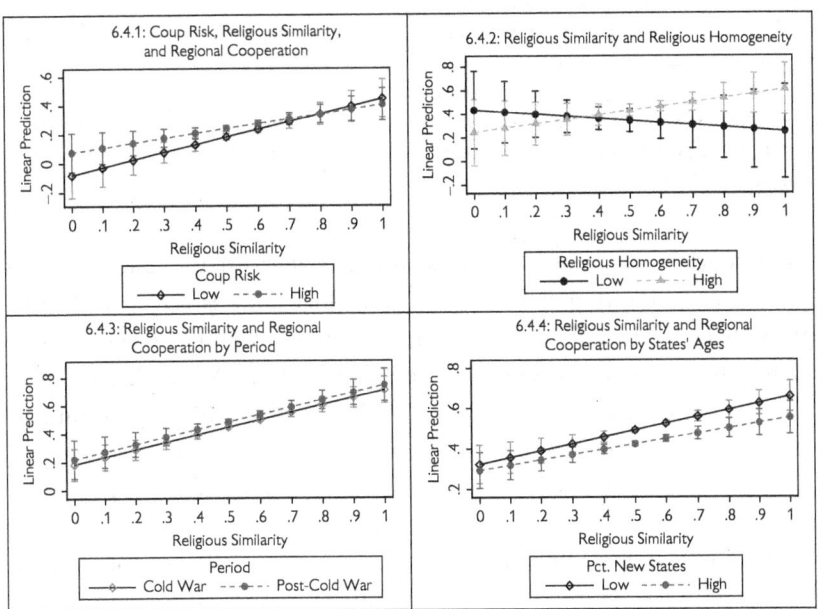

Fig. 6.4. Effects of intervening variables on regional cooperation

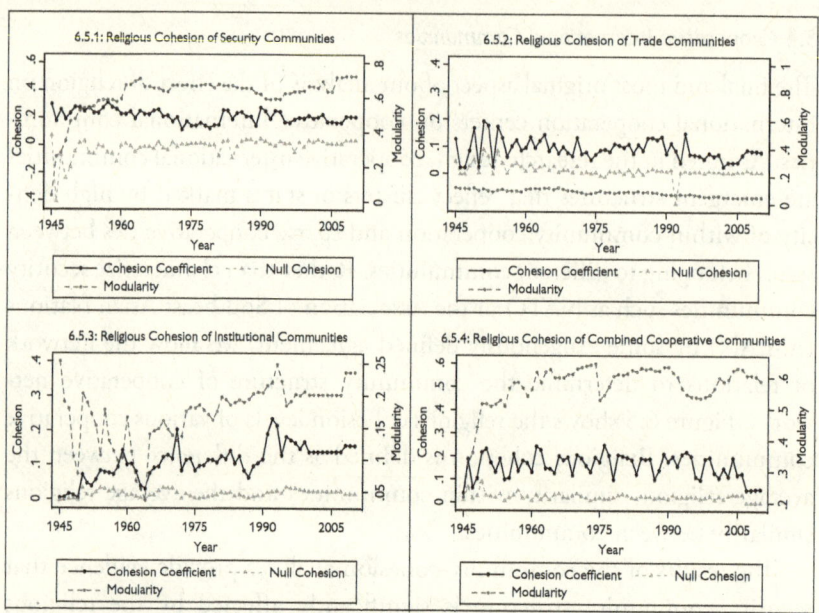

Fig. 6.5. Religious similarity and cooperative communities, 1945–2010

Note: The modularity coefficient provides an assessment of the "quality" of community structures. Specifically, it provides a difference between the actual community structure, and the community structure that would have been obtained by chance. The higher the modularity, the more reliable the community structure detected by the algorithm. The cohesion coefficient measures the extent to which within-community religious similarity is different (higher > 0, lower < 0) than between-community religious similarity. The null coefficient provides an assessment of the cohesion coefficient that would have been obtained by chance. The higher the difference between the actual cohesion coefficient and the null coefficient, the higher the impact of religious similarity on community formation.

communities—is quite high. This indicates that (a) the assignment of security community membership to individual states is very reliable and, given that, (b) the religious cohesion of such communities is significantly higher than what we would expect by chance alone. What that means is that security communities are marked by a high degree of religious similarity between members of such communities. At the same time, the degree of religious similarity between states belonging to one security community and states associated with another security community is relatively low.

The same applies, albeit to a lesser extent, to the religious composition of institutional communities and combined cooperation communities.

However, the modularity coefficient of economic and institutional communities is quite low, suggesting that inferences about community cohesion in these areas of international cooperation are not very reliable. Hence, we cannot make any strong inferences about the religious cohesion of economic, institutional, or combined cooperative communities.

The effect of religious cohesion on security communities is an interesting and important result; it also corroborates the previous findings suggesting that religious similarity has a significant impact on alliance formation and persistence. The results on the religious characteristics of economic and institutional communities seem to suggest that religious factors have played a very minor role in determining membership in such communities and their evolution over time.

6. Conclusion

This is one of the first, certainly the most general, forays into the relations between religion and various issue areas of cooperative international relations. As such, the results should be seen as preliminary. Additional research into the topics covered by this chapter would probably shed light on some of the key open questions. We summarize the results of the empirical analyses on religion and international cooperation in Table 6.5. The overall results suggest a mixed picture of the relationship between religious factors and international cooperation. However, some general conclusions emerge.

1. The principal and most robust finding is that religious similarity has a consistently strong effect on security cooperation. Religious similarity also tends to affect combined cooperation. These results hold across levels of analysis.
2. Secularism seems to positively affect security cooperation and overall cooperation at the nation, dyad, and regional level; however, we do not find consistent effects of secularism on cooperation across levels of analysis or across cooperative issue areas. In addition, these relationships are sensitive to model specification. Therefore, we urge caution in inferring a positive link between secularism and cooperation.

3. In general, religious factors tend to play a minor role in economic cooperation, and when they do, this effect is neither consistent nor robust.
4. Security communities show significant religious cohesion: the degree of religious similarity between members making up a given security community is considerably higher than the religious similarity of states belonging to different security communities. This is evident in the religious structure of such collective security organizations like the Organization of American States (OAS) or NATO (dominated by Christian states), on the one hand, and the Arab League (dominated by Sunni Muslim states), on the other. This effect seems to be fairly stable over time. *Ironically, this is precisely the type of community in which realists would expect to find the least religious cohesion.*
5. The religious organization of other, that is, economic, or institutional, communities seems to be neither as significant nor as stable as the religious organization of security communities.
6. Unlike the results on religion and conflict, there does not seem to be a robust or consistent interaction between political instability, religious similarity, and international cooperation. We do find, however, that this interaction produces results that support our hypothesis at the dyadic level. However, the same is not true of other levels of analysis.
7. States/Dyads with Christian or Muslim majorities tend to cooperate more in security affairs than either states with other religious majorities or dyads that do not share Christianity or Islam as their major religions. However, this effect does not extend to other cooperative domains.
8. While it may seem that the robust relationship between religious similarity and cooperative security ties (as well as combined cooperation) supports the CoC thesis, this is clearly not the case because the expectation of the CoC thesis is that this is a singular post–Cold War phenomenon. Our results strongly disconfirm this assertion. We find that the "religious similarity affinity" argument is much more a Cold War phenomenon than a post–Cold War one.
9. Likewise, we do not find support for the hypothesis derived from the constructivist perspective that the effect of religious similarity

Table 6.5 Religion and international cooperation—summary of empirical findings

Level of Analysis	Factor	Security Cooperation		Economic Cooperation		Institutional Cooperation	Overall Cooperation	Robustness
		Alliances	Commitment	Trade	PTAs			
Nation-Year	Religious Similarity w. PRIE	+	+	−	+	+	+	+
	Religious Homogeneity	+	+	−	−	+	+	+
	Pct. Christians	+	+	−	−	+	+	+
	Pct. Muslims	+	+	0	−	+	+	0
	Pct. Buddhists	0	0	0	0	0	0	0
	Pct. Hindus	0	0	0	0	0	0	0
	Pct. Non-religious	0	0	0	0	+	0	0
	State-Religion Relations	0	0	0	0	0	0	0
	Relig. Similarity#Coup-Risk	0	0	0	0	0	0	0
	Relig-State Rel.#Coup-Risk	+	+	0	0	0	+	+
Nation-History	Religious Similarity w. PRIE	+	+	0	0	0	+	+
	Religious Homogeneity	+	+	−	−	0	0	?
	State-Religion Relations	0	0	0	0	0	+	0
Dyad-Year	Religious Similarity	+	+	−	+	0	+	+
	Religious Homogeneity	+	0	−	−	0	−	?
	Major Religion Match	+	+	+	0	0	+	+ ?
	Major-Minor Relig. Match	−	−	0	0	0	−	
	Christian Majority	+	+	+	0	0	0	?
	Muslim Majority	+	+	0	0	0	+	?
	Christian-Muslim Dyad	0	−	0	0	+	−	?
	State-Religion Relations	+	+	+	−	0	+	+
Dyad-History	Religious Similarity	+	+	+	+	+	+	+
	Religious Homogeneity	+	+	−	−	0	+	+ ?
	State-Religion Relations	−	−	+	−	−	0	
Region-Year	Religious Similarity	+	+	+	+	0	+	+
	Religious Homogeneity	+	+	−	−	0	−	−
	State-Religion Relations	0	0	0	0	0	0	0
Community Structure	Religious Similarity	+	+	0	0	+	+	+

Key: + positive effect; − negative effect, 0 not statistically significant, ? Unclear on cooperation is characteristic of "young" states or dyads as opposed to more "mature" ones. When differences do exist, it seems that religious similarity affects cooperation between more mature states or dyads.

These results support our key hypotheses suggesting that religious factors play a key role in security and institutional cooperation but not in economic cooperation. They also provide some support (although hardly robust) for our contention that political leaders tend to use religious factors as mobilization tools when they feel politically insecure. This is particularly the case when there are strong ties between political and religious institutions.

The present study offers a rather nuanced and qualified picture of how, when, and to what extent religious factors affect international cooperation. Several important implications do follow, however. First, religious factors seem to matter most in areas where trust appears to be a critical component of the decision to form cooperative ties. If states pursue relative gains, as offensive realists would have us believe, then they tend to be more suspicious of each other when it comes to security cooperation than in other cooperative domains. In such situations, the notion of states cooperating against common enemies is valid. But having common enemies does not, in itself, induce trust. It appears that common religious values seem to be an important factor that increases trust. It is also possible—given our findings about religious differences and international conflict—that states that share religious values also tend to share enemies. This adds another layer—that of common interests—to the incentive to cooperate in international security affairs.

Second, the results about the religious cohesion of security cooperation and institutional communities are of particular importance. They suggest that the intentional design of security cooperation structures, such as multilateral alliances, takes place along religious lines. However, as we noted above, cooperative communities reflect not only formal structures formed and sustained by international treaties but also an emergent property due to the structure of dyadic, triadic, . . . , or k-adic, cooperative ties. The high degree of religious cohesion in security and institutional communities accentuates the significant impact of religion on international cooperation. Equally important is the result that religion has little or no effect on economic cooperation or on the structure of economic cooperation communities. This implies that economic transactions are based on principles that are fundamentally different from (although not necessarily independent of) institutional and security cooperation. We return to some of these points in the next chapters.

Overall, the results suggest interesting and previously unknown links between religion and various dimensions of international cooperation. These carry important implications for the theory and practice of international relations. We explore these implications in the concluding chapter.

Appendix to Chapter 6

1. Introduction

As in previous chapters, this appendix covers in more detail the methodological issues we have discussed in the chapter. Additional material, including replication data, is provided in the book's website. We focus here on additional issues—data, measures, and methods—that are specific to the study of religion and international cooperation and have not been discussed in the appendices to previous chapters. In particular, we focus here on community detection and on the measurement of the cohesion coefficients.

2. Data

In general, most of the datasets used for the study of religion and international cooperation were discussed in previous chapters. This applies also to the various measures of religious factors. However, in addition to the datasets used in previous chapters, we include a dataset on PTAs collected by Milner and Mansfield (2012). These data form a binary network where the presence of a PTA between two states is assigned a score of one for that year, and zero otherwise. Here we present the descriptive statistics for the cooperation measures used in the present study. The descriptive statistics of the religious factors have been provided in the appendix to chapter 5 above.

3. Methods and Measures

We discuss here three principal issues: the community detection process, the measurement of cohesion coefficients, and network effects.

3.1 Community Detection

A community is a subset of a network characterized by high density among community members and low density between members of a given community and members of any other community. There are a number of ways to detect communities in network analysis. We focus here on one of the common strategies of community detection developed by Newman and Girvan (2004) and extended by Leicht and Newman (2008) to community detection in directed networks.

Briefly, the detection algorithm does not require prespecification of the number of desired communities. Rather, this number is determined by the algorithm. The algorithm uses a number of computerized optimization methods such as the Travelling Salesman algorithm (Bektas 2006) or simulated annealing (Lancichinetti et al. 2009), to maximize the modularity coefficient, Q. The modularity coefficient is given by:

$$Q = \frac{\sum_{i=i}^{n-1}\sum_{j=i+1}^{n}\left[x_{ij} - \frac{do_i d_{ij}}{E}\right]\delta c_i c_j}{E}, \qquad [A6.1]$$

where x_{ij} is the presence (1) or absence (0) of an edge between nodes i and j, do_i and di_j are the out-degree of node i (the number of edges leaving node i—for example, the number of export partners of a state) and the in-degree of node j (the number of edges entering node j—for example, the number of import partners of node j), respectively, c_i and c_j are the community labels of nodes i and j, δ is the Kronecker delta (defined as 1 if $c_i = c_j$, and zero otherwise), and E is the number of edges in the network.

The community detection algorithm assigns nodes to communities iteratively. For each iteration, it measures the modularity coefficient. This process is repeated until the maximum modularity is found, and no subsequent community assignment produces a higher modularity coefficient. Intuitively, the modularity coefficient maximizes the difference between a given community structure and chance. This is done by subtracting the actual assignment of nodes to communities from what would be expected by randomly assigning such nodes to communities. The result is a community structure that ensures two community structure characteristics: (a) the maximum within-community density and the minimum between-community density, and (b) the maximum difference between the optimal community assignment (as defined in (a) above) and chance.

Once a community structure is defined, we can estimate the degree to which these communities are cohesive with respect to a certain attribute of the nodes (states). In this particular case, we examine the extent to which within-community religious similarity is higher (or lower) than between-community religious similarity. In other words, a high positive cohesion coefficient in the security cooperation network suggests that states that belong to a given community are more religiously similar than states that belong to different communities. A negative cohesion coefficient suggests that within-community religious similarity is *lower* than between-community religious similarity (that is, states tend to form alliances on the basis of factors other than religion).

For that purpose we use the religious similarity matrix. We partition the religious similarity matrix by community assignments of nodes, such that all nodes belonging to the first community appear as first rows and columns, followed by nodes belonging to the second community, and so forth. In order to demonstrate this process, consider the following example.

The left part of the table (labeled *Network*) is the network of nodes (states). A cell has a value of one if there exists an edge (tie) connecting the row node with the column node, and zero otherwise. The right-hand part of the table (labeled *Communities*) is the final community assignments of nodes. This part of the table consists of the ten nodes in the rows, and the community labels (in Roman numeral-labeled columns). An entry of 1 means that a node (row) is a member of a given community (column). In the current example, each node is a member of one community only, and no two communities share nodes in common. This is just a coincidence. In general, a node can be a member of multiple communities and two communities can have one or more nodes in common.

We can present these as graphs, as shown in Figure A6.1 below.

Table A6.1 A hypothetical cooperative network with community assignments

Network											Communities			
	1	2	3	4	5	6	7	8	9	10		I	II	III
1	0	0	0	0	1	1	1	0	1	1	1	1	0	0
2	1	0	1	1	1	1	0	0	1	1	2	0	0	1
3	1	1	0	0	1	0	1	1	1	0	3	0	0	1
4	1	0	0	0	0	0	0	1	0	1	4	1	0	0
5	0	0	0	0	0	0	0	0	1	1	5	0	1	0
6	0	1	0	1	0	0	0	1	1	1	6	1	0	0
7	0	1	0	0	1	1	0	0	1	0	7	0	1	0
8	1	0	0	0	0	0	0	0	0	0	8	1	0	0
9	0	0	0	0	1	1	1	0	0	0	9	0	1	0
10	1	0	1	0	1	1	1	0	1	0	10	1	0	0

Assume a hypothetical religious similarity matrix of the following type (Table A6.2).

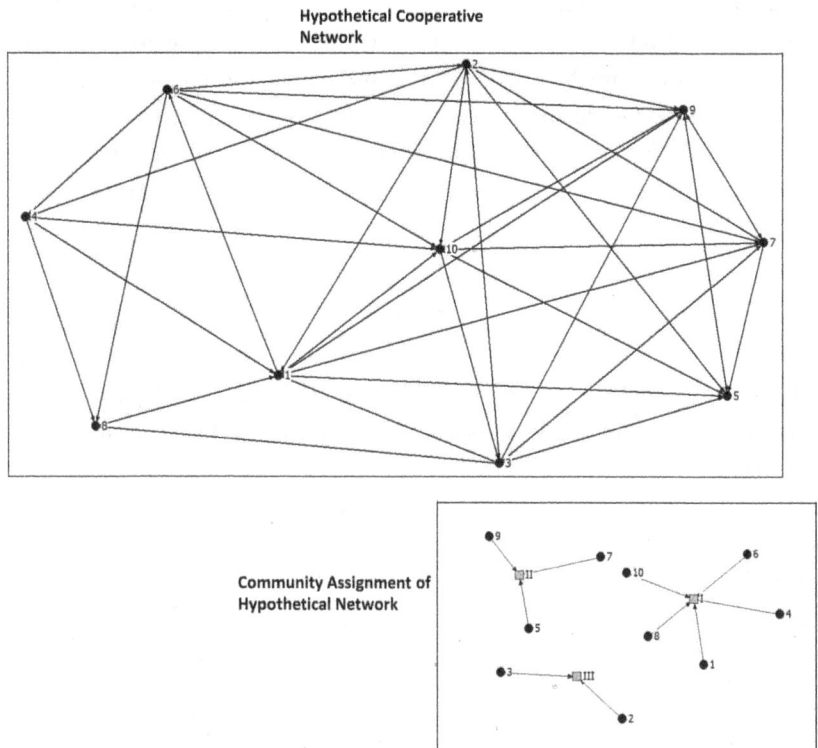

Figure A6.1. A graphical representation of the hypothetical network and community assignment

Table A6.2 Religious similarity of the states in the hypothetical cooperative network

Religious Similarity

State	1	2	3	4	5	6	7	8	9	10
1	0.7	0.5	0.6	0.45	0.6	0.4	0.6	0.5	0.6	0.55
2	0.5	0.45	0.4	0.55	0.5	0.4	0.5	0.6	0.5	0.55
3	0.6	0.4	0.33	0.65	0.5	0.6	0.6	0.5	0.5	0.55
4	0.45	0.55	0.65	0.89	0.55	0.55	0.35	0.75	0.45	0.5
5	0.6	0.5	0.5	0.55	1	0.8	0.7	0.5	0.6	0.35
6	0.4	0.4	0.6	0.55	0.8	0.44	0.6	0.3	0.4	0.25
7	0.6	0.5	0.6	0.35	0.7	0.6	0.62	0.5	0.6	0.45
8	0.5	0.6	0.5	0.75	0.5	0.3	0.5	0.12	0.5	0.55
9	0.6	0.5	0.5	0.45	0.6	0.4	0.6	0.5	0.55	0.65
10	0.55	0.55	0.55	0.5	0.35	0.25	0.45	0.55	0.65	0.88

We partition the network **X** by ordering nodes by community. This is given in Table A6.3. In this table, the order of rows and columns is not as in the original network matrix (i.e., by node id number). Rather it is ordered by the community membership of nodes. The first community is in the upper left quadrant of the matrix, the second community is in the middle quadrant, and so forth. Entries in this matrix are the religious similarity scores of the row node and the column node.

Based on the community partitioned religious similarity matrix, we generate a community cohesion matrix **CC**, with entries cc_{ij} defined as:

$$cc_{ij} = \frac{\sum_{i \in q} \sum_{j \in r} s_{ij}}{n_q n_r}, \qquad [A6.2]$$

where s_{ij} is the religious similarity score of nodes i and j, and n_q, n_r are the number of nodes in communities q and r respectively. In our example, we get the following **CC** matrix.

Table A6.3 Community-partitioned religious similarity

Partitioned Religious Similarity										
Community		I				II			III	
		1	4	6	8	10	5	7	9	2	3
I	1	0.7	0.45	0.4	0.5	0.55	0.6	0.6	0.6	0.5	0.6
	4	0.45	0.89	0.55	0.75	0.5	0.55	0.35	0.45	0.55	0.65
	6	0.4	0.55	0.44	0.3	0.25	0.8	0.6	0.4	0.4	0.6
	8	0.5	0.75	0.3	0.12	0.55	0.5	0.5	0.5	0.6	0.5
	10	0.55	0.5	0.25	0.55	0.88	0.35	0.45	0.65	0.55	0.55
II	5	0.6	0.55	0.8	0.5	0.35	1	0.7	0.6	0.5	0.5
	7	0.6	0.35	0.6	0.5	0.45	0.7	0.62	0.6	0.5	0.6
	9	0.6	0.45	0.4	0.5	0.65	0.6	0.6	0.55	0.5	0.5
III	2	0.5	0.55	0.4	0.6	0.55	0.5	0.5	0.5	0.45	0.4
	3	0.6	0.65	0.6	0.5	0.55	0.5	0.6	0.5	0.4	0.33

Table A6.4 Community cohesion matrix

Community Cohesion				Community Variance			
	Com1	Com2	Com3		Com1	Com2	Com3
Com1	0.51	0.53	0.55	Com1	0.0342	0.0136	0.0045
Com2	0.53	0.66	0.52	Com2	0.0136	0.0163	0.0014
Com3	0.55	0.52	0.4	Com3	0.0045	0.0014	0.0018

Consider first the left part of Table 5.5 labeled *Community Cohesion*. We denote the diagonal in this matrix as cc_{qq} and derive the cohesion coefficient C as:

$$C = \frac{\sum_{q=1}^{k}\left(cc_{qq} - cc_{qr}\right)}{k(k-1)}, \quad [A6.3]$$

where k is the number of communities. The cohesion coefficient in this case is C = -0.01.

To estimate the statistical significance of this coefficient, we generate a variance matrix from the partitioned community matrix. This matrix is given by the right-hand part of Table A6.4 labeled *Community Variance*. The question we wish to address when asking if the cohesion coefficient is statistically significant is this: to what extent are within-community cohesion scores significantly different (higher or lower) than between-community cohesion scores? To answer this question, we calculate the weighted within- and between-community means, and the within- and between-community variances, as follows:

$$w_m = \frac{\sum_{qq} cc_{qq} n_{qq}^2}{\sum_{qq} n_{qq}^2}, \quad [A6.4]$$

$$b_m = \frac{\sum_{q \neq r} cc_{qr} n_q n_r}{\sum_{qr} n_q n_r},$$

where w_m, b_m are the within- and between-community weighted means, "n_{qq} is the number" of nodes in community q, and n_{qr} is the product of the number of nodes in community q and the number of nodes in community r.

Likewise, weighted variances are calculated by:

$$w_v = \frac{\sum_{qq} cv_{qq} n_{qq}^2}{\sum_{qq} n_{qq}^2}, \quad [A.5.5]$$

$$b_v = \frac{\sum_{q \neq r} cv_{qr} n_q n_r}{\sum_{qr} n_q n_r},$$

where w_v, b_v are the within- and between-community weighted variances, and cv_{qq} is the within community variance of community q, and cv_{qr} is the cohesion variance of the nodes in community q and the nodes in community r.

The significance score is measured by a difference-of-means T-statistic given by

$$T = \frac{w_m - b_m}{\sqrt{\dfrac{w_v}{\sum_{q=r} n_{qq}^2} + \dfrac{b_v}{\sum_{q \neq r} n_q n_r}}}. \qquad [A6.6]$$

A T value of 1.96 or higher implies that a positive cohesion coefficient is statistically significant at the $p < 0.05$ level. Likewise, a T value of -1.96 or smaller implies that a negative cohesion coefficient is significant at the 0.05 level. In this particular example, $T = -0.654$, meaning that the cohesion coefficient is not statistically significant. So in this case, we can say that religious factors were probably not a key determinant of the emergence of cooperative communities.

3.2 Network Effects

When we analyze multiple cases, consisting of states deciding whether and with whom to cooperate at a given point in time, and repeatedly choosing whether to cooperate at a different point in time, we must consider two types of problems that may confound our results. The first type of factor is time dependence. The decision of a state about whether and with whom to cooperate at one point in time is not independent from its prior decisions (or the consequences of past decisions). This factor is controlled for, at least to a meaningful extent, in our analyses by the bootstrap sampling.

The second factor is spatial dependence—or what we describe as network effects. There is ample evidence that the decision of a state about whether and with whom to cooperate is not independent of the decision of other states, or of the ties each of these would-be partners have with third parties. This implies that the observations we try to explain are not independently and identically distributed (iid), as most estimation methods assume. Specifically the decision of state A to form a cooperative tie with another state B is dependent both on its own ties with third parties (C, D, E . . .), the ties between B and third parties (C, D, E . . .), the ties of those third parties with A, B, C, D, . . . , and so forth (Cranmer and Desmarais 2011, Warren 2010, Cranmer Desmaris and Menninga 2012).

Our network data reflect a sum total of cooperation decisions. However, they do not tell us directly how we got to a specific configuration of cooperative ties. Religion may have been a factor in defining whether or to what extent two states have a cooperative tie. However, other processes—endogenous to the structure of relations—may have been at work as well. For example, states may have opted to form ties with other states to the extent that the latter were "popular" or central. This is what network analysts call "preferential attachment." The reasoning is that if one forms a cooperative tie with a central state, one benefits from the ties of its partner. That is, it is exposed to more cooperative opportunities via its partner without having to pay the cost of forming or maintaining ties with the partners of the partner (Jackson and Wolinsky 1996). Likewise, if state A has a cooperative tie with state B and state B has a cooperative tie with state C, state A may have an incentive to close the triangle by forming a tie with C. This is what network analysts call "triadic closure." Such tendencies are apparent in alliance networks in which we observe a multitude of collective security arrangements like NATO, the Warsaw Pact, OAS, the Arab League, and so forth.

If we want to estimate the impact of such factors as religious similarity or state-religion relations on states' choices of partners for cooperative ventures, we must control for these network effects. If, controlling for endogenous network structural effects on the formation and maintenance of cooperative relations, religious factors have a significant impact on such relations, then we can be far more confident that religion plays a meaningful role in international cooperation. This means that we must estimate the probability of observing a given network structure by chance.

There are several methods for estimating network effects. These include exponential random graph models (ERGMs; Lusher et al. 2013, Cranmer and Desmarais 2011), econometric spatial lag models (Franzese and Hayes, 2007), or latent space analysis (Hoff and Ward, 2004).

Each of these approaches has some problems and is more suitable for one type of analysis than for others (e.g., ERGMs are particularly useful in dyadic analyses with binary dependent variables, whereas spatial lag models apply to continuous variables). We employ here a mixed approach. First, we extract several network statistics that are proxies for a number of endogenous network formation processes such as preferential attachment or homophily (Maoz 2012a). These include two- and three-star indicators, which measure the actual or expected number of two-star relations between members of a dyad. These are indicators of popularity effects. We also use the number of closed triangles associated with a dyad as an indicator of a triadic closure tendency (typically associated with homophilic processes). For the nation-year analyses, we use the average number of two stars or closed triangles of a state's network neighbors as potential network effects. For the dyad-year analyses, we use the actual two and three stars and closed triangles to estimate dyadic relations. However, for continuous dependent variables, we employ a network statistic developed by Joyce et al. 2015 and labeled expected value (EV). The EV variable is based on the degree distribution of the network and is measured by:

$$EV_{ij} = \frac{\sum_i x_{ij} \sum_j x_{ji}}{\sum_i \sum_j x_{ij}}, \quad [A6.5]$$

where x_{ij} and x_{ji} are the entries of the cooperative network associated with the ij (or ji) dyad, respectively. The expected value statistic is more general than the other network statistics in that it applies to both binary and weighted networks as well as to signed networks (which we do not analyze here).

CHAPTER 7

Religion and Civil War

1. Introduction

Scholars and practitioners have long been concerned with the relationship between political boundaries that mark the territory of a state and the composition of the society that resides within these boundaries. This relationship has many dimensions: geopolitical, social, economic, and cultural, to name just a few. Accordingly, the relationship between various groupings of people and the state in which they reside is of interest to economists, sociologists, cultural and religious scholars, and political scientists. In fact, the oldest subfield of political science, political philosophy, was focused almost exclusively on the relationships among individuals, groups, and governing institutions. One of the central concerns of political philosophers and modern political scientists has been the conditions under which law and order are maintained, or, stated differently, when, why, how, and under what circumstances individuals and groups organize to challenge political authority. More importantly, when and why do some of these challenges turn into violent confrontations?

States are a relatively recent phenomenon; they capture less than 20 percent of organized human history, according to a more conservative count, and less than 2 percent of human history, according to a more realistic estimate.[1] However, during this rather brief moment in human history, states were formed and functioned as long as they possessed three principal characteristics:

(a) a well-defined territory marked by physical and/or political boundaries

(b) a population residing within these boundaries
(c) internal sovereignty: a unified set of institutions that effectively make and enforce laws for this population.

From an IR perspective, there is a fourth condition of statehood: external sovereignty. External sovereignty requires that a minimum number of other states recognize the internal sovereignty and territorial integrity of that political unit. However, in terms of the actual functioning of a community as a state, the external sovereignty characteristic was neither a necessary nor a sufficient condition. For a very long time, states existed without being recognized as such—in many cases because they had been isolated in the international environment.[2] The importance of external sovereignty increased with the rise of international interdependence. When states ceased to be economically and militarily self-sufficient, thus requiring contact and collaboration with other states, recognition of their internal sovereignty became increasingly important. Interdependence required setting limits between international interactions, which operate within an anarchical system lacking central enforcement mechanisms, and internal authority, which is considered absolute according to this principle. This gave credence to the notion of external sovereignty and converted it into one of the few laws that survived the turns and tides of international relations over nearly 400 years.

The concept of sovereignty is a nominal creation of the Peace of Westphalia of 1648, which many IR scholars consider to mark the dawn of modern international relations. External sovereignty also implies the principle of noninterference in the internal affairs of a "legitimately recognized" state. Once a state was recognized as sovereign by other states, legally, its regime was pretty much free to do whatever it wanted to its citizens, and other states could do nothing about it—whether they liked it or not. While recent years have seen significant erosion in the external sovereignty concept, it is still widely accepted as a law of international politics (Krasner 2001).

The internal makeup of societies is multidimensional. Societies can be considered homogeneous on one dimension and heterogeneous on another. Members of a given society can share a single religion but speak many different languages. A society may be ethnically, racially, religiously, or linguistically cohesive, but economically or politically polarized. The multidimensionality of social fractionalization renders research into the social causes of civil violence complicated and, to a large extent, inconclusive. The jury is still out on the question of which specific aspects of social fractionalization cause civil violence. We do not pretend to resolve the debates in the literature on the causes of civil conflict. What this chapter does, however, is shed light on the role of religious factors in determining the outbreak, scope, extent, and outcomes of violent civil conflicts. Religious factors are rarely, if ever, the only or even the most important factors that foment civil violence. They are rarely the immediate triggers of such violence. However, they may establish underlying causes of social fractionalization that makes certain societies ex ante more prone to violent protests, rebellions, and civil wars than others.

2. Characteristics of Civil Violence in the Post–World War II Era

Before we discuss its characteristics, we need to define the concept of civil violence. As Sambanis (2004) points out, civil violence encompasses a broad range of actions that involve some degree of political disorder—from strikes, protests, and demonstrations, to full-fledged warfare between or among organized groups. In order to impose some degree of coherence on the events that we consider significant levels of civil conflict, we focus on the following characteristics of these phenomena:

1. *Organization.* The actors in civil violence are organized collectives, which operate under some form of central leadership. This leadership—an individual or group—directs the action of the collective and decides on the specific strategy that the collective uses.
2. *Government involvement.* One of the actors involved in the action is the government of the state that directs and operates various security forces—police, secret police, military, and (sometimes) paramilitary groups.
3. *Goal.* Civil violence may have many causes, as we discuss below. However, the events on which we focus involve, in one form or another, a struggle over the control of the state and its institutions.

4. *Lethality.* Civil resistance may be violent or nonviolent (Chenoweth and Stephan 2011). We focus on the former type. We measure violence by lethality. The data we use vary with respect to the lower bound of what is considered a lethal form of civil violence. Some of the data (e.g., Pettersson and Wallensteen 2015) that we are relying upon require relatively low levels of lethality. For example, one dataset used in this chapter—the Uppsala armed conflict dataset—defines civil conflict as violent confrontations resulting in a minimum of twenty-five fatalities per year of conflict. Other datasets (e.g., Fearon and Laitin 2003, Sarkees and Dixon 2015) require a minimum of 1,000 battle-related deaths per year to qualify as a "civil war." Regardless of which fatality threshold we use, lethality is a key characteristic of civil conflict. These vastly different lethality cutoffs and the associated labels (e.g., armed conflict, civil war) move us to use the term "civil conflict" to encompass any event that has a minimum threshold of lethality that also meets the other criteria stated above.

Thus, we define an incidence of civil violence as an *armed struggle between or among organized groups, one of which involves a government and its institutions, over the control of the state and its institutions that results in a minimum of twenty-five or more fatalities per year of struggle.* We distinguish between *low-level civil violence* that involves incidents resulting in fewer than 1,000 deaths per year of conflict, and *civil wars* that involve 1,000 or more deaths per year of conflict.

By focusing on the role of religious factors in civil violence, we are ignoring a large number of cases of nonviolent civil resistance (Chenoweth and Stephan 2011). This may be a serious limitation as nonviolent resistance movements may have important characteristics, some of which concern religious issues. However, our focus on violent civil conflict is in line with the major trends in the literature that regard such events as having significant international antecedents and even more important international implications.

A number of authors have pointed out the decline of political violence in the modern era (Mueller 2007, Pinker 2011). Even more research focuses on the decline of interstate war and the rise of domestic political violence—civil war being the more extreme type of such violence (Van Creveld 2009, Luttwak 2001, Gat 2006). However, from some perspectives, there are fundamental similarities between civil wars and interstate wars in the post–World War II era. The most striking similarity is that a vast majority of the states in the system have experienced little or no political violence of major magnitude, either internally or externally. By contrast, virtually all of the conflicts—domestic or international—were fought within or between a handful of states. This tendency of repeated fighting by the same states is what one of us has labeled "fightaholism" (Maoz 2004, 2009). We illustrate this skewed distribution of violent conflict in Figure 7.1.

The trends of civil wars and interstate wars are remarkably similar: between over 75 percent of the states in the international system experienced no severe conflict, that is, no major interstate or intrastate conflict during the period under examination. So that means about 25 percent of all states accounted for all civil and international wars, which suggests that

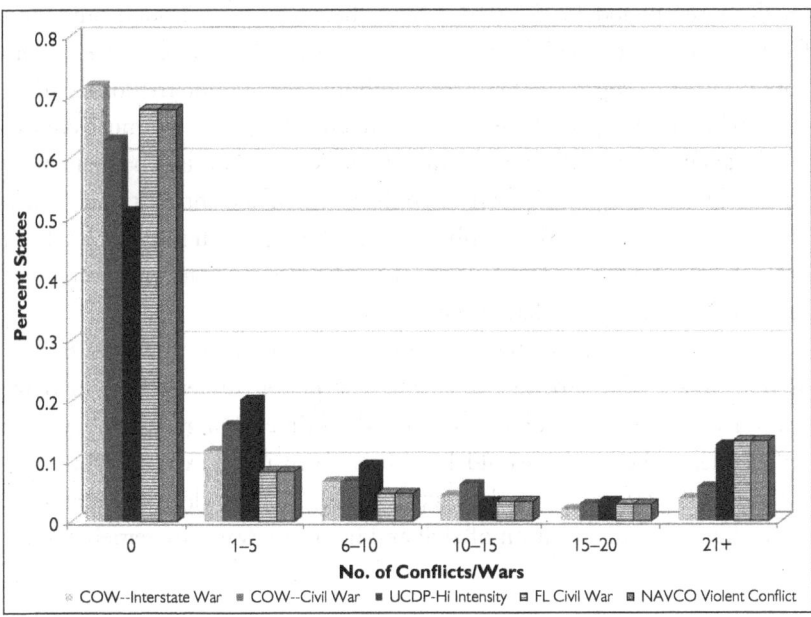

Fig. 7.1. The distribution of international and civil conflicts 1945–2010[23]

Key: Interstate war data and COW civil war data are from Sarkees and Wayman (2007); UCDP civil conflict data are from the Uppsala Department of Peace and Conflict Research and PRIO (Peace Research Institute, Oslo). FL is the Fearon/Laitin dataset (Fearon and Laitin 2003) updated to 2013, and NAVCO is the Non-Violent and Violent Campaigns and Outcomes (Chenoweth and Stephan 2013). The vertical axis is the percent of states experiencing a given range of civil conflict.

most of the states were pacific in terms of their international relations and their domestic political discourse. Only a handful of states accounted for all civil and interstate wars.

Another way to represent this inequality in the distribution of conflicts across states is by measuring it statistically. The Gini coefficient is one of the most commonly used indicators of inequality in the social sciences. It assumes the value of zero when the distribution of a specific variable (for example, income in a society) is completely equal, that is, each person's income is exactly the same as that of every other person's income. It assumes the extreme value of one when one person in the society controls all the income of that society, and all other people in the society control no income at all. In most cases, however, the Gini coefficient varies between these two extremes.[3] As its value increases, so does inequality. Before we present the statistical inequality in the distribution of civil and interstate wars, we must emphasize that the data shown in Figure 7.1 may be misleading. Some states have been around for the entire period 1945–2010, while others have been around only for a few years. Those that had longer periods of independence had, ex ante, more opportunities to engage in conflicts—both internal and international—than those with shorter periods of national independence. So we must control for the length of time during which each of the states was independent.[4] We do that by dividing the number of conflicts—civil and international—each state has experienced by the number of years during which the state has been independent. Figure 7.2 shows the Gini coefficients of the relative number of years during which states have been in conflict.

Here we look only at the conflict experience of states that had twenty or more years of independence during the period under study. Had we examined all states, regardless of the length of time during which they were independent, the results would have been even more extreme. But even without the "young" states, the picture is dramatically clear: the degree of inequality in the distribution of civil and interstate war is extremely high.

3. Theory and Evidence on the Determinants of Civil Conflict

3.1 *Key Themes in Research on Civil Conflict*

Research on the causes and consequences of civil conflict in the modern era is probably the dominant trend in the literature in IR in the last two

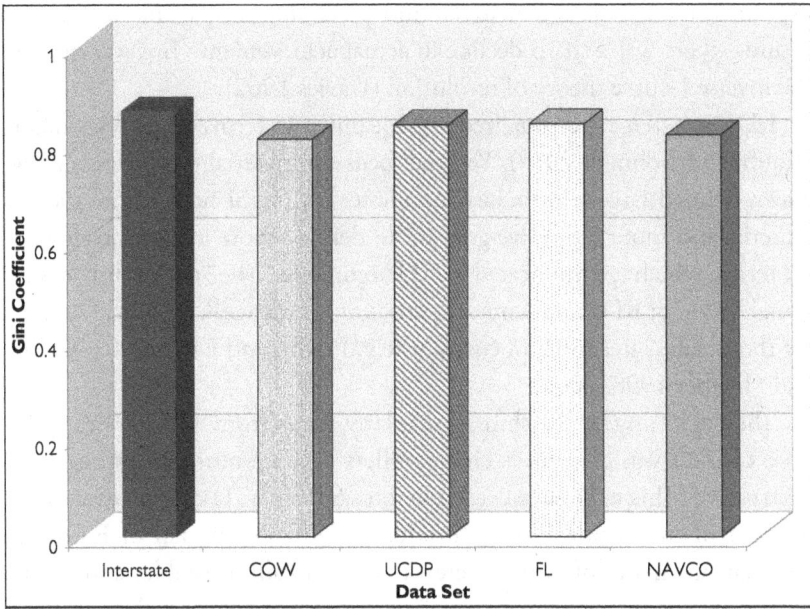

Fig. 7.2. The inequality of civil and interstate wars—Gini coefficients

Key: Gini coefficient—degree of inequality in the distribution of civil/interstate conflict. Datasets are as mentioned in Figure 7.1 above.

decades, largely outpacing research on interstate conflict or international cooperation. This trend reflects the growing level and lethality of domestic violence since the end of the Cold War, and a declining trend of interstate violence over the same period. As was the case in previous chapters, we do not provide a comprehensive review of this burgeoning literature. We do, however, lay out the key arguments on the determinants of civil violence and the evidence on these arguments.

During much of the Cold War era, the focus on civil conflict was almost exclusively the domain of comparative politics scholars. Perhaps the most significant theory of such conflict was found in the relative deprivation (RD) literature (Davies, 1962, Gurr 1970). The original RD arguments focused on perceived discrepancies between achievement and aspirations and the frustration that arose from this for individuals and groups. When individuals and groups found that their achievements lagged behind their aspirations, they were apt to rebel. This tendency was said to be most acute when—following a period of rising achievements, which induced high expectations of increased material and psychological payoffs in the near future—there was a sharp decline in actual achievement. This was dubbed the inverse J-curve theory of revolution (Davies 1962).

RD was often conceptualized and measured in terms of material factors (Koubi and Bohmelt 2014). Yet, the focus on material or objective grievances, defined largely in socioeconomic terms, might not capture the less material and more subjective grievances, defined more in sociopsychological terms, which are implicated in RD arguments. The "materialist" operationalization of RD arguments may account for the weak empirical support for these claims in studies of civil war (e.g. Fearon and Laitin 2003, Collier and Hoeffler 1998, 2004).

The beginning of the shift in scholarly focus from *inter*state to *intra*-state conflict was evident as civil conflicts became more widespread and destructive. This may have been due to two factors: 1) the increase in the number of independent states that emerged from the fall of European colonialism, many of which were often politically unstable, and 2) the increased incidence of "proxy wars" of the superpowers via their regional clients. The two superpowers sought to avoid direct confrontation for fear of escalation to nuclear war. Instead, they often managed their competition through third world state proxies, especially in Asia, Africa and the Middle East. These wars became more deadly through superpower provision of weapons to their combatant allies, often spreading to neighboring states as insurgents sought rear bases. Many such conflicts became protracted as a result of continuous resupply by the superpowers. The proxy wars in Vietnam, Angola, Mozambique, and Afghanistan, which began as civil wars, emerged as some of the most destructive conflicts of the Cold War era.

The salience of civil wars was reinforced in the early post–Cold War era as the former Soviet satellite states imploded into a number of often horrific civil wars. These were epitomized in the Yugoslav war and the subsequent war in Kosovo, in which NATO forces were deployed for the first time as a belligerent under the auspices of the 1949 treaty. These events demonstrated that, even in a post–Cold War context bereft of the ideological strife of the Cold War, internal conflicts could become internationalized just as Cold War era proxy wars had been. These substantive developments led IR scholars to increasingly focus on civil conflict (e.g., Brown 1996, Regan 1996, Rummel 1997, Benson and Kugler 1998). In effect, IR scholarship in the post–Cold War era appropriated the study of civil conflict from comparative politics scholars, who had produced the most significant work on such conflicts during the Cold War era (e.g. Eckstein 1964; Gurr 1970, 1980; Hibbs 1973; Gurr and Lichbach 1979; Horowitz 1985).[5]

Moreover, a number of theories proffered that religious rationales were supplanting the Cold War ideological struggles as precipitants and/or concomitants of these post-Cold War civil wars. The arguments advanced in these studies were that ethnic, racial, linguistic, and especially religious symbols were manipulated by political elites in order to provide justification for major armed conflicts against political opponents within states. The resultant armed conflicts were regarded as recent manifestations of timeless intractable battles rooted in primordial differences among the disputants (Posen 1993). Thus, many scholars viewed religious identity as a catalyst of major post–Cold War era civil wars. For example, the civil war in the former Yugoslavia—for both belligerents and allies—was not only a conflict over material resources and political values but it also pitted major religious groups against each other. It seemed that many Western Christian states supported Catholic Croats, while Russians and other Orthodox states sided with Serbs, and Islamic states such as Iran favored Bosnian Muslims. These fissures and alignments appeared to some as evidence of a "clash of civilizations," viewed mainly in religious terms.

A large number of quantitative studies of the role of religion in civil war were dominated by those focusing on several key theoretical themes. These included the clash of civilizations thesis (Huntington 1993), the post–Cold War emergence of religious based nationalism (e.g., Juergensmeyer 1993, 2017; Thomas 2005; Toft et al. 2011); and the religious dimensions of "ethnopolitical conflict" (Gurr 1994, Gurr and Harff 1994). Having discussed Huntington's thesis throughout this book, suffice it to point out here that the clash of civilizations applied to intrastate as well as interstate war. In fact, Huntington (2000) argued that the CoC thesis was more applicable to civil wars given that they had become more prevalent and destructive than interstate wars. His rendering argued that states bisected by civilizational fault lines, defined primarily in religious terms, were more likely to experience civil wars—and the most intense ones.

Juergensmeyer (1993) likewise implicated religious factors in the most intense armed conflicts in the post–Cold War era. In contrast to Huntington's thesis connecting CoC civil conflict to supranational "civilizational" divides,

Juergensmeyer's (1996) argument was tied more directly to religious nationalism. His focus was on "religionizing politics" exacerbated by the "geopolitical crisis" associated with the end of the Cold War. He noted that "as nations rejected the Soviet and American models of nationhood, they turned to their own past, and to their own cultural resources." Consequently, "politicized religious movements are the responses" (p. 19). These movements "religionize[d] politics" by putting "political issues and struggles within a sacred context" such that "compatability with religious goals becomes the criterion for an acceptable political platform" (p. 5). This put religious nationalists in conflict with secular nationalists—and even their nonnationalist coreligionists—in the former's aspiration to "religious statehood," leading to armed conflicts that were so much more frequent, intense, and widespread that they constituted a "new Cold War."

Gurr's (1994) focus on ethnopolitical conflicts in the post–Cold War era provided one of the first systematic analyses of Huntington's thesis, while also engaging aspects of Juergensmeyer's thesis. Drawing on his Minorities at Risk (MAR) dataset, Gurr found that while conflicts among ethnoreligious groups were more intense in the post–Cold War era, they were not more frequent. What appeared to be a greater incidence of ethnoreligious violence within states actually reflected the greater number of political transitions especially in post-Soviet states with the end of the Cold War, which had less to do with religious factors per se. Most quantitative analyses found little support for Huntington's claims regarding intrastate conflicts. Among the exceptions was Roeder's (2003, 517) study of the relationship between civilizational differences and the intensity of ethnopolitical conflict from 1980 to 1999. Roeder analyzed 1,036 ethnopolitical dyads and found that from 1990 to 1999, civilizational differences were significantly associated with the intensity of such conflicts, supporting Huntington's claim that religious differences were associated with more intense ethnopolitical conflicts in the post–Cold War era. In contrast, Henderson's (2004) study utilized two different civil war datasets (i.e., Regan 2000 and Sambanis 2000) and found that the period 1989–99 in comparison to 1978–88, witnessed fewer "clashes of civilizations" as a proportion of all civil wars or all "ethnic civil wars."

Licklider (1995, 685), relying on COW civil war data over the period 1945–93, divided civil wars "rather crudely into those primarily driven by ethnic-religious-identity issues and those driven by other concerns (primarily socioeconomic)." He found that 69 percent of the 91 civil wars were classified as identity wars. Utilizing five measures of intensity (i.e., continuance, length, casualty patterns, recurrence, and genocide), his analysis suggests that identity civil wars—of which religious wars are a subtype—"*are not clearly more intense than nonidentity ones*" [original emphasis] (p. 686). Both "identity" and "non-identity" civil wars "*are about equally likely to end in negotiated settlements*" [original emphasis] (p. 686). Mason and Fett (1996) found that civil wars "with an ethnic or religious component" (p. 558) were "no more or less susceptible to negotiated settlement than nonethnic conflicts." This, they argued was "at odds" with the "general notion that the indivisibility of the stakes in a civil war makes them more difficult to resolve by negotiations" (pp. 561–62). Walter's (1997, 356) analysis of COW civil wars from 1940 to 1990 not only differentiated between "identity" and "nonidentity" wars but also distinguished within the former between religious and ethnic civil wars. Her findings also suggest that "wars with strong ethnic underpinnings appear to be no more difficult to resolve than those fought over nonidentity issues," and "only very weak support was offered for the connection between religious wars and the absence of settlement."

Regan (1996) was the first major study to utilize the COW cultural dataset—a forerunner of the WRP data. Regan found that interventions in ethnic/religious civil wars had a higher probability of success than interventions in ideological civil wars (p. 349). In contrast, and more in keeping with the conventional wisdom, Doyle and Sambanis' (2000) study of 124 civil wars from 1944 to 1997, based mainly on COW and Uppsala data, found a lower probability of peacebuilding success in "identity wars," which they characterized as "ethnic and religious wars." Thus, the consensus of these early post–Cold War studies of civil conflicts was that while religious factors might play a role in these conflicts, they did not appear to operate along the lines implied by the CoC or the religious nationalism thesis. In fact, where religious factors seemed to influence the onset of civil wars, this impact was evident at least back to World War II—if not earlier—well before the presumed "explosion" of "religious conflicts" in a post–Cold War era "clash of civilizations."

While insightful, these studies were limited insofar as they often conflated religious, ethnic, racial and linguistic factors, and did not directly focus on the role of religion in the onset of civil wars. In fact, the first publication in what would become one of the most influential post–Cold War era research agendas on civil war—the greed-grievance framework—Collier and Hoeffler (1998) did not include a religion variable in the analyses.[6] Near the turn of the millennium, several studies began to address these broader shortcomings. Notably, drawing on an original dataset, which differentiated among the religious, ethnic, and linguistic attributes of all states from 1946 to 1992, Ellingsen (2000) found that religious fragmentation is positively and significantly associated with civil war onset, and states whose second largest religious group is medium size (between 5 percent and 20 percent of the population) are more likely to experience civil war. Focusing on African civil wars and those in other developing countries for 1960–99, Collier and Hoeffler (2002) also found that religious fractionalization increased the likelihood of civil war onset, and Hegre et al. (2001) found a similar relationship for all states from 1816 to 1992. Hegre et al. (2001) drew on Ellingsen's data for 1946–92, but although it disaggregated ethnicity, linguistic, and religious measures, it reported findings for only the ethnic heterogeneity variables. These findings corroborated Rummel's (1997) earlier results from his analysis of all states from 1932 to 1982 that the greater the number of religious groups in a society, the more intense its domestic collective violence, ranging from coups and purges to riots and internal war.

Fearon and Laitin's (2003) study of civil wars from 1945 to 1999 challenged these earlier results and found that neither religious fractionalization nor religious polarization was significantly associated with civil war onset. Religious diversity had at best a weak and inconsistent relationship with civil war onset. They also found that measures of state discrimination against religious minorities were not associated with a systematically higher risk of civil war onset. Montalvo and Reynal-Querol (2005) focused on 138 states from 1960 to 1999 and also found that religious fragmentation does not have a significant relationship with the incidence of civil war, but that religious polarization is positively and significantly associated with it. Drawing on a more expansive research design than their previous work, Collier and Hoeffler (2004) revised their earlier results and, like Fearon and Laitin (2003), found that neither religious fractionalization nor polarization was significantly associated with the onset of civil wars for 1960–99. Similarly, Wimmer and Min (2006) also found no significant relationship between religious fractionalization and civil war onset for all states from 1950 to 2001.

Hegre and Sambanis (2006) conducted a sensitivity analysis of earlier findings on civil war onset to determine the robustness of 88 candidate variables—including several religious factors—on the probability of intrastate conflict. They found that religious fractionalization is positively associated with the onset of internal armed conflict, but its impact is not robust for civil war. These results raised the intriguing question of why religious fractionalization would be significantly associated with less intense armed conflicts and not more intense ones, such as civil wars. Resonating with arguments from previous chapters on the importance of regional factors (i.e., PRIEs) in international conflicts, Hegre and Sambanis (2006) also found robust "neighborhood effects" influencing the onset of civil wars. Both whether a neighboring state was at war and the total number of neighboring states at war in a given year had robust positive effects on both internal armed conflicts and full-scale civil wars. The authors view these findings as supporting theses on the diffusion, contagion, or demonstration effects of civil war, although they emphasize that their analysis "cannot explain why or how civil wars spread across neighboring countries" (p. 532).

Relatedly, Miller (2007) argued that the "state-to-nation" balance, which reflects the degree of ethnic homogeneity within the boundaries of a given state, was a key cause of regional conflicts. A society within a state that is highly homogeneous in terms of ethnic, religious, and linguistic characteristics yields a "balanced" state. Such a state handles its external interactions using realist principles, and its foreign policy is not driven by domestic considerations. On the other hand, an ethnically heterogeneous state suffers from an imbalance in terms of the state-to-nation ratio. Such states are motivated by both domestic and external concerns when managing their foreign policies. First, they are internally unstable; leaders are invariably concerned with their political survival. Second, they are open to incitement and (overt or covert) intervention by other states and nonstate actors with affinity to some minority groups within such states. Viewing religion as an inherent part of ethnicity, this corresponds with an expectation of both lower internal and international stability in such regions.

Several scholars have focused on the relationship between external actors' religious affinity to rebel groups as a factor affecting the prospect and outcomes of intervention. San-Akca (2016) found that the probability of external state support for non-state armed groups (NAGs) in a civil conflict increases significantly with ideational affinities, based on ideological or religious similarities, between the external state and the NAG. Jackson, San-Akca, and Maoz (2020) find that actual or would-be rebel groups that anticipate support from external actors, including on the grounds of religious affinities between such groups and external actors, are more likely to rebel. The anticipation of such support also increases the probability of a violent uprising.

In their study of how civil wars may lead to international conflicts, Gleditsch et al. (2008) found that transnational linkages, including those that are associated with religious factors, influence the relationship between civil wars and MIDs; and this relationship was not mitigated when separating "ethnic" from "nonethnic" civil wars (also see Cunningham et al. 2009). Salehyan et al. (2011) found that transnational ties are significantly associated with increased support for rebels. These studies provide additional support for the importance of regions (e.g., PRIEs) in the analysis of civil wars, as well as the impact of civil wars on regions. Expanding on the research on "neighborhood effects" and the influence of regional factors in civil wars, Gleditsch (2007) found that transnational linkages and attributes of surrounding countries, including the regional dispersion of ethnic groups, operationalized to include religious heterogeneity, exerts a substantial impact on the risk of civil war onset.[7] Gleditsch's (2007) indicator may proxy religious heterogeneity in some cases, but in other cases it proxies any of its other social dimensions because it defines the largest ethnic group by the smallest of the dominant group shares on any of the indicators of ethnicity, which include race and nationality as well as religion. For example, Albania is coded as having a population that is 100 percent Caucasoid, 90 percent Albanian speaking, and 70 percent Muslim; therefore, its heterogeneity score is 100 - 70 = 30 since 30 percent of the population is not Muslim. If, instead, Albania were 90 percent Muslim and 60 percent Albanian speaking, then the heterogeneity score would also be 30 percent, but this would reflect its linguistic heterogeneity and not its religious heterogeneity.

Indicators such as these are often cross-temporally and even more so cross-nationally incomparable. Similarly, operationalizations from the Ethnic Power Relations (EPR) dataset that subsume "ethnoreligious groups" in categories that also include ethnolinguistic and ethnosomatic (or "racial") groups in a composite measure of ethnicity (e.g., Wimmer et al. 2009, Cederman et al. 2010, Koubi and Bohmelt 2014) may proxy religious characteristics for some states but not for others because (a) ethnicity and religion do not overlap and the EPR coding is based on a mix of religious, linguistic, and racial characteristics, and (b) the EPR coding is cross-nationally incomparable. With respect to the latter for example, people of European descent are characterized as "whites" in the United States, but people with the very same racial heritage are characterized as English, Scottish, Welsh, and so on in the United Kingdom. This precludes any meaningful cross-national affinity classification. In sum, they are cross-nationally incomparable for purposes of analyzing the religious correlates of wars.

Typically, such problems in the quantification of religion variables were extensions of those evident in early systematic studies of civil war onset that subsumed religious factors under broader "ethnicity" variables, or interactions of composite estimates of ethnic, linguistic, religious, or racial characteristics (e.g., Vanhanen 1999ab, Sambanis 2001, Collier and Hoeffler 2002, Elbadawi and Sambanis 2002, Regan and Norton 2005, among many others).[8] This did not allow us to discern the specific effects of religious factors on civil war onset. In addition, some of the early studies also distinguish and dichotomize "identity" wars, which are assumed to be ethnic and religious based, and "non identity" wars, which are assumed to be ideologically or resource driven (e.g., Regan 1996, 2000; Sambanis 2001; Reynal-Querol 2002). Even proponents of the latter scheme such as Sambanis (2002, 234) note that "there is no consensus in the literature on the theoretical validity and empirical applicability of these classifications." Nevertheless, scholars have continued to conflate religion with non-religion predictor variables (e.g., Gleditsch 2007, Jakobsen and De Soysa 2009, Cederman et al. 2010, Buhaug et al. 2014) and differentiate identity/religious and nonidentity/non-religious conflicts (Toft 2007, Kathman 2011, Basedau et al.'s 2016), which further complicates our ability to determine the actual religious correlates of civil war.

On the latter point, journalist Deborah Scroggins's (2004, 79–80) description of the civil war in Sudan reflects the multidimensionality of armed conflicts subsumed under the category of "religious" wars, and the often gross oversimplification associated with such characterizations:

> I have often thought that you need a . . . kind of layered map to understand Sudan's civil war. A surface map of political conflict, for

example—the northern government versus the southern rebels; and under that a layer of religious conflict—Muslim versus Christian and pagan; and under that a map of all the sectarian divisions within those categories; and under that a layer of ethnic divisions—Arab and Arabized versus Nilotic and Equatorian—all of them containing a multitude of clan and tribal subdivisions; and under that a layer of linguistic conflicts; and under that a layer of economic divisions—the more developed north with fewer natural resources versus the poorer south with its rich mineral and fossil fuel deposits; and under that a layer of colonial divisions; and under that a layer of racial divisions related to slavery. And so on and so on until it would become clear that the war, like the country, was not one but many: a violent ecosystem capable of generating endless new things to fight about without ever shedding any of the old ones.

Nevertheless, it is clear that even those who utilize such rubrics as "religious conflicts" admit that such conflicts are exceedingly rare and remain a minority of conflicts into the present decade. For example, Svensson (2007, 938) notes that among the civil wars from 1989 to 2003, only 48 of the 217 conflict dyads involve a religious incompatibility, while 169 (78 percent)—the vast majority—are *intra*religious, involving parties belonging to the same religious tradition. Toft (2007) reports that of the 133 civil wars fought from 1940 to 2000, 42 (32 percent) were religious civil wars. Basedau et al. (2016) notes that out of a total of 138 armed conflict onsets between 1990 and 2010, less than half (n = 60) are interreligious conflicts in which warring factions differed greatly in their religious affiliations, and only 41 were theological conflicts in which at least one of the belligerents had explicit religious aims.[9]

Each of these major studies of "religious wars" indicates that although religion plays a role in civil wars, religious civil wars are a minority of all civil wars. Moreover, branding certain wars as "ethnic," "religious," or "identity" and then testing whether ethnicity, religion, or identity factors affected their character and/or outcome biases the results in favor of the hypotheses. It is akin to drawing the target around the hits. Consequently, our focus on the relationship between religion and armed conflict should not employ arbitrarily truncated datasets restricted to often dubious categories of "ethnic/religious/identity wars." These terms obscure broader and more anodyne outcomes associated with religious factors. With respect to the latter point, for example, De Juan (2015) is simply one of many scholars who acknowledge the pacifying impact of religious factors. In an analysis of more than 60,000 villages in Indonesia, he found a statistically significant negative relationship between the density of local religious institutions and the probability of mass fighting. Interestingly, an important qualification was that the pacifying effect of religious institutions was weak or absent in conflicts that evolved along explicitly religious cleavages, reminding us, even in this example, of the tensions that are at times attendant to religious differences. This argument extends to analyses that impute the "relevance" or "salience" of religion in armed conflicts, which is often imposed quite idiosyncratically.

For reasons similar to the difficulty of differentiating "ethnic" civil wars (Kalyvas 2001), the extent to which a civil war is "religious" as opposed to "non-religious" is exceptionally difficult to determine in a systematic way. Our theory suggests that religion can be mobilized to advance political, territorial, or personal goals. Branding certain wars as "religious," almost by definition eliminates our ability to discern these tendencies.

Importantly, we do not reject coding schemes that include religious factors among their list of social incompatibilities. Rather, we argue that we need to consider a more refined way of isolating religious factors from other factors that operate in civil conflicts, many of which have multiple grievance dimensions at any given time. Moreover, religious differentiation is important given that many civil wars have a dynamic nature, which includes significant changes in the relative importance of various factors. The grievances that cause people to rebel may be different from those that cause them to sustain the fight or to terminate it at some point. In the course of civil conflicts, groups may rise and fall, and so may their specific causes (Henderson and Singer 2002). For example, the uprisings in Egypt and Syria in 2011 were concerned with political and economic freedoms and development. They were spearheaded by liberal groups; religious groups and institutions took a backseat to secular prodemocracy popular sentiments. However, these soon were converted into struggles involving highly contentious religious issues. In Egypt, the secular revolution was appropriated by the Muslim Brotherhood and the Salafis who were elected in popular elections and attempted to impose religious laws on the country. This led to resistance by liberal groups, and ultimately resulted in the takeover of power by the Egyptian military. In Syria, the civil war was quickly converted into a complex web of groups fighting both against the regime and against each other—in many cases on religious and ethnic grounds.

The early phases of the Israeli–Palestinian rivalry were primarily nationalist and anticolonial. The Palestinian national movement was led by a semisecular nationalist organization, Fatah (and smaller Marxist organizations such as the Popular Front of the Liberation of Palestine, PFLP). On the Israeli side, the conflict was largely managed by a political system led by secular parties such as the Labor Party and Likud. In the 1980s, Palestinian religious groups such as Hamas and Islamic Jihad started gaining influence among the Palestinians, and this influence has deepened considerably since then. On the other hand, the rise of the religious right in Israel has also been influential in Israeli politics. These trends have converted this conflict into one that has taken on an increasingly religious character, largely superimposed on (and sometimes superseding) the nationalist orientation of this conflict.

Scholars also examined the impact of religious factors on a range of other civil war outcomes. Among the most prominent were civil war duration and severity/intensity, the latter typically measured in terms of numbers killed. For example, Collier, Hoeffler and Söderbom (2004) found that religious fractionalization did not have a significant relationship with the duration of civil wars from 1960 to 2000. Fox (2004a, 57) found that "ethnic" and "revolutionary wars" characterized by religious differences among the belligerents—which at their highest levels are civil wars—were more intense than "non-religious conflicts," and, in a related study (Fox 2004b, 727), showed that religious homogeneity was negatively and significantly associated with the number of fatalities—his primary indicator of conflict intensity—in civil wars from 1965 to 1999.

Pearce's (2005) study using data on 278 cases of territorial conflict phases in both intrastate and interstate armed conflicts between 1946 and 2001 found a weak relationship between the extent of religious differences of the belligerents and intensity (measured in terms of the number of conflict-related deaths and the duration of the conflict), and this weak relationship washed out when "religious relevance" was considered. In contrast to these studies, Lacina (2006) found no significant correlation between religious heterogeneity or religious polarization and the severity of civil war for 1946–2002, utilizing Lacina and Gleditsch's (2005) fatalities data on 114 civil wars.

Analysts examined the role of religion in other aspects of civil wars, as well, such as international peacekeeping, negotiation, and terrorism. For example, Mullenbach (2005) did not find that religious issues have a significant impact on the establishment of peacekeeping missions for civil conflicts, from 1945 to 2002. Svensson (2013) found that intrastate conflict dyads from 1989 to 2003 are significantly less likely to be terminated through negotiated settlement when governments or rebel groups have made explicit religious claims. At the same time, whether the primary parties come from different religious traditions does not affect the chances for negotiated settlement. De Soysa and Nordås (2007) analyzed data for 141 countries with over one million inhabitants for the period 1980–2000 to determine whether Muslim societies were associated with higher levels of political terrorism and concluded that "public and scholarly discussion seems to be wrong about the uniqueness of Islam for predicting levels of dissent and repression, and they may have overemphasized religion over other, more important, factors based on political economy" (p. 936). In contrast, Toft (2007) claims that Islam played a disproportionally high role in "religious" civil wars between 1940 and 2000 (thirty-four out of forty-two "religious" wars). Her explanation for this disproportionate participation of Islamic governments or rebels in such wars involves geography (proximity of Islam's holiest sites to Israel) and resources, particularly oil, which are more structural. However, she also identifies jihad—unique to Islam—as a phenomenon that both religious actors and political elites can manipulate to boost mobilization.

Returning to our main focus on religious heterogeneity and civil war onset, near the turn of the decade, Regan and Bell (2010) found no significant relationship between religious fractionalization and civil war onset for all states from 1949 to 1999, including 110 civil war onsets after removing anticolonial wars. Similarly, Gubler and Selway (2012), using cross-national data from over 100 countries, found that religious fractionalization had no significant impact on civil war onset when controlling for the combination of geographic, income, and religious cross-cutting cleavages in the society. They find that civil war onset is on average nearly twelve times less probable in societies where ethnicity is crosscut by socioeconomic class, geographic region, and religion. More recently, Basedau et al.'s (2016) analysis of 130 developing countries over the period 1990–2010 found a negative and significant relationship between religious fractionalization, religious polarization, and religious overlap with ethnicity, on the one hand, and the onset of armed intrastate conflict. By contrast, they found a positive and significant relationship between religious dominance and armed conflict.

3.2 Debates and Issues in the Research on Civil Conflict: Ethnicity, Linguistic, and Religious Factors

This review suggests that the main division in the literature on the sources, processes, and outcomes of civil conflict is between those who believe that identity factors play an important role in such processes, and those who suggest that conflicts, in general, and civil conflict, in particular, are driven by materialistic factors. The greed-grievance framework, popularized by Collier and Hoeffler (1998, 2004), offers a window into this theoretical and empirical fault line. The concept of greed as a cause of civil conflict concerns a struggle for tangible resources; civil conflict is about the redistribution of wealth or the means of production (e.g., land). Grievance concerns high economic inequality, political repression, and ethnic and religious divisions in the society (Collier and Hoeffler 2004). An alternative interpretation of this framework differentiates between motivations and opportunities. Motivations reflect underlying factors that make individuals or groups dissatisfied with the political, social, or economic status quo in a society. Opportunities reflect access to resources that are necessary for social mobilization.

What is common to both sides of this debate is the notion that a principal motivation for the outbreak of such conflicts is some deep satisfaction with a social, political, or economic status quo. The basic idea is that a motivation for government change emerges when people are unhappy with their lives and when they attribute this unhappiness to government policies. These situations emerge when people's *absolute* utility gains are low—for example, when they suffer from low income, unemployment, or lack of opportunities to practice their way of life. However, these situations can also arise when the *relative* utility of individuals or groups is low, that is, when a person's own group's lot is relatively lower than that of other individuals or relevant reference groups. In the latter case, people may have basic resources that sustain them, or they can be free to pursue cultural or spiritual values, yet they feel that their conditions are unjustly disadvantaged compared to the conditions of equivalent people or groups. This is akin to what Gurr (1970) called "relative deprivation." Collier and Hoeffler (2002) argue insightfully that if people define their attitude toward a given status quo based on such a comparison, there will always be individuals or groups that are dissatisfied and motivated to change it.

The concept of relative deprivation may be seen in a different light, however. Grievances may arise due to gaps between a group's value aspirations and their actual capabilities. This discrepancy has been taken as an important precipitant of civil conflict (Davies 1962, Gurr 1970).[10] Yet one way of assessing a group's actual accomplishment is not based on absolute utility analysis—how much do I get relative to what I expect?—but rather, how much do I get relative to others in groups that serve as my reference groups? Relative deprivation can be interpreted as a precipitant of civil conflict in both relative utility and absolute utility frameworks.

Dissatisfaction with the status quo can operate on an individual level, and there may be a lot of individuals who are dissatisfied with the prevailing status quo. However, civil conflict requires organization, so individual motivations for change need to be channeled through some group mechanism. Several studies suggest that a common group identity (e.g., ethnicity, race, language, religion) and a sense that a community is disadvantaged in absolute or relative terms makes for a powerful organizational mechanism (Basedau et al. 2016, Cederman et al. 2011).

Even if individuals are both motivated to change the status quo and are sufficiently organized to convert their individual dissatisfaction into group action, the question of opportunity is critical. People who feel that a social order threatens their identity or values may have many options to act. In some cases—principally in democratic states—they may organize as political parties and replace the government via elections. In other cases, they may choose nonviolent resistance tactics such as peaceful demonstrations, strikes, or nonparticipation (Chenoweth and Stephan 2011). And some may choose not to act because the expected costs of resistance—government repression and violence—are expected to outweigh the benefits of resistance. The willingness-opportunity framework (Most and Starr 1989) that has been applied primarily to interstate conflict (Siverson and

Starr 1991) seems equally applicable as a way of explaining the outbreak of violent civil conflict.

Research on processes of resource mobilization and political opportunity focuses on the changed opportunities created by transformations in the politico-economic environment that alter the costs and benefits of rebellion for individuals (Olson, 1965) and collectives (e.g., Tilly, 1978). Empirical analyses drawing on either perspective have yielded varying degrees of success. Both approaches have theoretical limitations that are framed nicely by Lichbach (1995, 13): "Given the ubiquity of grievances, for Gurr (1970) the problematique is to explain why people do not rebel . . . [and] given the ubiquity of free riding, Olson's (1965) problematique is to explain why people do rebel."

A key issue with the greed-grievance framework is that it is actually a political opportunity approach, in contrast to the grievance-based perspectives. It argues, inter alia, that the prospects for looting and securing rents from primary commodity exports allow rebel leaders to overcome collective action problems and gain recruits and retain them. This approach faced significant empirical and theoretical critiques. Such critiques were based on, among other things, the inability of scholars to replicate some of the main findings on the relationship between the primary proxy of greed—resource extraction—and civil war onset (Fearon 2005, De Soysa and Neumayer 2007). Other critiques centered on assumptions regarding incentives for looting (Kalyvas 2001), the coding and interpretation of grievance variables (Nafziger and Auvinen 2002), and the conceptualization of the mechanism for rebellion in terms of greed-driven rebels engaged in a criminal enterprise (Humphreys 2005, De Soysa and Neumayer 2007).

These critiques led Collier and Hoeffler to abandon the "greed" reference and rename it the "opportunity" model (Collier and Hoeffler 2004), then rephrase it as the "feasibility" thesis (Collier et al. 2009). This moniker simply notes that civil wars are more likely where they are most feasible. In effect, the "feasibility" thesis, which they contrast with "motivation" factors, is simply a restatement of their original distinction between "greed" and "grievance." Now "greed" is assigned to a number of possible motivations for civil war along with grievances, and opportunities are represented by an array of institutional, political, cultural, and economic factors.

Religious factors are viewed as providing a basis for grievance as well as an organizational apparatus and impetus to coordinate collective action.

Thus, religious factors have been incorporated into each of these perspectives to account for civil war outcomes, but with largely inconsistent results. As Murshed and Tadjoeddin (2009, 95) point out, "the content of their [Collier and Hoeffler's] previous 'greed' hypothesis (now part of motivation) is almost identical with what they now re-phrase as 'feasibility'"; and "if feasibility is about opportunity, greed is also about opportunity"; therefore, "the basic arguments and empirical evidence are much the same as before." Thus more than a decade of theorizing and testing of the "greed versus grievance" framework simply returns the attention of many political scientists to the status quo ante differentiation between political opportunity/resource mobilization and relative deprivation explanations of civil war.

The weak or insignificant findings on the relationship between religious fractionalization or religious discrimination and civil war (e.g., Fearon and Laitin 2003, Collier and Hoeffler 2004, Hegre and Sambanis 2006) were often framed as refuting "grievance"-based arguments. These results also challenged the view that religious factors were important aspects of resource mobilization and political opportunity arguments, as well. For example, religious groups may have lower costs of rebellion than nonidentity groups such as those based on class. Religious groups can more easily recruit from within their identity group (just as ethnic, linguistic, and racial groups do); they can draw on shared religious symbols and norms to rally coreligionists. And, more than most other identity groups, religious groups can utilize the suspicion and mistrust often rooted in doctrinal differences and exacerbated by discrimination between different religious groups to overcome collective action problems, especially when this discrimination is generated by the state (Koubi and Bohmelt 2014, 22).

The ability of religious groups to overcome collective action problems resonates with Esteban and Ray's (2008a) argument that, in the presence of economic inequality, ethnoreligious groups more than class-based groups are more likely to resort to conflict. This is so, in part, because ethnoreligious alliances generate a "perverse synergy" that induces the rich within the group to supply the resources for conflict and the poor to supply the labor. By contrast, in class-based conflict this synergy is largely absent given that the rich have little incentive to initiate a redistribution effort, and the poor have exceptionally high opportunity costs for resources (p. 2186). Gill (2011) also emphasizes the ability of religious mobilization to overcome collective action problems in the case of suicide bombings. But he argues that the religious mobilization strategy is far more general than the more limited and far less common case of suicide bombings.

The seemingly weaker support for relative deprivation explanations of civil war onset was criticized on theoretical and empirical grounds. Buhaug et al. (2014) argued that theoretical misspecification and measurement problems contributed to the inconsistent findings on the relationship between grievances and civil war. For example, Stewart (2008) focused on the largest discriminated group in a state—which in some cases refers to a religious group—rather than the total excluded population, and used a measure of relative deprivation emphasizing "horizontal inequality," which denotes inequalities between groups, rather than "vertical inequality," which refers to inequality between individuals within an otherwise homogeneous population.[11] In their analyses of civil war onsets from 1960 to 2005, Buhaug et al. (2014) find that political and socioeconomic disparities associated with grievance increase the risk of civil war onset primarily when they overlap with horizontal cleavages among groups (also see Koubi and Bohmelt 2014).

Cederman et al. (2010, 114) argue that "proper" conceptualizing and measuring of "ethnic politics" would allow researchers to identify "those ethnic constellations of power that are particularly war prone." They analyzed 124 "ethnic conflicts" fought between 1946 and 2005—half of which were full-fledged civil wars (p. 102)—focusing on whether representatives of a "politically relevant ethnic group" are discriminated against, are powerless, or have regional or separatist autonomy (see Wimmer et al. 2009). Importantly, for our analysis, their conceptualization of ethnicity included "ethnolinguistic, ethnosomatic (or 'racial'), and ethnoreligious groups," which suggests that in certain cases it captures religious characteristics of groups (p. 99). They noted that "without denying the relevance of feasibility mechanisms," there is support for grievance-based claims grounded in issues of ethnic discrimination as explanatory factors in civil wars. Large politically relevant ethnic groups—which can include religious groups— that are either underrepresented in government or excluded from state power, are more likely to pursue violent domestic conflict. Specifically, they "demonstrate empirically how the logics of contention and mobilization lead ethnically defined actors who are excluded from state power into armed conflict," and note that "roughly half of the conflicts fought since the

Second World War can be linked to this dynamic of ethnopolitical struggle for state power" (p. 114).

Esteban et al. (2012) analyzed 138 countries over the period 1960–2008. They relied on an update of Fearon's (2003) dataset, which identifies over 800 "ethnic and ethnoreligious" groups in 160 countries, but without relying on "income-based groups or income-based measures." They find support for grievance-based arguments, suggesting a relationship between economic inequality and domestic conflict. They conclude that "this is not to say that conflict is fundamentally noneconomic," but that "there is an equal possibility that the economics of conflict finds expression across groups that are demarcated on other grounds: religion, caste, geography, or language" (Esteban et al., 2012, 1137). These findings dovetail with those of Basedau et al.'s (2016) analysis of 130 developing countries from 1990 to 2010. Basedau et al. (2016) differentiate among armed conflicts in general; "interreligious" armed conflicts, in which warring factions differ in terms of their religious affiliation (e.g., the Hindu government vs. Christian rebels in Nagaland in India; the Christian government vs. Muslim rebels in the Philippines, and the Buddhist government vs. Hindu rebels in Sri Lanka); and "theological" armed conflicts, which are differentiated by the presence/relevance of an incompatibility over religious ideas between the government and rebels (e.g., the introduction of religious law). The authors employed variables to explicitly proxy religious grievances such as religious fractionalization, religious polarization, and religious overlap with ethnicity and the use of violent religious rhetoric. They suggest that such variables are positively and significantly associated with "interreligious" or "theological" conflicts, but not with armed conflict, in general.[12]

The latter point is supported by findings that assert the greater relevance of psychological over economic-based grievances in "religious" conflicts. For example, Canetti et al. (2010) reject what they view as the tendency to rely mainly on economic resource loss in estimations of relative deprivation, given that psychological, not economic, resources seem to mediate the relationship between religion and support of violence. Their analysis of a sample of 545 Israeli Jews and Muslims found that the relationship between religion and support of political violence is mediated by relative deprivation based in psychological rather than economic resource loss. They argued that "even acute economic deprivation can hardly explain the tendency of certain individuals to support violence while others remain peaceful." This "suggests that the typical tendency to focus on economic resource loss is over simplistic." Instead, "it is the loss of psychological, not economic, resources that mediates the relationship between religion and support of violence" (pp. 583–84). They also note that "group differences between religions seem to matter more than differences between levels of religiosity within the same religion" (p. 583).

Isaacs's (2016) study of the relationship between religious rhetoric and violence using annual data on 495 organizations worldwide from 1970 to 2012 suggests that an organization's recent participation in conflict, and the intensity and duration of the conflict, substantially increased the likelihood that the organization would adopt religious rhetoric (p. 222). Religious rhetoric became more likely with both more intense and longer conflicts. He concluded that violent organizations strategically adopt religious rhetoric to resolve logistical challenges associated with resource mobilization and the recruitment and retention of members. Such rhetoric assists political entrepreneurs in "gain[ing] an edge over their rivals" (p. 222). Isaacs's findings, in demonstrating the endogeneity of religious rhetoric and violence, provide empirical support for the contention that "various logistical challenges associated with participation in violence encourage the adoption of religious rhetoric" (p. 222).

A key focus of the recent literature connecting religion to conflict focuses on religious discrimination as a motivating factor for rebellion. Akbaba (2006), Akbaba and Taydas (2011), and Fox, James, and Li (2009), for example, find that religious discrimination increases motivations for violence and therefore the probability of the onset of violent domestic conflict. However, the causal motivation outlined in these studies seems quite underspecified, because it does not focus on opportunities and on the relationship between religious grievances based on discrimination and other grievances.

Perhaps the most direct and relevant research on the causal factors that connect religion to civil war comes from the work of Basedau and his colleagues (Vüllers et al. 2015, Basedau et al. 2016, Basedau et al. 2017) using a dataset on religion and conflict in 130 developing countries from 1990 to 2010. This group establishes a causal mechanism connecting religion to both motives and opportunities. The argument is that religion as a political component has two aspects: practices and structures (Basedau et al. 2016, 231–36). If the practice of religion is somehow hampered or oppressed by political and social constraints, this may invoke feelings of discrimination among believers, thereby generating motivation to change the conditions that produce discrimination. Such perceptions of discrimination breed motivation for violence. Second, religious institutions, and the overlap of religious and other social identities, help would-be rebels overcome the collective action problem. Religious leaders may assist organization and mobilization by calling for rebellion and violence, thereby increasing the opportunities that arise from mass mobilization. As these authors argue, this framework does not fit all civil conflicts. It applies to specific types of conflict. In particular, they argue that religious factors affect conflict onset when the conflict possesses a religious or theological component (p. 236). Likewise, religious identity overlaps increase the risk of interreligious armed conflict, and interreligious discourse increases the risk of theological armed conflict.

3.3 Problems with the Extant Literature

Although we reviewed and critiqued some of the studies of religion and civil conflict in chapter 2, the current literature review of civil conflict goes well beyond that focus, embedding the religion-civil conflict nexus in broader theoretical frameworks. Our review of this broader literature highlights several issues that we find troubling. We point out at the outset that our review of the literature suggests that the jury is still out when it comes to adjudicating the greed-grievance or the relative deprivation/resource mobilization frameworks. This also applies to the role of religious factors in fomenting and sustaining civil conflict. There may be ample reasons for this lack of consensus on some of the fundamental factors that might affect the onset and characteristics of civil conflict. We pointed out some of the reasons for this diversity of findings above. However, several issues need clarification before we discuss our theory.

First, the discussion of religion in this literature was, more often than not, embedded in broad classifications of social groupings. In many cases, religious factors were conflated with other elements of group identity such as ethnicity and language. Relatively few analyses singled out religious factors and theorized about the causal mechanism that makes religious identities more or less prone to violence.[13] The theorizing about these aspects of the religion-civil violence nexus was not separated from other types of identity markers. As we pointed out above, religion can be a powerful group identity marker, a motivating grievance, and an organizational tool (both via invocation of common grievances based on values and on organizational characteristics of religious institutions).

Second, most of the studies focusing on religion as a motivating or mobilizing factor center on religious discrimination and the mobilization capacity of religious groups. However, very few studies examine how religion can be manipulated by ruling political elites to advance specific goals—including oppressing and discriminating against religious groups—especially religious minorities. Such actions are often justified by political elites (sometimes with the help of religious elites) by pointing out—correctly or incorrectly—the rebellious intentions of such minorities. Another common argument that political elites use to justify discriminatory practices against religious groups concerns the affinity between such groups and external enemies of the state. For example, Israel practices nominal religious freedom and provides equal political rights to the Arab-Palestinian minority within its pre-1967 borders. However, political elites have often depicted this minority as a fifth column. On election day of March 17, 2015, the Israeli prime minister, Benjamin Netanyahu, who at the time was trailing in some polls, posted on his Facebook page the following: "The rule of the right-wing [led by Netanyahu] is at risk. Arab voters are moving in droves to the polling stations. The left-wing NGOs drive them to the polling stations in buses . . . Go and vote, bring your friends and family members. With your help, and with God's help . . . we will form a national government that would protect the state of Israel." This is a typical racist mobilization tactic applied by political elites in states characterized by strong affinities between excluded religious groups and hostile neighboring states.

Third, partly because of the tendency to conflate religion with other identity markers, the relationship between religious institutions and state institutions as a precipitant of conflict remains unexplored. Specifically, are states that have a tight relationship between religious and political institutions more or less likely to experience civil war than states that explicitly separate religion from politics? The measurement of religion was done primarily to identify the degree of fractionalization in a society, or the access of certain groups to power. However the institutionalization of religion was not really understood as a factor in the emergence of civil conflict. Even in studies using the religion and state dataset, the focus was on the linkage between discrimination and conflict rather than on the institutionalized relations between religion and state (for example, on the degree of religious legislation and religious regulation) in states and the likelihood of civil violence. Institutionalization of religion by political elites elevates the opportunity of those elites to mobilize religious leaders and religious institutions to oppress and discriminate against other religious groups; as a result, creating both conditions for, and helping motivate such groups to rebel. Thus, the causal mechanism of Basedau and his collaborators, and of Akbaba, Fox, and their coauthors linking discrimination to civil conflict seems to cover only part of the story, conceptually. We focus on the work of Fox and Akbaba on religious discrimination, and of Basedeau and his colleagues on the more general causal mechanism connecting religious practices and religious institutions to the outbreak of political violence not because they are unique in these regards, but because they exemplify the main concerns we discuss herein.

Additionally, as we pointed out in chapter 2, methodologically, there is a problem with many of these studies insofar as they truncate civil conflict in a manner that creates selection bias and, possibly, predetermines their results. There are two related issues here. First, conflict has several distinct characteristics that are, and should be, treated as independent of the causes of these phenomena. By selecting a subset of cases on the basis of presumed underlying causal mechanisms—thereby branding such conflict as ethnic, ethnoreligious, religious, or theological—researchers may predetermine the outcome of their investigation. If such conflicts already constitute a fraction of all conflicts that are selected by independent criteria (e.g., degree of participation, lethality), then the probability of a hypothesis being supported by the data is not due to the accuracy of the theory but to the fact that cases were selected on the independent variable (King, Keohane, and Verba 1994). To alleviate such selection bias, we need to test hypotheses connecting *specific* motivations to fight to *all* types of civil conflict. Saying that a set of motivations (e.g., religious discrimination) fits religious conflict amounts to equating a concept to itself. This does not constitute scientific evidence of anything. Explaining civil conflict requires selecting a set of cases on criteria that are independent of the possible causes of such conflicts.

Further, the subset of studies that focuses on the dimensions of civil conflict (e.g., duration, outcome, or form of settlement) and ties religious factors to these conflicts offers some interesting insights. However, without studying the conflicts that *did not* occur, we cannot really say that religious conflicts are more intense, last longer, or are more difficult to settle peacefully than other types of conflicts. The opportunity for conflict within a given state exists all the time, but only a small fraction of all states experience civil conflict. It is quite possible that there exist a large number of conflicts that have zero intensity, last no time at all, and have been resolved peacefully. These are the conflicts that did not happen. And without knowing the religious, economic, social, or political characteristics of the dogs that did not bark, we cannot say much that would be credible about the dogs that did. A credible analysis must include the opportunity for conflict outbreak and distinguish between those conflicts that did break out and those that did not. We address this issue below.

Despite the deep disagreements in, and the inherent problems of, the literature on civil conflict, this literature provides some meaningful guides and points of departure to our theorizing and empirical analyses. We therefore move to a discussion of key theoretical linkages between religion and civil conflict.

4. Religion and Civil Conflict

4.1 *The Religious Structure of Societies*

The extant literature on the causes of civil war provides much of the theorizing on the relationship between religion and civil conflict, either as a distinct variable or as part of the broader category of ethnic fractionalization. These theories center on two central themes: motivations and opportunities. We connect these theoretical themes and their analytic frameworks that guided our research thus far.

Another way of framing the manner by which various factors—including, but not restricted to, religious ones—affect the probability and magnitude of civil conflict, is to distinguish between underlying causes and immediate (proximate) causes of conflict (Levy and Thompson 2010, Miller 2007). This typology of causes also captures the interaction between motivations (or grievances), and opportunities that characterizes much of the relevant literature. Underlying causes of conflict refer to basic, entrenched, and long-term factors that elevate the expected probability of conflict. They also indicate whether a given actor is at a higher or lower risk of conflict involvement or conflict outbreak than another actor. Analogous to the science of predicting earthquakes and volcanic eruptions, geologists typically can identify areas, regions, or specific locations that are more prone to experience such disasters. These predictions are general, in the sense that they are based on tectonic structures, magma buoyancy, crust thickness, and so forth. Based on the mapping of these and other factors, geologists can identify high-risk areas. In the case of civil conflict, underlying factors refer to relatively stable characteristics of societies associated with an elevated risk of conflict outbreak in a more general sense.

However, underlying causes do not allow more precise explanation of *when* conflict will occur. Geologists using underlying factors typically cannot predict when earthquakes will take place, or when a volcano will erupt. To provide such predictions, geologists typically rely on more proximate indicators, such as frequency of tremors, magmatic activity, and other geological factors. Yet even those proximate indicators do not allow for accurate predictions of the timings of such disasters, or even their locations. Proximate causes of civil conflicts may include specific triggers (for example, a specific dispute over a holy shrine; the assassinations of Martin Luther King Jr. or Indira Gandhi; or the immolation of Mohammed Boazzizi in Tunisia on October 17, 2010), but more broadly, they refer to specific processes such as the mobilization of groups, specific policies, short-term hardships, or other processes that transform these underlying causes into actual violence. Motivations typically cover underlying causes of conflict, whereas opportunities cover more immediate or proximate causes. This typology allows us to make better sense of the causal mechanisms associated with the various frameworks that form the common theoretical thread of this study.

Starting with the primordialist framework, it views religious diversity as a fixed factor; it does not change very much over time within a given state. Likewise, the same can be said for the relationship between religion and state. Therefore, when considering the predictions that can be derived from the primordialist perspective, it is analytically reasonable to connect religious diversity to a general propensity of states to become embroiled in civil conflict. The fact that there is a structural disparity in civil war experience across states suggests that the primordialist account of structural instability in religiously diverse societies may be quite compelling. The inequality of civil conflict across states also attests to the importance of understanding the underlying conditions leading to civil war propensity.

But, as we have seen in the literature review, many—if not most—civil conflicts implicate the interaction of motivations and opportunities. So, how does religion factor into this process? The short answer is that civil war is more likely when there is a convergence of religious and economic discrimination. Specifically, the probability of civil war in a state increases when one religious group controls a disproportionate share of political, social, and economic resources, largely at the expense of other religious groups. Likewise, relative deprivation is most commonly connected with civil violence when the material gap between aspirations and achievements is framed in both economic and ideational terms. In other words, civil war is more likely when one religious group experiences a significantly higher gap between aspirations and achievements than other groups. This is especially the case when the former's sense of relative deprivation is high, whereas the latter's is low or negative (that is, their aspirations match or outpace their achievements).

Political and economic inequality can be prevalent in both religiously homogeneous and religiously diverse societies. In religiously homogeneous societies, civil wars are typically not about religion. Indeed, many civil wars broke out in relatively homogeneous societies for example, the Russian Revolution, the Spanish Civil War, or even the American Civil War. Indeed, as we documented in the literature review, evidence suggests that most civil wars are not about religion. The key stakes in these wars are political disputes or economic grievances. However, religion may become an issue in diverse societies when one or more groups feel that they are exploited or discriminated against because of their religion or other cultural characteristics that are connected to religious beliefs.

4.2 The Mobilizing Power of Religion

It is important to clarify that religion operates as a group identifier more than as an independent motivator of civil resistance. Even in societies where the practice of certain religions is severely curtailed by policies and legislation, religious discrimination in itself may not be the critical factor driving rebellion. Rather, it is the combination of discrimination on religious, political, and economic matters that pushes disadvantaged groups to rebel. As noted, religion may be a powerful mobilization mechanism if a community has a common identity marker and at the same time feels that discrimination is both cultural and economic.

From the primordialist perspective, the combination of economic discrimination and religious identity fuels the grievances of a community more than either of them taken separately. This point also provides a baseline for the expectations of the instrumentalist perspective. Mass mobilization is necessary in order to stage mass civil protest. When economic grievances overlap with religious discrimination, leaders of a protest movement may find it practical to use religious symbols to mobilize social protest. It is important to note that protest, in and of itself, does not entail violent uprising; it can include peaceful demonstrations and other acts of civil disobedience (Chenoweth and Stephan 2011). Violence in such cases may result from government's use of force to crush nonviolent resistance (Sutton, Butcher, and Svensson 2014, Rorbaek and Knudsen 2017). In cases where protesters are organized along religious lines, the government can use its own religious symbols to mobilize support of its winning coalition members against the threat emerging from different religious groups. It can depict the struggle as a fight for preserving the state's identity vis-à-vis a religious enemy.

A religiously divided society is also a prescription for trouble according to the constructivist perspective. Divided states are less likely to form a unique national (or corporate) identity than religiously homogeneous states. Nationalist ideas that establish a unity of people, territory, and political institutions compete with divisive ideas about religious or other aspects of cultural affinity. The loyalty of people to the state and its political institutions depends on the extent to which they identify with other people in the territory controlled by such institutions. Mobilizing populations for national projects that are financially and humanly costly is difficult under the best social and political circumstances; mobilizing a divided society where some groups feel that the demands imposed on them far exceed the benefits they get from playing by the rules is even more difficult. In religiously diverse societies, the ability of group leaders to mobilize disadvantaged groups against the ruling elite is far greater than in homogeneous societies in which leaders may share the religious beliefs of their constituents.

Recall that constructivists argue that interaction shapes identity. This is true for both interstate interactions that shape national identities, and for intrastate interactions among various groups that shape group identity. Marginalization of certain groups may create a stronger sense of group identity and increase group mobilization. Likewise, groups that benefit from a given status quo might develop an identity based on entitlement. This raises the degree of group awareness and increases the probability that disagreements among people from different groups will be perceived as intergroup conflict, and that instability is presumed to follow.

It also follows that as the level of social secularization—the number of people in a society who do not ascribe to absolute values associated with religious beliefs—increases, it is more difficult to mobilize resistance to ruling elites or prevalent policies along religious markers. Such societies might also experience political instability, but when that happens, this is more likely to result from economic hardships and inequalities than from cultural discrimination.

Our integrative theory contends that politics within a society are shaped by a relationship between two variables: the degree of religious homogeneity/heterogeneity and the degree to which religious affairs are separated from political, social, and economic affairs (the separation of religion and state). The interaction between these factors provides the context for mobilization opportunities by political elites and counterelites. Religious homogeneity and religion-state relations may also provide a context for religious-based grievances in the society. For example, recall that Type I states are characterized by religiously homogeneous societies that lack separation between religion and politics (e.g., Saudi Arabia and Iran). In such states, religion plays a pivotal role in domestic politics. Religion affects leader selection (since political leaders need to be acceptable to religious institutions and to religious leaders). Religion also defines the legal system in which religious laws play a powerful role. Loyalty to the state and loyalty to the prevailing religion are viewed as synonymous. Secularism is either disallowed or marginalized. In such states, it is unlikely that religion would play an important role in fomenting internal conflict. The ability to use religious symbols or to mobilize one group against another is very limited. Religion is a unifying force, not a divisive one. Even religious discrimination against minority religious groups may not be a cause of internal conflict. In religiously homogeneous societies, the minority groups are typically too weak and reluctant to use their religious identity as a mobilizing force. Doing that would unify and solidify their opponents' ability to defeat them and increase the already rampant discriminatory practices. Only coalitions among different groups that are formed to mitigate other economic, political, or social grievances, would give rebels a fighting chance. Therefore, civil conflicts in such societies—to the extent that they break out—would tend to be about non-religious grievances.

Type II states are religiously homogeneous societies that have separated religion from state (e.g., Scandinavian states, Turkey during the post-Ataturk but pre-Erdogen period). Such states minimize the formal role of religion in politics via a constitution or a civil legal system. Religious beliefs and practices of candidates for political office can still play an important role in their election or selection. Although religious discrimination is outlawed, attitudes toward religious minorities may be mixed if not outright suspicious. In such states, too, religion cannot be a powerful unifier because it is difficult to claim that institutionalized practices induce religious discrimination. Therefore, the ability to mobilize groups around religious grievances is quite limited, and the use of religious values to mobilize minorities may in fact be counterproductive.

Type III states are religiously heterogeneous but do not separate religion from state (e.g., Sudan during the Islamic regime, 1989–2008; Myanmar since the early 1990s). In such states, one religious group's rules, principles, and legal values tend to dominate those of other groups, and political leaders are selected from those identified with the "state religion." Religious discrimination is rampant and systematic, privileging the narrow religious identity of the dominant group. This happens even though religious freedom may be a nominal legal right. In these societies, religious civil conflict is most likely. The combination of religious diversity and religious discrimination creates potential for grievances that center on religious issues or the combination of religious grievances and economic or political ones. Religious diversity may lead several discriminated religious groups to form coalitions against the discriminating practices of the state. These are the kinds of societies that display a linkage between religious discrimination and civil conflict (Akbaba 2006, 2011; Fox et al. 2009; Ozdamar and Akbaka 2014).

Finally, Type IV states are religiously diverse societies with separation of religion and state (e.g., United States). In these societies, national identity is formed around non-religious symbols and affinities; political leadership criteria are largely secular; and the role of religious factors in political discourses is minimal. While these states manifest some tensions between different religious communities, other factors, such as secular ideological similarities (e.g., classical liberalism, neoliberalism), define political attitudes. Here, too, the likelihood of religious factors affecting civil conflict is low because it is difficult to show explicit or legal limits on practicing religious beliefs. It is also difficult to use religion to mobilize mass rebellion because of the religious diversity.

One may argue that these sociopolitical characteristics of states are logically prior to the socioeconomic and sociopsychological processes that the relative deprivation and resource mobilization/political opportunity perspectives emphasize in generating conflict. In fact, relative deprivation and resource mobilization processes are embedded in the sociopolitical characteristics of states. However, both primordialism and, to a lesser extent, constructivism emphasize underlying and structural conditions that make some societies more prone to internal conflict than other societies. They are less useful in explaining when conflict will break out in such societies. So we need a more dynamic account of civil conflict outbreak.

4.3 *Proximate Determinants of Civil Conflict*

To answer questions about when (rather than where) civil conflict is likely to occur, we have to consider factors that are less time invariant than the religious homogeneity of societies. As discussed in chapter 3, our integrative theory posits that religious factors affect political processes when the religious characteristics of a society interact with other factors. Accordingly, we suggest that religious factors become prominent determinants of internal conflict when they interact with (a) political and economic factors, (b) the relations between political and religious institutions, and (c) the religious affinities between domestic groups and the politically relevant external environment of the state. We discuss each of these interactions in turn.

We accept the idea that religiously diverse societies are more prone to internal friction than homogeneous societies. The key question, however, concerns the specific conditions under which religious groups can be mobilized to oppose governments' policies and laws. First, religion may become a mobilizing instrument when economic conditions deteriorate. This may be the case when economic conditions are particularly worse for specific religious communities, especially when compared with the economic lot of other religious communities. We also agree that the overlap of religious identities with class identity helps mobilize communities along religious lines. Fox et al. (2017) point out that objective measures of religious discrimination do not predict grievances. Rather, it is the ability of religious and political leaders to mobilize communities around common grievances that helps predict political action. This finding dovetails with our argument that mobilization requires a combination of conditions that would make people angry and willing to risk their lives for a common goal. Using religion as a mobilization strategy requires a perception by members of a community that it is the linkage between their religious beliefs and their economic and political conditions that is responsible for the perceived disadvantaged, oppressed, or otherwise exploited condition of their community.

Mobilizing communities for political action along religious lines requires the support of religious authorities. This is true for both governments and rebels. A government that has close ties with religious elites can mobilize its religious allies against challenges stemming from both religious and other economic, political, or social groups. Governments that have separated religion from state face two challenges when confronting opposition. First, they cannot mobilize religious elites to support their policies. Second, religious elites may have antigovernment sentiments precisely because of this separation of religion from state. By contrast, religious elites of communities that suffer from religious and other discriminatory practices can mobilize antigovernment groups. This is facilitated by policies and laws that cause discrimination and economic or social hardships. Under such conditions, religious elites can use group grievances as a mobilization instrument not only against specific government policies but also against the system of political and religious institutions that perpetuates discrimination.

4.4 The External Dimension of Civil Conflict

One of the more neglected aspects of mobilization in the civil conflict literature concerns the strategic anticipation of external support. The calculus of rebellion involves a strategic assessment of risks and benefits. The benefits of victory and the utility of the status quo define the motivation for rebellion. If the status quo is deemed satisfactory compared to the expectation of political, social, or economic change following rebels' victory, then there is no reason to rebel. The status quo offers more benefits than any expectation of change. On the other hand, if the status quo is seen as deeply damaging, then the motivation for changing it increases.

However, motivation to preserve or change a given status quo requires assessment of the risks associated with such a change. A rebellion may result in victory or defeat; in either case rebels pay a price. Therefore the probability of victory is a key to a decision whether to rebel and what strategy to use. The mobilization literature is important in that it tells us not only who can be mobilized and for what causes, but also how many can be mobilized, what resources can be used to advance rebels' strategy, and, ultimately, how all this affects the prospect of victory. Highly motivated communities that lack the resources to succeed in protesting the government's policies are unlikely to rebel, no matter the depth and magnitude of their grievances. Unfortunately, while there exists a significant body of literature on third-party intervention in civil conflict, most of it focuses on post-uprising intervention. There is little work on the anticipation of external support as part of the calculus of uprising (Jackson, San-Akca, and Maoz, (2020). We argue that would-be rebels assess not only factors that concern the relative capabilities of the disputants before they decide whether to rebel but also the balance of external support for uprisings as an important factor in their risk assessment.

Jackson, San Akca, and Maoz (2020) outline a strategic assessment of anticipated external support for an uprising by potential rebels. This assessment is based on a set of strategic, political, and ideational affinities between (a) would-be rebels and external actors, and (b) the government and external actors. Religious factors enter into the equation when potential rebels share affinities with external actors. In such cases, would-be rebels can anticipate some support for their cause by external actors. If such external actors also share some degree of enmity with the government of the focal state, the likelihood of support for a rebellion by such external actors increases. This pre-rebellion calculus of external support has an effect on the balance of risks associated with an uprising. Typically, the balance of capabilities between would-be rebels and the government tilts heavily in favor of the latter. Anticipation of external support—in the form of material support or through political and diplomatic support—can either narrow this balance of capabilities or alter it in favor of the rebels.[14]

We can summarize these ideas by the following propositions.

H1. All else being equal, the probability of civil conflict increases with the interaction between
   a. the religious diversity of a state and the relations between religious and political institutions, and
   b. the religious diversity of the state and the degree of religious discrimination and religious intolerance.
H2. The probability of civil conflict decreases with the proportion of the secular population in the state.
H3. The probability of civil conflict decreases with the degree of religious similarity between the major religious group in a given state and the religious makeup of the state's PRIE. Conversely, the probability of civil conflict increases with the degree of religious similarity between the largest minority religious group and the religious makeup of the state's PRIE.

Note that in H3, we focus on the religious similarity between two religious groups in a given state and the makeup of the state's PRIE. We assume that states are usually governed by political leaders who belong to the largest religious group. This is not a general case, but it is a reasonable assumption. Likewise, we assume that the second-largest religious group in a state is more likely to be excluded from power than the largest religious group. Again, this is not a general case, but it is quite common. We discuss these assumptions in the next section and take measures to control for other confounding factors. H3 suggests—in the spirit of Jackson, San Acka, and Maoz (2020) argument—that the religious affinity between the ruling elites and the state's PRIE suggests to would-be rebels that the ruling elites may get outside support in the case of an uprising. Conversely, if there is high religious similarity between the would-be rebels and actors in the state's PRIE, would-be rebels can expect outside support for their cause.

Before turning to a discussion of the research design to test these propositions, it is important to return to the issue of selection bias in the treatment of the types of civil wars (i.e., religious versus non-religious). Most students of civil conflict tend to lump together the probability of civil conflict with the attributes of civil conflicts such as its type (e.g., religious versus non-religious), intensity, duration, or outcome. This is wrong on both theoretical and methodological grounds. Societies "select" themselves into civil conflict. As we have seen in section 2 above, most states have little or no civil conflict. Those that do, tend to have such conflict repeatedly. This means that there is some—potentially systematic—set of factors that causes states to "select" themselves into such conflict. Civil conflicts can be more or less intense only if they actually occur. Therefore, the argument that religious conflicts are more intense, last longer, and are less likely to end in a negotiated settlement needs to take into account the probability that such conflict would break out in the first place. This requires us to estimate selection models that account for such processes (more below).

Although, as we mentioned in chapter 2, we are uncomfortable with the partition of civil conflicts into religious and non-religious ones and we do not endorse "religious-based" classificatory schema of armed conflicts, we nevertheless realize that many students of religion and civil conflict rely heavily on such distinctions (e.g., Toft 2007; Toft, Philpott, and Shah 2011; Svensson 2007, 2013; Pearce 2005, 2006; Fox, 2004a, 2004b, 2015; Bormann et al. 2017; Wucherpfennig et al. 2012). Therefore, we examine which factors account for these so-called "religious" civil conflicts as opposed to allegedly "non-religious" ones, as well. We also use the type of war as a variable that is expected to account for the attributes of the war such as its duration and intensity. Finally, we examine the effects of war type and various religious factors on the type of war termination.

Hypotheses on these matters are as follows:

H4. Religious polarization increases the likelihood of "religious war."
H5. The similarity between the majority religious group in the focal state and the majority religious group in the state's PRIE reduces the probability of "religious war."
H6. The similarity between the second-largest religious group in the focal state and the majority religious group in the state's PRIE increases the probability of "religious war."
H7. "Religious wars" are
  a. more severe than "non-religious wars,"
  b. last longer than "non-religious wars," and
  c. are less likely to end in a negotiated settlement than "non-religious wars."

5. Research Design

We discuss the structure of the data analysis briefly here. A more detailed discussion is provided in the appendix to the chapter.

Data. Our principal data source for religious factors in civil wars is the WRP dataset. These data allow us to determine the composition of a society in terms of the distribution of religious groups in that society. In order to examine the relations between religion and state, we combine, as discussed in previous chapters, the religion-state dataset (Fox 2016) with the Comparative Constitutions Project (CCP) of Elkins et al. (2014). We discuss the religion-state measure below.

Civil Conflict Datasets. Our dependent variables concern civil conflict. Here we employ four different datasets: the COW Intrastate Wars dataset (Sarkees and Wayman 2010, Sarkees and Dixon 2015), the UCDP Armed Conflict dataset (UCDP 2014), a dataset collected by Fearon and Laitin (2003), and the Non-violent and Violent Campaigns and Outcomes (NAVCO) data (Chenoweth and Lewis 2013). The datasets differ substantially. The COW intrastate war dataset covers civil wars defined as "any armed conflict that involved (1) military action internal to the metropole of the state system member; (2) the active participation of the national government; (3) effective resistance by both sides; and (4) a total of at least 1,000 battle-deaths during each year of the war" (Sarkees and Wayman 2010, 43; Dixon and Sarkees 2015). In other words, the COW intrastate war dataset focuses on cases properly characterized as "civil wars," that is, large-scale armed conflicts between the government of a state and organized elements of its population that involve high levels of violence resulting in substantial (at least 1,000) fatalities. The COW civil war dataset covers the period 1816–2015, and we use the COW data for the period 1945–2010.

The UCDP armed conflicts project defines an internal armed conflict as any series of engagements between nongovernment groups/individuals and government forces, or between different nongovernmental groups. The UCDP project has two levels of armed conflict. Low-scale conflicts are those that result in 25–999 fatalities per year of conflict. High-scale conflicts involve 1,000 or more fatalities per year of conflict. The UCDP civil conflict dataset covers the period 1945–2010.

The Fearon and Laitin dataset (hereafter FL dataset) defines civil wars as involving incidents of

1. fighting between agents of (or claimants to) a state and organized groups who sought either to take control of a government, take power in a region, or use violence to bring about a change in government policies;
2. a conflict that killed or has killed at least 1,000 [people] over its course; and
3. at least 100 of the dead being on the side of the government (including civilians attacked by rebels). This last condition is intended to rule out state-led massacres where there is no real organized or effective rebel opposition (Fearon and Laitin 2003).

The FL dataset covers the period 1945–2010.[15]

The NAVCO 3.0 dataset covers violent and nonviolent campaigns. A campaign is defined as "a series of observable, purposive, mass-tactics or events in pursuit of political objectives" (Chenoweth and Lewis 2013, 416), that involve 1,000 or more participants. The NAVCO dataset covers 290 violent and 161 nonviolent country-year campaigns over the period 1945–2012.

Data on war attributes—duration and intensity—are derived from these datasets.

War type. We use Toft's (2009) and Toft, Philpott, and Shah's (2011, 145) classification of civil wars as religious or non-religious. These are matched with the civil conflict datasets, so that any civil war that appears in Toft's list and also in one of the other datasets is designated "religious" or "non-religious" based on Toft's coding. We also match this with Svensson's (2007) data, so that any war that is coded "religious" by Toft or as involving religious issues (due to Svensson's coding), is coded "religious" in our dataset.

Termination type. We use Hartzell's (2009) data on war termination. Hartzell classifies war termination types as military victory, negotiated settlement, or truce. We code the first category as zero and the last two categories as one—negotiated termination.

Levels of analysis. We focus on the nation-year and the nation-history unit of analysis. For the nation-history level, we include only states that had a history of independence of ten or more years during the period under observation.

Measures. We use several measures of the dependent variable. For the nation-year unit of analysis, we employ the following measures of civil war.

1. *Civil war occurrence.* This variable is assigned a score of one for each year a civil war was underway and zero otherwise.
2. *Civil war duration.* This is the number of days during which civil war was underway for a given year.
3. *Civil war severity.* This is the log of battle deaths for the entire period of the civil war.[16] Analyses on this variable were conducted once for a given civil war.

As noted above, *war type* is assigned a value of one (i.e., "religious war") if the issues in contention involved religious factors, following the criteria of Toft (2006, 97). These factors may involve conflict over the status and role of religion or religious institutions in social, economic, or political affairs, or conflict between or among religious groups over things like holy places, religious liberties/privileges, or religious practices.

In order to provide a more general assessment of selection effects (as well as to conserve space), we combine the dependent variables for the analyses of civil conflict attributes as follows:

1. In the analysis of war type, we define a civil conflict as any nation-year during which any of the datasets listed above indicated an ongoing civil conflict.
2. In the analysis of civil conflict duration and civil conflict intensity, we used the maximum score of duration and intensity of any of these datasets. Since intensity was measured differently in the various datasets, we used the UCDP levels to indicate intensity (that is low intensity was given a score of one if the number of deaths due to civil conflict in a given year was between 25 and 999, and a score of two if the number of deaths was 1,000 or more. We also assigned an intensity value of three if the number of deaths in a given year exceeded 10,000—mostly based on COW battle deaths data.).
3. For civil conflict settlement, we used Hartzell's (2009) data on negotiated settlements, following her coding rules.

For the nation history. The same three variables were aggregated over the entire state's history and divided by the number of years during which a given state was independent. This gave us a mean frequency, duration, and severity per year of history.

Note that we do not follow much of the convention in the religion-civil conflict literature to focus on the outcomes of civil conflict. Our theory does not have anything specific to say about this linkage. As we noted above, we view the truncation of civil conflict types (i.e., into religious conflict, ethnic conflict, etc.) in this literature to be fundamentally biased and methodologically inappropriate.

Independent Variables. We used a number of measures of religious factors. The first set of factors concern the degree of religious diversity, polarization, or fractionalization. We do so because of a debate in the relevant literature about the way in which diversity/fractionalization/polarization is measured, and the extent to which different measures affect the results (Cederman and Girardin 2007; Fearon, Kasara, and Laitin 2007; Esteban, and Ray 2008b). We use the following measures:

1. *Religious diversity.* We used the IQV as in previous chapters. Here we use a normalized IQV over the valid number of religious groups in a given state. We also applied a normalized IQV for religious families. As in the previous chapters, we trichotomize this index into low/medium/high homogeneity values using the same breakpoints as before. We also conducted analyses using the continuous version, and these results are reported in the book's website.

2. *Religious polarization.* We employ a measure developed by Maoz (2006, 2010) of the degree of group religious polarization in society as:

$$gpol = \frac{\sum_{i=1}^{k}(1-p_i)p_i}{.25k},\qquad [7.1]$$

where k is the number of valid (nonzero) religious groups in the society and p_i is the percentage of religious group i in the state's population.[17] This measure varies between zero (when there is one group that includes the entire population, that is, a single religious group within a state) and one. Maximum polarization (*gpol* = *1*) occurs when the society is strictly bipolar: it is divided into only two groups, each of which controls exactly 50 percent of the population.

3. *Religious fractionalization.* We use the measure employed by Fearon and Laitin (2003):

$$RF = \sum_{i=1}^{k} p_i p_j.$$ [7.2]

As we show in the appendix to this chapter, these measures are highly correlated. Therefore, in the analyses in the body of the chapter, we focus on the fractionalization and group polarization (GPOL) measures.

4. *Secularism.* We measure secularism as the percentage of non-religious members of a society. This does not include the residual category of other religions. Rather, it reflects the proportion of people who do not practice a given religion (including atheists, agnostics, and other nonpractitioners).
5. *Affinity of minority group with members of a state's relevant environment.* As noted in previous chapters, a state is surrounded by politically relevant neighbors. These include all of the states that are contiguous to the focal state, as well as regional powers with regional reach capacity and major powers with global reach capacity (Maoz 2010). This is the focal state's PRIE. Hypotheses H3–H5 require data on the religious composition of the ruling elite and potential or actual opposition groups in states. Unfortunately, we do not have such data, so we use a less refined measure here.[18] We assume that the majority religious group in a country is likely to be associated with the ruling elite, whereas the second-largest group is likely to be associated with the opposition. Under this assumption, we focus on two types of relationships between religious groups within the focal state and religious groups in its PRIE. First, we focus on the affinity between the majority religious group in the focal state and the majority religious group in the state's PRIE. This is an indicator of the potential support a regime may expect to receive if religion-based mobilization occurs

in the focal state. Second, we examine the affinity between the second-largest religious group in the focal state and the majority religious group in the state's PRIE. This is an indicator of the expected support the opposition can receive from neighboring states.

These measures are as follows: (a) major-major match (*Match State-PRIE Maj. Relig. Groups*); this variable is the sum of states in a focal state's PRIE whose modal religious group is the same as the modal religious group in the focal state; (b) minor-major match (*Match State-PRIE Min-Maj. Relig. Groups*); this variable is the sum of states in a focal state's PRIE whose modal religious group is the same as the second-largest religious group in the focal state.

Note that for any given composition of a PRIE, both the regime and the opposition may expect to receive support from PRIE members. Some states in one's PRIE may be matched on religious majorities; other states in one's PRIE might be matched on the state's religious minority. When these two variables receive high value, the expectation is that the probability of severe civil conflict will increase.

Control Variables.

1. *Democracy.* We measure democracy in the same way as in previous chapters. The general expectation is that democracies are less vulnerable to violent civil unrest because publics have legitimate avenues for expression of dissent and grievances. If certain segments of the public are unhappy with government policies, they can protest or replace the government in the elections. In autocracies, even peaceful protest against government policies is not likely to be tolerated and therefore violent opposition is more likely.
2. *Log. per capita GDP.* This is a commonly used control that measures overall economic wealth. The expectation is that wealthier countries are less vulnerable to civil unrest than poor ones. We log-transform this magnitude to prevent exceedingly small coefficient estimates.
3. *Change in per-capita GDP.* This is a three-year moving average of the annual percent change in per-capita GDP. This measures the change in economic conditions over the previous three-year

period. When the economy is growing, people are more likely to be satisfied with the government than when the economy is stagnating or shrinking.
4. *Log population.* Again, the size of the population was considered in many previous studies of civil conflict to be an important factor in civil wars. Large populations typically imply more potential grievances and weakened state capacity (an ability to extract resources and to protect law and order, lower reach capacity to various segments of the population).
5. *External conflict.* We measure external conflict as the three-year moving average of MIDs involving the focal state. Exposure to external conflict may make a state either more or less vulnerable to civil conflict: the former may result from discontent within the state from the government's handling of the external conflict; and the latter from the benefits to the state of a "rally around the flag" effect that encourages greater support for the government.
6. *Ethno-religious excluded population.* We use the EPR dataset (Wimmer et al., 2009, Cederman et al. 2010). This dataset contains an ethnic breakdown of states, with an assessment of the extent to which ethnic groups share equal access to political power. We use a variable of the proportion of ethnically excluded population as a control on religion, under the assumption that ethnicity and religion do not usually overlap. The average correlation between this variable and religious fractionalization/polarization is in the range of $0.05 \leq r \leq 0.125$, which suggests that this is a reasonable control.
7. *Past civil war/conflict.* Due to the skewed distribution of civil conflict onset, it is important to include the number of past years during which a civil war occurred. Just as studies of recidivism show, this is expected to have a very powerful impact on civil war recurrence.

5.1 *Estimation.*

We use a number of different methods to estimate the equations that stem from the various hypotheses, depending on the structure of the data and the nature of the dependent variable. For the nation year, we use logit models with nonevent years and cubic splines when the dependent variable is the occurrence or nonoccurrence of a given event. For the duration of civil wars, which is an event count, we use cross-sectional time-series negative binomial regression. For the intensity (log battle deaths), we use cross-sectional time-series regression. Because of the skewed distribution of civil wars over states, we cannot use fixed-effects models. These models would drop all states with zero civil wars during their history—a huge proportion of the entire sample; therefore, we are compelled to use random-effects models. A generalized least-squares model with an ar(1) autocorrelation structure produces similar results. For the nation-history unit of analysis, we use OLS estimation.

As noted in the literature review and the previous section, analyses of civil conflict type and civil conflict attributes require "screening" of the ex-ante probability of conflict outbreak. For that reason, we employ a Heckman selection model estimation. The Heckman selection modeling strategy is an approach that allows examining for bias in the sample under analysis. Since the outbreak of civil war is nonrandom, the probability that a given state finds itself embroiled in a civil conflict is a function of a set of factors. Hence, from a causal inference perspective, the "treatment sample" is not randomly assigned. The factors that account for the outbreak of civil conflict may have an impact on the attributes and outcomes of such conflicts. Heckman selection models proceed in two steps. The first step estimates the bias in the selection process. This step involves estimation that is quite similar to the single-step logit equations (except that it uses probit estimation). The second step augments the test of the attributes of the civil conflict with the inherent bias in the selection process (represented by a significant *rho* value) so that the estimates of the attributes of the civil conflict correct for the bias in the "selection" of the state into the conflict. This allows for a more credible estimate of the type, duration, and intensity of the conflict, given the (potential) bias in states' selection into such conflicts. It also allows us to test the effect of such biases in terms of settlement types.

6. Results

6.1 *War outbreak*

We start our analysis at the nation-year level of analysis. Table 7.1 shows the results of factors affecting civil war outbreak. The full results are presented in the book's website.

Table 7.1 Civil war occurrence

	COW	UCDP	FL	NAVCO
Religious Homogeneity	0.089	0.161**	-0.023	0.311**
	(0.064)	(0.06)	(0.063)	(0.062)
Relig-State Relations	-0.306**	-0.052	-0.035	-0.107
	(0.074)	(0.07)	(0.076)	(0.072)
Match State-PRIE Maj. Relig. Groups	0.016**	0.005	0.018**	0.02**
	(0.004)	(0.005)	(0.005)	(0.005)
Match State-PRIE Min-Maj. Relig. Groups	-0.015*	0.023**	0.014	0.009
	(0.007)	(0.008)	(0.007)	(0.007)
Secularism	**-1.756****	**-4.119****	**-4.994****	**-4.432****
	(0.549)	**(0.736)**	**(0.795)**	**(0.602)**
Pct. Christians	-0.497**	-0.163	-0.162	-0.673**
	(0.184)	(0.203)	(0.222)	(0.189)
Pct. Muslims	-0.59**	0.057	0.278	-0.832**
	(0.208)	(0.217)	(0.237)	(0.215)
Pct. Hindus	0.315	0.001	0.006	0.557
	(0.348)	(0.399)	(0.478)	(0.443)
Democracy	-0.388**	-0.492**	-0.622**	-0.376*
	(0.144)	(0.153)	(0.172)	(0.151)
Per-Capita GDP (logged)	-0.846**	-0.726**	-1.124**	-0.843**
	(0.131)	(0.122)	(0.136)	(0.128)
Change in PC GDP	-6.935**	-5.818**	-4.002	-4.047
	(1.993)	(2.111)	(2.049)	(2.552)
Pct. Excluded Population (EPR)	0.969**	1.215**	0.675**	1.034**
	(0.179)	(0.159)	(0.173)	(0.17)
Past Conflict	0.626**	0.134**	0.167**	0.042**
	(0.039)	(0.007)	(0.007)	(0.002)
Spatial Diffusion	0.058**	0.003	0.052**	0.091**
	(0.006)	(0.004)	(0.005)	(0.005)
Log Population	0.516**	0.483**	0.752**	0.611**
	(0.082)	(0.078)	(0.085)	(0.081)
Constant	-2.369**	-2.394**	-3.116**	-4.737**
	(0.518)	(0.5)	(0.525)	(0.515)
Statistics				
N	6,952	6,704	6,865	6,952
Chi-Square	742.10	780.65	1,100.00	1,100.00
R-Squared	0.216	0.377	0.433	0.371

Notes: Numbers in parentheses are robust standard errors.
Cubic splines omitted due to space considerations
*p < 0.05; **p < 0.01

The results suggest that religious homogeneity and religion-state relations do not have a consistent and significant effect on the occurrence of civil conflict. This runs contrary to the expectations of all the key theories linking religious factors to civil conflict. The degree of secularism—measured as the percent of the non-religious population—is the only variable that is indicative of a consistent and robust relationship between the religious characteristics of societies and the probability of civil war occurrence. We also do not find a consistent relationship between the religious makeup of societies and the religious makeup of their politically relevant environments. Nor did we find a consistent relationship between a given religion and civil conflict.

There are several reasons for the apparent nonrelationship between religious factors and civil conflict. First, the percentage of excluded population based on the EPR dataset as well as the log of total population wash out the relationship between religious-state relations (and in some cases between religious homogeneity) and civil conflict. Since the coding of ethnic groups in the EPR dataset converges in many cases with the religious breakdown of societies, this may account for some of these results. Indeed, if we drop the percent excluded population, we find a statistically significant effect of religion-state relations on the outbreak of civil conflict in three out of the four datasets. (UCDP, FL, and NAVCO. See results in book website.)

As noted above, past civil conflict has a consistent effect on current civil conflict occurrence. In addition, economic wealth, measured by per-capita GDP, and change in economic conditions, measured by per-capita GDP change, as well as democracy have a significant dampening effect on civil conflict. On the other hand, total population (logged) and spatial diffusion have significant positive effects on civil conflict occurrence. This is consistent with the extant empirical literature on this subject.

The findings up to this point suggest that approaches that propose a simplistic religion-conflict nexus probably are not capturing these alternately conflict exacerbating, conflict dampening, or nonconflictual relationships borne of the particularity of these interactions in individual states. In particular, the interplay of exclusion and specific political, social, and economic conditions that results in more bellicose propensities, is more likely rooted in the specific conflict histories of individual states, which is evident in the robustness of that variable in our analyses. This may explain why the inclusion of the state's conflict history does so much to diminish the salience of the religion variables in our analyses as compared to previous findings on the relationship between religious factors and civil conflict in the literature.

6.2 Civil Conflict Attributes

How do religious factors affect the attributes of civil conflicts? The analyses on these matters are given in Table 7.2. The first and most important

Table 7.2 Heckman selection models of religious factors and civil conflict attributes

Variable	War Type[1]	Duration	Intensity[2]	Settlement[1]
War Type		0.100**	0.863**	-0.232*
		(0.029)	(0.092)	(0.097)
Religious Polarization	1.993**	0.025	-1.173**	0.562*
	(0.23)	(0.088)	(0.318)	(0.277)
Religion-State Relations				
Some Relation	0.516**	-0.119**	0.177	-0.358**
	(0.099)	(0.039)	(0.116)	(0.101)
Cohabitation	1.084**	-0.371**	-0.241	-0.411**
	(0.113)	(0.046)	(0.137)	(0.120)
Match State-PRIE Maj. Relig. Groups	0.006	-0.001	-0.001	-0.024**
	(0.004)	(0.002)	(0.006)	(0.009)
Match State-PRIE Min-Maj. Relig. Groups	0.021**	-0.013**	-0.012	-0.016**
	(0.005)	(0.002)	(0.008)	(0.006)
Secularism	**0.791***	**0.899***	**0.001**	**0.232**
	(0.336)	**(0.147)**	**(0.431)**	**(0.413)**
Democ	-0.006**	-0.002**	-0.002	0.000
	(0.001)	(0.000)	(0.001)	(0.001)
Per-Capita GDP	-0.311**	0.24**	-0.236	0.177
	(0.099)	(0.04)	(0.121)	(0.109)
GDP Change	1.858	-0.252	-2.096	-4.323
	(2.001)	(0.842)	(2.554)	(2.354)
Pct. Excluded Population	-0.061	-0.275**	0.418*	0.644**
	(0.141)	(0.062)	(0.168)	(0.154)
Constant	0.152	2.554**	-0.835*	-1.22**
	(0.315)	(0.131)	(0.400)	(0.355)
Statistics				
N	6,457	6,478	6,478	6,478
N_selected	1,455	1,476	1,476	1,476
Chi Square	221.777	196.424	138.179	107.218
Rho	-0.668	-0.891	0.33	-0.32
p(Rho)	0.000	0.000	0.0000	0.005

Notes: First-stage results (civil conflict outbreak) are not presented; they are similar to those in Table 7.1 above.
1 Heckman probit model
2 Ordered Heckman probit model

evidence provided by Table 7.2 is the significant selection bias that is observed in the analyses of civil war attributes. This is evidenced by the significant *rho* statistics measures for the Heckman selection models. This vindicates our suspicion that states select themselves systematically into repeated civil conflicts. Specifically, past civil conflict and global spread of civil conflict, as well as state-specific conditions (e.g., excluded populations, low economic development), have an important impact on such selection processes. Consequently, studying the attributes of only those civil conflicts that broke out leads to potentially flawed inferences about the factors that affect such conflict attributes in the first place, due to such selection mechanisms.

Once we control for selection bias, the results of Table 7.2 provide important insights into the effects of religious variables on the attributes of civil conflict. They corroborate some previous analyses of these matters, but cast doubt on others. We start with a discussion of the type of war outbreak. First, we find that the regime score reduces the probability of "religious" conflicts. Civil conflicts on religious issues tend to be fought in states with less democratic characteristics than in democracies.

Second, religious polarization has a positive impact on "religious conflict" outbreak. When a society approximates a bipolar religious structure (two large religious groups, each controlling close to half of the population), the probability of a civil conflict over religious issues increases significantly. This is so even though the probability of civil war is not consistently related to religious polarization in general. Again, states that select themselves into civil wars in general appear to evince a tendency to fight over religious issues when their populations are highly polarized in terms of religious affiliation. Yet, given the methodological and inferential problems we have noted regarding the classification of "religious wars," it is just as likely that conflict in religiously polarized states is more likely to be categorized as "religious conflict."

Third, we find that religious-state relations increase the probability of civil conflict over religious issues. We tested the specific dimensions of religious-state relations (religious discrimination, religious regulation, and religious legislation, Fox 2016) and found significant effects of each of these dimensions on the probability of "religious" civil conflict. Interestingly, while these factors were associated with a significantly lower likelihood of peaceful settlements, they were associated with relatively shorter conflicts, which were not significantly more or less intense than "non-religious" conflicts. The latter may be contrasted with the effects of the percentage of excluded populations, in general, which is associated with significantly more severe conflicts, and that, nonetheless, are more likely to reach a negotiated settlement.

Fourth, we find that when the second-largest religious group in a state is matched with the religious majority groups in the state's PRIE, the probability of a civil conflict over religious conflict increases. This supports the argument of Jackson, San-Akca, and Maoz, (2020) that potential or actual opposition groups that expect the support of neighbors with religious affinity are more likely to rebel.

We also find that secularism increases the probability of conflict over religious issues. This may well be a reaction of religious groups to growing secularization. It may also stem from the dissatisfaction of secular populations with the status of relations between political and religious institutions.

Economic development reduces the probability of civil conflict over religious issues. However, economic growth is not related to the issues at stake in such conflicts. We also did not find a significant effect of the percent of excluded groups on the probability of a "religious" civil conflict.

Looking at the characteristics of civil conflicts, given selection bias, we find that civil conflicts that are waged on religious issues are more intense and last longer than those conflicts that are about non-religious issues. We also find, in line with previous research, that civil conflicts that are fought over religious issues are less likely to end in a negotiated settlement than those fought over other issues.[19]

A key result concerns the effect of the relations between political and religious institutions on the outbreak of "religious war." We find that once states that maintain close ties between religious and political relations select themselves into civil conflict, the likelihood of "religious conflict" increases significantly. The difference between states that separate religion from politics, and states that maintain a close relationship between religious and political institutions is especially stark in this respect. This is demonstrated by Figure 7.3, which shows that as religious polarization increases—especially in states that are characterized by close ties between political and religious institutions—the probability of civil war increases significantly. At levels of 0.7 or higher of religious polarization, in such states the probability is that, accounting for selection bias, all wars that break out are likely to be over religious issues.

Religious polarization does not have a significant effect on the duration of civil conflicts, but it tends to reduce their intensity. Interestingly, religious polarization increases the probability of a negotiated settlement in civil conflicts. State-religion relations reduce the duration of civil conflict, but also reduce the probability of negotiated settlements.

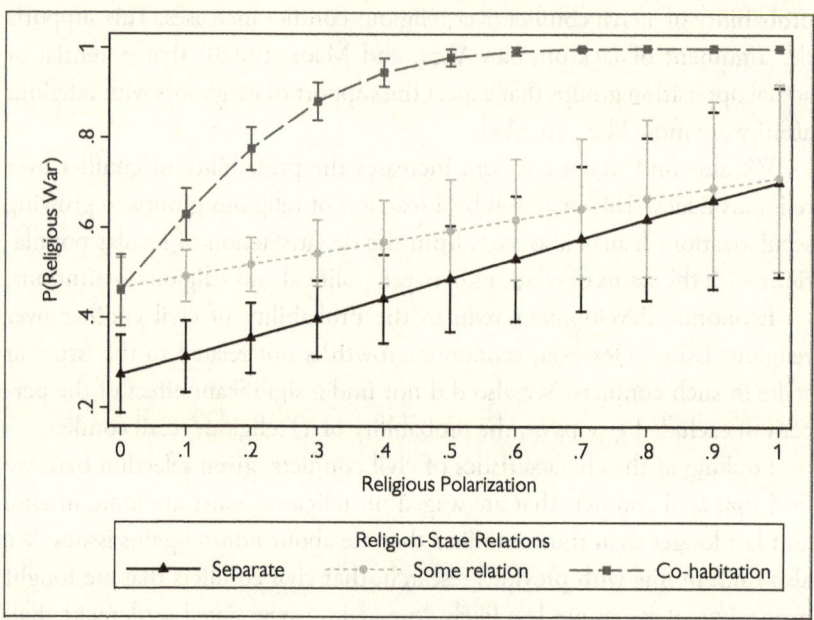

Fig. 7.3. Religious polarization, religion-state relations, and the probability of religious war outbreak (marginal effects based on Heckman probit selection model)

A match between the major religious group in a society and the other majority groups in the focal state's PRIE, and a match between the second-largest religious group and the majority group in the state's PRIE both reduce the probability of a negotiated settlement. This suggests that when the dominant religious group of the focal state shares high religious affinity with dominant groups in neighboring states, the likelihood of a negotiated settlement declines. The same applies to cases where the second-largest religious group in a state shares high affinity with majority groups in the focal state's PRIE.

In the book's online appendix (Table A7.2), we repeat the analyses of Table 7.2, including estimates of the impact of the percent population in a country practicing a specific religion, focusing in particular on the four most common types of religious affiliation: Christianity, Islam, Hinduism, and secular. The reason for that is that, in contrast to previous analyses where we did not find that the size of a specific religious group in a country increases its propensity to fight external or internal wars, here we find some contrasting results. These results resonate with our previously stated concerns regarding the greater likelihood of Type 1 errors in research designs that rely on categorization of "religious wars."

We find some differences between religious groups in terms of civil war attributes. As the proportion of Christians increases, the propensity for civil conflict over religious issues declines. By contrast, increasingly larger Muslim populations increase the propensity of civil conflict on religious grounds. Both Christian and Muslim populations reduce the duration of civil conflict, and Muslim populations also tend to reduce the intensity of such conflicts. However, the probability of negotiated settlements decreases in states with a large Muslim population.[20]

These findings may simply represent what they seem to: provisional support for theses proposing a positive relationship between religious factors and "religious war," but it also may be that religious factors only appear to be salient in "religious wars" because the categories themselves are constructed using the very criteria that their subsequent models presumably are attempting to detect.

The key takeaway from this set of analyses is that the process by which states select themselves into civil conflicts has a significant impact on the type of wars they fight, on the duration and severity of such wars, and on the manner by which they end. This offers important insights into the literature on civil war in general, and on the impact of religious factors on such wars in particular.

6.3 Nation History

We now turn to an analysis of the entire history of states. This analysis is germane in light of the highly skewed distribution of civil conflicts over different states. We focus on the general civil-conflict proneness of states over their entire history. The significance of these analyses is threefold. First, it allows assessment of a general propensity of states for civil conflict. Because of the high inequality of civil war occurrence across states, it is useful to qualitatively distinguish between war-prone states in terms of civil war occurrences and those that have had few or none. Second, this enables us to assess the effect of the more stable religious characteristics of states (e.g., percent of certain religious adherents, religious homogeneity) on civil war propensity. Third, this analysis, as in previous chapters, allows for a robustness test of our nation-year results. Specifically, do the aggregate characteristics of states account for their propensity for political instability?

Table 7.3 provides the results of the marginal effects of the same independent variables over the civil war participation of states during their entire history, or over the period 1945–2010.

When we examine the general propensity of states to engage in civil conflict, we find that the only religious (or rather non-religious) factor that consistently reduces the degree of civil conflict in states is the average degree of secularism in the state over its history. States that averaged a higher proportion of nonreligious people were significantly less likely

Table 7.3 The effects of religious characteristics on state's civil conflict history—OLS analysis (only states with 10+ years of independence included)

	COW	UCDP	FL	NAVCO
Religious Homogeneity				
Medium	0.03	0.134	0.062	0.091
	(0.025)	(0.092)	(0.043)	(0.053)
High	0.015	-0.002	0.023	0.006
	(0.02)	(0.056)	(0.044)	(0.041)
Relig-State Relations				
Some Relation	0.006	0.073	0.061	0.05
	(0.019)	(0.052)	(0.042)	(0.039)
Cohabitation	-0.006	0.149	0.042	0.064
	(0.023)	(0.101)	(0.047)	(0.057)
Match State-PRIE Maj. Relig. Groups	-0.001	-0.003	-0.002	-0.001
	(0.001)	(0.003)	(0.003)	(0.003)
Match State-PRIE Min-Maj. Relig. Groups	0.003**	0.004	0.002	0
	(0.001)	(0.003)	(0.002)	(0.002)
Democracy	0.017	0.384*	0.137*	0.143
	(0.025)	(0.186)	(0.055)	(0.082)
Per-Capita GDP	-0.068**	-0.343*	-0.168**	-0.167**
	(0.019)	(0.14)	(0.044)	(0.061)
GDP Change	-1.772	7.024	1.375	0.509
	(2.299)	(9.254)	(4.298)	(4.928)
Secularism	**-0.143***	**-0.725***	**-0.508***	**-0.444***
	(0.057)	**(0.241)**	**(0.148)**	**(0.128)**
Pct. Excluded Population	0.162**	0.385*	0.286**	0.284*
	(0.062)	(0.168)	(0.101)	(0.114)
MIDs	0.033**	0.125**	0.112**	0.067**
	(0.012)	(0.046)	(0.03)	(0.025)
Constant	0.253**	1.073**	0.556**	0.569**
	(0.065)	(0.435)	(0.148)	(0.201)
N	150	150	150	150
F-Statistic	9.571	5.571	7.001	5.246
R-Squared	0.336	0.275	0.382	0.264
RMSE	0.095	0.387	0.192	0.222

to engage in civil conflict than states that had a larger proportion of believers—regardless of the distribution of such beliefs across different religions. This result holds across all of the datasets, thereby corroborating the nation-year analyses.

Other religious factors do not distinguish between civil conflict-prone states and those that are less prone to resolve political, economic, or social difference through violence. In particular, at this level of analysis we corroborate the findings of Fearon and Laitin (2003, 2007) and of Collier and Hoeffler (2004) that religious fractionalization (and our measure of religious polarization) does not significantly impact the civil conflict propensity of states. Likewise, we do not find any meaningful correlation between religious homogeneity and civil conflict, or between religion-state relations and civil conflict.

As was the case in previous chapters, we find no statistically significant association between any religion and civil war propensity (see online appendix). Whether a state is populated by a high percentage of Christians, Muslims, Hindu, Buddhists, or Jews has no effect on its propensity to experience civil conflict. This refutes a persistent and popular idea in both the academic literature and in popular discourse. In particular, it challenges Huntington's (1996, 258) widely publicized claim that "Islam's borders are bloody and so are its innards."

With respect to other determinants of civil conflict proneness, we find that the size of the economic system consistently affects civil conflict propensity. Developed countries—not surprisingly—tend to experience significantly lower levels of civil conflict than developing ones. There is also support for the relationship between external and internal conflict, but this result is not robust over datasets and model specifications. Interestingly, the average regime score (or the proportion of the period during which a state was a democracy) had no effect on civil conflict proneness.

The percent of excluded population has a positive and significant effect on civil war propensity, and this result is robust with respect to different conflict datasets and model specifications. Since excluded population can be grouped along ethnic, racial, class, religious or linguistic lines, there may be some latent evidence that religious discrimination affects civil war propensity. However, using the Fox religious discrimination measure suggests that religious discrimination does not have a significant impact on civil war propensity, and this result is also quite general across datasets. As noted above, one inference seems clear: exclusion, by itself, may provide motivation for conflict. But motivation must be accompanied by opportunity, and such opportunities are typically not captured by measures of religious, ethnic, or racial discrimination. Such factors are those rooted in the conflict histories of individual states that are myriad in the abstract and specific to each state's conflict history in the particular—and even these myriad factors may interact in particular ways (and in specific time periods)—in the affected countries to increase the probability of civil war.[21] This is why the state's conflict history does so much to wash out the impact of the otherwise heretofore significant variables in the religion-conflict literature in our analyses.

7. Conclusion

The key point in this chapter is that—contrary to the expectations of the theories connecting religion to conflict—civil conflict is not typically about religion. First, we find that over the period 1945–2010, religious civil conflicts, that is, civil conflicts that pit different religious groups against each other, or which are focused on a religious issue, accounted for about a third of civil conflicts (See Figure A7.1 in book website). While there has been a rise in the number of "religious conflicts" during the post–Cold War era, the claim that this is "God's Century" is an obvious exaggeration. It is clearly not supported by empirical evidence. Second, with respect to the outbreak of civil conflicts, our analyses lend support to the argument made by several authors (Cederman and Wimmer 2009, Wimmer and Cederman 2009, Wucherpenning et al. 2012, Cederman et al. 2013) that systematic exclusion of ethnic groups from power is a consistent predictor of conflict. We have not been able to ascertain, however, the extent to which ethnic exclusion overlaps with religion and exclusion of religiously defined communities. Our measures of religious diversity, religious homogeneity, or religious polarization do not correlate with the measure of exclusion that affects civil war outbreak. Therefore, we cannot conclude with confidence that religious factors do not affect civil conflict.

We do find, however, fairly strong evidence for three religion-related issues. First, secularism tends to dampen civil-conflict proneness. This is clearly evidenced by our analyses of nation histories. Second, virtually all our analyses suggest that the dominance of a specific religious group in a given state does not affect its propensity to engage in civil conflict. Nor does any specific religious group affect the attributes of civil conflict. Third, taking into account our reservations with respect to labeling some civil conflicts "religious" in the sense that they may be fought over religious issues, we find that civil conflicts designated as "religious" tend to be more severe, last longer, and be less likely to end in peaceful settlements than "nonreligious" conflicts.

There may be (and typically are) other possible correlates of civil war outbreak, including inequalities that overlap across economic, social, and cultural identity dimensions. We have not presumed to cover the entire spectrum of possible causes of civil wars. What we do find is that religious factors do not have a prominent effect on either the probability of civil conflict outbreak, on their attributes, or on the general propensity of states to engage in repeated civil conflicts.

What does this tell us about the relationship between religion and civil conflict? Clearly, some of the central civil conflicts in the second half of the twentieth century and first decade of the twenty-first century have been between religious groups: the Israeli–Palestinian conflict, the Iraqi–Kurdish conflict, the "Golden Temple" conflict between the Indian government and Sikhs, the massacre of Shiites by the Sunni military of Saddam Hussein at the end of the first Gulf War and the continued sectarian civil war in Iraq after the US invasion, the civil war between the Muslim north and the Christians/animists in the former Sudan, the Christian–Muslim conflicts in the former Yugoslavia, the conflict in Northern Ireland, and so forth. However, intrareligious conflicts during this time were just as numerous (as most advocates of religious-conflict theses acknowledge, see chapter 2), no less vicious (e.g., in overwhelmingly Christian Rwanda and Liberia, in the overwhelmingly Muslim countries of Libya, Syria, and Yemen), and just as long (e.g., in predominantly Catholic Colombia, and predominantly Hindu Nepal). Moreover, there were quite a few religiously diverse or polarized societies that managed their political conflict without resort to violence.

So, a look at a select list of highly visible civil conflicts may form an impression that they are about religion and/or ethnicity. Yet, a more systematic analysis of the relationship between religion and civil conflict suggests that religious factors have little effect on the outbreak of civil conflicts in general. At the same time, once we control for the selection bias in civil war outbreak, it turns out that religious factors have a significant impact on the attributes of civil wars. Our analysis casts some doubt on previous studies of civil war outbreak that suggest the importance of religious factors regarding when and whether such wars break out. To the extent that it appears to vindicate studies that suggest that religion plays a role in determining the type of war and in affecting its attributes, one is reminded of our concern that it may simply be that conflicts in states with certain religious characteristics are more likely to be categorized as "religious" by construction.

Some of the results do suggest a puzzle: as the level of secularism in societies increases, the propensity for civil conflict declines. However, secularism—the proportion of atheists, agnostics, or nonbelievers in a society—does not necessarily imply that the society does not possess meaningful religious groups. In fact, the average secularism in states is only slightly more than 5 percent. This means that most societies contain one or more well-defined religious groups. So why is it that the structure of society in terms of religious groups is not correlated with civil wars, but secularism is? One possible answer is that secularism is correlated with other factors that mitigate the propensity for civil conflict. If secularism is related to national wealth or economic growth—or non-economic attributes of states such as "quality of life"—and these latter characteristics of a society reduce the propensity for civil conflict, that might explain this puzzle. To explore this issue further, we need to examine the relationship between religious factors and various aspects of the quality of life in states. This is the topic of the next chapter.

Appendix to Chapter 7

1. Introduction

This appendix outlines some technical methodological issues that expand on the issues discussed in the research design section in the chapter. Also see the online appendix for detailed tabular and graphical results, beyond those presented in the body of the chapter.

2. Measures

Measures of religious diversity/fractionalization and polarization require a brief discussion. There are multiple measures of fractionalization or diversity, as well as a few measures that claim to measure polarization. Fearon and Laitin (2003) conceive fractionalization to be the probability that a given person practicing a given religion (or speaking a certain language or belonging to a specific ethnic group) will encounter another person from the same religion by chance. Measures developed by Reynal-Querol (Montalvo and Reynal-Querol 2005, Reynal-Querol 2002) are based on a similar conception. The correlation between the Reynal-Querol and the WRP IQV measure is quite high ($r = 0.859$). The religious fractionalization measure is also very highly correlated with the IQV measure we have used in previous chapters ($r = 0.993$) so these are virtually equivalent.

On the other hand, the polarization index is significantly different from the other two. As one of us showed elsewhere (Maoz 2010), this measure is maximized when the network—in our case the society—is split into exactly two groups of the same size.[22] The correlation between the network polarization index and the other measures of polarization and dispersion is moderate (correlations range between 0.676 and 0.760 with the other indices).

CHAPTER 8

Religion and Quality of Life

1. Introduction

We have analyzed the ways in which the religious characteristics of states, dyads, and regions, relate to international conflict and cooperation. We have also examined the effect of the religious characteristics of states on their domestic conflict experience. Throughout our analyses we focused on the internal characteristics of states as well as the characteristics of their relevant political environment. We found that both sets of attributes—domestic and international—have a significant impact on the domestic and foreign policy behavior of states. In this chapter we focus on the relationship between the religious attributes of states and a novel conceptualization of security—human security or, more broadly conceived—quality of life. The key question of this chapter is *to what extent do the characteristics of the state and society—in particular their religious characteristics—correlate with the quality of life of its citizens?*

Since the late 1980s, mainstream IR scholars began to formulate alternative and more expansive notions of security. While scholars such as Matthews (1989) and Homer Dixon (1991) expanded the notion vertically to include resource, environmental, and demographic issues, feminist scholars such as Enloe (1989) and Tickner (1992) broadened the concept horizontally to address issues of women's rights. In so doing, they advanced notions of human security that focused on individual security and well-being as well as the social welfare of marginalized social groups more generally. Combining aspects of both vertical and horizontal expansions of mainstream conceptions of international security, IR scholars in what became known as the Copenhagen School of security studies (Buzan 1983, 1991; Waever et al. 1993, Buzan et al. 1998) argued for a multidimensional approach to security, emphasizing the political construction of threats across several sectors (military security, political security, economic security, societal security, and environmental security). In this way, the Copenhagen School expands on the primarily military and state-centric concept of security. Even more expansively, IR scholars associated with the Aberystwyth School of security studies, often drawing on critical theorists of the Frankfurt School, cast international security squarely at the individual level of analysis, explicitly concentrating on human security. In their critical conception, human security could be realized through the emancipation of the individual from oppressive social structures and the transformation of political communities (e.g. Wyn Jones 1999, Booth 2005).

These conceptions not only expand but challenge traditional notions of security that focus on military power, technology, or economic foundations of national power. In contrast, human security focuses on factors and processes at the individual and group levels of analysis. Such a reconceptualization of security was necessitated by the realization that many of the threats and vulnerabilities in the global system in the post-Cold War era were dramatically different than those that dominated the Cold War era and often beyond the scope of the state to address effectively. As the threat of nuclear war declined with the end of the superpower standoff that marked the Cold War, the rise of transnational challenges such as globalization, climate change, or communicable diseases such as HIV, were beyond the scope of individual states to resolve.

Further, the post-Cold War era witnessed genocidal conflicts in Europe, Africa, and Asia, as well as a proliferation of violent transnational drug cartels and terrorist groups. These processes evolved even as a new wave of democratization began to buttress an expanding international regime of human rights which mandated international humanitarian intervention. (Of note, the first deployment of NATO troops into hostilities was not in a Cold War armed conflict, but in response to the atrocities committed by Serbian forces in Kosovo in 1999.) Global economic inequality was such that some regions were characterized by persistent stultifying poverty and some regimes were unable or unwilling to provide basic services, institutions, and infrastructure to their populations and became "failed states."

Such states tended to devolve into internal wars which often spread beyond single states, targeted non-combatants, utilized child soldiers, employed rape as a weapon of war, and utilized international trade networks to finance the fighting which increased its longevity and lethality.

In such a context, observers recognized that the concept and content of international security needed to be reconsidered; and the primary focus of both should be on security for the individual: human security. "Human security," the International Commission on Intervention and State Sovereignty (ICISS) insisted, "means the security of people – their physical safety, their economic and social well-being, respect for their dignity and worth as human beings, and the protection of their human rights and fundamental freedoms" (ICISS 2001: 15). This approach recognized that "[t]he fundamental components of human security—the security of *people* against threats to life, health, livelihood, personal safety and human dignity—can be put at risk by external aggression, but also by factors within a country, including "security forces"(p. 15) [original emphasis]. In fact being hamstrung by narrow state-centric and militarily focused conceptions of " 'national security' may be one reason why many governments spend more to protect their citizens against undefined external military attack than to guard them against the omnipresent enemies of good health and other real threats to human security on a daily basis" (p. 15).

Human security became prominent among policymakers with publication of the UN Development Program's (UNDP's) *Human Development Report* which argued that "[t]he world can never be at peace unless people have security in their daily lives;" moreover, "it will not be possible for the community of nations to achieve any of its major goals…except in the context of sustainable development that leads to *human security*" (UNDP 1994: 1) [emphasis added]. They maintained that human security reflected "[t]he growing recognition worldwide that concepts of security must include people as well as states" (UNDP 1994: 15); and "[f]or most people today, a feeling of insecurity arises more from worries about daily life than from the dread of a cataclysmic world event" (p. 3). Thus, human security is people centered: "concerned with how people live and breathe in a society, how freely they exercise their many choices, how much access they have to market and social opportunities and whether they live in conflict or in peace" (p. 23).

While human security is clearly related to human development it is not synonymous with it. In fact, human security engages with and in some cases encompasses each of the aspects of security laid out in Buzan's (1983, 1991) scheme (i.e. military, political, economic, environmental, societal); and while it transcends traditional state-centric military security issues it implicates them as well. Where it does so unequivocally is in its challenge to state sovereignty and justification of military intervention in those countries where regimes are substantially violating the human rights of their citizens. This is expressed in the notion of the international community's "responsibility to protect" (R2P). R2P arises from the report by that name of the International Commission on Intervention and State Sovereignty (ICISS 2001). Like the UNDP, it recognized that "[t]he meaning and scope of security have become much broader since the UN Charter was signed in 1945" (p. 15). The basis for this international circumvention of state sovereignty is that "the protection of human security, including human rights and human dignity, must be one of the fundamental objectives of modern international institutions" (p. 6). Human security, "including concern for human rights—but broader than that in its scope—has also become an increasingly important element in international law and international relations," R2P is one of the most prominent and provocative justifications that derive from this framework (p. 6).

Thus, issues related to human security affect not only the domestic politics of a state, but its international relations as well. In this way, human security, in highlighting individual level factors, nonetheless, extends our conception of security to the global system itself. Nevertheless, human security begins from individual and collective well-being or quality of life. Clearly the breadth of human security is not captured in a single indicator; but, previous scholarship investigating its correlates has attempted to measure its key components, especially as they relate to what's come to be call "human development". With respect to the latter, the Human Development Index (HDI) is a composite index designed by the UNDP since 1990 (UNDP 2014). This index captures a wide array of quality-of-life indicators including public health variables, education indices, and economic variables. Due to criticism of early versions of this index (Hicks 1997, Sharma 1997), the HDI was expanded to control for general social inequalities and, more specifically, gender inequalities. However, due to political sensitivities, the HDI does not incorporate such things as political freedoms, civil liberties, institutional democracy, racial or ethnic equality, and so forth. Nor does it capture human security from internal violence, both political and criminal, or external threats. Yet clearly, quality of life is affected by these factors as well.

These and other limitations notwithstanding, the human security conception offers an expanded view of the similarities and differences among people in different parts of the globe. Accordingly, it is important to understand the possible connections that may exist between the religious characteristics of societies and the quality of life of their members. This is the focus of the present chapter. Specifically, we examine the following issues:

1. What do we mean by human development? Why is this important?
2. Why should we expect a relationship between religion and human development?
3. How does religion affect human development?
4. Does human development affect religious freedoms and secularism?

2. Human Security—Measuring the Quality of Life in Societies

As noted above, the concept of human security is based on a bottom-up perspective of what constitutes security and well-being. It focuses on the basic needs each of us requires to conduct a normal, peaceful, and productive life. These needs are physical and psychological. Physical needs include basic access to health resources, food, and clothing (and the means to access them); shelter; and protection from physical harm by other individuals or groups. Psychological needs include those related to access to educational resources that allow people to develop their skills and spirits. Both physical and psychological needs may converge in the civic realm with respect to civil rights and liberties such as freedom of expression and of assembly, and the voicing opinions and grievances under the protection of law. An important aspect of political and social freedom concerns freedom of religion: the ability to exercise one's religious rituals and practices under the protection of law (as long as these rituals and practices do not directly infringe on the religious freedom of other groups).

The underlying idea of human security is that states are supposed to nurture, develop, and protect those basic needs from both domestic and external threats. Advocates of human security would not deny that protecting the state's sovereignty and territorial integrity is an important aspect of security; however, they insist that a state's functioning is incomplete if it fails to provide people with basic needs and does not protect their basic rights. This is not simply an idealist conception; it is also instrumental and rational. Deficient human security has an adverse effect on state capacity. The ability of the state to mobilize human and material resources for national security is gravely impaired if the nonmilitary aspects of human security are missing or weak. Low state capacity increases the likelihood of deficient performance in the international system. It increases the likelihood of the state becoming prey to outside predators; it reduces the incentive of external actors to trade with or invest in the state and weakens it even further. It also decreases the job security of political leaders in the state.

States differ widely in terms of the ability and willingness of their political and social institutions to provide for human security. In some cases, political leaders have a sincere interest in promoting human security, but they lack the resources for doing so. In other cases, resources are available but the will is lacking, primarily due to leaders' fear that the promotion of human security will endanger their political survival. Specifically, the concern that the rise of a middle class that would challenge traditional elites often results in the suppression of political and economic freedoms, blocking access to public health and education, and promoting policies that provide unfair advantage to some social groups at the expense of others. In such cases, state capacity is based either on rents (e.g., land ownership, natural resources) that are under the control of some political and social elites, or on the coercive extraction of human and capital resources. Other leaders whose rule rests on a tenuous domestic legitimacy, "abjure political institutionalization out of fear of the development of potentially rival centers of power that might be used by counterelites to threaten their authority. Instead, they opt for the creation of sinecures and prebends over efficient administration and for loyalty over merit in the selection of administrators." Such leaders have little commitment to actual political mobilization or the formal institutionalization of an administrative infrastructure to facilitate effective governance, much less provide for social welfare, or in many cases to provide for the protection of personal integrity rights of their citizens (Henderson 2015: 134).[1]

The concept of human security is based on a fundamental notion of individual needs and rights. It attempts to identify indicators of the quality of life in a society. Yet, there is little agreement on what it includes, how it differs from traditional notions of security, and how it should be measured (Martin and Owen 2010, Newman 2010, Breslin and Christou 2015, Eliott 2015). An Internet search for "quality of life" produces multiple listings and indicators, each set of indicators emphasizing different dimensions of this concept. However, two points stand out upon examining these different indicators. First, all of these concepts focus on the individual level of analysis. The key questions addressed by these notions concern the factors that affect individual well-being and protect people's basic needs and rights. A given conception of human security may emphasize a different set of factors (or assign different weights to the same set of factors) compared to another conception. But the common denominator of all these conceptions is the same: a person and/or a community requires certain things to feel physically and spiritually secure and to be able to function efficiently. The extent to which they have access to these things is what defines human security. This contrasts with traditional notions of security that focus on the state level of analysis and, in particular, on the relations between a given state and its external environment (Buzan et al. 1998).

Second, in general there exists a very high correlation among the factors that comprise the various schemes quantifying this concept. States that rank high on one set of indicators (e.g., economic development) tend to rank high on another set of indicators (e.g., access to education, public health). There is also a moderately high correlation between the more common indicators of human security (e.g., economic, health, education) and other indicators showing the extent to which certain meaningful subsets of the population (e.g., women) have equal opportunities compared to other subsets (e.g., men).

For these reasons, we chose to use the HDI and some major modifications of that index as key indicators of the quality of life across the globe. We supplement these indices by using regime-related indicators that emphasize civil and political liberties. These measures enable us to assess the extent to which the religious characteristics of societies are related to various quality-of-life indicators.

Before we enumerate the key elements of the quality of life and human security indices we use to address these questions, it is imperative that we highlight an inherent bias in the concept of quality of life. This concept is fundamentally tilted toward Western notions of what constitutes a "good life." This index relies on the premise that things like wealth, high life expectancy, low infant mortality, and advanced formal education are "good," while lack of wealth (but availability of resources that afford for subsistence) or low formal education somehow diminish peoples' happiness. This premise may reflect a particular worldview. However, people can be quite happy as long as they can provide food and shelter for their family, rather than accumulating that which is not considered essential for survival and well-being. Likewise, people can be uneducated but perfectly happy in their circumstances. Not all cultures agree that high life expectancy is a desirable property of a society. Elderly people in some cultures become a burden on their families when they cannot participate in life-sustaining economic activities. So the concept of human security—or more accurately its quantitative manifestations—may be culturally bound.

The modifications to the HDI over time also seem to be culturally bound. Two important factors highlighted in the literature (Despotis 2005, Hicks 1997, McGillivray 1991, Noorbakshish 1998)—economic inequality and gender inequality—are correlated with the other factors that make up the composite HDI. They do convey new information, but this information also reflects what many consider a Western bias. Other concepts that many Western values associate with human development concern civil liberties and political freedom (Freedom House 2016, Marshall, Jaggers, and Gurr 2010). Here, too, despite the lip service generally paid to democracy, it is not clear that civil liberties and political freedoms are always desirable. In some cases, the transition from a regime that lacks these properties involves instability, violence, economic hardship, and social fragmentation.

Because of this cultural bias—which also results in high correlations among the indicators of human security—the concept does not acknowledge social, political, and cultural diversities that lead to different, sometimes extremely divergent, conceptions of human development and human security. This important criticism notwithstanding, it is important to note that the concepts of human development and human security do emphasize important aspects of personal and communal security and well-being. And the fact that they correlate quite highly with alternative measures that focus on mere subsistence (e.g., energy intake, undernourishment, infant mortality) suggests that they tap some of the more fundamental and universal human needs for survival. For that reason it makes sense to examine the possible relationship between religion and quality of life or human security.

3. Religion and Human Security: Theoretical Expectations

Religions vary in terms of the degree to which their directives apply to different aspects of everyday life. They also vary in terms of their attitude toward political institutions. Some religions prescribe quite detailed directives about dietary issues, marital issues, economic transactions, and even political structures. Other religions have very little to say about day-to-day life and social processes. As we mentioned in chapter 4, religions vary in terms of their level of institutionalization. Some religions have hierarchical institutional structures; others have more diversified structures; still others have very minimal institutionalization.

However, virtually all religions place a high premium on tradition and view social and political change with suspicion. Modernity, however, embraces change that emerges from education, science, technology, and greater contact among people(s). Virtually all major world religions view gender equality with suspicion. For many religions, women cannot serve as religious leaders; their roles are typically assigned to childbearing and housework. In many cases, their marital rights and independence in terms of education or work are restricted. This, of course, is in sharp contrast to what modern societies regard as personal security and well-being (and this may reflect a modern Western bias of the concept of human security). Other religious restrictions—such as dietary restrictions, certain economic transactions, rituals—can also infringe on economic and social opportunities that might be available either to nonbelievers or to members of other religions.

The "religious economy" model (Gill 2001, 2007, 2013) suggests that it is not so much the strictness of religion that affects human development; rather, it is the extent to which the religious market is free for competition. This has to do with religious diversity, which, in turn, affects the propensity of political elites to allow for religious freedom. It is, therefore, religious freedom—not the extent to which religious groups are cosmopolitan or restrictive in terms of their rules and rituals—that affects the degree of human development. Gill (2013, 9) suggests that "the 'religious economy' perspective has demonstrated that when regulation on religious activity is decreased, religious pluralism and religious activity increase, and overall religious participation increases . . . *To the extent that religious activity is what people desire . . . religious freedom does add directly to the economic wellbeing of society* (defined in the broad sense of the word 'economic growth)." [original emphasis][2]

The religious economy model offers compelling insights into the relationship between religious factors and human development. However, it has some important limitations. First, it suggests quite sensibly that the religious homogeneity/heterogeneity of the society affects the extent of religious freedom, and that it is this linkage among diversity, religious freedom, and human development that we need to examine. However, here too, one can overstate the role of religious institutions in affecting religious freedom and, in turn, human development. Political and social groups—especially ones that pursue non-religious values that may or may not parallel those of religious groups—can affect both religious freedoms and human development.

Grim and Finke (2011) offer a more comprehensive model of religious freedom/persecution. To begin with, both their study and that of Fox (2016) provide important data on religious freedoms or, more importantly, various restrictions on religious freedom around the world. The descriptive part of these studies is illuminating.[3] Grim and Finke (2011) and Sarkissian (2015) suggest that there exist fundamental regional and political differences in terms of religious persecution. They find that both governmental and societal restrictions on religious freedoms increase the probability and magnitude of religious persecution. They report a significantly higher propensity of Muslim-majority countries to engage in religious persecution of minorities. Most important, they offer a complex model of religious freedom and religious persecution. This model suggests a cycle between social restrictions on religious freedom that affects government-imposed restrictions on religious freedom, which leads to violent religious restrictions. These, in turn, increase social restrictions on religion. This cycle can be positive—a constantly escalating cycle. This can happen if the factors that increase social and/or government tendencies to restrict freedom of religion offset those that drive societies and governments to ensure religious freedom. These factors include civilizational divides, religious laws that require religious monopoly, or percent Muslims. If, however, social and political factors that promote social and government tolerance toward religious diversity are prominent, then this cycle can be negative, fostering religious tolerance and stability. Factors that tend to promote social and government tolerance of religious activities and religious diversity include gender equality, democracy, percent Christians, and economic growth.

Grim and Finke's analysis focuses on the determinants of religious freedom and the effects of these determinants on religious persecution. They do not focus on the broader social and human effects of religious freedom. Gill, on the other hand, offers a linkage between religious freedom and other factors that shape human security—such as economic development.

We build on these ideas to provide a concrete theoretical linkage between religious factors and human security. In order to test for the effects of religious factors on human security, we need to account—as Gill, and Grim and Finke suggest—for the factors that affect religious freedom. Structural factors, such as the religious diversity of a society, may have both a direct effect on human security and an indirect effect via religious freedom. As Gill suggests, the religious diversity of a society and its level of political openness affect the probability that the society and the government will tolerate diverse religious beliefs. It is also more likely that social tolerance toward religious freedom will increase. Consequently, if religious factors affect human security, they should affect it via the degree of religious freedom. This level tends to fluctuate over time, as both social norms change and as government policies toward religion undergo significant modifications.

Also, if we are to accept the correlation between religious freedom and political stability that both Fox (2016) and Grim and Finke (2011) observe, then religious freedom should correlate with human security. Therefore, our theory should go beyond a simple first-order direct effect of structural attributes of societies and their level of human security. If religious factors are to affect human security, we must relate them to the structure of relations between political and religious institutions. These, as we demonstrate below, are closely linked to the level of religious freedom.

Accordingly, our theory suggests the following propositions:

H1.1. As religious diversity increases, the degree of religious freedom increases.
H1.2. As the degree of religious freedom increases, so does the level of human security.

The effect of religion on everyday life in a society depends on the degree to which people in that society are religious. Secularism is not necessarily the opposite of religious prevalence. People may believe in God/s, but not follow the guidelines of religious scriptures or religious institutions on a strict basis. However, in societies marked by a high proportion of non-religious people—including atheists, agnostics, and generally non-religiously affiliated—the effect of religious values and directives is minimal. Even if a society is fundamentally religious, the role of religion in everyday life may be restricted. In such societies, legal, social, and other interactions are guided by other values. These values may well be more open to change, progress, and opportunity to all people regardless of their religious or non-religious values and beliefs. This is the essence of modernity theory. Accordingly, we expect the following:

H2. The more secular a society, the higher the level of human security of its members.

The structural characteristics of a society, specifically, the level of religious diversity, also affect its human security. Religiously diverse societies require governments to build winning coalitions among multiple religious groups. Their ability to rely on a single religious group is reduced compared to governments ruling religiously homogeneous societies. Religious institutions and religious leaders also attempt to influence leader selection in different ways. When a society is diverse, competition between religious groups requires building coalitions across groups because no single group can guarantee that a favorable candidate would be elected or selected to political leadership. In homogeneous societies, on the other hand, dominant religious groups can and often do endorse candidates who are loyal to religious institutions and are willing to support and provide private goods to such institutions. Thus, religious diversity is expected to have both a direct and indirect—via reduced restrictions on religious freedom—impact on human security.

This leads to the third hypothesis.

H3. Religious diversity is positively correlated with human security.

4. Research Design

4.1 *Data and Units of Analysis*

Data on the HDI is available for the last ten years (UNDP 2017). However, using the nation-year unit of analysis on these data is inappropriate for a number of reasons. First, meaningful changes in human development indicators are extremely difficult to achieve within a decade. Most of the indicators comprising the HDI—economics, health, education, and even gender equality—exhibit little change over time. Other indicators not included in the HDI—such as political and civil liberties, political and criminal violence rates—are prone to more rapid fluctuations. However, even these are quite stationary for most states. As noted in previous chapters, the right-hand side of the equation also contains fairly stationary variables, most importantly, various indicators of religion. Consequently, we perform a cross-sectional analysis comparing general characteristics of states accumulated or averaged over a long period to the most recent indicators of human security. Below we detail the key variables used in these analyses.

In order to measure political freedoms, we use the Freedom House (2016) civil liberties measure as well as the POLITY IV democracy index defined in previous chapters (Marshall, Jaggers, and Gurr 2010). We also employ the Fox (2012b) dataset on religion and state and the Comparative Constitutions dataset (Elkins et al. 2014). In order to gauge religious freedom, we employ the religious freedom dataset (ARDA 2017). Finally, in order to gauge religiosity in societies, we rely on the World Values Survey (WVS 2016). We use waves 5 (2005–9) and 6 (2010–14), including two sets of questions that are asked in both surveys: whether a person is religious, and the importance of God in one's life. We calculate average values of these variables for all respondents in a given country (employing only valid responses and ignoring responses such as "don't know" or "not asked"). We replace missing entries in wave 6 by nonmissing values in wave 5, to increase the number of cases.

4.2 *Dependent Variables*

Human Development Index (HDI). The HDI is measured as a geometric mean of a standardized set of indicators, including gross national income per capita (GNI), life expectancy at birth, and expected and mean years of schooling (UNDP 2015). This is the "raw" HDI. As noted, the HDI was criticized for heavy emphasis on GNI; consequently, it has been modified in two ways. First, the HDI was modified to account for inequality in the distribution of the various components of the HDI over the international system. This is the *Inequality-Adjusted HDI* (UNDP 2015). Second, HDI was adjusted to reflect gender inequalities in societies. This was done by breaking up each of the indicators into gender categories. For example, life expectancy at birth was separated into male and female life expectancy figures. Then the HDI was adjusted by modifying each of the indices to reflect differences between males and females in a society, taking into account the proportion of each gender category in the population. This enabled a generation of a gender development index (GDI). The GDI is obtained by dividing the female HDI by the male HDI. It approaches one when there is a high level of gender equality, and zero when male HDI vastly outpaces female HDI. The overall HDI can then be adjusted by multiplying it by the GDI. We use both the gender-adjusted HDI and the GDI as indicators.[4] This is the *Gender-Adjusted HDI*.

Gender development index. This measures the ratio of female to male in HDI indicators. Ratios smaller than one indicate male advantages; ratios close to one indicate relative male-female equality; and ratios higher than one indicate female advantages.

Civil liberties. This index is not reflected in the HDI, but it is an important aspect of human security. We use the Freedom House (2016) seven-point index of political liberties. Two aspects of this scale are particularly important for our purposes: civil liberties index and political rights index. The two variables are highly correlated ($r = 0.929$), so we employ the civil liberties variable. The civil liberties index ranges from 1 to 7 with higher numbers indicating fewer civil liberties. This index is based on expert ratings of a range of civil liberties, including "freedoms of expression, assembly, association, education, and religion." This also includes a fair legal system—including an independent judiciary—freedom of economic activity, and equality in terms of gender and minority groups (Freedom House 2016). We inverted this index so that higher numbers reflect higher levels of civil liberties to facilitate interpretation. This variable is not captured in the other (and more general) measure of regime score based on the POLITY IV dataset (Marshall, Jaggers, and

Gurr 2010). The correlation between the civil liberties index and the Maoz-Russett (1993) regime score is 0.834 (N = 141, $p < 10^{-7}$).

In order to match the value of this index with the other dependent variables, we use the cumulative distribution scores of states on this index (with states that have the same value getting the same cumulative score). Analyses run with the raw value of the index and the cumulative value yield the same results.

4.3 Independent Variables

Religious diversity. We use the IQV and religious fractionalization measures to gauge religious diversity.

Religiosity. We use two different measures to gauge religiosity. The first is the proportion of the population that is not affiliated with any religion or that is atheist/agnostic, based on the WRP. The second is the response to the importance of God in one's life extracted from the WVS. The number of valid cases for the latter variable is much lower than the number of valid cases for the first variable. However, generally speaking, the latter variable offers a more valid index of religiosity in a society than the former.

Religious legislation. We use the religious legislation index (Fox 2012b) as a formal measure of legislation based on religious principles. This reflects an institutionalized influence of religious principles on the legal system.

Religious freedom. This index combines a number of variables based on the US State Department Religion Freedom Reports (USCIRF 2016). We use an average of two variables in that dataset: aggregate government restrictions on religion and aggregate social restrictions on religion. Here, too, we invert this variable to reflect increased levels of freedom. It varies from zero (absolute lack of religious freedom) to ten (full freedom of religion).[5]

4.4 Control Variables

Interstate war. We use the number of dyadic wars per year through 2010. It is reasonable to expect that wars affect all the factors that make up the HDI, so the intuitive expectation is that of a negative impact of war proneness on HDI, but not necessarily on civil liberties and regime score.

Civil war. We use the number of civil war years through 2010 as an indication of the level of domestic unrest in the country. We expect a negative relationship between civil war frequency and human security.

4.5 Estimation

In order to capture the complex relationship between religious freedom and human security, as noted by previous authors (Gill 2013, Grim and Finke 2011), a simple regression model relating religious freedom to human security is inappropriate. The argument is that social factors that promote religious freedom will ultimately affect the relationship between religious freedom, on the one hand, and economic, political, and social development, on the other. Therefore, we use three-stage least squares estimation to first estimate the factors that affect religious freedom, and then estimate the effect of religious freedom on human security indices.

In order to estimate religious freedom, we use log population as an instrument. Log population is not correlated with any of the human security indices (see appendix), but it is negatively correlated with religious freedom, so it seems to offer a reasonably good instrument.

We also ran separate equations of human security without first estimating religious freedom. The results are dramatically different from the more complex estimation that controls for the endogeneity of religious freedom. We discuss both sets of results below.

An important note about time-related issues is in order. The equations are cross-sectional. There is no temporal dependence here because the human security indices are point estimates (at 2015 for the HDI and GDI-related measures) and at 2008 for the religious freedom index. Accordingly, we have used 2007 indices for the independent and control variables in order not to confound the time of measurement of the dependent and independent variables.

5. Results

Table 8.1 reports the results of the three-stage least-squares (3SLS) analyses using the percent non-religious as an indicator of secularism. Table 8.2 reports the results of the same analyses employing a smaller sample where we use the "importance of God" indicator from the WVS as a proxy of secularism. The appendix reports the results of the separate equations of human security.

We start with the first set of equations where we regress religious freedom on a number of indicators. First, we note that log population has a consistent negative impact on religious freedom. Countries with large

Table 8.1 Religion and human security—three-stage least-squares

Religious Freedom

	Model 1	Model 2	Model 3	Model 4	Model 5
Civil Liberties	0.099**	0.076**	0.089**	0.096**	0.317**
	(0.013)	(0.014)	(0.014)	(0.014)	(0.048)
Civil Wars	0.001	0.001	-0.001	-0.001	0.001
	(0.002)	(0.002)	(0.002)	(0.002)	(0.003)
Interstate Wars	-0.002	-0.003	-0.001	0.001	0.002
	(0.002)	(0.002)	(0.002)	(0.002)	(0.003)
Log Per-Capita GDP	0.1*	0.166**	0.125**	0.045	-0.455**
	(0.048)	(0.047)	(0.048)	(0.049)	(0.124)
Log Population	-0.003*	-0.003*	-0.003*	-0.003*	0.002*
	(0.001)	(0.001)	(0.001)	(0.001)	(0.001)
Religious Diversity	0.161*	0.226**	0.122	0.094	0.222*
	(0.075)	(0.079)	(0.078)	(0.076)	(0.11)
Secularism	-0.569**	-0.576**	-0.537**	-0.489**	-0.423
	(0.192)	(0.193)	(0.19)	(0.191)	(0.276)
Religious Legislation	-0.015**	-0.014**	-0.016**	-0.018**	0.007
	(0.003)	(0.003)	(0.003)	(0.003)	(0.005)
Constant	-0.084	-0.225	-0.108	0.178	0.596*
	(0.154)	(0.159)	(0.158)	(0.16)	(0.246)
Chi-Square	185.706	126.007	168.026	183.714	90.826
R-Squared	0.542	0.466	0.528	0.557	0.136

Human Security

	HDI 2015	Inequality HDI	Gender HDI	Gender Dev. Index	Civil Liberties
Religious Freedom	0.204*	0.394*	0.360*	0.151*	11.289**
	(0.102)	(0.181)	(0.175)	(0.071)	(2.468)
Religious Diversity	-0.153**	-0.225**	-0.16**	-0.03	-0.748
	(0.042)	(0.064)	(0.047)	(0.022)	(0.597)
Secularism	0.456**	0.704**	0.552**	0.208**	3.363*
	(0.104)	(0.155)	(0.114)	(0.053)	(1.399)
Religion-State Relations					
Some Relation	-0.026	0.001	-0.031	0.003	0.861
	(0.026)	(0.038)	(0.029)	(0.014)	(0.442)
Co-Habitation	0.061	0.068	0.041	-0.01	4.551**
	(0.059)	(0.095)	(0.062)	(0.03)	(1.52)
Democracy	0.049	0.057	0.062*	0.009	
	(0.026)	(0.034)	(0.029)	(0.014)	
Past Civil Wars	-0.001	-0.001	-0.001	0	0.012
	(0.001)	(0.002)	(0.001)	(0.001)	(0.015)
Past Interstate Wars	0.002	0.003	0.001	0	-0.011
	(0.001)	(0.002)	(0.002)	(0.001)	(0.018)
Coup Risk	-1.895**	-1.318**	-2.204**	-0.81**	-2.898
	(0.279)	(0.373)	(0.303)	(0.147)	(3.766)
Constant	0.632**	0.347*	0.598**	0.908**	-4.387
	(0.091)	(0.164)	(0.099)	(0.047)	(2.400)
N	148	129	136	136	153
Chi-Square	159.991	108.231	179.924	104.876	224.32
R-Squared	0.512	0.405	0.561	0.395	0.39

Note: $^*p < 0.05$; $^{**}p < 0.01$
Parameters for the religious freedom equations are different across models due to differences in sample sizes (N) and model specification for the civil liberties equation.

Table 8.2 Religion and human security—inequality, gender development, and political freedoms

Variable	Model 1	Model 2	Model 3	Model 4	Model 5
Religious Freedom					
Civil Liberties	0.823**	0.69**	0.797**	0.788**	1.25**
	(0.102)	(0.113)	(0.102)	(0.101)	(0.177)
Religious Diversity	0.134	0.194	0.131	0.119	0.21*
	(0.091)	(0.099)	(0.094)	(0.091)	(0.097)
God Important	0.036*	0.04*	0.038*	0.036*	0.061**
	(0.016)	(0.018)	(0.016)	(0.016)	(0.018)
Religious Legislation	-0.013**	-0.014**	-0.014**	-0.015**	-0.002
	(0.003)	(0.003)	(0.004)	(0.003)	(0.003)
Log Per-Capita GDP	-0.044	0.098	-0.017	-0.045	-0.074
	(0.078)	(0.084)	(0.078)	(0.077)	(0.084)
Past Civil War	0.001	0.001	0.001	0.001	0.001
	(0.002)	(0.002)	(0.002)	(0.002)	(0.002)
Past Interstate War	-0.001	-0.002	-0.001	-0.001	0
	(0.002)	(0.002)	(0.002)	(0.002)	(0.003)
Constant	0.032	-0.447	-0.055	0.092	-0.447
	(0.348)	(0.38)	(0.35)	(0.342)	(0.302)
Chi-Square	151.673	113.576	146.212	146.212	114.697
R-Squared	0.643	0.589	0.592	0.672	0.703

Human Security					
Variable	HDI	Inequality HDI	Gender HDI	Gender Development	Civil Liberties
Religious Freedom	0.044	0.218	0.068	0.025	0.833
	(0.104)	(0.141)	(0.132)	(0.076)	(0.516)
Religious Diversity	-0.098*	-0.13*	-0.1*	-0.016	-0.178*
	(0.04)	(0.06)	(0.051)	(0.029)	(0.072)
God Important	-0.029**	-0.048**	-0.037**	-0.015**	-0.05**
	(0.006)	(0.009)	(0.008)	(0.004)	(0.017)
Religion-State Relations					
Some Relation	-0.015	0.03	-0.002	0.009	0.006
	(0.033)	(0.041)	(0.041)	(0.024)	(0.082)
Co-Habitation	0.016	0.068	0.001	-0.03	0.045
	(0.057)	(0.072)	(0.071)	(0.041)	(0.294)
Democracy	0.035	0.001	0.028	-0.016	#DIV/0!
	(0.037)	(0.046)	(0.046)	(0.027)	(0)
Past Civil War	-0.003**	-0.002	-0.002*	0	-0.002
	(0.001)	(0.001)	(0.001)	(0.001)	(0.002)
Past Interstate War	0.002*	0.003	0.002	0	0.001
	(0.001)	(0.002)	(0.001)	(0.001)	(0.002)
Coup Risk	-3.112**	-2.644**	-3.089**	-0.646	-1.427
	(0.649)	(0.849)	(0.819)	(0.471)	(0.854)
Constant	1.045**	0.937**	1.067**	1.084**	0.581
	(0.107)	(0.154)	(0.135)	(0.078)	(0.593)
N	69	61	68	69	69
Chi-Square	119.167	93.205	95.755	31.943	224.76
R-Squared	0.643	0.589	0.592	0.290	0.703

Note: * $p < 0.05$; ** $p < 0.01$
Parameters for the religious freedom equations are different across models due to differences in sample sizes (N) and model specification for the civil liberties equation.

populations tend to have a lower degree of religious freedoms than countries with smaller populations. This is hardly surprising. Since religious freedom is a component of civil liberties, we should be surprised if there is no significant relationship between the two indices. Second, we find—not surprisingly—that civil liberties have a significant positive effect on religious freedom, and that the extent of religious legislation has a negative effect on religious freedom. In this respect as well, the magnitude of religious legislation is aimed at curbing religious freedom and subjecting the legal system to religious principles. This typically works in favor of dominant (or more influential) religious groups, against non-religious groups, and at the expense of other religious groups.

Third, as suggested by Gill, religious diversity tends to increase religious freedom. This supports his contention that in diverse societies, it is more difficult for both governments and religious actors to curb religious interaction and competition. The result is typically higher levels of religious freedoms. This inference may be misleading, however, as we discuss below. Thus, interpreting the relationship between religious diversity and religious freedom as supporting the causal mechanism put forth by the religious economy model may not be appropriate.

Secularism appears to have a negative impact on religious freedom. This is surprising at first sight, but on reflection, a society can be either religiously diverse or religiously homogeneous, but also have few non-religious people. Likewise, a society may have a high number of non-religious people, but it is its diversity that accounts for the level of religious freedom. The global average level of secularism in 2007 was roughly 7 percent, and the median was significantly lower (2.5 percent), and the highest fraction of non-religious groups was either in highly democratic societies (e.g., Belgium, Germany, Canada, Australia, New Zealand) or in highly authoritarian societies (e.g., Vietnam, China, North Korea). However, the percent non-religious in the latter states far exceeds that of the former type of states. Atheism, as we have demonstrated in Chapter 4, was an imposed social norm in the communist world. So the highly atheist communities in the surviving communist states coincide with their low level of religious freedom.

We now turn to a discussion of our key dependent variable: human security. The first and most important observation is that secularism—defined either as the percent non-religious in a society or the percent WVS respondents who claim that God does not play an important part of their daily life—consistently affects human security indices. The more secular a society, the higher its human security. Second, religious freedom does not consistently affect HDI-related measures, but it does positively affect HDI and inequality-adjusted HDI.

Religious diversity has a negative effect on human security. One of the reasons for that is that HDI indices are heavily influenced by economic indicators. This pits rent-based countries, for example, the Organization of the Petroleum Exporting Countries states, that are highly homogeneous against the high HDI indices. At the same time it places low-income but religiously diverse countries, for example, most African states, at the bottom of the HDI ladder.

This suggests one of the reasons why religious diversity positively affects religious freedom but negatively affects human security. Specifically, many religiously diverse countries are also characterized by low political capacity. This deficiency in political capacity may be due partly to the diverse social makeup. At the same time, low political capacity may result from extreme resource scarcity. Consequently, there are few resources available for government extraction. There is also a historical legacy of weak political capacity in such states, suggesting that governments cannot overcome the communal loyalties of individuals and groups. These governments find it difficult to forge a unifying national identity that is above and beyond factional loyalties. Religious discrimination, religious legislation, and restrictions on religious practices in such cases amount to political suicide for ruling elites. This explains the positive effect of diversity on religious freedom and, at the same time, it accounts for the negative relationship between religious diversity and human security.

On the other hand, consistent with our expectations, religious freedom has a positive and significant effect on civil liberties and on gender development. States that practice a high level of religious freedom seem to allow more opportunities for women in health, education, and employment. For that reason, we find that religious freedom has a positive effect on human security that is not directly tied to wealth.

As we can see in Figure 8.1, secularism has a significant effect on the various indices of human security. However, the large spread at higher levels of secularism suggests that at that level (above the median level of secularism), there are a number of high-secularism outliers. These are communist states in which secularism may be a state-induced myth rather than a practical reality. The general correlation between secularism and human security indices is in the range of $0.39 \leq r \leq 0.45$. ($145 \leq N \leq 182$.). However, when

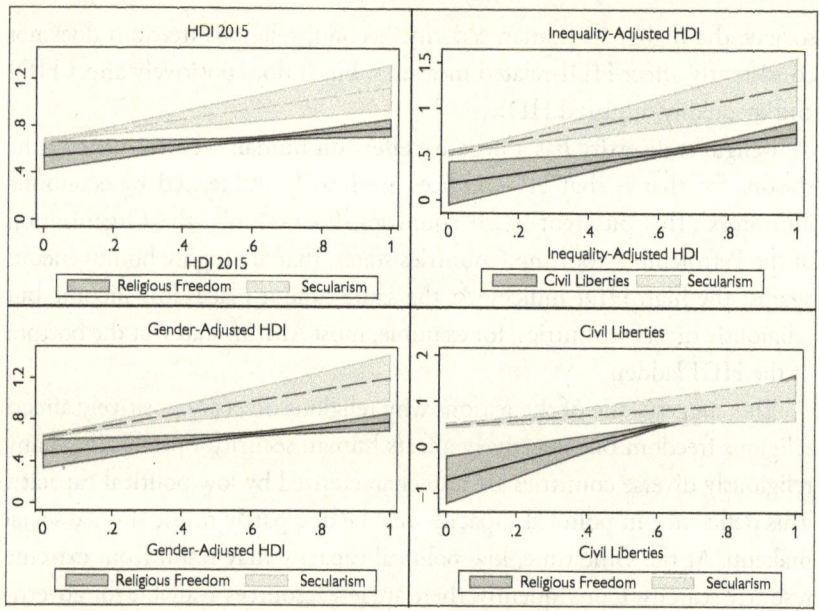

Fig. 8.1. Secularism, civil liberties, religious freedom, and human security

we limit secularism to less than 0.4, thus omitting the highly secular outliers, correlations increase to $0.41 \leq r \leq 0.65 (138 \leq N \leq 174)$.

Note that religious freedom is negatively correlated with religion-state relations (see appendix for correlations). This suggests that the effects of religion-state relations on human security are not significant when we use HDI-based measures of human security.

Overall, we find support for the argument that religious diversity increases religious freedom and reduces the degree of religion-state cohabitation. We also find limited support for the effect of religious freedom on gender development and on civil liberties. But religious freedom and religion-state relations do not seem to affect HDI-based indices of human security. The principal reason for that is the heavy reliance of these indices on economic indicators; these are spread widely over different religious freedom characteristics of states.

By contrast, we find strong support for the effect of secularism on human security. This effect is even stronger if we omit the outlier states that tend to "induce" secularism as a matter of regime policy—not necessarily due to truly atheistic beliefs of the population (as we have seen following the collapse of communism in Eastern Europe and Central Asia). Secularism has long been a favorite straw man of scholars of religion and politics. However, even small changes in secularism seem to have a marginally strong effect on human security.

6. Conclusion

In this chapter we highlighted the concept of human security: the extent to which a state provides for basic human physical and psychological needs, and the ability of individual members to access health, education, economic, and political resources that ensure their physical and psychological well-being. The human security literature contends that it is the role of the state to provide for these basic needs, beyond protecting its citizens from external or internal threats to their survival. The extent to which states perform this duty faithfully is captured by a wide array of measures of human development, political rights, and gender and income equality. These indices are important not only as a scientific tool that allows comparing societies; they are also important because they allow governments to detect fundamental deficiencies in their social and economic policies, to learn from one another, and to potentially improve their policies.

Measures of human development and human security are not unbiased; nevertheless, they are manifestly better than subjective assessments of quality of life in societies. More important, they are transparent in the way they are generated and explicit about what they include and what they omit. As such, they offer an important window into human security from a global perspective.

Some governments work hard to protect and improve human development and human security. Others work hard to suppress access to health, education, economic opportunities, and political rights for all or some of their citizens. Human development, economic well-being, education levels, and public health are highly correlated; these aspects of human development are also correlated with gender development, and moderately correlated with civil liberties and democracy. This suggests that governments that are effective in promoting or protecting one dimension of human security are also fairly effective in protecting other dimensions.

But just as we can see the half-full part of the glass in these correlations, we can see also the half-empty part of the glass. The factors making up human security may have been identified correctly by the various composite measures (such as HDI or its gender, or inequality modifications). However, the weights that we assign to various indicators may be different. What is more important is that different governments may and typically do assign different priorities to different aspects of human security. In many cases, the resources that are supposed to go toward the promotion of human security are appropriated for other goals such as public order or national security. This may happen quite often because there is objective need to address national security challenges or public order problems prior to ensuring opportunities for education, health, or gender equality. But quite a few governments work under the notion that the promotion of human security risks their political or economic survival. These governments deliberately work to constrain different aspects of human security in order to protect the sectors in the society that safeguard their tenure. Other governments suppress some aspects of human security as a matter of social, political, or religious beliefs. It is the latter type of beliefs we have focused on in the present chapter.

We argued that religion typically cannot be a force for the promotion of human security. However, religion can and often does serve as an instrument used by governments to constrain, stall, or dampen different aspects of human security. This can happen when governments (and in most cases religious institutions) use religious values to halt or slow down economic progress, gender equality, democracy, and income equality. The notion of "God's will" is the epitome of complacency and acceptance of a status quo that might be hurtful, unjust, and exploitative. The finding that the importance of God in one's life (although available only for less than half of the states in our sample) has a strong negative impact on human security is quite telling in this respect.

The headline of this chapter is that secularism—more than any other religious characteristic of societies—affects modernization and human security. The central hypothesis we have put forth in this chapter receives strong and robust confirmation.

Interestingly, however, the institutionalized structure of religion—the degree of religious discrimination, or the institutional or legal constraints on religious freedom—does not appear to have a robust effect on human security. Religious diversity has an adverse impact on some aspects of human security but not on others. It appears that, contrary to our expectations, more homogeneous societies tend to have a higher degree of human security. This relationship is not robust and is potentially biased. Some highly homogeneous societies can have high levels of economic wealth due to resource-based rents that affect their HDI score. By contrast, diverse but poor societies can have high religious freedom (partly due to low state capacity, partly due to constraints imposed on governments by virtue of such diversity) and low human security scores.

Religious diversity has a positive impact on religious freedom and a negative impact on religious discrimination, religious legislation, and religious regulation, making for a relatively separate relationship between religious and political institutions. This conforms to the religious economy model. But here, too, a word of caution is in order. The causal mechanism specified by the religious economy model—diverse societies make it difficult for governments to impose religious restrictions because such restrictions risk the government's survival—may be true in some cases but misleading in other cases. The combination of religious diversity with low political capacity may be due to unrelated reasons such as the arbitrariness of boundaries of postcolonial powers with regard to the cultural makeup of their societies. The low state capacity and the religious diversity of such societies are joint outcomes of such processes. The real test of the causal mechanism linking religious diversity to religious freedom must be performed in high political capacity states, and there, this relationship is not as strong as the model suggests.

Given the growing importance of human security in both theory and practice, the linkage between secularism and human security becomes all the more apparent in contemporary international politics. Religious groups in many countries have increased both their political power and their level of activity. In some regions, such as the Middle East and parts of Africa and South Asia, religious groups engage in rampant violence aimed at establishing theocratic governments, and run them using violence and the suppression of individual rights, political liberties, women's rights, gay rights, and economic opportunities. However, even in more advanced industrial countries, religious extremism is on the rise. If such groups prevail, not only will they have a dramatic effect on international security, but they will also have a profound impact on human security, individual liberties, and economic prosperity. The evidence from this chapter suggests not only the linkage between secularism and human development; it also highlights the risks associated with religious domination in domestic social and political affairs.

Appendix to Chapter 8

1. Introduction

The appendix provides additional details about the data and analyses. We start with descriptive statistics of the variables under analysis. This is given in Table A8.1.

We continue with Table A8.2, which provides correlations among the dependent variables. Finally, Table A8.3 shows the correlations between measures of religious freedom and religion-state relations.

Table A8.1 Descriptive statistics

Variable	Obs	Mean	Std. Dev.	Min	Max
HDI 2015	187	0.698	0.155	0.352	0.949
Ineq. Adjusted HDI	151	0.559	0.189	0.199	0.898
Gender-Adjusted HDI	159	0.667	0.178	0.258	0.943
Gender Development Index	146	0.930	0.074	0.600	1.030
Civil Liberties	164	4.502	1.742	1.000	7.000
Democracy	165	0.406	0.493	0.000	1.000
Cumulative Interstate Wars	240	2.383	10.175	0.000	83.000
Cumulative Civil War Years	240	4.983	12.345	0.000	111.000
Log Population	161	3.819	0.657	2.541	5.954
Log Per-Capita GDP	159	3.422	0.449	2.253	4.424
Religious Freedom	194	5.970	2.477	0.333	10.000
Pct. Non-religious	195	0.075	0.158	0.000	1.000
God Important	72	7.779	1.955	3.482	9.906
Religious Legislation	161	8.640	6.987	0.250	42.000

Table A8.2 Correlations among dependent variables

	HDI	IneqHDI	GendHDI	GenDev	Civil Lib.	Regime	Log Pop.
HDI 2015	1.000						
Ineq. Adjusted HDI	0.979	1.000					
Gender-Adjusted HDI	0.985	0.970	1.000				
Gender Development index	0.708	0.711	0.811	1.000			
Civil Liberties	0.569	0.681	0.598	0.506	1.000		
Maoz-Russett Regime	0.382	0.570	0.416	0.334	0.853	1.000	
Log Population	0.102	0.119	0.035	-0.079	-0.002	0.116	1.000

Note: Statistically significant correlations (*p* > .05) are **boldfaced**.

Table A8.3 Correlations between measures of religious freedom and religion-state relations

	Rel. Free	Rel. Discrim	Rel. Regulat	Rel. Legislat.	
Religious Freedom	1				
Religious Discrimination	-0.761	1			
Religious Regulation	-0.543	0.700	1		
Religious Legislation	-0.685	0.574	0.355	1	
Combined Religion-State	-0.7851	0.9376	0.8474	0.7012	1

Note: Statistically significant correlations ($p > .05$) are in **bold**.

CHAPTER 9

The Complex Role of Religion in World Politics

1. Introduction

This study is a systematic empirical analysis of the linkages between religious factors and politics. These linkages have attracted much interest from scholars and practitioners, especially since the end of the Cold War. Consequently, the number of theoretical and empirical forays into this topic have been on the rise over the last two decades. We have focused on scientifically assessing the empirical validity of some of the more central and most popular theories on this subject. Our approach to this topic contributes to the study of religion and politics in several important respects.

The first distinguishing aspect of our study is its theoretical scope. We examined several theories on religion and politics. Identifying both the compelling arguments of existing theoretical frameworks and their logical and evidentiary weaknesses, we offered an integrative approach that combined structural and situational factors. We draw on the structural characteristics of societies, as well as the political, economic, and social conditions under which political elites are likely to invoke and manipulate religious factors, religious groups, and religious markers of national identity. We also tied the characteristics of societies to those of their politically relevant international environment, an aspect that most studies of religion and politics have overlooked.

Second, we based our empirical investigations on multiple and highly diverse datasets and on multiple levels of analyses. At the center of our investigation is a novel and systematically derived dataset on the religious composition of the international system since 1945, the WRP dataset. We draw on these data to provide a much more extensive and nuanced analysis of religion's impact on politics than previous research focused on individual states, pairs of states, groups of states, regions, and the global system as a whole.

Third, we examined multiple dimensions of the religion-politics linkage. Specifically, we focused on both interstate relations and on intrastate processes; both international conflict and cooperation; and the previously understudied relationship between religion and human security. In each of these dimensions of the present study we expanded the scope of the theoretical claims linking religious factors to the range of political behaviors of states. We noted that virtually all of the literature linking religion to international conflict addresses—favorably or critically—the clash of civilizations (CoC) thesis. We offered more nuanced ideas about how religion affects conflict. Likewise, in the chapter on religion and international cooperation, our ideas went well beyond the structural notions of "similarity attracts, differences repulse" embedded in the few extant theories that address the linkages between religious factors and cooperation. While we have developed our own ideas about the linkages between religion and international behavior, either conflictual or cooperative, we attempted to examine multiple theories that address these issues in order to evaluate their relative merit. We offer a general appraisal of these theories below.

Fourth, we provided several methodological innovations not only in variable construction but in research design. Recognizing the stationarity of many of the variables analyzed in the study of religion and political outcomes we employed much more rigorous tests of the putative relationships utilizing bootstrapping techniques that required greater consistency and robustness among the variables before they'd achieve a threshold whereby we were satisfied that the relationships reported actually obtained in the data.

A key element in our empirical analysis is the notion of religious similarity. This concept features prominently in all of the different perspectives we have discussed and tested in this study. We are certainly not the first to emphasize this concept, and are also not the first to test the connection between religious similarity and conflict (although we are not aware of a lot of empirical research connecting religious similarity to cooperative interactions). Our original contribution, however, is in the way we measure this concept. In contrast to the cruder measures of religious similarity in the myriad studies of religion and international conflict, and religion and civil conflict, we measure similarity in terms of the degree of overlap of distributions of religious adherents in societies. Two societies may be similar in that the modal religious groups in both are the same, but they are, in fact, different if one has a single religious group and the other has many other religious groups, and the largest religious group accounts only for a fraction of the state's population. For example, the variation in the majority religious group if the largest religious group was Christian was from 0.26 to 1. When the largest religious group was Muslim, this variation was between 0.36 and 1. And when the largest religious group was Hindu, this variation was between 0.44 and 0.81. So, saying that two societies have the same largest religious group may be vastly misleading when the largest religious group in one society is about one-third of the population and the largest religious group in the other society accounts for 90 percent of its population. We find that, in general, the higher resolution religious similarity index we use in most of our analyses provides a more precise description of cross-national comparison than the more coarse indices used in most of the previous studies. We believe that this renders a more credible inference of the relationship between religious similarity, on the one hand, and international conflict, international cooperation, and civil conflict, on the other.

This chapter briefly summarizes our study of religion and world politics. The next section provides a summary of the key results. The third section assesses the key theoretical perspectives we have examined throughout the present study in light of these results. The fourth section discusses the theoretical implications of our study. The final section discusses some policy implications and identifies directions for future research.

2. Summary of Key Results

A general summary of the results is provided in Table 9.1, which outlines the effects of the key religious factors on conflict, cooperation, and quality of life. As can be seen, the results are illuminating in some respects and mixed in others. We start by outlining the major insights about religion and world politics that we can garner from this comprehensive empirical study.

Table 9.1 Summary of key findings by topic

Religious Factor	Effect on					
	International Conflict	International Cooperation	Civil Conflict		Quality of Life	Robustness
			Outbreak	Attributes		
Religious Similarity	–	++	+	+	NA	H
Coup-Risk Interaction with Religious Factors	+	+	NA	NA	NA	MH
Environmental Effects—Religious similarity State-PRIE	—	++	+	+	NA	MH
Religious Homogeneity	++	++	NA	NA	–	M
Religious Polarization	NA	NA	+	+	NA	NA
Secularism	–	+	–	?	++	M
State-Religion Relations	+	0	0	+	?	M
Specific Religions	0	0	0	+	0	0

Key:
1. Effect types: ++ Robust positive effect, + Some positive effect— not robust, – – Robust negative effect, – Some negative effect— not robust, 0 No significant effect ? Inconsistent results
2. Robustness of effects across issue areas
H High, MH Medium-High, M L Low, 0 Null

1. Religion is one of the key attributes of the cultural identity of states. As such, it is among the most important factors that shape their domestic politics and their behavior in the international arena. This does not mean that religious factors trump other factors that shape states' behavior and politics—factors associated with either realist or liberal perspectives. What our findings indicate, however, is that culture matters; it shapes identity, defines affinities and enmities, and affects politics within and among nations. Culture, or at least the religious aspects of culture, should be included in any attempt to understand world politics.
2. Religious factors: religious homogeneity/diversity, religion-state relations, and the degree of similarity between states and their relevant environment, are fairly stationary over time. The extent to which they affect more volatile and diverse relations between and among states—such as conflict or cooperation—depends on the ability and willingness of political elites to invoke religion as a mobilization strategy. We find that political elites, particularly in authoritarian states, are significantly more likely to use religion to mobilize support for foreign adventures when they believe that their job security is at risk. This applies mostly with respect to the use of religion in potential or actual conflict situations. At the same time, however, the evidence also suggests that political elites tend to invoke religious similarities and dissimilarities to justify costly cooperative ventures such as high-commitment alliances.
3. Contrary to popular theses such as the clash of civilization, we did not find evidence that the post–Cold War era is shaped by a struggle between or among civilizations marked by religious factors. In fact, struggles within religions are as or more common than struggles between religions. Moreover, in many of our analyses on both conflict and cooperation we found that religious factors were more active in the Cold War era than in the post–Cold War era. Nor did we find a greater degree of within-civilizational cooperation during the post–Cold War era compared to the previous period. We discuss this thesis at greater length in the next section.
4. Our evidence also fails to support the constructivist notion that the behavior of newly established states is shaped by their religious identity more than the behavior of older and well-established

states. We are not claiming that there is no inherent antagonism among different cultures; however, when examined closely, this antagonism is, on average, overshadowed by common interests along other aspects of their political interactions. Importantly, the notion that religions do not possess factors that cause animosity and hatred among believers is fundamentally flawed. Some of the most violent and intractable conflicts are intrareligious while some of the more surprising and persistent forms of cooperation are among states of different religious makeup.

5. Perhaps the most robust finding is a negative one: we did not find consistent evidence linking a particular religion to bellicosity and conflict—domestic or international. Nor did we find consistent evidence that one particular religion is more benign and cooperative than other religions. Branding one religion as violent and another as benign and peaceful is not rooted in the empirical reality of the global system in the post–World War II era. The same applies to the role of religion in the domestic politics of states. We did not find evidence that a given religion or religious combination is related to domestic instability, or that countries dominated by a specific religion enjoy higher levels of human security than other countries.

6. We remind the reader that characterizing certain conflicts as "religious wars" is problematic. This suggests that it is just as likely that what previous analyses are uncovering is the relationship between their variables of interest and the probability of being classified among so-called religious wars. For example, the finding of a positive relationship between religious polarization and "religious war" onset says more about the probability of violent conflicts within religiously polarized states being categorized as "religious wars" in the first place. The same can be said about conflicts in states that might inordinately identify with the major religions. Conversely, the finding of a negative relationship between democracy and so-called religious wars may be more likely the result of the low probability that conflicts in democracies will be classified as "religious conflicts." A caveat is that, once we control for the inherent bias in civil conflict involvement, we find the most populous religious groups on the planet—Christianity, Islam, Hinduism, and

non-religious—to be highly prone to the outbreak of conflict on religious grounds. We also find that these religious groups tend to be less likely to settle their civil conflicts via negotiated settlements. These results seem to provide some support for arguments about the "dangerous" nature of religion. They are, however, restricted to specific types of civil conflicts, and are not generalizable to other types of conflictual or cooperative behaviors, the latter comprising the overwhelming majority of such interactions.

7. Several "positive" results that are generalizable across the dimensions of domestic and international politics that emerge from our study are the following:

   a. The religious similarity between states and their external environments—their immediate geographic or their substantive (strategic reference) neighborhoods—reduces the level of conflict of individual states, dyads, and, to a lesser extent, regions. Religious similarity also increases the degree of cooperation between states—primarily in areas that exact high transaction costs (such as security cooperation). There is also some evidence that religious similarity between majority religions within states and their relevant environment reduces the focal state's propensity for civil conflict.

   b. Secularism also has mixed effects on international politics. Secular states, that is, states that have substantial numbers of non-religious citizens, are not less likely to fight each other, nor are they more likely to cooperate with each other than are "religious" states. However, secularism reduces the likelihood of civil conflict within states and has a positive effect on human security and quality of life. Secular states are less likely to experience domestic disturbances than "religious" states, and when such disturbances occur, they are likely to be less severe and enduring than in "religious" states. The citizens of "secular" states are better educated, have better access to health services and enjoy longer life expectancy, and have generally higher standards of living than the citizens of "religious" states.

8. The manner in which religious factors affect international relations and domestic politics is rather complex. The theories linking religion to politics attempt, as many other theories do, to portray

a rather simple and straightforward relationship. But even when a consistent relationship seems to exist, it is context dependent. The context, as we show in this study, refers to the specific type of behavior one examines. In reality, the impact of religion on international relations and the domestic structure of states is more nuanced. We have observed this nuanced relationship both when we focused on conflict behavior (domestic and international), and on international cooperation, as well as on the quality of life of individuals within states (i.e. human security). The implication is that we should be careful in assigning simplistic and all-encompassing roles to religious factors. Just as we should not ignore culture as a factor shaping political processes, we should avoid attributing to culture a simple, direct, and autonomous role in domestic and international politics. One of the points we made early on is that studies of religion and political behavior tend to focus on a single behavioral aspect. And even if several studies focus on the same behavioral domain, they do not always agree on whether and which religious factors affect this type of behavior. When we cast a wider net—covering multiple behavioral domains—we find that sweeping generalizations are inappropriate in the general case, and sweeping generalizations about religious factors are even less justifiable.

3. Religion and World Politics: Theory Meets Evidence

How do theories on religion and politics fare in light of the evidence? We have repeated the point that these theories offer complementary predictions about specific associations between religious factors and different aspects of international relations. This makes evaluation of the insights of such theories even more difficult. However, we can afford an admittedly qualified evaluation of these theories.

3.1 *Primordialism*

The key argument of the primordialist perspective is that religion is an inherent, constant, and crucial aspect of national identity. The extent to which it forms a central part of national identity is a function of two factors: the religious homogeneity of the state and the degree to which political and religious institutions are closely linked. Religiously homogeneous societies and states in which religion and politics cohabitate make religion a central identity marker, often forming the foundation of nationalism. This defines the nation's outlook on its international environment, framing friends and foes in terms of religious similarity, and forming an important determinant of the state's behavior. Moreover, a highly homogeneous society in which religious and state institutions are closely linked tends to be politically stable. If civil conflict breaks out, it is likely to be on issues that have little or nothing to do with religious disputes.

Some of our results lend support to this perspective. In particular, we found that religious homogeneity increases the propensity of conflict behavior of individual states. We also found religious similarity to be a consistent pacifier when it comes to dyadic and regional conflict, and a consistent incentive when it comes to security and institutional cooperation. We also found evidence that the cohabitation of religious and political institutions tends to increase the risk of interstate conflict behavior.

However, this theory emphasizes relatively stationary linkages between religion and state. The religious composition of societies does not change much over time. Nor does the relationship between religious and political institutions fluctuate significantly over time. This suggests that the more direct tests of the theory focus on general propensities rather than on annual fluctuations. When we examine the nation-history or dyad-history results, many of the expectations of the theory are not supported. For example, we do not find support for the argument that religious homogeneity has a direct effect on conflict. We also do not find consistent evidence of the extent to which the relationship between religious and political institutions affects the conflict propensity of states or dyads. The same applies to civil conflict patterns. Religiously homogeneous states are no more likely to experience civil conflicts than religiously diverse ones. Similarly, the relationship between religious and political institutions does not have a significant effect on the propensity of states to experience civil conflict.

Our evaluation of this theory on several issues is decidedly incomplete. For example, data limitations do not permit us to study the relationship between state-religious relations and international behavior or domestic conflict over the entire time span of 1945–2010. Nor could we ascertain whether political leaders in homogeneous societies belonged to or practiced the same religion as the majority of the population over the postwar timespan. For example, about 74 percent of Syria's population are Sunni Muslims. However, since 1966, Syria has been ruled by an Alawite minority accounting for roughly 13 percent of the population.[1] In states governed by communist regimes, the population was largely affiliated with various religions. However, these societies were governed by atheist political leaders, so the sharp drop in the number of "seculars," that is, atheists, agnostics, and other nonbelievers in such societies following the fall of communism suggests that atheism was not prevalent.[2] Thus, there is some evidence supporting this perspective and also a fair amount of evidence that is inconsistent with primordialist arguments. Therefore, what we can suggest is that there are certainly primordialist factors that are significantly associated with the outcomes we examine in this study; however, the role of religion in these outcomes is only superficially captured by the factors that are emphasized by primordialism.

3.2 Instrumentalism.

The central argument of the instrumentalist perspective on religion and politics is that religion is a political tool used by political elites to advance their aims. The more static aspects of the instrumentalist predictions are almost identical to the primordialist ones. So, in terms of these aspects, the evidence offers neither strong explicit support nor unequivocal refutation of this perspective. However, the relative empirical support of the theory's main claims is more robust and more meaningful than the primordialist perspective. The negative impact of regime stability on conflict behavior along with the negative effect of regime similarity on conflict behavior receives considerable support. Specifically, political leaders who feel politically threatened are likely to invoke religious loyalties to mobilize their populations for external adventures if the social conditions are "right." Likewise, the impact of political stability on cooperation toward religiously similar states also provides support for the instrumentalist perspective.

The fact that religious similarity is a strong determinant of security cooperation, but not of economic cooperation, also adds credence to this perspective. Moreover, we find that security communities are significantly more religiously cohesive than other types of cooperative communities. This result is also consistent with instrumentalism. The underlying logic of this argument is that alliances are politically risky ventures and involve more transaction costs than trade, PTAs, or membership in IGOs. Alliances require commitment of human and material resources in support of other states at times of war. Forming alliances require more intensive mobilization. Another layer of evidence in support of instrumentalism concerns the finding that secularism reduces the likelihood of civil conflict and elevates human security. This suggests that when a substantial proportion of the population is not susceptible to the manipulation of religious ideas in support of certain groups or certain policies, more people in the society seem to benefit; they get higher levels of education, more economic equality, and more open political systems.

However, as in the case of primordialism, instrumentalism's predictions are not supported in the case of civil wars and in terms of some key aspects of conflict behavior. On the whole, empirical evidence lends more support to instrumentalist predictions—in particular, the dynamic aspects of these predictions—than the more static predictions of primordialism. At the same time, we do not have sufficient evidence to claim that this perspective provides a comprehensive explanation of the linkages between religious factors and key aspects of world politics in the modern era.

3.3 *Constructivism.*

Like primordialism and instrumentalism, constructivism claims that religion can become (or can be manipulated to be) a central national identity marker when a society is highly homogeneous and when there is little or no separation of religion from state. The key difference between constructivism and the other two approaches is that national identity is not a constant, but rather changes as a result of the state's interaction with its environment, and as a result of prevailing "international cultures."

Constructivism implies that religious factors are more important determinants of identity when states lack interactive experience. In such cases—and this applies to newly formed states—leaders attempt to form a sense of national identity via shared social values. Once the state acquires interactive experience, its self-perception, as well as its perception of friends and foes, begins to reflect the lessons of such experience and the role of shared social values in defining its national identity declines. The empirical evidence connecting states' age to their conflict or cooperative behavior does not support this inference. We could not find any significant differences between national (or dyadic) age and conflict behavior. Nor could we find consistent evidence that religion plays a higher role in determining cooperation between "young" states more or less than it affects cooperation between "mature" states. We argue, therefore, that there is not enough evidence to support most of the propositions deduced from the constructivist perspective regarding the role of religion in world politics.

3.4 The Clash of Civilization (CoC) Thesis

The CoC thesis argues that civilizational factors define the key divides in post–Cold War politics. Accordingly, we deduced that religious differences tend to fuel conflict, and that religious similarities tend to promote cooperation. Religious divides may also be driving forces in post–Cold War domestic conflicts in factionalized societies. Our evidence lends at best partial support for this perspective in that religious differences seem to play an important role in fomenting conflict, and—at least in the security cooperation domain—similarities tend to attract. By contrast, we did not find evidence supporting this thesis in the case of intrastate conflict. We tend to be highly critical of arguments that religious divides make some societies more prone to civil conflict because these arguments tend to truncate such conflict into religious/ethnoreligious/or ethnic conflicts versus other types of civil conflict. This typology is methodologically misguided, as we argued repeatedly. Once we examine the role of religious factors in civil conflicts across all types of civil conflicts (where such conflicts are defined by their behavioral attributes rather than by the types of groups that fight each other or by the types of claims and grievances expressed by such groups), we find little evidence in support of the intrastate clash of civilizations.

In general, Huntington's thesis rests on a central temporal claim: civilizational divides are characteristics of post–Cold War politics. During the Cold War era, the ideological, strategic, and economic struggle between the two superpowers overshadowed intercivilizational tensions. While such tensions presumably existed under the surface, they did not emerge before the US–Soviet competition receded. This argument has received virtually no support in our analyses. In fact, we found that religious factors played a more important role in international conflicts during the Cold War era than during the post–Cold War era, which is diametrically opposed to CoC claims (see Henderson 2004: 550).

All told, while we cannot unequivocally reject the CoC arguments, we certainly can reject that aspect which suggests that the post–Cold War period signals a new era of clashing civilizations across religious fissures. It clearly does not. The degree of confidence one places in the CoC thesis depends to a large extent on the relative centrality of the temporal nature of the thesis compared to the overall claim about civilizational divides. And in terms of this specific expectation, we can confidently state that there is no support for the CoC thesis.

3.5 The Integrative Theory of Religion and World Politics

Our integrative theory of religion and world politics builds on the common themes of these often-competing perspectives. However, it adds two important elements. First, it connects the static factors that emphasize social structure and identity markers with specific political conditions, pointing out that the convergence of static social and political-situational conditions brings religious factors to the fore of international and internal processes. Second, it emphasizes the cultural interaction between the focal state and its international environment (i.e., its PRIE), which determines to a large extent its potential targets for both conflict and cooperation. Our theory focuses on the interaction between three sets of factors: the religious structure of the state, the religious structure of the state's PRIE, and the specific political conditions prevailing in both the focal state and its PRIE. The integrative theory claims that political leaders are more likely to invoke religious factors as a mobilization strategy when they feel that their job security is under threat. Religion can be used as an instrument of political mobilization if the religious structure of the society permits.

We find relatively robust support for the claims of this theory in terms of the linkages between religion and international conflict. We also find fairly consistent support for the propositions of the theory in the case of certain types of cooperative ventures—security cooperation in particular. We find less support for the theory's propositions in the case of civil conflict outbreak, but we do find support for the effect of religious polarization, religion-state relations, and state-environment religious similarity on several attributes of civil war, such as type of war and type of war settlement. It seems that religious motivations for uprisings may be confounded with other—economic or political—motivations. Also the effect of ethnic exclusion on civil conflict may overlap with religious exclusion since many "excluded" ethnic groups may also be religiously distinct from the included and dominant groups.

Overall the support for our theory is reasonably robust if we also consider the environmental effect on conflict, cooperation, and civil war. Clearly, the integrative nature of our theory tends to combine the more compelling parts of the other perspectives. As such, the overall support for our theoretical expectations is marginally better than any of its individual parts. In particular, we find the interaction of structural conditions, political circumstances, and the structure of PRIEs to offer more theoretical and empirical insights into the nature of the linkages between religion and world politics than any of these components taken independently and separately.

4. Implications for Scholarship on Religion and World Politics

It is not surprising that our study does not result in a grand theme regarding religion and world politics as previous forays into this subject (e.g., Toft, Philpott, and Shah 2011, Huntington 1996, Fox and Sandler 2004).

The reasons for the lack of a grand theme in our study are manifold; they seem to reside in some of the more substantial differences between our study and previous ones. First, our study is theoretically more nuanced than previous investigations. We do not focus on a single theory of religion and politics. Rather, we attempt to discern several perspectives linking religion to different aspects of politics. As we have seen several times throughout this book, different theories overlap significantly when it comes to making predictions about how the religious characteristics of states affect their behavior. This does not make these theories identical. Rather, they tend to differ in terms of some key elements.

Second, our analyses of the various aspects of religion and world politics are much more extensive and multilayered than any of the previous forays into this subject. To be sure, a limited set of analyses on a limited set of questions is far more likely to result in what appear to be clear answers than a comprehensive and multilayered analysis such as ours. Actually, the scope, depth, and complexity of our analyses reveal that the relationships between religious factors and different aspects of world politics are contingent—and rarely simplistic: they vary by dimension of behavior and by levels of analysis. We have used multiple indicators of religious identity and religious similarity, as well as multiple indicators of the conflict or cooperation phenomena under investigation. We applied our analysis to multiple units of analysis. All this suggests that our empirical tests are far more demanding than previous investigations. The likelihood that a given religious factor will be robust across all these different types of analysis is significantly lower than what one would find in the studies we have reviewed in the book.

Third, unlike most previous investigations that focus on a single-issue area in which religion is said to be operative, our analyses cover multiple issue areas. Consequently, factors that positively affect conflict behavior do not necessarily negatively affect cooperative behavior. Factors that affect one dimension of cooperation do not necessarily affect other dimensions of cooperation. Factors that are influential in an international context are not necessarily influential in a domestic context. Here, too, the likelihood that we can find consistent relationships between religious factors and a very broad array of international and domestic processes is low. Hence, these contingent effects of religious factors on different behavioral aspects should not come as a surprise.

Several implications follow. First, we can categorically support the argument that religion is a force in world politics. It has been a force even during the Cold War era, a period that was seemingly dominated by a struggle between two secular ideologies and worldviews: liberalism and communism. Existing theories linking religion to various aspects of conflict and cooperation leave a lot to be desired. This means we need a more nuanced understanding of the role religious factors play in international behavior. But it clearly does not mean we need to abandon the focus on religion in favor of more tangible factors that have been emphasized by the strictly materialistic perspectives of politics. If indeed, our theory combining structural conditions with situational political factors and environmental (structural characteristics and situational processes) seems to provide a reasonable explanation of religion and politics, we must explain not only how political leaders manipulate religious beliefs, but also why and under what conditions people follow such manipulations.

There is a growing dialogue between scholars of religion and politics. This dialogue is not always coherent; it involves a great deal of polemics and relatively little concerted effort to empirically connect religion to multiple aspects of international and domestic politics. We believe that a major implication of this study is to invigorate a debate on these issues that (a) is more logically and theoretically coherent, (b) covers multiple facets of international behavior rather than a single theme, (c) is more explicit in terms of the causal mechanisms linking religious factors to behavioral patterns, (d) is more explicit in terms of methodological strategies, and (e) is more systematic and replicable with respect to hypothesis testing, data transparency, and inferences.

We do not claim to have resolved all issues regarding these implications, but we believe we offer a direction in terms of these desiderata for future research, and we are open to concerns, questions, criticisms, and replications. The book's website offers the data, programs, and extensive analyses that will hopefully help anyone who wishes to follow up on what we have done.

5. Policy Implications

In terms of policy, one of the appealing aspects of the CoC thesis, for some, especially after the September 11, 2001, terrorist attacks, and perhaps even more so with the rise of ISIS terrorism, is the branding of a specific religion as inherently bellicose. Our research demonstrates that arguments that single out a specific religion, such as Huntington's claim that "Islam has bloody borders," are patently false. Islamic states—states with majority Muslims—are neither more bellicose nor more benevolent than states with Christian, Jewish, Hindu, Buddhist, or secular majorities. One thing that we can say about religion and bellicosity, though, is that religious beliefs can be manipulated regardless of the kind of God, prophet, scripture, or shrine people worship. This means that we should be careful when political or religious leaders call us to rally around a certain flag against infidels, or against people who share a different set of religious ideals. We should also be wary of religious leaders working for or against a given religion politically. These calls and these policies have hidden agendas. Religion may be an important part of people's belief systems. However, the politicization of religion can be quite dangerous.

We did not find that the promotion of religious freedom, separation of political and religious institutions, and secularism is an unequivocal force for stability, prosperity, or peace. Although some of our results do suggest that such a connection may exist, we must be very careful about calls for more religious influence or about advocacy for less religious influence in politics. Societies should establish their own equilibria on these matters; there is no single policy prescription that fits all. What we do claim is that social institutions—communities, media, political and economic institutions—should be conspicuous when political leaders start using political and religious symbols to mobilize support for militarized conflict or for oppressing segments of their own or other societies. Social checks and balances against such manipulations are important and need to be developed and safeguarded—religiously.

Notes

Preface

1. Our datasets are publicly available for use. They can be found at the two organizations that helped us generate them. The ARDA website is at http://www.thearda.com/Archive/Files/Descriptions/WRDGLOBL.asp. The Correlates of War Project hosts our dataset at http://www.correlatesofwar.org.

Chapter 1 Religion and World Politics—Theory and Evidence

1. The only exception to this is the Esther story in the Old Testament, which is a story about a plot to eliminate the Jewish community in Persia. Another explicit tale of religious warfare concerns the Maccabee books that take place in the second century BCE. However, these books did not make it into the Old Testament.

2. It is important to note two things about this comparison. First, we chose title-word combinations rather than topic-word combinations because the former selection algorithm reflects a more precise focus of the publication on the particular word combination. Second, many of these publications have no direct IR content. For example, the combination of power and world politics produces titles such as "Cuba as a World Medical Power: The Politics of Symbolism (Feinsilver 1989), or "New World States and Empires: Politics, Religion, and Urbanism" (Smith and Schreiber, 2006), where "New World" refers to the Americas and the article is an archeological study. WOS allows filtering of such titles by discipline, thus limiting the number of irrelevant works that come up in the search. However, this precludes comparison to the more general search enabled by GS. Nevertheless, a filtering of WOS search by discipline, limiting this to only works in political science and IR, reveals similar difference ratios as in the more general search.

3. Shah and Philpott (2011, 46–50) argue that the rise of religious factors in modern international relations began in 1967, due to the disappearance of prominent secular leaders such as Nehru and Nkrumah and the defeat of Nasserist secular pan Arabism by Israel in the Six Day War. While they may be correct about the factual rise of religious factors in the practice of international relations, this did not resonate in mainstream

theories of IR until much later. One of the reasons for that may be that the leading paradigms of IR were and still are dominated by Western liberal thought (Fox and Sandler 2004).

4. We calculate this statistic to reflect changes in the number of publication venues and the search engines' ability to detect publications in the latter (1991–2017) period compared to the earlier (1945–90) period.

Chapter 2 Scholarship on Religion and World Politics: A Critical Review of the Literature

1. For reviews of the role of religion in IR theories, or more precisely the lack of the role of religion in these theories, see Snyder (2011); Shah and Philpot (2011); Toft, Philpott, and Shah (2011); Fox and Sandler (2004, 1–32); Sandal and Fox (2013).

2. Cited in Shah (2012, 1–2). No source is given. Italics in original.

3. Richardson (1985, 104) noted that "secularization theory served as something of a 'sacred canopy' for most research in the social sciences of religion."

4. Anecdotally, however, Lebow's (2016) book, which offers a critique of the concept of national identity, does not even have an index entry for "religion." His discussion of the concept of self-induced (as opposed to attributed) national identity focuses on history and political vision, all encapsulated in a conception of "role." Culture, in general, and religion, in particular, play no role in this "role" conception.

5. Note that the table in appendix 4 (pp. 32–37) of that study has a code of identity type but none of the variables in this table is explained anywhere in the text or appendix.

6. Note that empirical evidence (e.g., Svensson 2013, 23) shows that a vast majority of the cases in his sample involve civil conflict between government and rebels from the same religion. Likewise, religious incompatibility does not appear to be a critical issue in most of the cases in that sample (p. 36).

7. Source: Jonathan Fox (2020). The Religion and State Project https://www.thearda.com/ras/downloads/. Data cover the period of 1990-2014 and include 1976 that match the COW state list and Fox's data.

8. This is a key argument of Philpott (2007), Toft (2007), and Fox (2015), as well as that of the religious economy model (Gill 2007, 2013).

Chapter 3 Religion and World Politics: An Integrated Theoretical Perspective

1. Conversion to Judaism is possible through a certain process that involves significant learning and preparation, and is conducted under the supervision of rabbis who are specifically trained for this matter. It is also a source of acute conflict among the various families of Judaism (Orthodox, Conservative, Reform).

2. Clearly, the relationship between religious and political institutions may fluctuate over time within a society. They also may be a source of domestic as well as international conflict, as some groups may wish to change the relationship between religion and state, and other groups may wish to sustain them as they are.

3. These rational orientations, such as the social contract theses that underwrite realism, liberalism, and constructivism, may delimit similar "othering" of communities through a "scientific" racism (see Henderson 2013).

4. Beyond the Old Testament, there is a debate among scholars regarding the dates of this invasion, but the range of dates are somewhere between the fifteenth and thirteenth centuries BCE.

5. Although in this case, the modern incarnation of Jewish nationalism, Zionism, emerged out of a long period of persecution of Jews, primarily in Eastern and Central Europe. Moreover, the principal thinkers and activists of the Zionist movement were largely secular (Sachar 2007). However, the idea of a Jewish homeland in Palestine rests on the theological bond between the Jewish religion and Judea/Israel (Palestine).

6. Interestingly, some Jewish communities in Ethiopia and Central and East Asia survived for centuries despite constant persecution and harassment by their surrounding communities (Baron 1983, Ehrlich 2009).

7. However, religion can be invoked to incite action against certain political figures or groups if the society is highly religious and the leaders are perceived as secular or in violation of religious values, such as in the Iranian Revolution and Ayatollah Khomeini's incitement of the overwhelmingly Shia Iranians against the laicity of the Shah of Iran, or the prominently Catholic Solidarity union's successful struggle against nominally atheistic communist rule in Poland, which appealed to and received assistance from Pope John Paul II. This is a utilitarian twist of Philpott's (2007) concept of "political theology," further suggesting that political theology is not a factor that is independent of political goals. Rather, it is a device whereby political elites legitimate collective action against the regime or another state.

8. Galtung's theory of neoimperialism (1971) is an apt description of this process.

9. Miller focuses on national characteristics, emphasizing ethnicity. We focus on religion as a key determinant of shared affinities among people comprising a given state.

10. For example, Mustafa Kemal (Ataturk) changed the Turkish/Ottoman legal system to base it on secular laws and separated religion from educational and political practices. By contrast, the imposition of Islamic laws in Iran after the Iranian revolution changed the relationship between religious and political institutions. These are dramatic, "revolutionary" changes. However, they do not happen very often even after fundamental regime changes.

11. Nevertheless, in our shorter-term analysis we draw on responses to World Values Survey questions on the importance of God in one's life to derive a more valid index of religiosity in a society.

12. Maoz (1996, 39 and 2010) provides a list of states that satisfy criteria (ii) and (iii) above. Empirical research (Lemke and Reed 2001, Maoz 1996, Bennett and Stam 2004) showed that most conflicts (about 82 percent to 85 percent of all militarized interstate disputes (MIDs) take place between members of PRIEs). Evidence also suggests that politically relevant dyads are about three times more likely to form an alliance

and twice more likely to trade with each other than what is expected by chance alone. We will return to these results in subsequent chapters.

Chapter 4 The Religious Landscape of the World, 1945–2010

1. This is an expanded and updated version of an article that appeared in *International Interactions* (Maoz and Henderson 2013). We thank the editor and the publisher for their permission to use the materials from the article.

2. A list of sources is provided on the project's website at: http://correlatesofwar.org.

3. This definition is used by other studies in the literature on religion and politics (e.g., Toft, Philpott, and Shah 2011, 21; Toft 2012, 133).

4. A useful example of how this criterion operates is available on the ARDA website with respect to Christian denominations in the United States. See http://www.thearda.com/Denoms/Families/trees.asp.

5. The statistical description may be slightly different from that in Maoz and Henderson (2013). This is because the current analyses are based on version 1.1 of the WRP which employs a wider and a more precise array of sources than version 1.0 on which Maoz and Henderson (2013) was based.

6. For example, average record reliability scores in 2010 are twice those of 1950.

7. This ratio has changed since 2010. By 2013, Israeli Jews constituted the single largest Jewish group in world Jewry, their share rising to roughly 50 percent of the world Jewish population.

8. In subsequent chapters, we compare this measure to other measures of fractionalization (Fearon and Laitin) and polarization (Maoz 2010), and show that this measure is very similar to these other measures. We use this measure here and in subsequent chapters because it has some advantages over these others. We discuss these differences in greater detail in the appendix to chapter 7. One caveat about *IQV* is that when a society contains only one religious group, this measure converges to infinity as the denominator ($k - 1$) becomes zero. We arbitrarily convert this to zero in such cases, as clearly there is no variation in such a society.

9. We define religious similarity precisely in the next chapter. Here, however, the data reflect the average degree to which the populations of any two states in a given region are distributed similarly in terms of their religious beliefs.

10. Also, as mentioned above, postcommunist or post-Soviet states tended to report more religious affiliations than during the Soviet/communist era. This accounts, to a large extent, for the growth in reporting of Islamic beliefs among post-Soviet republics.

11. For a complete list of sources, see the annotated bibliography on the project's website at: http://correlatesofwar.org. The website also contains a detailed coding manual.

12. This would be 1945 for states that existed at that time, or the first half-decade year for states that were formed after this point.

13. We kept this category because it featured prominently in the actual data on religious affiliation. The lumping together of this category with the religions turned out to be confusing in the survey (more below).

14. We allowed multiple categories here, so categories are not mutually exclusive and do not sum to 100 percent.

Chapter 5 Religion and International Conflict

1. These COW data were first utilized in published work by Regan (1996) to code religious characteristics of third-party interventions into civil war; and also by Lai and Reiter (2000) and Lai (2006) to code religious similarity in alliance making and Middle Eastern conflicts, respectively.

2. Huntington's (pp. 47–48) civilizations are not precisely religious designations (e.g., Western, Sinic, Japanese, African, and Latin American include diverse religious traditions), and where they are specifically religious, they are broadly so, arbitrarily subsuming major doctrinal or denominational groups (e.g., Islamic—as opposed to Sunni and Shia).

3. Generalizations from the findings of both Tusicisny (2004) and Charron (2010) are limited by the studies' research design flaws: the former relies mainly on cross-sectional bivariate analyses without theoretically relevant statistical controls. The latter study focuses only on the post–Cold War era, and therefore fails to compare the relative likelihood of fault-line conflicts to earlier periods, in contrast to earlier studies (e.g., Henderson 2004). As noted, studies that relied on a more long-term time span found that states of different civilizations straddling a fault line were significantly more likely to fight each other both during and after the Cold War era.

4. Average change in the percentage of a given religious group over a five-year period is about two-tenths of one percent. When considering this change over a single year, as would be the case in most studies that use the dyad-year unit of analysis, the annual percent change of the size of religious groups is less than five-hundredths of one percent (0.0005).

5. The same applies to some of the common controls used in such analyses such as contiguity/distance, major/minor power status, and even joint democracy dummy variables.

6. For example, several scholars, following Maoz and Russett (1993), have focused on a sample of politically relevant dyads, that is, dyads that are made up of contiguous states, or dyads that consist of at least one major power.

7. There are, however, systemic shocks that may alter the religious identity of societies. For example, we saw in chapter 3 how the collapse of communism in Eastern Europe and the disintegration of the Soviet Union increased the level of religious identity in the postcommunist states, and established states that have become more religiously homogeneous than their predecessor states (e.g., in Central Asia, the former Yugoslav republics). However such systemic shocks are rare, and part of the implications of such shocks are captured in P2.

8. We use Maoz's (2010) definition of major and regional powers and his list of such powers. Data are in Maoz's website at: http://maoz.ucdavis.edu/datasets.html.

9. Note that in cases of disagreement between RS and CCS datasets, we follow the former, which is more detailed regarding practical aspects of religion-state relations, in contrast to the more textual basis of the latter.

10. Here, too, we use the continuous coup-risk variable in some of the analyses; the results are largely the same. The need to generate an ordinal coup-risk measure arises from interactions between coup risks and religious similarity state-PRIE.

11. We have also tested the extent to which Judeo-Islamic dyads are more likely to engage in conflict. We find no significant relationship there as well. We do find some evidence that Hindu-Islamic dyads are more likely to fight each other than other types of religious combinations. However, this is also not a robust result.

12. Maoz (2010) offered a new list of major and regional powers. See online appendix to *Networks of Nations* at http:// maoz.ucdavis.edu/ datasets.html.

Chapter 6 Religion and International Cooperation

1. Examples of such social dilemmas include the Prisoner's Dilemma (Flood 1952, Axelrod 1984), the Stag Hunt (Jervis 1978), and the tragedy of the commons (Hardin 2009).

2. We define "substantial" trade between two states as trade from state i to state j greater than 0.1 percent of its GDP. On the "Catch-22" relationship between trade and conflict, see Barbieri and Levy (1999).

3. Here, too, we define "substantial" overlap in IGO membership between two states if their shared membership in IGOs was higher than the average dyadic overlap in IGO membership for that year.

4. We provide data on this point in the appendix to this chapter.

5. Some of the seminal systematic theses on international cooperation are not easily fitted into extant paradigms of world politics, such as Deutsch et al.'s (1957) thesis on amalgamated and pluralistic security communities.

6. Trend data on these figures are given in the book's website.

7. The paradox is more severe, however. The state that dragged its ally into an unwanted war, sometimes bails out of the war and leaves its ally to fight alone against a third party with whom it had no quarrel before the alliance was formed.

8. Powers (2006) observes exceptions in the case of PTAs in Africa, which largely emerged as attempts at economic cooperation, and which ramified into security cooperation, epitomized in the embedding of security agreements in the trade treaties (also see Henderson 2015).

9. Note that Wendt identifies a Hobbesian culture—a "warre of all against all"—in which no cooperation is possible. However, he claims that this is a hypothetical culture and has no historical equivalent.

10. One may argue, particularly so, given both the significance of race (Mills 1997) and gender (Pateman 1988) in Kant's original conception; and in the common conception of anarchy drawn from social contract theorists' view of the state of nature (Henderson 2013, 2015).

11. Haas (1992, 3) defines an epistemic community in terms of a group of individuals with shared norms and beliefs that have expertise with respect to some issue domain.

12. See Maoz (2010, Ch. 2) as well as the appendix for technical details.

13. All states with the same cooperative rank (e.g., with the same number of allies) get the same rank.

14. This is even more necessary here than in the study of conflict, because we do not have a meaningful filter (such as the concept of political relevance) to reduce the size of the population. In principle, any state can cooperate with any other state, regardless of distance or reputational status. By contrast, the probability of conflict is strongly conditioned by distance and reputational status. This generates, for cooperative behavior, a population size of over 800,000 undirected dyads over the period 1945–2010.

15. This resonates with Powers (2006) and Henderson's (2015) findings on the greater likelihood of African states to create PTAs with embedded security agreements.

16. Henderson (2015) provides a fuller discussion of the differential process of socialization on newly independent states in the post-WWII era and its impact on their international relations.

Chapter 7 Religion and Civil War

1. The conservative estimate considers the dawn of human communities as the Neolithic period, roughly 10,000 years ago, when farming developed. The more realistic estimate considers significant parts of the era of hunter-gatherers, which ranges for over three million years. See Gat (2008), Cioffi-Revilla (1991).

2. Japan, up to the Meiji Restoration (1868), is a prime example, but other examples in Africa and Asia prior to the expansion of colonialism and imperialism in the nineteenth century also apply.

3. The Gini coefficient has an upper limit of $1-1/N$ (Ray and Singer 1973).

4. In principle, it is possible to include extrasystemic—imperial and colonial—wars. However, we focus on the interactions within and between independent states, so we do not include those here.

5. The turn of focus for quantitative-oriented IR scholars was facilitated by publication of the COW project's data on civil wars from 1816 to 1980 (Small and Singer 1982). The first published study utilizing these civil war data appears to have been Altfeld and Sabrosky (1990).

6. Although they found that ethnolinguistic polarization was significantly associated with the onset and duration of civil wars, for 1960–92.

7. For an alternative view implicating realist factors (i.e., neopatrimonial balancing) in these relationships for African cases, see Henderson (2015).

8. A number of early post–Cold War era studies that took as one of their concerns the impact of "ethnicity" on civil war (e.g., Collier and Hoeffler 1998, Henderson and Singer 2000) did not include specific religion variables.

9. Using Toft's (2009, Appendix 1) and Toft, Philpott, and Shah's (2011, 154) designation of civil wars as "religious" or "non-religious," and applying this designation to our civil war data (discussed below), we find that 33 percent of the COW civil wars were "religious," 32 percent of the UCDP civil conflicts were "religious," 37 percent of the civil wars identified by Fearon and Laitin (2004) were "religious," and 26 percent of the violent resistance campaigns identified by the NAVCO project (Chenoweth and Stephan 2013) were "religious." This suggests a fairly robust result indicating that religious civil wars constitute a rather hefty minority of all civil wars over the period 1945–2010.

10. Much of this literature was spurred by the racial and civil rights conflicts in the United States during the 1950s and 1960s—and the domestic opposition to the Vietnam War.

11. They operationalize grievances in terms of the largest discriminated group within a country rather than the total excluded population and the inequality among groups by comparing the relative wealth of the poorest and richest groups to the country average.

12. As noted above, we focus on the work of Fox and Akbaba on religious discrimination, and of Basedau and his colleagues on the more general causal mechanism connecting religious practices and religious institutions to the outbreak of political violence. These exemplify the main concerns we discuss herein.

13. In Africa, the site of a disproportionate number of civil conflicts and the original focus of the greed versus grievance framework (i.e. Collier and Hoeffler 1998), this assessment of the potential for anticipated external support has been theorized by Henderson (2015) as a form of "neopatrimonial balancing," whereby neopatrimonial elites realize that the most likely source of their downfall—and that of other neopatrimonial leaders in the region—is domestic. Balancing power in such a context is aimed at supporting rival regimes' rebels who constitute the greatest potential threat to their rule. State A's support of state B's rebels typically results in state B's reciprocal support of state A's rebels, which is a form of balancing power among African dyads: neopatrimonial balancing.

14 We thank James Fearon for making the updated dataset available to us.

15. Note that if a state experienced more than one civil war in a given year, the duration and severity variables were aggregated over all civil wars fought during that year.

16. This is part of a more general measure of network polarization and is a product of two components: group polarization (GPOL) and group cohesion (GC). However, for a set of discrete groups, as is the case with religious affiliation, the network polarization index reduces to GPOL because the group overlap (proportion of people practicing more than one religion) is—with some minor exceptions—zero. Therefore, group cohesion is assigned uniformly a value of 1.

17. The EPR dataset (Wimmer et al. 2009) outlines the access of various ethnic groups to political power in states. The problem, as we have already pointed out, is that ethnicity and religion are not synonymous and their measures are not consistently comparable across states.

18. Note that the relationship between war type (religious/non-religious) and settlement becomes statistically insignificant if we use a simple logit estimation, without taking into account selection bias.

19. We applied a number of analyses on religious groups' effect on war type. The table reports results for measures of the relative size (percent) of the specific religious group in the state's population. We found similar results when we used only dummy variables for a majority religious group (i.e., a majority Christian country is one where 50 percent+ of its population practice Christianity, and so forth). The results for the specific religious groups are the same. The only exception is the non-religious group; the effect of this group (when counting only instances of majority non-religious country years) is washed out given this type of measure.

20. For example, considering the plethora of civil wars that resulted from or in the direct aftermath of anti-colonial armed struggles, racial difference and racist discrimination are candidate variables in analyses of those wars; but they may be less salient as precipitants of civil war in the country's later post-independence era where issues and policies related to personalist (neopatrimonial) leadership, political survival, and third party support of the regime or its dissidents may exacerbate domestic tensions and lead to civil war.

21. And the groups do not overlap, which—with two national exceptions, Haiti and Japan—is always the case.

22. Data sources are listed in the chapter's appendix.

Chapter 8 Religion and Quality of Life

1. Prior to Bueno de Mesquita et al's more famous usage, Migdal (1988) had characterized the calculus of leaders of such political systems as the "politics of survival" (Henderson 2015).

2. Gill (2013) reviews other models of religion and economic development. He also warns that the path to religious freedom can, and often does, go through religious and political conflict, as some religious groups lose their preferential status and some seek to gain hegemony, and politicians often form alliances with one group or another. The bottom line, however, is "the case for religious freedom has greater appeal if it is tied to some tangible benefit . . . If there is one thing other than raw political power that captures the attention of rulers, it is the accumulation of economic resources" (p. 18).

3. The work of Sarkissian (2015) is also notable in this regard. Unfortunately, both Grim and Finke's and Sarkissian's data are primarily cross-sectional, and therefore of limited usage in a more general context. Moreover, Sarkissian's focus is on authoritarian regimes, and hence his data do not represent the entire spectrum of states. However, for this particular aspect of our study, both the data and the substantive arguments about the determinants of religious freedom/repression are extremely useful.

4. We offer a detailed explanation of the measurement process of the various HDI-related indices in the appendix to this chapter.

5. The correlation between these variables (see appendix) is $r = -0.785$, $N = 193$, $p < 10^{-7}$. We have also analyzed each of these variables separately. The results are largely the same.

Chapter 9 The Complex Role of Religion in World Politics

1. Lai (2006) examines the impact of such relationships where leaders and populations in the Middle East have distinct religious affiliations.

2. As noted, such datasets as the EPR contain an assessment of the access to power of different social groups; however, they mix ethnicity, religious, racial and linguistic characteristics of groups, thus making it difficult to single out religious groups' access to political power.

Bibliography

Abernethy, D. B. 2000. *The Dynamics of Global Dominance.* New Haven, CT: Yale University Press.
Adler, E. 2005. *Communitarian International Relations: The Epistemic Foundations of International Relations.* New York: Routledge.
Adler, E., and M. Barnett 1998. "Security Communities in Theoretical Perspective, edited by E. Adler and M. Barnett. *Security Communities,* 3–28. Cambridge: Cambridge University Press.
Adler, E., and P. M. Haas. 1992. "Epistemic Communities, World Order, and the Creation of a Reflective Research Program." *International Organization* 46: 367–90.
Akbaba, Y. 2006. "Understanding Ethnoreligious Conflict: The State, Discrimination and International Politics," PhD diss., University of Missouri.
Akbaba, Y., and Z. Taydas. 2011. "Does Religious Discrimination Promote Dissent? A Quantitative Analysis." *Ethnopolitics* 10, no. 3–4: 271–95.
Alston, W. P. 1967. "Religion." In *Encyclopedia of Philosophy,* edited by P. Edwards, 140–45. New York: Macmillan.
Anievas, A., N. Manchanda, and R. Shilliam, eds. 2015. *Confronting the Global Colour Line: Race and Racism in International Relations.* London: Routledge.
Appleby, S. R. 1999. *The Ambivalence of the Sacred: Religion, Violence, and Reconciliation.* Lanham, MD: Rowman & Littlefield Publishers.
ARDA. 2017. Association of Religion Data Archives. http://thearda.org
Aslan, R. 2011. *No God But God: The Origins, Evolution, and Future of Islam.* New York: Random House.
Axelrod, R. 1984. *The Evolution of Cooperation.* New York: Basic Books.
Axelrod, R., and R. O. Keohane. 1985. "Achieving Cooperation under Anarchy: Strategies and Institutions," *World Politics* 38, no. 1: 226–54.
Baccini, L., and W. M. Chow. 2018. "The Politics of Preferential Trade Liberalization in Authoritarian Countries." *International Interactions* 44, no. 2: 189–216.
Baez, J. E. 2011. "Civil Wars beyond Their Borders: The Human Capital and Health Consequences of Hosting Refugees." *Journal of Development Economics* 96, no. 2: 391–408.
Barbieri, K., and J. Levy. 1999. "Sleeping with the Enemy: The Impact of War on Trade." *Journal of Peace Research* 36, no. 4: 463–79.

Barbieri, K., O. Keshk, and B. Pollins. 2009. "Trading Data: Evaluating Our Assumptions and Coding Rules." *Conflict Management and Peace Science* 26, no. 5: 471–91.

Baron, S. 1983. *Social and Religious History of the Jews*. New York: Columbia University Press.

Barrett, D., G. Kurian, and T. Johnson. 2011. *World Christian Encyclopedia: A Comparative Study of Churches and Religion in the Modern World*. New York: Oxford University Press.

Basedau, M., B. Pfeiffer, and J. Vüllers. 2016. "Bad Religion? Religion, Collective Action, and the Onset of Armed Conflict in Developing Countries." *Journal of Conflict Resolution* 60, no. 2: 226–55.

Basedau, M., J. Fox, and J. H. Pierskalla. 2017. "Does Discrimination Breed Grievances—and Do Grievances Breed Violence? New Evidence from an Analysis of Religious Minorities in Developing Countries." *Conflict Management and Peace Science* 34, no. 3: 217–39.

Beach, E. C., and J. Snyder 2011. "Religion's Contribution to International Relations Theory." In *Religion and International Relations*, edited by J. Snyder, 200–10. New York: Columbia University Press.

Bektas, T. 2006. "The Multiple Traveling Salesman Problem: An Overview of Formulations and Solution Procedures." *Omega* 34, no. 3: 209–19.

Bennett, D. S., and A. Stam III. 2004. *The Behavioral Origins of War*. Ann Arbor: University of Michigan Press.

Benson, M. A. 2005. "The Relevance of Politically Relevant Dyads in the Study of Interdependence and Dyadic Disputes." *Conflict Management and Peace Science* 22, no. 2: 113–33.

Benson, M., and J. Kugler. 1998. "Power Parity, Democracy, and the Severity of Internal Violence." *Journal of Conflict Resolution* 42, no. 2: 196–209.

Bercovitch, J., and A. S. Kadayifci-Orellana. 2009. "Religion and Mediation: The Role of Faith-Based Actors in International Conflict Resolution." *International Negotiation* 14, no.1: 175–204.

Berger, P. 1968. "A Bleak Outlook Is Seen for Religion." *New York Times*, April 25, 3.

Besley, T., and T. Persson. 2010. "State Capacity, Conflict, and Development." *Econometrica* 78, no. 1: 1–34.

Blainey, Geoffrey. 1988. *The Causes of War*. 3rd ed. New York: Free Press.

Bolks, S., and R. Stoll. 2003. "Examining Conflict Escalation within the Civilizations Context." *Conflict Management and Peace Science* 20, no. 2: 85–109.

Booth, K., ed. 2005. *Critical Security Studies and World Politics*. Boulder, CO: Lynne Rienner.

Bormann, N-C., L-E. Cederman, and M. Vogt. 2017. "Language, Religion, and Ethnic Civil War." *Journal of Conflict Resolution* 61, no. 4: 744–71.

Bremer, S. 1980. "The Trials of Nations." In *The Correlates of War II: Testing Some Realpolitik Models*, edited by J. D. Singer, 3–35. New York: Free Press.

Bremer, S. 1992. "Dangerous Dyads: Conditions Affecting the Likelihood of Interstate War, 1816–1965." *Journal of Conflict Resolution* 36, no. 2: 309–41.

Breslin, S., and G. Christou. 2015. "Has the Human Security Agenda Come of Age? Definitions, Discourses and Debates." *Contemporary Politics* 21, no. 1: 1–10.

Brown, M. E., ed. 1996. *The International Dimensions of Internal Conflict.* Cambridge, MA: MIT Press.
Brownlee, J., T. Masoud, and A. Reynolds. 2015. *The Arab Spring: Pathways of Repression and Reform.* New York: Oxford University Press.
Buck, l. P., and J. P. Zophy, eds. 1972. *The Social History of the Reformation.* Columbus: Ohio State University Press.
Buckley, D. T. 2015. "Beyond the Secularism Trap: Religion, Political Institutions and Democratic Commitments." *Comparative Politics* 47, no. 4: 439–58.
Bueno de Mesquita, B., J. D. Morrow, R. M. Siverson, and A. Smith 1999. "An Institutional Explanation of the Democratic Peace." *American Political Science Review* 93: 791–807.
Bueno de Mesquita, B., J. D Morrow, R. M. Siverson, and A. Smith. 2003. *The Logic of Political Survival.* Cambridge, MA: MIT Press.
Bueno de Mesqiuta, B., R. Siverson, and G. Woller. 1992. "War and the Fate of Regimes." *American Political Science Review* 86: 638–46.
Buhaug, H., L. Cederman, and K. Gleditsch. 2014. "Square Pegs on Round Holes: Inequalities, Grievances, and Civil War." *International Studies Quarterly* 58, no. 2: 418–31.
Buzan, B. 1983. *People, States, and Fear.* Chapel Hill: University of North Carolina Press.
Buzan, B. 1991. *People, States, and Fear.* 2nd ed. Colchester, UK: Harvester Wheatsheaf.
Buzan, B., O. Wæver, and J. de Wilde. 1998. *Security: A New Framework for Analysis.* Boulder, CO: Lynne Rienner Publishers.
Cabral, A. 1972. *Revolution in Guinea: Selected Texts by Amilcar Cabral.* New York: Monthly Review.
Canetti, D., S. Hobfoll, A. Pedahzur, and E. Zaidise 2010. "Much Ado about Religion: Religiosity, Resource Loss, and Support for Political Violence." *Journal of Peace Research* 47, no. 5: 575–87.
Carlson, J. D. 2014. "What Is Christian about Christian Realism? Reinhold Biebuhr. In *Religion and the Realist Tradition*, edited by J. Troy, 37–62. London: Routledge.
Carlson, J. D., and E. C. Owens 2003. *The Sacred and the Sovereign: Religion and International Politics.* Washington, DC: Georgetown University Press.
Cederman, L. E., A. Wimmer, and B. Min 2010. "Why Do Ethnic Groups Rebel? New Data and Analysis." *World Politics* 62, no. 1: 87–119.
Cederman, L. E., and A. Wimmer 2010. Ethnic Power Relation Dataset. Retrieved 2/9/2018, from http://www.epr.ucla.edu/
Cederman, L. E, and L. Girardin. 2007. "Beyond Fractionalization: Mapping Ethnicity onto Nationalist Insurgencies." *American Political Science Review* 101: 173–85.
Cederman, L-E., K. S. Gleditsch, and H. Buhaug. 2013. *Inequality, Grievances, and Civil War.* Cambridge: Cambridge University Press.
Cederman, L-E., N. B. Weidmann, and K. S. Gledtisch. 2011. "Horizontal Inequalities and Ethnonationalist Civil War: A Global Comparison." *American Political Science Review* 105, no. 3: 478–95.
Cesari, J. 2016. "Revisiting the Secular Assumptions" In *Routledge Handbook of International Political Sociology*, edited by X. Guillaume and P. Bilgin, 214–22. New York: Routledge.

Cesari, J., and J. Fox 2016. "Institutional Relations Rather Than Clashes of Civilizations: When and How Is Religion Compatible with Democracy?" *International Political Sociology* 10, no. 3: 241–57.

Charron, N. 2010. "Déjà Vu All Over Again: A Post–Cold War Empirical Analysis of Samuel Huntington's 'Clash of Civilizations' Theory." *Cooperation and Conflict* 45, no. 1: 107–27.

Cheibub, J. A, J, Gandhi, and J, R, Vreeland. 2010. "Democracy and Dictatorship Revisited." *Public Choice* 143, no. 2–1: pp. 67–101.

Chenoweth, E., and M. J. Stephan. 2011. *Why Civil Resistance Works: The Strategic Logic of Nonviolent Conflict.* New York: Columbia University Press.

Chenoweth, E., and O. A. Lewis. 2013. "Unpacking Nonviolent Campaigns Introducing the NAVCO 2.0 Dataset." *Journal of Peace Research* 50, no. 3: 415–23.

Chiozza, G. 2002. "Is There a Clash of Civilizations? Evidence from Patterns of International Conflict Involvement, 1946–97." *Journal of Peace Research* 39, no. 6: 711–34.

Chow, W. M., and D. Y. Kono. 2017. "Entry, Vulnerability, and Trade Policy: Why Some Autocrats Like International Trade." *International Studies Quarterly* 61, no. 4: 892–906.

Cioffi-Revilla, C. 1991. "The Long-Range Analysis of War." *Journal of Interdisciplinary History* 21, no. 4: 603–29.

Cleveland, W. L., and M. Bunton. 2012. *A History of the Modern Middle East.* Boulder, CO: Westview Press.

Cohen, R. 1997. *Negotiating across Cultures: International Communication in an Interdependent World.* Washington, DC: United States Institute of Peace Press.

Colaresi, M. P, K. A. Rasler, and W. R. Thompson. 2008. *Strategic Rivalries in World Politics: Position, Space and Conflict Escalation.* Cambridge: Cambridge University Press.

Colgan, J. D. 2013. *Petro Aggression: When Oil Causes War.* Cambridge: Cambridge University Press.

Collier, P., A. Hoeffler, and D. Rohner. 2009. "Beyond Greed and Grievance: Feasibility and Civil War." *Oxford Economic Papers* 61, no. 1: 1–27.

Collier, P., A. Hoeffler, and M. Söderbom. 2004. "On the Duration of Civil War." *Journal of Peace Research* 41, no. 3: 253–73.

Collier, P., and A. Hoeffler 1998. "On Economic Causes of Civil War. *Oxford Economic Papers* 50, no. 4: 563–73.

Collier, P., and A. Hoeffler. 2002. "On the Incidence of Civil War in Africa." *Journal of Conflict Resolution* 46, no. 1: 13–28.

Collier, P., and A. Hoeffler. 2004. "Greed and Grievance in Civil War. *Oxford Economic Papers* 56, no. 4: 563–95.

Collier, P., and N. Sambanis. 2005. *Understanding Civil War, Evidence and Analysis*, vol.1: *Africa.* Washington, DC: World Bank.

Correlates of War. 2008 Military Capabilities of Nations, 1816–1986. Retrieved November 15, 2009, from http://www.correlatesofwar.org/.

Cranmer, S. J., and B. A. Desmarais. 2011. "Inferential Network Analysis with Exponential Random Graph Models." *Political Analysis* 19, no. 1: 66–86.

Cranmer, S. J., B. A. Desmarais, and E. J. Meninga. 2012. "Complex Dependencies in the Alliance Network." *Conflict Management and Peace Science* 29: 279–313.

Cunningham, D.E., Gleditsch, K. S. and Salehyan, I., 2009. It takes two: A dyadic analysis of civil war duration and outcome. *Journal of Conflict Resolution*, 53, no. 4: 570–597

Davies, J. 1962. "Toward a Theory of Revolution." *American Sociological Review* 27, no. 1: 5–19.

De Juan, A., J. Pierskalla, and J. Vüllers. 2015. "The Pacifying Effects of Local Religious Institutions: An Analysis of Communal Violence in Indonesia." *Political Research Quarterly* 68, no. 2: 211–24.

De Soysa, I., and E. Neumayer. 2007. "Resource Wealth and the Risk of Civil War Onset: Results from a New Dataset of Natural Resource Rents, 1970–1999." *Conflict Management and Peace Science* 24: 201–18.

De Soysa, I., and R. Nordås. 2007. "Islam's Bloody Innards? Religion and Political Terror, 1980–2000." *International Studies Quarterly* 51, no. 4: 927–43.

Desmarais, B. A., and S. J. Cranmer. 2012. "Statistical Mechanics of Networks: Estimation and Uncertainty." *Physica A* 391: 1865–76.

Despotis, D. K. 2005. "A Reassessment of the Human Development Index via Data Envelopment Analysis." *Journal of the Operational Research Society* 56, no. 8: 969–80.

Deutsch, K., S. Burrell, R. Kann, M. Lee, M. Lichterman, R. Lindgren, F. Lorwenheim, and R. VanWagenen. 1957. *Political Community and the North Atlantic Area*. Princeton, NJ: Princeton University Press.

Diehl, P. F., and G. Goertz. 2000. *War and Peace in International Rivalry*. Ann Arbor: University of Michigan Press.

Doyle, M. 1986. "Liberalism and World Politics." *American Political Science Review* 80, no. 4: 1151–61.

Doyle, M., and N. Sambanis. 2000. "International Peacebuilding: A Theoretical and Quantitative Analysis." *American Political Science Review* 94, no. 4: 779–801.

Du Bois, W. E. B. 1915. "The African Roots of War." *Atlantic Monthly* 115: 707–14.

Dunn, R. S. 1979. *The Age of Religious Wars, 1559–1715*. New York: W. W. Norton.

Eckstein, H., ed. 1964. *Internal War: Problems and Approaches*. New York: Free Press of Glencoe.

Ehrlich, A. M. 2009. *Encyclopedia of the Jewish Diaspora: Origins, Experience, and Culture*. Santa Barbara, CA: ABC Clio Press.

Elbadawi, I., and N. Sambanis. 2002. "How Much War Will We See? Explaining the Prevalence of Civil War." *Journal of Conflict Resolution* 46, no. 3: 307–34.

Elkins, Z., T. Ginsburg, and J. Melton. 2014. The Comparative Constitutions Project. Retrieved August 30, 2019, from http://comparativeconstitutionsproject.org/ccp-data–downloads/.

Ellingsen, T. 2000. "Colorful Community or Ethnic Witches' Brew?" *Journal of Conflict Resolution* 44, no. 2: 228–49.

Ellingsen, T. 2006. "Toward a Revival of Religion and Religion Clashes?" In *Religion in World Conflict*, edited by J. Fox and S. Sandler, 11–38. New York: Routledge.

Elliott, L. 2015. "Human Security/Environmental Security." *Contemporary Politics* 21, no. 1: 11–24.

Elster, J. 1985. *Making Sense of Marx*. London and New York: Cambridge University Press.

Enloe, C. 1989. *Bananas, Beaches, and Bases: Making Feminist Sense of International Relations*. Berkeley: University of California Press.

Esteban, J., and D. Ray. 2008a. "On the Salience of Ethnic Conflict." *American Economic Review* 98, no. 5: 2185–202.

Esteban, J., and D. Ray. 2008b. "Polarization, Fractionalization and Conflict." *Journal of Peace Research* 45, no. 2: 163–82.

Esteban, J., L. Mayoral, and D. Ray. 2012. "Ethnicity and Conflict: An Empirical Study. *American Economic Review* 102, no. 4: 1310–42.

Farber, H. S., and J. Gowa. 1995. "Polities and Peace." *International Security* 20, no. 2: 123–45.

Fearon, J. 2003. "Ethnic and Cultural Diversity by Country." *Journal of Economic Growth* 8, no. 2: 195–222.

Fearon, J. 2005. "Primary Commodity Exports and Civil War." *Journal of Conflict Resolution* 49, no. 4: 483–507.

Fearon, J., and D. Laitin. 2003. "Ethnicity, Insurgency, and Civil War." *American Political Science Review* 97, no. 1: 75–90.

Fearon, J. D., K. Kasara, and D. D. Laitin. 2007. "Ethnic Minority Rule and Civil War Onset." *American Political Science Review* 100, no. 1: 187–93.

Feinsilver, J. M. 1989. "Cuba as a 'World Medical Power': The Politics of Symbolism." *Latin American Research Review* 24, no. 2: 1–34.

Finnemore, M. 1996. "Norms, Culture, and World Politics: Insights from Sociology's Institutionalism. *International Organization* 50, no. 2: 325–47.

Fitzgerald, T. 2011. *Religion and Politics in International Relations*. Cambridge: Cambridge University Press.

Flood, M. 1952. "Some Experimental Games," Research Memorandum RM-789-1. Santa Monica, CA: RAND Corporation.

Fordham, B. O. 2010. "Trade and Asymmetric Alliances." *Journal of Peace Research* 47: 685–96.

Fox, J. 1997. "The Salience of Religious Issues in Ethnic Conflicts: A Large-n Study." *Nationalism and Ethnic Politics* 3, no. 3: 1–19.

Fox, J. 2001. "Religious Causes of International Intervention in Ethnic Conflicts." *International Politics* 38, no. 4: 515–32.

Fox, J. 2002. *Ethnoreligious Conflict in the Late 20th Century: A General Theory*. Lanham, MD: Lexington Press.

Fox, J. 2004a. *Religion, Civilization, and Civil War: 1945 through the New Millennium*. Lanham, MD: Lexington Press.

Fox, J. 2004b. "Religion and State Failure: An Examination of the Extent and Magnitude of Religious Conflict from 1950 to 1996." *International Political Science Review* 25, no. 1: 55–76.

Fox, J. 2004c. "The Rise of Religious Nationalism and Conflict: Ethnic Conflict and Revolutionary Wars, 1945–2001." *Journal of Peace Research* 41, no. 6: 715–31.

Fox, J. 2008. *A World Survey of Religion and the State*. New York: Cambridge University Press.

Fox, J. 2012a. *An Introduction to Religion and Politics: Theory and Practice*. New York: Routledge.

Fox, J. 2012b. The Religion and State Project. Retrieved July 3, 2013, from http://www.religionandstate.org/.

Fox, J. 2012c. "The Religious Wave: Religion and Domestic Conflict from 1960 to 2009." *Civil Wars* 14, no. 2: 141–58.

Fox, J. 2015. *Political Secularism, Religion, and the State: A Time-Series Analysis of Worldwide Data*. Cambridge: Cambridge University Press.

Fox, J. 2016. *The Unfree Exercise of Religion: A World Survey of Discrimination against Religious Minorities*. Cambridge: Cambridge University Press.

Fox, J., and S. Sandler, eds. 2004. *Bringing Religion into International Relations*. New York: Palgrave Macmillan.

Fox, J., and S. Sandler. 2006. "The Question of Religion and World Politics." In *Religion in World Conflict*, edited by J. Fox and S. Sandler, 1–10. New York: Routledge.

Fox, J. and S. Sandler, eds. 2014. *Religion in World Conflict*. New York: Routledge.

Fox, J., C. Bader, and J. M. McClure. 2017. "Don't Get Mad: The Disconnect between Religious Discrimination and Individual Perceptions of Government." *Conflict Management and Peace Science* 31, no. 3: 217–39.

Fox, J., P. James, and Y. Li. 2009. "State Religion and Discrimination against Ethnic Minorities." *Nationalism and Ethnic Politics* 15, no. 2: 189–210.

Franzese, R. J., and J. C. Hays. 2007. "Spatial Econometric Models of Cross-Sectional Interdependence in Political Science Panel and Time-Series-Cross-Section Data." *Political Analysis* 15: 140–64.

Freedman, L., and E. Karsh. 1995. *The Gulf Conflict, 1990–1991: Diplomacy and War in the New World Order*. Princeton, NJ: Princeton University Press.

Freedom House. 2016. Freedom in the World. From https://freedomhouse.org/about-us.

Furedi, F. 1998. *The Silent War: Imperialism and the Changing Perception of Race*. New Brunswick, NJ: Rutgers University Press.

Galtung, J. 1971. "A Structural Theory of Imperialism." *Journal of Peace Research* 8, no. 2: 81–117.

Gartzke, E., and K. S. Gleditsch. 2004. "Why Democracies May Actually Be Less Reliable Allies." *American Journal of Political Science* 48, no. 4: 775–95.

Gartzke, E., and K. S. Gleditsch. 2006. "Identity and Conflict: Ties That Bind and Differences That Divide. *European Journal of International Relations* 12: 53–87.

Gat, A. 2006. *War in Human Civilization*. New York: Oxford University Press.

Geller, D. S., and J. D. Singer. 1998. *Nations at War: A Scientific Study of International Conflict*. Cambridge: Cambridge University Press.

Ghosn, F., G. Palmer, and S. Bremer. 2004. "The MID3 Data Set, 1993–2001: Procedures, Coding Rules, and Description." *Conflict Management and Peace Science* 21, no. 2: 133–54.

Gibler, D. M. 2007. *International Military Alliances, 1648–2008*. Washington, DC: CQ Press.

Gill, A. 2001. Religion and Comparative Politics. *Annual Review of Political Science* 4, no. 1: 117–38.

Gill, A. 2007. *The Political Origins of Religious Liberty*. Cambridge: Cambridge University Press.

Gill, A. 2011. "Religion and Violence: An Economic Approach" In *The Blackwell Companion to Religion and Violence*, edited by A. R. Murphy, 35–49. Malden, MA: Wiley-Blackwell.

Gill, A. 2013. "Religious Liberty and Economic Development: Exploring the Causal Connections." *The Review of Faith & International Affairs* 11, no. 4: 5–23.

Gill, S. 1993. *Gramsci, Historical Materialism and International Relations*. Cambridge: Cambridge University Press.

Gilligan, M. J., and L. Johns. 2012. "Formal Models of International Institutions." *Annual Review of Political Science* 15: 221–43.

Gleditsch, K., I. Salehyan and K. Schultz. 2008. "Fighting at Home, Fighting Abroad: How Civil Wars Lead to International Disputes." *Journal of Conflict Resolution* 52, no. 4: 479–506.

Gleditsch, K. S. 2002. "Expanded Trade and GDP Data." *Journal of Conflict Resolution* 46, no. 5: 712–24.

Gleditsch, K. S. 2007. "Transnational Dimensions of Civil War." *Journal of Peace Research* 44, no. 3: 293–309.

Gleditsch, K. S., and M. D. Ward. 2001. "Measuring Space: A Minimum Distance Database." *Journal of Peace Research* 38, no. 4: 749–68.

Gochman, C. S., and Z. Maoz. 1984. "Militarized Interstate Disputes, 1816–1976: Procedures, Patterns, Insights." *Journal of Conflict Resolution* 29, no. 4: 585–615.

Goertz, G. 2006. *Social Science Concepts: A User's Guide*. Princeton, NJ: Princeton University Press.

Gorski, P. S., and G. Türkmen-Dervişoğlu. 2013. "Religion, Nationalism, and Violence: An Integrated Approach." *Annual Review of Sociology* 39, no. 1: 193–210.

Gowa, J. 1995. *Allies, Adversaries, and International Trade*. Princeton, NJ: Princeton University Press.

Gowa, J. 1999. *The Elusive Democratic Peace*. Princeton, NJ: Princeton University Press.

Gowa, J., and E. D. Mansfield. 1993. "Power Politics and International Trade." *American Political Science Review* 87, no. 2: 408–20.

Gowa, J., and E. D. Mansfield. 2004. "Alliances, Imperfect Markets, and Major-Power Trade." *International Organization* 58, no. 4: 775–805.

Grim, B. J., and R. Finke. 2006. "International Religion Indexes: Government Regulation, Government Favoritism, and Social Regulation of Religion." *Interdisciplinary Journal of Research on Religion* 2, no. 1: 3–40.

Grim, B. J., and R. Finke. 2011. *The Price of Religious Freedom Denied: Religious Persecution and Conflict in the Twenty-First Century*. New York: Cambridge University Press

Gubler, J. R., and J. S. Selway. 2012. "Horizontal Inequality, Crosscutting Cleavages, and Civil War." *Journal of Conflict Resolution* 56, no. 2: 206–32.

Guilhot, N. 2010. "American Katechon: When Political Theology Became International Relations Theory." *Constellations* 17, no. 2: 224–53.

Gurr, T. 1970. *Why Men Rebel*. Princeton, NJ: Princeton University Press.

Gurr, T. 1980. "On the Outcomes of Violent Conflict." In *Handbook of Political Conflict*, edited by T. Gurr, 238–94. New York: Free Press.

Gurr, T. 1993. *Minorities at Risk: A Global View Of Ethnopolitical Conflict*. Washington, DC: US Institute of Peace.

Gurr, T. 1994. "People against States: Ethnopolitical Conflict and the Changing World System." *International Studies Quarterly* 38: 347–78.

Gurr, T, and B. Harff. 1994. *Ethnic Conflict in World Politics*. New York: Westview.

Gurr, T., and M. Lichbach, 1979. "Forecasting Domestic Political Conflict." In *To Augur Well: Early Warning Indicators in World Politics*, edited by J. D. Singer and M. Wallace, 153–93. Beverly Hills, CA: SAGE.
Haas, P. 1992. "Introduction: Epistemic Communities and International Policy Coordination." *International Organization* 46, no. 1: 1–35.
Hall, P., and S. R. Wilson. 1991. "Two Guidelines for Bootstrap Hypothesis Testing." *Biometrics* 47, no. 2: 757–62
Hanson, E. 2006. *Religion and Politics in the International System Today*. Cambridge: Cambridge University Press.
Hardin, G. 2009. "The Tragedy of the Commons." *Journal of Natural Resources Policy Research* 1, no. 3: 243–53.
Hartzell, C. A. 2009. "Settling Civil Wars: Armed Opponents' Fates and the Duration of the Peace." *Conflict Management and Peace Science* 26, no. 4: 347–65.
Hasenclever, A., and V. Rittberger. 2000. "Does Religion Make a Difference? Theoretical Approaches to the Impact of Faith on Political Conflict." *Millennium* 29, no. 3: 641–74.
Hasenclever, A., and V. Rittberger. 2003. "Does Religion Make a Difference?" In *Religion in International Relations: The Return From Exile*, edited by F. Petito and P. Hatzopoulos, 107–45. New York: Palgrave Macmillan.
Hassner, R. E. 2009. *War on Sacred Grounds*. Ithaca, NY: Cornell University Press.
Hassner, R. E. 2011. "Blasphemy and Violence." *International Studies Quarterly* 55, no. 1: 23–45.
Haynes, J. 2007. *Introduction to International Relations and Religion*. New York: Pearson Longman.
Haynes, J. 2008. *Development Studies*. Cambridge: Polity.
Heckman, J. 1976. "The Common Structure of Statistical Models of Truncation, Sample Selection and Limited Dependent Variables and a Simple Estimator for Such Models." *Annals of Economic and Social Measurement* 5, no. 4: 475–92.
Hegre, H., and N. Sambanis. 2006. "Sensitivity Analysis of Empirical Results on Civil War Onset." *Journal of Conflict Resolution* 50, no. 4: 508–35.
Hegre, H., T. Ellingsen, S. Gates, and N. P. Gleditsch. 2001. "Towards a Democratic Civil Peace? Democracy, Political Change, and Civil War, 1816–1992." *American Political Science Review* 95, no 1: 33–48.
Henderson, E. A. 1997. "Culture or Contiguity: 'Ethnic |Conflict,' the Similarity of States, and the Onset of War, 1820–1989." *Journal of Conflict Resolution* 41, no. 5: 649–68.
Henderson, E. A. 1998. "The Democratic Peace through the Lens of Culture." *International Studies Quarterly* 42, no. 3: 461–84.
Henderson, E. A. 2004. "Mistaken Identity: Testing the Clash of Civilizations Thesis in Light of Democratic Peace Claims." *British Journal of Political Science* 34, no. 2: 539–63.
Henderson, E. A. 2005. "Not Letting Evidence Get in the Way of Assumptions: Testing the Clash of Civilizations Thesis with More Recent Data." *International Politics* 4, no. 4: 458–69.

Henderson, E. A. 2013. "Hidden in Plain Sight: Racism and International Relations Theory." *Cambridge Review of International Affairs* 26, no. 1: 71–92.

Henderson, E. A. 2015. *African Realism? International Relations Theory and Africa's Wars in the Postcolonial Era*. Lanham, MD: Rowman and Littlefield.

Henderson, E. A., and J. D. Singer. 2000. "Civil War in the Post-Colonial World 1946–92." *Journal of Peace Research* 37, no. 3: 275–99.

Henderson, E. A., and J. D. Singer. 2002. "'New Wars' and Rumors of 'New Wars.'" *International Interactions* 28, no 2: 165–90.

Henderson, E. A., and R. Tucker. 2001. "Clear and Present Strangers: The Clash of Civilizations and International Conflict." *International Studies Quarterly* 45, no. 2: 317–88.

Hendrix, C. S. 2010. "Measuring State Capacity: Theoretical and Empirical Implications for the Study of Civil Conflict." *Journal of Peace Research* 47, no. 3: 273–85.

Henir, B. J. 2012. "Why Religion? Why Now?" In *Rethinking Religion and World Affairs*, edited by T. Shah, A. Stephan, and M. D. Toft, New York: Oxford University Press, pp. 15–24.

Henne, P. S. 2012a. "The Ancient Fire: Religion and Suicide Terrorism." *Terrorism and Political Violence* 24, no. 1: 38–60.

Henne, P. S. 2012b. "The Two Swords: Religion-State Connections and Interstate Disputes." *Journal of Peace Research* 49, no. 6: 753–68.

Henne, P. S., and D. H. Nexon. 2014. "One Cheer for Classical Realism, or Toward a Power Politics of Religion." In *Religion and the Realist Tradition: From Political Theology To International Relations Theory and Back*, edited by J. Troy, 164–75. Oxford: Routledge.

Hibbs, D. 1973. *Mass Political Violence*. New York: Wiley.

Hicks, D. A. 1997. "The Inequality-Adjusted Human Development Index: A Constructive Proposal." *World Development* 25, no. 8: 1283–98.

Hoff, P. D., and M. D. Ward. 2004. "Modeling Dependencies in International Relations Networks." *Political Analysis* 12, no. 2: 160–75.

Hoffmann, S. 1965. *The State of War: Essays in the Theory and Practice of International Relations*. New York: Praeger.

Homer Dixon, T. 1991. "On the Threshold: Environmental Changes as Causes of Acute Conflict." *International Security* 16, no. 2: 76–116.

Horowitz, D. 1985. *Ethnic Groups in Conflict*. Berkeley: University of California Press.

Humphreys, M. 2005. "Natural Resources, Conflict, and Conflict Resolution: Uncovering the Mechanisms." *Journal of Conflict Resolution* 49, no. 4: 508–37.

Huntington, S. 1993. "The Clash of Civilizations." *Foreign Affairs* 72, no. 3: 56–73.

Huntington, S. 1996. *The Clash of Civilizations and the Remaking of World Order*. New York: Simon and Schuster.

Huntington, S. 2000. "Try Again: A Reply to Russett, Oneal & Cox." *Journal of Peace Research* 37, no. 5: 609–10.

Huntington, S. P. 1971. "The Change to Change: Modernization, Development, and Politics." *Comparative Politics* 3, no. 3: 283–322.

Hurd, E. S. 2004. "The Political Authority of Secularism in International Relations." *European Journal of International Relations* 10, no. 2: 235–62.

Hurd, E. S. 2008. *The Politics of Secularism in International Relations.* Princeton, NJ: Princeton University Press.

Hurd, E. S. 2012. "International Politics after Secularism." *Review of International Studies* 38, no. 5: 943–61.

Hurd, I. 1999. "Legitimacy and Authority in International Politics." *International Organization* 53, no. 2: 379–408.

Iannaccone, L. R. 1990. "Religious Practice: A Human Capital Approach." *Journal for the Scientific Study of Religion* 29, no. 3: 297–314.

Iannaccone, L. R. 1998. "Introduction to the Economics of Religion." *Journal of Economic Literature* 36, no. 3: 1465–95.

ICISS (International Commission on Intervention and State Sovereignty). 2001. *The Responsibility to Protect.* Ottawa: International Development Research Center.

Ireland, R. 1988. *The Challenge of Secularization.* Melbourne, Australia: Collins Dove.

Isaacs, M. 2016. "Sacred Violence or Strategic Faith? Disentangling the Relationship between Religion and Violence in Armed Conflict." *Journal of Peace Research* 53, no. 2: 211–25.

Jackson, J., B. San-Acka, and Z. Maoz. 2020. "International Support Networks and the Calculus of Uprising." *Journal of Peace Research* (in press).

Jackson, M. O., and A. Wolinsky. 1996. "A Strategic Model of Social and Economic Networks." *Journal of Economic Theory* 71, no. 1: 44–74.

Jakobsen, T., and I. De Soysa. 2009. "Give Me Liberty, Or Give Me Death! State Repression, Ethnic Grievance and Civil War, 1981–2004." *Civil Wars* 11, no. 2: 137–57.

Jervis, R. 1978. "Cooperation under the Security Dilemma." *World Politics* 30: 167–213.

Jervis, R. 1982. "Security Regimes." *International Organization* 36, no. 2: 357–78.

Johns, R., and G. A. Davies. 2012. "Democratic Peace or Clash of Civilizations? Target States and Support for War in Britain and the United States." *Journal of Politics* 74, no. 4: 1038–52.

Johnston, D., and C. Sampson. 1995. *Religion, The Missing Dimension of Statecraft.* New York: Oxford University Press.

Johnston, I. 1995. *Cultural Realism: Strategic Culture and Grand Strategy in Chinese History.* Princeton: Princeton University Press.

Jones, D. M., S. Bremer, and J. D. Singer. 1996. "Militarized Disputes, 1816–1992: Rationale Coding Rules and Empirical Patterns." *Conflict Management and Peace Science* 15, no. 2: 163–212.

Joyce, K. A., J. Hammond, and Z. Maoz. 2015. "A Simple Algorithm for Estimating Network Effects: The Expected Value." Mimeographed: University of California, Davis.

Juergensmeyer, M. 1993. *The New Cold War? Religious Nationalism Confronts the Secular State.* Berkeley and Los Angeles: University of California Press.

Juergensmeyer, M. 1996. "The Worldwide Rise of Religious Nationalism." *Journal of International Affairs* 50, no. 1: 1–20.

Juergensmeyer, M. 2003. *Terror in the Mind of God: The Global Rise of Religious Violence*, 3rd ed. Berkeley and Los Angeles: University of California Press.

Juergensmeyer, M. 2017. *Terror in the Mind of God: The Global Rise of Religious Violence.* 4th ed. Berkeley and Los Angeles: University of California Press.

Juergensmeyer, M., M. Kitts, and M. Jerryson, eds. 2013 *The Oxford Handbook of Religion and Violence*. New York: Oxford University Press.

Kalyvas, S. 2001. "'New' and 'Old' Civil Wars: A Valid Distinction?" *World Politics* 54, no. 2: 99–118.

Karsh, E., and I. Rautsi. 2007. *Saddam Hussein: A Political Biography*. New York: Grove/Atlantic.

Kathman, J. 2011. "Civil War Diffusion and Regional Motivations for Intervention." *Journal of Conflict Resolution* 55, no. 6: 847–76.

Kemp, B. J. 2006. *Ancient Egypt: Anatomy of a Civilization*. New York: Routledge.

Keohane, R. O. 1984. *After Hegemony: Cooperation and Discord in the World Political Economy*. Princeton, NJ: Princeton University Press.

Keohane, R. O., and L. Martin. 1995. "The Promise of Institutionalist Theory." *International Security* 20, no. 1: 39–51.

Keshk, O. G., B. Pollins, and R. Reuveny. 2004. "Trade Still Follows the Flag: The Primacy of Politics in a Simultaneous Model of Interdependence and Armed Conflict." *Journal of Politics* 66, no. 4: 1155–79.

King, G., R. Keohane, and S. Verba 1994. *Designing Social Inquiry Scientific Inference in Qualitative Research*. Princeton, NJ: Princeton University Press.

Kinne, B. J. 2014. "Network Dynamics and the Evolution of International Cooperation." *American Political Science Review* 107, no. 4: 766–85.

Kitchen, K. A. 2003. *On the Reliability of the Old Testament*. Grand Rapids, MI: Wm. B. Eerdmans Publishing.

Klugman, J., F. Rodriguez, and H. J. Choi. 2011. "The HDI 2010: New Controversies, Old Critiques." *Journal of Economic Inequality* 9, no. 2: 249–88.

Knutsen, T. L. 1994. "Re-reading Rousseau in the Post–Cold War World." *Journal of Peace Research* 31, no. 3: 247–62.

Koremenos, B., C. Lipson, and D. Snidal. 2001. "The Rational Design of International Institutions." *International Organization* 55, no. 4: 761–99.

Koubi, V., and T. Böhmelt. 2014. "Grievances, Economic Wealth, and Civil Conflict." *Journal of Peace Research* 51, no. 1: 19–33.

Koubi, V., G. Spilker, and T. Bohmelt. 2014. "Do Natural Resources Matter for Interstate and Intrastate Armed Conflict?" *Journal of Peace Research* 51, no. 2: 227–43.

Krasner, S. D. 1982. "Regimes and the Limits of Realism—Regimes as Autonomous Variables." *International Organization* 36, no. 2: 497–510.

Krasner, S. D. 2001. "Rethinking the Sovereign State Model." *Review of International Studies* 27, no. 1: 17–42.

Lacina, B. 2006. "Explaining the Severity of Civil Wars." *Journal of Conflict Resolution* 50, no. 2: 276–89.

Lacina, B., and N. P. Gleditsch. 2005. "Monitoring Trends in Global Combat: A New Dataset of Battle Deaths." *European Journal of Population* 2–3: 145–66.

Lai, B. 2006. "An Empirical Examination of Religion and Conflict in the Middle East, 1950–1992." *Foreign Policy Analysis* 2, no. 1: 21–36.

Lai, B., and D. Reiter. 2000. "Democracy, Political Similarity, and International Alliances, 1816–1992." *The Journal of Conflict Resolution* 44, no. 2: 203–27.

Lancichinetti, A., F. Radicchi, J. J. Ramasaco, and S. Fortunato. 2011. "Finding Statistically Significant Communities in Networks." *PLOS ONE* 6, no. 4: 1–18.

Lancichinetti, A., S. Fortunato, and J. Kertész. 2009. "Detecting the Overlapping and Hierarchical Community Structure in Complex Networks." *New Journal of Physics* 11: 033015.

Lebow, R. N. 2016. *National Identities in International Relations*. Cambridge: Cambridge University Press.

Leeds, B. A. 2003. "Alliance Reliability in Times of War: Explaining State Decisions to Violate Treaties." *International Organization* 57, no. 3: 801–27.

Leeds, B. A. 2005. "Alliance Treaty Obligations and Provisions (ATOP) Codebook." Rice University, http://atop.rice.edu/home.

Leeds, B. A., A. G. Long, and S. McLaughlin-Mitchell. 2002. "Alliance Treaty Obligations and Provisions, 1815–1944." *International Interactions* 28, no. 3: 237–60.

Leicht, E., and M. J. Newman. 2008. "Community Structure in Directed Networks." *Physical Review Letters* 100: 1–4.

Lemke, D., and W. Reed. 2001. "The Relevance of Politically Relevant Dyads." *Journal of Conflict Resolution* 45, no. 1: 126–44.

Levy, J. S. 1989. "The Diversionary Theory of War: A Critique." In *Handbook of War Studies*, edited by M. Midlarsky, 259–88. Boston: Unwin Hyman.

Levy, J. S., and W. R. Thompson. 2010. *Causes of War*. New York: Wiley-Blackwell.

Lichbach, M. I. 1995. *The Rebel's Dilemma*. Ann Arbor: University of Michigan Press.

Licklider, R. 1995. "The Consequences of Negotiated Settlements in Civil Wars, 1945–1993." *American Political Science Review* 89, no. 3: 681–90.

Lusher, D., J. Koskinen, and G. Robins. 2013. *Exponential Random Graph Models for Social Networks*. New York: Cambridge University Press.

Luttwak, E. 2001a. "Blood and Computers: The Crisis of Classic Military Power in Advanced Postindustrialist Societies and the Scope of Technological Remedies." In *War in a Changing World*, edited by Z. Maoz and A. Gat, 49–76. Ann Arbor: University of Michigan Press.

Luttwak, E. 2001b. *Strategy: The Logic of War and Peace*. Cambridge: Harvard University Press.

Luttwak, E. N. 1979. *The Grand Strategy of the Roman Empire*. Baltimore: Johns Hopkins University Press.

Lynch, C. 2009. "A Neo-Weberian Approach to Religion in International Politics." *International Theory* 1, no. 3: 381–408.

Mansfield, E. D., and H. V. Milner. 2012. *Votes, Vetoes, and the Political Economy of International Trade Agreements*. Princeton, NJ: Princeton University Press.

Mansfield, E. D., and J. Pevehouse. 2003. "Institutions, Interdependence and International Conflict." In *Globalization and Armed Conflict*, edited by G. Schneider, K. Barbieri and N. P. Gleditsch, 233–50. Lanham, MD: Rowman and Littlefield.

Mansfield, E. D., and R. Bronson. 1997. "Preferential Trading Arrangements, and International Trade." *American Political Science Review* 91, no.1: 94–107.

Mansfield, E. D., H. V. Milner, and P. B. Rosendorff. 2000. "Free to Trade: Democracies, Autocracies, and International Trade." *American Political Science Review* 94, no. 2: 305–21.

Mansfield, E. D., H. V. Milner, and P. B. Rosendorff. 2002. "Replication, Realism, and Robustness: Analyzing Political Regimes and International Trade." *American Political Science Review* 96, no. 1: 167–69.

Maoz, Z. 1982. *Paths to Conflict: Interstate Dispute Initiation, 1816–1976.* Boulder, CO: Westview Press.

Maoz, Z. 1989. "Joining the Club of Nations: Political Development and International Conflict, 1816–1976." *International Studies Quarterly* 33, no. 2: 199–231.

Maoz, Z. 1990a. *National Choices and International Processes.* Cambridge: Cambridge University Press.

Maoz, Z. 1990b. *Paradoxes of War: On the Art of National Self-Entrapment.* Boston: Unwin Hyman.

Maoz, Z. 1996. *Domestic Sources of Global Change.* Ann Arbor: University of Michigan Press.

Maoz, Z. 1998. "Realist and Cultural Critiques of the Democratic Peace: A Theoretical and Empirical Reassessment." *International Interactions* 24: 3–89.

Maoz, Z. 2000. "The Street-Gangs of World Politics: The Origins, Management, and Termination of International Alliances." In *What Do We Know about War?*, edited by J. A. Vasquez. 114–41. Lanham, MD: Rowman and Littlefield.

Maoz, Z. 2002. "Paradoxical Functions of International Alliances: Security and Other Dilemmas." In *Realism and the Balancing of Power: A New Debate*, edited by J. A. Vasquez and Colin Elman, 200–21. New York: Pearson.

Maoz, Z. 2004. "Pacifism and Fightaholism in International Politics: A Structural History of National and Dyadic Conflict, 1816–1992." *International Studies Review* 6, no. 2: 107–33.

Maoz, Z. 2006. "Network Polarization, Network Interdependence, and International Conflict, 1816–2002." *Journal of Peace Research* 43: 391–411.

Maoz, Z. 2009a. "Primed to Fight: The Can/Must Syndrome and the Conflict Proneness of Nations." *Conflict Management and Peace Science* 26, no. 5: 1–26.

Maoz, Z. 2009b. "The Effects of Strategic and Economic Interdependence on International Conflict across Levels of Analysis." *American Journal of Political Science* 53: 223–40.

Maoz, Z. 2010. *Networks of Nations: The Evolution, Structure, and Impact of International Networks, 1816–2001.* New York: Cambridge University Press.

Maoz, Z. 2012a. "Preferential Attachment, Homophily, and the Structure of International Networks, 1816–2003." *Conflict Management and Peace Science* 29, no. 3: 341–69.

Maoz, Z. 2012b. "Normal Science and Open Questions: Reflections on the Study of War and Peace, 2001–2011." In *What Do We Know About War?*, edited by J. A. Vasquez, 271–80. New York: Rowman and Littlefield.

Maoz, Z. 2015. "Alliance Reliability: A Network Approach." Mimeographed: University of California, Davis.

Maoz, Z. 2017. "Democracy and International Networks." In *The Oxford Handbook of Political Networks*, edited by J. Victor, A. Montgomery, and M. Lubell, 733–60. New York: Oxford University Press.

Maoz, Z., and B. Russett. 1992. "Alliance, Contiguity, Wealth and Political Stability: Is the Lack of Conflict among Democracies a Statistical Artifact?" *International Interactions* 17, no. 3: 245–67.

Maoz, Z., and B. Russett. 1993. "Normative and Structural Causes of Democratic Peace, 1946–1986." *American Political Science Review* 87, no. 3: 624–38.

Maoz, Z., and B. D. Mor. 2002. *Bound by Struggle: The Strategic Evolution of Enduring International Rivalries*. Ann Arbor: University of Michigan Press.

Maoz, Z., and E. A. Henderson. 2013. "The World Religion Dataset 1945–2010: Logic, Estimates, And Trends." *International Interactions* 39, no. 3: 265–91.

Maoz, Z., L. Terris, R. Kuperman, and I. Talmud. 2007. "What Is the Enemy of My Enemy: Causes and Consequences of Imbalanced International Relations, 1816–2001." *Journal of Politics* 69: 100–15.

Maoz, Z., P. Johnson, J. Kaplan, F. Ogunkoya, and A. P. Shreve. 2018. "The Dyadic Militarized Interstate Disputes (Mids) Dataset Version 3.0: Logic, Characteristics, and Comparison to Alternative Datasets." *Journal of Conflict Resolution* 63, no. 3: 811–835.

Marshall, M., K. Jaggers, and T. Gurr. 2010. "Polity IV Project: Political Regime Characteristics and Transitions, 1800–2010." Retrieved 8/17/2014, from www.systemicpeace.org/polity/polity4.htm.

Martin, D. 1997. *Does Christianity Cause War?* New York: Oxford University Press.

Martin, M., and T. Owen. 2010. "The Second Generation of Human Security: Lessons from the UN and EU Experience." *International Affairs* 86, no. 1: 211–24.

Mason, T. D., and P. Fett. 1996. "How Civil Wars End: A Rational Choice Approach." *Journal of Conflict Resolution* 40, no. 4: 546–68.

Matthews, J. 1989. "Redefining Security." *Foreign Affairs* 68, no. 2: 162–77.

Mazrui, A. 1988. *The Africans: A Triple Heritage*. Boston: Little, Brown.

McGillivray, M. 1991. "The Human Development Index: Yet Another Redundant Composite Development Indicator?" *World Development* 19, no. 10: 1461–68.

Mearsheimer, J. J. 2001. *The Tragedy of Great Power Politics*. New York: W.W. Norton.

Mearsheimer, J. J. 1990. "Back to the Future: Instability in Europe after the Cold War." *International Security* 15, no. 1: 5–56.

Mearsheimer, J. J. 1994/5. "The False Promise of International Institutions." *International Security* 19, no. 3: 5–49.

Migdal, J. 1988. *Strong Societies and Weak States*. Princeton, NJ: Princeton University Press.

Miller, B. 2007. *States, Nations, and the Great Powers: The Sources of Regional War and Peace*. Cambridge: Cambridge University Press.

Mills, C. 1997. *The Racial Contract*. Ithaca, NY: Cornell University Press.

Milner, H. W. 1992. "International Theories of Cooperation among Nations: Strengths and Weaknesses." *World Politics* 44, no. 3: 466–98.

Mollov, B. 2014. "The Influence of the Jewish experience on the Liberal Realism of Hans J. Morgenthau." In *Religion and the Realist Tradition: From Political Theology to International Relations Theory and Back*, edited by J. Troy, 21–36. London: Routledge.

Montalvo, J. G., and M. Reynal-Querol. 2005. "Ethnic Polarization, Potential Conflict, and Civil Wars." *American Economic Review* 95, no. 3: 796–816.

Mooney, Christopher Z., and Robert D. Duval. 1993. *Bootstrapping: A Nonparametric Approach to Statistical Inference*. Beverly Hill, CA: SAGE.

Morrow, J. D. 1994. "Alliances, Credibility, and Peacetime Costs." *Journal of Conflict Resolution* 38, no. 2: 270–97.

Morrow, J. D. 2000. "Alliances: Why Write Them Down?" *Annual Review of Political Science* 3: 63–83.

Morrow, J. D., R. Siverson, and T. Tabares. 1998. "The Political Determinants of International Trade: The Major Powers, 1907–1990." *American Political Science Review* 92, no. 2: 649–61.

Most, B. A., and H. Starr. 1989. *Inquiry, Logic, and International Politics.* Columbia: University of South Carolina Press.

Muehlenbeck, P., ed. 2012. *Religion and the Cold War: A Global Perspective.* Nashville, TN: Vanderbilt University Press.

Mueller, J. 2007. *The Remnants of War.* Ithaca, NY: Cornell University Press.

Mullenbach, M. 2005. "Deciding to Keep Peace: An Analysis of International Influences on the Establishment of Third-Party Peacekeeping Missions." *International Studies Quarterly* 49, no. 3: 529–55.

Murshed, S. M., and M. Z. Tadjoeddin. 2009. "Revisiting the Greed and Grievance Explanations for Violent Internal Conflict." *Journal of International Development* 21, no. 1: 87–111.

Nafziger, E. W., and J. Auvinen. 2002. "Economic Development, Inequality, War, and State Violence." *World Development* 30, no. 2: 153–63.

Neumayer, E., and T. Plümper. 2009. "International Terrorism and the Clash of Civilizations." *British Journal of Political Science* 39, no. 4: 711–34.

Newman, E. 2010. "Critical Human Security Studies." *Review of International Studies* 36, no. 1: 77–94.

Newman, M. E., and M. Girvan. 2004. "Finding and Evaluating Community Structure in Networks." *Physical Review* 69, no. 2: 1–16.

Nexon, D. H. 2009. *The Struggle for Power in Early Modern Europe: Religious Conflict, Dynastic Empires, and International Change.* Princeton, NJ: Princeton University Press.

Nexon, D. H. 2011. "Religion and International Relations: No Leap of Faith Required." *Religion and International Relations Theory*, edited by J. Snyder, 141–67. New York: Columbia University Press.

Nexon, D. H., and T. Wright. 2007. "What's at Stake in the American Empire Debate." *American Political Science Review* 101, no. 2: 253–71.

Noorbakhsh, F. 1998. "A Modified Human Development Index." *World Development* 26, no. 3: 517–28.

Norris, P., and R. Ingelhart. 2011. *Sacred and Secular: Religion and Politics Worldwide.* New York: Cambridge University Press.

O'Neill, K., J. Balsiger, and S. D. VanDeveer. 2004. "Actors, Norms, and Impact: Recent International Cooperation Theory and the Influence of the Agent-Structure Debate." *Annual Review of Political Science* 7: 149–75.

Olson, M. 1965. *The Logic of Collective Action: Public Goods and the Theory of Groups.* Cambridge, MA: Harvard University Press.

Oren, I. 2003. *Our Enemies and Us: America's Rivalries and the Making of Political Science.* Ithaca, NY: Cornell University Press.

Özdamar, Ö., and Y. Akbaba. 2014. "Religious Discrimination and International Crises: International Effects of Domestic Inequality." *Foreign Policy Analysis* 10, no. 4: 413–30.

Pabst, A. 2012. "The Secularism of Post-Secularity: Religion, Realism, and the Revival of Grand Theory in IR." *Review of International Studies* 38, no. 5: 995–1017.

Pateman, C. 1988. *The Sexual Contract*. Cambridge: Polity Press.

Pearce, S. 2005. "Religious Rage: A Quantitative Analysis of the Intensity of Religious Conflicts." *Terrorism and Political Violence* 17, no. 3: 333–52.

Pearce, S. 2006. "Religious Rage: A Quantitative Analysis of the Intensity of Religious Conflict." In *Religion in World Conflict*, edited by J. Fox and S. Sandler, 39–58. New York: Routledge.

Pearse, M. 2007. *The Gods of War: Is Religion the Primary Cause of Violent Conflict?* Nottingham, UK: InterVarsity Press.

Pettersson, T., and P. Wallensteen. 2015. "Armed Conflicts, 1946–2014." *Journal of Peace Research* 52, no. 4: 536–50.

Pevehouse, J., and B. Russett. 2006. "Democratic International Governmental Organizations Promote Peace." *International Organization* 60, no. 4: 969–1000.

Pevehouse, J., T. Nordstrom, and K. Wranke. 2004. "The Correlates of War 2: International Governmental Organizations Data, Version 2." *Conflict Management and Peace Science* 21: 101–19.

Phillips, A. 2011. *War, Religion and Empire: The Transformation of International Orders*. New York: Cambridge University Press.

Philpott, D. 2002. "The Challenge of September 11 to Secularism in International Relations." *World Politics* 55, no. 1: 66–95.

Philpott, D. 2007. "Explaining the Political Ambivalence of Religion." *American Political Science Review* 101, no. 3: 505–25.

Philpott, D. 2009. "Has the Study of Global Politics Found Religion?" *Annual Review of Political Science* 12: 183–202.

Philpott, D. 2013. "Religion and Violence from a Political Science Perspective." In *The Oxford Handbook of Religion and Violence*, edited by M. Juergensmeyer, M. Kitts, and M. Jerryson, 397–409. New York: Oxford University Press.

Pinker, S. 2011. *The Better Angels of Our Nature: Why Violence Has Declined*. New York: Penguin.

Posen, B. R. 1993. "The Security Dilemma and Ethnic Conflict." *Survival* 35, no. 1: 27–47.

Powell, J. M., and C. L. Thyne. 2011. "Global Instances of Coups From 1950 to 2010: A New Dataset." *Journal of Peace Research* 48, no. 2: 249–59.

Powers, K. 2004. "Regional Trade Agreements as Military Alliances." *International Interactions* 30, no. 4: 373–95.

Powers, K. 2006. "Dispute Initiation and Alliance Obligations in Regional Economic Institutions." *Journal of Peace Research* 43, no. 4: 453–71.

Preston, A. 2012. *Sword of the Spirit, Shield of Faith: Religion in American War and Diplomacy*. New York: Anchor Books.

Putnam, R. D., and D. E. Campbell. 2010. *American Grace: How Religion Divides and Unites Us*. New York: Simon and Schuster.

Putnam, R. D., and D. E. Campbell. 2012. *American Grace: How Religion Divides and Unites Us*. New York: Simon and Schuster (Second printing).

Quackenbush, S. L. 2006. "Identifying Opportunity for Conflict: Politically Active Dyads." *Conflict Management and Peace Science* 23, no. 1: 37–51.

Randall, V. 1999. "The Media and Religion in Third World Politics." In *Religion, Globalization and Political Culture in the Third World*, edited by J. Hayes, 45–68. New York: Palgrave Macmillan.

Randall, V., and R. Theobald. 1985. *Political Change and Underdevelopment: A Critical Introduction to Third World Studies*. Durham, NC: Duke University Press.

Ray, J., and J. D. Singer. 1973. "Measuring the Concentration of Power in the International System." *Sociological Methods & Research* 1, no. 4: 403–37.

Regan, P. 1996. "Conditions of Successful Third-Party Intervention in Intrastate Conflicts." *Journal of Conflict Resolution* 40, no. 2: 336–59.

Regan, P. 2000. *Civil Wars and Foreign Powers: Interventions and Intrastate Conflict*. Ann Arbor: University of Michigan Press.

Regan, P., and D. Norton. 2005. "Greed, Grievance, and Mobilization in Civil Wars." *Journal of Conflict Resolution* 49, no. 3: 319–36.

Regan, P., and S. R. Bell. 2010. "Changing Lanes or Stuck in the Middle: Why Are Anocracies More Prone to Civil Wars?" *Political Research Quarterly* 63, no. 4: 747–59.

Reimer, A. J. 2010. *Christians and War: A Brief History of the Church's Teachings and Practices*. Minneapolis: Fortress Press.

Reuther, R. R., and H. J. Reuthers. 2002. *The Wrath of Jonah: The Crisis of Religious Nationalism in the Israeli–Palestinian Conflict*. Minneapolis: Fortress Press.

Reynal-Querol, M. 2002. "Ethnicity, Political Systems, and Civil Wars." *Journal of Conflict Resolution* 46, no. 1: 29–54.

Richardson, J. 1985. "Studies of Conversion: Secularization or Re-Enchantment?" In *The Sacred in a Secular Age: Toward Revision in the Scientific Study of Religion*, edited by P. E. Hammond, 104–21. Berkeley and Los Angeles: University of California Press.

Richardson, L. F. 1960. *Statistics of Deadly Quarrels*. New York: Boxwood Press.

Robinson, A. L. 2014. "National versus Ethnic Identification in Africa: Modernization, Colonial Legacy, and the Origins of Territorial Nationalism." *World Politics* 66, no. 4: 709–46.

Roeder, P. 2003. "Clash of Civilizations and Escalation of Domestic Ethnopolitical Conflicts." *Comparative Political Studies* 36, no. 5: 509–40.

Rogan, A. 2009. *The Arabs: A History*. New York: Basic Books.

Rørbæk, L. L., and A. T. Knudsen. 2017. "Maintaining Ethnic Dominance: Diversity, Power, and Violent Repression." *Conflict Management and Peace Science* 34, no. 6: 640–59.

Rubin, B. 1990. "Religion and International Affairs." *The Washington Quarterly* 13, no. 2: 51–63.

Rudolph, S. H., and J. Piscatori. 1996. *Transnational Religion and Fading States*. Boulder, CO: Westview Press.

Rummel, R. 1997. "Is Collective Violence Correlated with Social Pluralism?" *Journal of Peace Research* 34, no. 2: 163–75.

Russett, B., and J. Oneal. 2001. *Triangulating Peace: Democracy, Interdependence, and International Organization*. New York: W. W. Norton.

Russett, B., J. Oneal, and M. Cox. 2000. "Clash of Civilizations, Or Realism and Liberalism Déjà Vu? Some Evidence." *Journal of Peace Research* 37, no. 5: 5583–608.

Sachar, H. 2007. *A History of Israel: From the Rise of Zionism to Our Time*. 3rd ed. New York: Alfred A. Knopf.
Sagar, A. D., and A. Najam. 1998. "The Human Development Index: A Critical Review." *Ecological Economics* 25, no. 3: 249–64.
Saggi, K. 2006. "Preferential Trade Agreements and Multilateral Tariff Cooperation." *International Economic Review* 47, no. 1: 29–57.
Saiya, N. 2016. "Religion, State, and Terrorism: A Global Analysis." *Terrorism and Political Violence* 31, no. 2: 204–223.
Saiya, N., and A. Scime. 2015. "Explaining Religious Terrorism: A Data-Mined Analysis." *Conflict Management and Peace Science* 32, no. 5: 487–512.
Salehyan, I., 2011. *Rebels without borders: transnational insurgencies in world politics*. Ithaca: Cornell University Press.
Saleyhan, I., K. Gleditsch and D. Cunningham. 2011. "Explaining External Support for Insurgent Groups." *International Organization* 65, no. 4: 709-744.
Sambanis, N. 2000. "Partition as a Solution to Ethnic War: An Empirical Critique of the Theoretical Literature." *World Politics* 52 no. 4: 437–83.
Sambanis, N. 2001. "Do Ethnic and Non-Ethnic Civil Wars Have the Same Causes? A Theoretical and Empirical Inquiry Part 1." *Journal of Conflict Resolution* 45, no. 3: 259–82.
Sambanis, N. 2002. "A Review of Recent Advances and Future Directions in the Quantitative Literature on Civil War." *Defence and Peace Economics* 13, no. 3: 215–43.
Sambanis, N. 2004. "What Is Civil War? Conceptual and Empirical Complexities of an Operational Definition." *Journal of Conflict Resolution* 48, no. 6: 814–58.
San-Akca, B. 2016. *States in Disguise: Causes of State Support for Rebel Groups*. New York: Oxford University Press.
Sandal, N., and J. Fox. 2013. *Religion in International Relations Theory: Interactions and Possibilities*. New York: Routledge.
Sandal, N. A. 2011. "Religious Actors as Epistemic Communities in Conflict Transformation: The Cases of South Africa and Northern Ireland." *Review of International Studies* 37, no. 3: 929–49.
Sandal, N. A., and P. James. 2011. "Religion and International Relations Theory: Towards a Mutual Understanding." *European Journal of International Relations* 17, no. 1: 3–25.
Sanín, F. G., and E. J. Wood. 2014. "Ideology in Civil War: Instrumental Adoption and Beyond." *Journal of Peace Research* 51, no. 2: 213–26.
Sarkees, M., and F. W. Wayman. 2010. *Resort to War: Civil and International Wars, 1816–2007*. Washington, DC: CQ Press.
Sarkees, M., and J. Dixon. 2015. *Guide to Intrastate Wars: A Handbook on Civil Wars*. Washington, DC: CQ Press.
Sarkissian, A. 2015. *The Varieties of Religious Repression: Why Governments Restrict Religion*. New York: Oxford University Press.
Schelling, T. C. 1963 *Arms and Influence*. New Haven, CT: Yale University Press.
Schelling, T. C. 1978. *Micromotives and Macrobehavior*. New York: W. W. Norton.
Scroggins, D. 2004. *Emma's War*. New York: Vintage.
Seiple, R. A., and D. Hoover. 2004. *Religion and Security: The New Nexus in International Relations*. Lanham, MD: Rowman and Littlefield.

Senese, P., and J. Vasquez. 2008. *The Steps to War: An Empirical Study*. Princeton, NJ: Princeton University Press.

Shah, T. 2012. "Introduction." In *Rethinking Religion and World Affairs*, edited by T. S. Shah, A. Stephan, and M. D. Toft, 1–14. New York: Oxford University Press.

Shah, T., A. Stephan, and M. D. Toft, eds. 2012. *Rethinking Religion and World Affairs*. New York: Oxford University Press.

Shah, T., and D. Philpott. 2011. "The Rise and Fall of Religion in International Relations: Theory and History." In *Religion and International Relations Theory*, edited by J. Snyder, 24–59. New York: Columbia University Press.

Sharma, S. D. 1997. "Making the Human Development Index (HDI) Gender-Sensitive." *Gender & Development* 5, no. 1: 60–61.

Shaw, I. 2003. *The Oxford History of Ancient Egypt*. New York: Oxford University Press.

Sheikh, M. K. 2012. "How Does Religion Matter? Pathways to Religion in International Relations." *Review of International Studies* 38, no. 2: 365–92.

Singer, J. D. 1971. "Modern International War: From Conjecture to Explanation." In *The Search for World Order*, edited by A. Lepawsky, E. H. Buehrig, and H. D. Lasswell, 47–71. New York: Appleton-Century-Crofts.

Singer, J. D. 1990. "Reconstructing the Correlates of War Data Set on Material Capabilites of States, 1816–1985." In *The Correlates of War*, edited by J. D. Singer and P. F. Diehl, 53–72. Ann Arbor: University of Michigan Press.

Singer, J. D. 1997. *Cultural Composition of Interstate System Members*. Ann Arbor, MI: Correlates of War Project.

Siverson, R. M., and H. Starr. 1991 *The Diffusion of War*. Ann Arbor: University of Michigan Press.

Smart, N. 1998. *The World's Religions*. Cambridge: Cambridge University Press.

Smith, A. 1995. "Alliance Formation and War." *International Studies Quarterly* 39, no. 4: 405–25.

Smith, M. E., and K. J. Schreiber. 2006. "New World States and Empires: Politics, Religion, and Urbanism." *Journal of Archaeological Research* 14, no. 1: 1–52.

Snyder, G. H. 1997. *Alliance Politics*. Ithaca, NY: Cornell University Press.

Snyder, J. 1991. *Myths of Empire: Domestic Politics and International Ambition*. Ithaca, NY: Cornell University Press.

Snyder, J., ed. 2011. *Religion and International Relations Theory*. New York: Columbia University Press.

START. 2017. Global Terrorism Dataset. Retrieved October 28, 2017, from https://www.start.umd.edu/gtd/terms-of-use/citinggtd.aspx.

Stewart, F., ed. 2008. *Horizontal Inequalities and Conflict: Understanding Group Violence in Multiethnic Societies*. Basingstoke, UK: Palgrave Macmmillan.

Sudduth, J. K. 2017. "Coup-risk, Coup-Proofing, and Leader Survival." *Journal of Peace Research* 54, no. 1: 3–15.

Sun–Tzu. 1994 [circa 512 BC]. *The Art of War*. New York: Barnes and Noble.

Sutton, J., C. R. Butcher, and I. Svensson. 2014. "Explaining Political Jiu-Jitsu: Institution-Building and the Outcomes of Regime Violence against Unarmed Protests." *Journal of Peace Research* 51, no. 5: 559–73.

Svensson, I. 2007. "Fighting with Faith." *Journal of Conflict Resolution* 51, no. 6: 930–49.

Svensson, I. 2013. *Ending Holy Wars: Religion and Conflict Resolution in Civil Wars*. St. Lucia, Queensland: University of Queensland Press.

Tabatabai, A. 2017. "Preserving the Iran Nuclear Deal: Perils and Prospects." Cato Institute. Policy Analysis, August 15. no. 818.

Thomas, S. M. 2005. *The Global Resurgence of Religion and the Transformation of International Relations*. New York: Palgrave Macmmillan.

Thompson, W. R. 2001. "Identifying Rivals and Rivalries in World Politics." *International Studies Quarterly* 45, no. 4: 557–86.

Thompson, W. R., and D. Dreyer. 2011. *Handbook of International Rivalries*. Washington, DC: CQ Press.

Thucydides. 1943. *The Peloponnesian Wars*. New York: Oxford University Press.

Tickner, J. 1992. *Gender in International Relations: Feminist Perspectives on Achieving International Security*. New York: Columbia University Press.

Tilly, C. 1978. *From Mobilization to Revolution*. Reading, MA: Addison-Wesley.

Toft, M. D. 2007. "Getting Religion? The Puzzling Case of Islam and Civil War." *International Security* 31, no. 4: 97–131.

Toft, M. D. 2009. *Securing the Peace: The Durable Settlement of Civil Wars*. Princeton, NJ: Princeton University Press.

Toft, M. D. 2012. "Religion, Terrorism and Civil Wars" In *Rethinking Religion and World Affairs*, edited by T. Shah, A. Stephan, and M. D. Toft, 127–48. New York: Oxford University Press.

Toft, M. D., D. Philpott, and T. S. Shah 2011. *God's Century: Resurgent Religion and Global Politics*. New York: W. W. Norton.Troy, J., ed. 2014. *Religion and the Realist Tradition*. New York: Routledge.

Tusicisny, A. 2004. "Civilizational Conflicts: More Frequent, Longer, and Bloodier?" *Journal of Peace Research* 41, no. 4: 485–98.

UCDP (Uppsala Conflict Data Program). Armed Conflict dataset UCDP 2014.

UNDP (United Nations Development Programme). 2014. The Human Development Index. Retrieved April 19, 2016, from http://hdr.undp.org/en/content/human–development–index–hdi.

UNDP. 2015. Technical Report HDI in http://hdr.undp.org/sites/default/files/hdr2015_technical_notes.pdf.

Unger, L. K. 2013. *Networks and Human Rights: An Examination of Human Rights Treaties and the Influence of Dependence on States' Human Rights Practices*. Ph.D. Dissertation: University of California. Davis, CA.

US Commission on International Religious Freedom. 2016. *2015 Annual Report*. From http://www.uscirf.gov/reports–briefs/annual–report/2015–annual–report.

Van Creveld, M. 2009. *Transformation of War*. New York: Simon and Schuster.

Vanhanen, T. 1999a. "Domestic Ethnic Conflict and Ethnic Nepotism: A Comparative Analysis." *Journal of Peace Research* 36, no. 1: 55–73.

Vanhanen, T. 1999b. *Ethnic Conflicts Explained by Ethnic Nepotism*. Stamford, CT: JAI Press.

Vasquez, J. A. 1993. *The War Puzzle*. Cambridge: Cambridge University Press.

Vijayaraghavan, V. S., P. Andre-Noelle, Z. Maoz, and R. M. D'Souza. 2015. "Quantifying Dynamical Spillover in Co-Evolving Multiplex Networks." *Scientific Reports* 5: 15142.

Vüllers, J., B. Pfeiffer, and M. Basedau. 2015. "Measuring the Ambivalence of Religion: Introducing the Religion and Conflict in Developing Countries RCDC) Dataset." *International Interactions* 41, no. 5: 857–81.

Wæver, O., B. Buzan, M. Kelstrup, and P. Lemaitre. 1993. *Identity, Migration and the New Security Agenda in Europe*. London: Pinter.

Wallace, M., and J. D. Singer. 1970. "Intergovernmental Organization in the Global System, 1815–1964: A Quantitative Description. *International Organization* 24, no. 2: 239–87.

Walter, B. 1997. "The Critical Barrier to Civil War Settlement." *International Organization* 51 3: 335–64.

Waltz, K. 1958. *Man, the State, and War*. New York: Columbia University Press.

Waltz, K. 1979. *Theory of International Politics*. Reading, MA: Addison-Wesley.

Ward, M. D., J. S. Ahlquist, and A. Rozenas. 2013. "Gravity's Rainbow: A Dynamic Latent Space Model for the World Trade Network." *Network Science* 1: 95–118.

Warren, T. C. 2010. "The Geometry of Security: Modeling Interstate Alliances as Evolving Networks." *Journal of Peace Research* 47: 697–709.

Wasserman, S., and K. Faust. 1994. *Social Network Analysis: Methods and Applications*. 2nd ed. New York: Cambridge University Press.

Wendt, A. 1992. "Anarchy Is What States Make of It: The Social Construction of Power Politics." *International Organization* 46, no. 2: 391–425.

Wendt, A. 1999. *Social Theory of International Politics*. Cambridge: Cambridge University Press.

Wendt, A. 2003. "Why Is a World State Inevitable?" *European Journal of International Relations* 9: 491–542.

Wilson, P. H. 2011. *The Thirty Years War: Europe's Tragedy*. New York: Belknap Press.

Wimmer, A., and B. Min. 2006. "From Empire to Nation-State: Explaining Wars in the Modern World, 1816–2001." *American Sociological Review* 71, no. 6: 867–97.

Wimmer, A., L. E. Cederman, and B. Min. 2009. "Ethnic Politics and Armed Conflict: A Configurational Analysis of a New Global Dataset." *American Sociological Review* 74, no. 2: 316–37.

World Values Survey. 2016. World Values Survey wave 6 2010–2014 official aggregate v.20150418. World values survey association. Aggregate file producer: asep/jds, madrid spain." from http://www.worldvaluessurvey.org/wvsdocumentationwv6.jsp.

Wucherpfennig, J., N. W. Metternich, and L-E. Cederman. 2012. "Ethnicity, the State, and the Duration of Civil War." *World Politics* 64, no. 1: 79–115.

Wyn Jones, R. 1999. *Security, Strategy and Critical Theory*. Boulder, CO: Lynne Rienner.

Zimmerman, J. C. 2008. "Islam and War: A Review Essay." *Terrorism and Political Violence* 20, no. 3: 434–59.

Index

Page locators in italics indicate figures or tables.

Abernethy, D. B., 7, 64, 397
Aberystwyth School, 345
Abrahamic religions, 74, 76
absolute gains, 233, 235, 237, 239
Adler, E., 240, 252, 397
Afghanistan, 12, 52;
 population, 144;
 terrorism, 57;
 wars, 12, *222*, 290
Africa, 7, 48, 49–50, 64, 86, 89, 124, 128, 130, 132, 136, 137, 180, 199, 200, 266, 290, 294, 345, 363, 367, 391n2, 393n2, 393n7, 394n13;
 PTAs, 392n8, 393n15
Ahmadis, 3
Akbaba, Y., 308, 311, 317, 397, 412
al-Assad, B, 81
Alawites, 3, 91, 102, 128, 397
Albania, 296
Allah, 64
Al Qaeda, 30, 33, 46, 53, 57
Alston, W. P., 117, 119, 379, 397
America, 7, 68, 151, 244;
 Civil War, 314;
 exceptionalism, 33;
 imperialism, 33;
 nationhood, 292. *see also* United States
American Civil War, 314
Americas, 64, *135*, 387n2
Anarchy, 11, 84, 163, 232, 233, 392n10;
 international, 91, 107, 233
Anatolia, 74
Anglicanism, 7, 120, 139, 152
Angola, *220*, *221*, 290

Anievas, A. 64, 397
Arabian Peninsula, 74, 75
Arab–Israeli conflict, 7, 8, 82, 83, 159
Arab League, 107, 251, 270, 281
Arab nationalism, 107, 298
Arab-Palestinian minority, 310
Arab voters, 310
Arab world, 107
ARDA. *see* Association of Religion Data Archives
Argentina, 213, *221*
Armenia, *221*
Armenia–Azerbaijan war, 12
ASEAN. *See* Association of Southeast Asian Nations
Asia, 64, 75, 86, 92, 124, 128, 131, 266, 290;
 Central, 50, 364, 391n7;
 civilization, 6;
 colonialism, 180, 393n2;
 conflicts, 199, 345;
 East, 7, 132;
 Islamic population, 137;
 Jewish communities, 389n6;
 Muslims, 133, 137;
 nontheistic religions, 76;
 non-religious population, 133;
 population, 132;
 religious similarity, 136, 265;
 societies, 6, 7;
 South, 7, 132–33;
 Southwest, 5;
 Western colonialism, 180
Aslan, R., 75, 397

Association of Religion Data Archives
  (ARDA), vii, 7, 139, 356;
  website, 387n1, 390n4, 397
Association of Southeast Asian Nations
  (ASEAN), 267
atheism, 68, 137, 264
Australia *219*, *220*, *222*, 362
Austria-Hungary, 7
Auvinen, J., 304, 412
average religious similarity scores across
  regions, 1945–2010, *135*
Axelrod, R., 226, 231, 232, 237,
  392n1, 397
Ayatollah Khomeini, 39, 389n7, 362, 379
Azerbaijan, 12, *221*

Baccini, L., 249, 397
Balkans, 50
Barbieri, K., *195*, *202*, *204*, *251*, *208*,
  210, *211*, 392n2, 397–398
Barbados, 216
Barnett, M., 240, 252, 397
Baron, S., 389n6, 398
Barrett, D., 144, 398
Basedau, M., 297, 298, 301–2, 303,
  307, 308, 311, 398, 417
battle deaths, 150, 323, 325, 330
Bektas T., 275, 398
Belgium, *219*, 264, 362
belief systems: civil uprising, 43;
  political, 35;
  religious, 1, 34, 38, 42, 44, 57,
    63–64, 76, 93, 117, 118, 119, 121,
    248, 385
Bektas T., 275, 398
Bell, S. R., 301, 414
bellicosity, 375, 385
Bendix, R., 28
Bennett, D. S., 7, 106, 197,
  389n12, 398
Benson, M., 106, 290, 398
Berger, P., 28, 398
bipolar, 11, 154, 264, 327, 334
Blainey, G., 59, 398
Boazzizi, M., 313
Bohmelt, T, 290, 296, 305, 306, 408

Bolivia, 213
Bolks, S., 151, 398
Booth, K., 345, 398
bootstrapping, 174, *182*, 217, 222,
  257, 371
Bormann, N-C., 322, 398
Bosnia, 52, *221*, 291
Boston Marathon bombing, 79
Brazil, *66*, 67, 213, *219*
Bremer, S., 153, 197, 199, 398,
  403, 407
Breslin, S., 350, 398
Brexit, 12
Britannica Book of the Year, 116
Brown, M. E., 290, 399
Brownlee, J., 39, 399
Buck, I. P., 76, 399
Buddha, 77
Buddhism, 3, 26, 64, 75, 76, 77, 89,
  116, 119, 126, *131*, 132, 133, 134,
  140, *142*, 191, *203*, 307, 385
Bueno de Mesquita, B., 71, 237, 249,
  395n1, 399
Buhaug, H., 297, 306, 399
Bulgaria 145, *219*
Bunton, M., 64, 75, 400
Buzan, B., 345, 347, 350, 399, 418
Byzantine Empire, 74, 75

Cabral, A., 28, 399
Cambodia, 8, *220*, 221
Campbell, D. E., 116, 413
Canada, *219*, *221*, *222*, 362;
  Protestant population, 216;
  –US dyad, 198
Canetti, D., 307, 399
Caribbean, 86, 89
Carlson, J. D., 32, 399
Catholic, 2, 3, 7, 33, 38, 47, 48, 49, 52,
  64, 67, 78, 120, *127*, 128, 129, 132,
  139, *140*, *142*, 152, 160, 171, 201,
  214, 216, 246, 291, 341, 389n7. *See
  also* Roman Catholic Church
Catholicism, 46, 52, 120, 160, 246
Cederman, L-E., 296, 297, 303, 306,
  326, 329, 340, 398, 399, 418

Central Asia, 50, 364, 391n7
Chad, 52, 197, 221
Charron, S., 151, 391n3, 400
Chenoweth, E. 286, *287*, 303, 315, 323, 324, 393n9, 400
Chile, 213
China, 199, 213, *219, 220, 221,* 264, 362;
  Japan rivalry, 159
China (PRC), *220*
Chiozza, G., 151, 152, 400
Chow, W. M., 249, 397, 400
Christianity, 3, 26, 46, 74, 75, 76, 77, 102, 116, 120, 121, 123, 124, 126, 129, 134, 137, 149, 151, 152, 153, 183, 191, 214, 216, 259, 264, 270, 336, 337, 339, 354, 372, 375, 394n19;
  Africa, 132;
  Bulgaria, 145;
  Catholic (*see* Catholic);
  "Christian" realism, 32;
  "doubly affiliated," 139;
  Eastern Orthodox (*see* Eastern Orthodox);
  Europe, 129;
  European colonization, 64;
  Hindu government, 307;
  Jerusalem, 43;
  Mexico, 201;
  Muslim conflict, 6, 92, 192, 298, 307, 341 (*see also* Crusades);
  Orthodox, 52, 126, 139;
  Palestine, 78;
  Protestant (*see* Protestant);
  religious families in Christianity and Islam, *127*;
  right evangelical, 12;
  superiority, 7;
  Turkey, 68;
  United States, 390n4;
  US foreign policy, 31;
  West, 11, 291
Christian states, 7, 183, 216, 270, 291
Church of England, 38
The CIA World Factbook, 116

Cioffi-Revilla, C., 393n1, 400
civil war and religion, 283–343;
  appendix, 343;
  characteristics of civil violence in post–World War II era, 285–88;
  civil conflict attributes, 325, 330, 332–37, *333*;
  civil war duration, 300, 325;
  civil war occurrence, 325, 329, *331, 332, 336,* 337;
  civil war severity, 325;
  conclusions, 340–42;
  debates and issues in research on civil conflict, 302–9;
  estimation, 329–30;
  ethnicity, linguistic, and religious factors, 302–9;
  extant literature problems, 309–12;
  external dimension of civil conflict, 319–22;
  introduction, 283–85;
  key themes in research on civil conflict, 288–302;
  mobilizing power of religion, 314–18;
  nation history, 337–40, *338*;
  proximate determinants of civil conflict, 318–19;
  religion and civil conflict, 312–22;
  religious structure of societies, 312–14;
  research design, 323–29;
  results, 330–40;
  theory and evidence on determinants of civil conflict, 288–312;
  war outbreak, 330–32
clash of civilizations (CoC) thesis, 12, 13, 23, 90, 91, 92, 147, 149, 151–52, 153, 371, 381–82;
  civil wars, 291;
  conflict in post–Cold War, 192, 154;
  cooperation, 248;
  definition, 93;
  hypotheses, 250–51, 259, 262;
  intercultural conflict, 248;

clash of civilizations (CoC) thesis (*Continued.*)
    international conflict, 164–65, 371;
    monadic conflict—differences between Cold War and post–Cold War patterns, *179*;
    policy implications, 385;
    predictions, 178–79;
    religious aspects, 291, 374;
    religious conflict more prominent since end of Cold War, 184–85, *185*, 293;
    religious similarity, 186, *187*, 187–88, 191, 270
Cleveland, W. L., 64, 75, 400
CoC thesis. *See* clash of civilizations (CoC) thesis
codes of moral conduct, 3
coercion, 38, 77
Cohen, R., 70, 400
Colaresi, M., 159, 400
collective action problem, 78, 104, 304–6, 309
collective instrumentalism, 73, 74, 75, 77, 78
collective rituals, 2, 63, 119
Collier, P., 290, 294, 297, 300, 302, 303, 304, 305, 339, 393n8, 394n13, 400
Colombia, *219*, 341
colonialism 6, 30, 49, 86, 87, 98, 106, 163–64, 167, 180, 213, 264, 290, 298, 393n2, 393n4, 395n20
combined cooperation, 255–56, 258, 259, 260, 261, 265, 268, 269, 270
common class of beliefs, rituals, and practices, 119
communal behaviors, 2, 94
communal identity markers, 35, 65
communism, 11, 68, 128, 133, 154, 361, 363, 364, 379, 384, 391n7;
    communist bloc, 11;
    Poland, 389n7;
    postcommunist, 126, 137, 390n10, 391n7;
    Soviet, 390n10

community structure, 254, 275
Comparative Constitution Project, 170, 191, 323, 356
Comte, A., 8, 238
conflict history of nations, *181*
Confucianism, 8, 77, 92, 119
Congress of Vienna, 197
constructivism, 13, 33, 45, 58, 62, 83–89, 90, 94, *96*, 112, *253*, 263, 318, 380–81, 389n3;
    paradigm, 239–42;
    propositions, 162–64, 192
cooperation, international, 224–73;
    and constructivism 239–42;
    economic 228;
    general 229;
    institutional 228;
    and liberalism 236–39;
    and realism, 233–36;
    security 227–28;
    types of 227–30
cooperative international communities, 225, 267–69, *268*;
    religion, 251–52
Copenhagen School, 345
corporate identities, 84, 85, 240, 241, 315
Correlates of War (COW): 7, 116, 144–45, 149, 152, 168, 391n1;
    battle deaths, 325;
    civil war data, 287, 190–93, 292–94, 323, *331*, *338*;
    civil wars, 393n9;
    civil wars, 1816–1980, 393n5;
    definition of system membership, 122;
    Intrastate Wars, 323;
    national capabilities, 205, 210, 211
Costa Rica, 197
Council of Nicea, 74
coup risk, 171–72, 173, 174, 177, *177*, 178, 180, *181*, *182*, 183, *184*, *185*, *187*, 249, *258*, 259, *260*, 270
COW. *see* Correlates of War
Cox, M., 151, 152, 414
Cranmer, S., 223, 281, 400

critical omission, 59–60
Croatia, *221*
Croats, 52, 291
Crusades, 6, 64, 75, 78, 92
Cuba, *221*
Cultural Composition of Interstate System Members dataset, 149
Cunningham, D., 296, 400
Cyprus *220*
Czechoslovakia, 123, 157, 197, 199

Damascus, 74
Davies, G. A., 151, 152, 407
Davies, J., 289, 290, 303, 401
decolonization, 180
De Juan, A., 299, 401
Democratic Republic of the Congo, *221*
Demographic Yearbook, 116
Desmarais, B., 223, 281, 400
De Soysa, I., 297, 301, 304, 401, 407
Despotis, D.K., 351, 401
Deutsch, K. 392n5, 401
Diehl, P.F. 159, 401
disaggregated empirical evidence, 60–61
distribution of major world religions, 1945–2010, *123*
Dixon, J., 286, 323, 415
domestic conflicts, 17, 36, 43, 83, 88, 111, 306, 307, 308, 344, 378, 381
domestic political conflict and religious factors, 22, 25, 112. *see also* religion and civil war
dominant religion, 66, 67, 79, 88, 104, 105, 112, 129, 158, 336, 355
Dominican Republic, 214, 216
Doyle, M., 9, 28, 293, 401
Du Bois, W. E. B., 7, 64, 401
dual religions, 144, 201
Dunn, R. S., 6, 401
Duval, R., 217, 411
dyad-history level of analysis, 148, 173, *186*, 186–87, 191, 198, 199, 216, 253, 378

East Asia, 7, 389n6
Eastern Orthodox, 3, 120, 126, 128, 129
Eckstein, H., 291, 401
economic cooperation, 224, 228, 229, 236, 238, 244, 247, 250, 255, 256, 270, 272, 273, 379, 392n8
Ecuador, 66, 67, *221*
Egypt, 38, 39, 53, 74, 75, 107, 159, 201, 213, *219*, *220*, *221*, 299, 300;
ancient, 4, 5;
constitution, 39;
government, 74;
Jordan relations, 201;
Judaism, 74;
Israel relationship, 159;
Lower, 4;
military, 53, 300;
Muslim Brotherhood, 38, 299;
political elites, 107;
politics, 39, 53;
PRIE, 201, 213;
royalty, 5;
Salafis, 299;
Saudi Arabia relations, 201;
United Kingdom relations, 213;
Upper, 4;
uprisings, 299
Ehrlich, A. M. 389n6, 401
Eighty Years' War, 6
Eisenstadt, S. N., 28
Elbadawi, I. 297, 401
elite instrumentalism, 73, 77, 78–79
Elkins, Z., 170, *195*, 323, 356, 401
Ellingsen, T., 48, 49, 50, 51, 52, 53, 116, 150, 152, 294, 401, 405
Elster, J., 9, 401
El Salvador *220*
emergence, 93;
of cooperative communities, 254, 267, 272, 280;
implications of international cooperation, 242, 251;
properties of international relations, 225;
properties of religious factors, 225;
structures, 251, 267

endogenous cooperative communities, 21, 230, 251, 252, *253*
England, 12. *see also* United Kingdom
English School, 45
Enlightenment, 8, 27, 73
Enloe, C., 344, 401
EPR. *see* Ethnic Power Relations
Eritrea, *221*
Esteban, J., 305, 307, 326, 401, 402
Esther, 387n1
Ethiopia, 123, *219*, *221*, 389n6
ethnic civil wars, 292, 293, 296, 299
ethnicity, 87, 150, 163, 294, 295, 297, 298], 301, 341, 389n9, 393n8, 395n2;
  and civil war, 302–309;
  indicators of, 296;
  and language, 309;
  measures of, 296;
  and religion, 297, 302, 307, 329, 394n17
ethnic kinship, 87
Ethnic Power Relations (EPR) dataset, 296, 297, 329, 332, 394n17, 395n2
Europe, 5, 37, 38, 75, 76, 78, 128, 136, 137, 152, 160, 199, 266;
  Catholicism, 129;
  Christianity, 64, 129;
  colonialism, 64, 87, 290;
  ethnicity, 297;
  genocidal conflicts, 345;
  imperialism, 7;
  Islamic influence, 132;
  medieval wars, 6;
  Muslims, 132;
  non-religious, 133;
  Orthodox, 7;
  pagan religions, 75;
  Protestantism, 6;
  religious diversity, 137, 152;
  religious warfare, 6;
  Turkey relations, 67;
  white supremacy, 7. *see also* Eastern Europe
European Union, 67–68
exceptionalism, 33

Falkland Islands, *221*
Farber, H. S., 235, 244, 402
failed states, 345
Fatah, 300
Faust, K. 213, 418
Fearon, J., 286, *287*, 290, 294, 304, 305, 307, 323, 324, 327, 339, 343, 393n9, 394n14
Feinsilver, J. M., 389, 402
feminism, 344
Fertile Crescent, 74, 199
Fett, P., 293, 411
final data cleaning, 144–45
Finke, R., 103, 353, 354, 395n3, 404
Finnemore, M., 85, 402
Fitzgerald, T., 26, 34, 55, 402
Flavius, 5
Flood, M. 392n1, 402
Fordham, B. J., 225, 402
Fox, J., 26, 28, 30, 34, 35, 36, 39, 41, 42, 43, 44, 45, 46, 47–48, 55, *56*, 65, 82, 85, 98, 116, 169, 191, *195*, *203*, *205*, *207*, *209*, *211*, 300, 308, 311, 317, 319, 322, 323, 334, 339, 353, 354, 355, 356, 358, 383, 388n3, 388n2, 388n7, 388n8, 398, 400, 401, 402–3, 413, 415
fractionalization, ethnic, 312;
  religious, 294–95, 300–302, 305, 307, 326, 327, 329, 339, 343, 358, 390n8;
  social, 285, 310
France, 6, *219*, *220*, *221*, *222*, 264
Franseze, R., 281, 403
Frankfurt School, 345
Freedman, L., 107, 403
Freedom House, 356, 357
friends and foes, 41, 240, 378, 380;
  definition, 74, 241;
  interests, 164
fundamentalism, 42, 45
Furedi, F. 7, 403

Galtung, J., 389n8, 403
Gandhi, I., 313
Gartzke, E., 70, 88, 150, 152, 403

Gat, A., 4, 286, 393n1, 403, 409
Gaza, 57
gender, 26, 84;
  categories, 357;
  development, *361*, 363, 364, 365;
  equality, 41, 352, 354, 356, 357, 365;
  inequality, 347, 351, 357, 366
Gender-Adjusted HDI, 357
gender development index (GDI), 357
general cooperation, 229
genocide, 143, 293
Germany 7, *219*, *221*, 362
Gibler, D. M., *195*, 403
Gill, A., 28, 39, 40–41, 65, 79, 103, 305, 352–53, 354, 359, 362, 388n8, 395n2, 403–4
Gilligan, M., 230, 404
Ginsburg, T., 170, *195*, 323, 356, 401
Girvan, M., 254, 275, 412
Gleditsch, K. S., 70, 88, 150, 152, *195*, *206–7*, *208*, *211*, 296, 297, 301, 399, 403, 404, 405, 407, 409
global patterns in world religions, 1945–2010, 122–29
global religious diversity, 1945–2010, *134*
Gochman, C. S., 199, 404
The Godfather, 245, 246
God/s, 1, 3, 8, 46, 48, 64, 70;
  belief, 355;
  different, 74;
  help, 310;
  importance, 356, 358, 359, 362, 366, 389n11;
  kind of, 385;
  "true mind of," 64;
  will, 366
God's Century, 24, 193, 340
Goertz, G., 106, 159, 401, 404
"Golden Temple" conflict, 341
Google Scholar, 9, *10*, 387n2
Gowa, J., 108, 225, 235, 238, 244, 402, 404
Gramscian approaches, 28
Greece, 199, *219*
Grim, B. J., 39, 103, 353, 354, 359, 395n3, 404

Grotius, H., 8
GS (Google Scholar), 9, *10*, 387n2
Gubler, J. R., 301, 404
Guilhot, N., 28, 32, 404
Gulf War: first, 12, 341
Gurr, T., *209*, 289, 291–292, 303, 304, 351, 356, 358, 404–5, 411
Gusfield, J., 28

Haas, P. M., *219*, 392n11, 397
Haiti, 201, 395n22
Hall, P. 222, 405
Hamas, 57, 300
Hammond, J., 282, 407
Hanson, E., 27, 47, 405
Hardin, G., 392n1, 405
Hartzell, C. A., 324, 325, 405
Hasenclever, E., 85, 405
Hassner, R. E., 42, 43, 160, 405
Hayens, J., 29, 405
Hays, J. C., 281, 403
HDI. *see* UN Human Development Index
Heckman, J., 174, 330, 333, *333*, *336*, 405
Hegre, H., 294, 295, 305, 405
Henderson, E. A., 6, 86, 98, 149, 150, 151, 169, 180, *195*, *202*, *205*, *206*, *207*, *210*, *211*, 229, 292, 299, 349, 381, 389n3, 390n1, 390n5, 391n3, 392n8, 392n10, 393nn15–16, 393n8, 395n1, 405–6, 411;
  "neopatrimonial balancing," 393n7, 394n13
Henir, J. B., 31, 406
Henne, P. S., 32, 154, 406
Henry VIII, 38
Hibbs, D., 291, 406
Hicks, D. A., 347, 351, 406
Hinduism, 116, 119, 153, 336, 375
Hindus, 89, 123, 132, 372;
  government, 307;
  Nepal, 341;
  rebels, 307
historical development, 119
history of religions, 2–3

HIV, 345
Hizbollah, 30, 57
Hobbes, T., 8
Hobbesian culture, 8, 392n9
Hobfoll, S. 307, 399
Hoeffler, A., 290, 294, 297, 300, 302, 303, 304, 305, 339, 393n8, 394n13, 400
Hoff, P., 281, 406
Hoffmann, S., 8, 406
holy places, 1, 6, 42, 43, 65, 78, 82, 160, 171, 325
Homer: *Iliad*, 5
Homer Dixon, T., 344, 406
Honduras, *220*
Horowitz, D., 281, 406
Human Development Index. *See* UN Human Development Index
human security, 17, 22, 23, 35, 47, 58, 60, 61, 95, 345, 356, 362–63, 365–66, 367, 371, 375;
  civil liberties index, 357;
  civil war, 358;
  definition, 346–48;
  HDI-based measures, 364;
  human development, 365;
  inequality, gender development, and political freedoms, *361*;
  measuring the quality of life in societies, 348–52;
  political diversity, 363;
  promotion, 366;
  religion-state relations, 364;
  religious diversity, 363, 366;
  religious freedom, 24, 359, 363;
  secularism, 363, 364, *364*, 365, 366, 376, 377, 380;
  social welfare, 16;
  theoretical expectations, 352–55;
  three-stage least-squares, *360*
Humphreys, J., 304, 406
Hungary, 7, *219*, *220*
Huntington, S., vi, 6, 28, 29, 383, 400, 406;
  clash of civilizations, 11–12, 89–90, 91, 92, 149–50, 154, 186–87, 189, 191, 192, 248, 291–92, 381, 391n2;
  definition of civilization, 89, 91–92, 248, 391n2;
  "Islam has bloody borders," 24, 178, 339, 385;
  thesis, 381
Hurd, E. S., 26, 31, 34, 44, 406–7
Hussayni rebellion, 6
Hussein, Saddam, 39, 81, 107, 341
hypothetical cooperative network with community assignments, *276*, *277*

ICISS. *see* International Commission on Intervention and State Sovereignty
idealism, 27, 349, 385
identity, 27, 49, 69, 71, 81, 83, 84, 88, 156, 158, 161, 163, 194, 240, 241, 244, 264, 302, 310, 374, 382, 388n5;
  civilizational, 12;
  common, 247, 253, 262, 315;
  communal, 35, 41, 65, 163, 164, 315;
  conflict/wars, 49–50, 57, 293, 297, 298;
  constructivism and 13, 34, 83–89, 90, 163, 240–41, 244, 253, 380–81;
  corporate, 84, 85, 240, 241, 315;
  cultural, 84, 89, 94, 241, 341, 374;
  definition, 65;
  experiential elements, 163, 241, 380;
  group, 63, 303, 305, 309, 316;
  individual, 2;
  interaction-based, 49, 88, 94, 241, 316, 380;
  international, 240–41;
  linguistic, 65;
  Muslim, 68;
  national 65, 66, 68, 70, 84, 86, 87, 89, 90, 91, 94, 157, 163, 164, 190, 240, 244, 315, 317–18, 363, 370, 377, 380, 388n4;
  political, 65;
  primordialism and, 63–71, 76, 247, 377–78;

religious, 2, 12, 34, 45, 47, 65, 68, 88, 89, 108, 110, 113, 150, 153, 157, 164, 180, 184, 247, 291, 292, 298, 309, 315, 317, 319, 374, 383, 391n7;
religious markers of, 16, 27, 69, 70, 85, 88, 98, 160, 162–63, 165, 310, 370, 378
IGO. *see* intergovernmental organizations
imperialism, 5, 6, 7, 27, 30, 33, 74, 393n2, 393n4;
neoimperialim, 107, 389n8
Index of Qualitative Variation (IQV) 133–34, 135, 169, 200, 201, *202*, *212*, 326, 343, 358, 390n8
India, 132, *219*, *220*, *221*, 307, 341
Indonesia, 299
Indo–Pakistani war, 7, 8, 12, 83, 159
infidels, 3, 39, 46, 64, 101, 107, 161, 385
institutional cooperation, 11, 224, 228–29, 235, 236, 238, 243, 244, 247, 250, 255, 259, 265, 266, 272, 378
institutional structure, 28, 76, 98, 99, 119, 352
institutions: definition, 118–19
instrumentalism, 71–83, 94, *96*, 112, 161–62, 379–80;
collective, 73, 74, 75, 77, 78;
cooperation, 247–48;
elite, 73, 77, 78–79
integrative theory, 16, 24, 62, 95–112, *111*, 174, 192, 193, 382–83;
civil war, 316;
dyad-history unit of analysis, 187, *187*;
effect of international environment, 106–9;
international conflict, 165–66;
international cooperation, 248–51;
political and religious institutions relationships, 103–6;
religious influences on foreign and domestic policy, 109–12;

social structure, 100–103, 318;
temporal differences, 180
interaction-based, 87, 88, 94
interests, 3, 27, 34, 65, 68, 84, 236, 239;
definition of, 164;
in constructivism, 239–40;
economic, 28, 39, 236;
material, 34, 239–40;
national, 58, 156, 236–37;
political, 3, 86, 235;
religious, 88;
self, 40;
shared, 108, 235, 236, 238, 241, 244, *253*, 272, 375
intergovernmental organizations:
definition, 229;
memberships, 172, 173, 227, 232, 254, 255, 256, 260, 261–62, 380, 392n3
International Commission on Intervention and State Sovereignty (ICISS), 346–47, 407
international conflict and religion, 146–223;
appendix, 194–223;
clash of civilizations, 164–65, *179* (*see also* clash of civilizations);
constructivist propositions, 162–64, 192;
determinants of international conflict, *188*;
dyadic level of analysis, *182*, 182–90, *184*, *185*, *186*, *187*;
effects of religious characteristics of states, 1945–2020, *176*;
effects of religious factors on conflict history of nations, *181*;
effects of religious variables on conflict, *186*;
effects of religious similarity and period on dyad history, *187*;
empirical literature, 149–55;
implications, 192–93;
instrumentalist propositions, 161–62;

international conflict and religion
(*Continued.*)
  integrative theory, 165–66;
  interaction between political instability and religion-state relations, 191–92;
  introduction, 146–49;
  national level of analysis, 175–81;
  political instability and effects on conflict propensity of nations, *177*;
  primordialist proposition, 155–60;
  religious homogeneity, 191;
  religious similarity, *187*, *189*, 190–91;
  research design, 166–75;
  research design, estimation methods, 173–75;
  research design, key measures, 168–73;
  research design, units of analysis, 166–68;
  results, 175–90;
  secularism, 192;
  specific religions more conflict prone, 192;
  theory, 155–66;
  unstable regimes, 191
international cooperation and religion, 21–22, 224–82;
  appendix, 274–82;
  attraction, 242, 243–44;
  clash of civilizations, 248;
  communities, 251–52;
  community cohesion matrix, *278*;
  conclusion, 269–73;
  constructivist paradigm, 239–42;
  cooperative international communities, 267–69, *268*;
  definition, 226–27, 231;
  dyadic analyses, 261–65, *263*, *264*;
  empirical findings, *271*;
  hypothetical cooperative network with community assignments, *276*, *277*;
  instrumentalism, 247–48;
  integrative theory, 248–51;
  international cooperation—state of the art, introduction, 224–42;
  liberalism, 236–39;
  nation-level analyses, 257–61, *258*, *260*, *261*;
  need, 242–43;
  network effects, 280–82;
  prevention, 242, 244–45;
  primordialism, 246–47;
  realism, 233–36;
  regional analyses, 265–66, *266*, 267;
  religious cohesion of cooperative communities, 256–57;
  research design, 252–57;
  research design, estimation, 257;
  religious similarity, *277*, *278*;
  research design, key variables, 254–55;
  research design, units of analysis, 253–54;
  results, 257–69;
  theories, 242–52;
  trust, 242, 245–46
international culture, 91, 240, 241, 242, 380
International Relations (IR) theories, 6, 9, 10–11, 13, 19, 25, 26, 59, 151, 284, 288–89, 290–91, 387nn2–3, 388n1;
  central themes of religion and IR literature, 35–48;
  modernization and classical paradigms, 27–34;
  quantitative-oriented, 393n5;
  security, 344, 345;
  traditional, 46, 47, 58
Iran, 39, *66*, 67, 88, 104, 132, 159, *221*, 250, 291, 316;
  Revolution, 389n7, 389n10
Iraq, 81;
  Arab League target, 107;
  desert, 74;
  Iran–Iraq war, 39;
  Shi'a, 132;
  terrorism, 57;
  war, 12
Iraqi Shi'ites, 39
Ireland, R., 29, 407

Isaacs, M., 308, 407
ISIS, 46, 53, 385
Islam, 3, 6, 43, 74, 77, 82, 116, 126,
    134, 191, 388n1;
  –Kurdish conflict, 341;
  nonradical, 12;
  radical, 12;
  religious families in Christianity and
    Islam, *127*
Islamic Jihad, 300
Islamic Republic, 39;
  of Iran, 67, 88;
  of Saudi Arabia, 88
Israel, 57, *66*, 201, 213, *220*, *221*, *222*,
    222, 310, 387n3, 389n5;
  –Arab wars, 7, 8, 82, 159, *219*;
  holy sites, 43, 301;
  Jewish state, 74;
  Jews, 132, 390n7;
  "Little Satan," 39;
  non-Jewish communities, 68;
  –Palestinian conflict, 36, 82, 83, 102,
    300, 341;
  Palestinian peace settlement, 43;
  religious freedom, 310
Israelites (antiquity), 5, 74

Jackson, J., vii, 108, 296, 320, 321, 335,
    407
Jackson M.O., 281, 407
Jaggers, K., 351, 356, 357, 411
Jainism, 76, 119, *140*, 142, *212*
Jakobsen, T., 297, 407
James, P., 26, 34, 308, 415
Japan, 7, 89, 92, 391n2, 393n2, 395n21;
  China relations, 159;
  dual religions, 201;
  Pearl Harbor attack, 190
Jerusalem, 6, 43, 75
Jervis, R., 107, 231, 251, 392n1, 407
Jewish: community in Central and East
    Asia, 389n6;
  community in Ethiopia, 389n6;
  community in Persia, 387;
  community in Russia, 75;
  homeland in Palestine, 389n5;

intra-conflicts, 82;
Israeli group, 390n7;
majorities, 385;
majority in Israel, 102;
nationalism, 389n5;
person is born to a Jewish mother, 64;
population, 132, 390n7;
religious leaders, 5;
settlers against Palestinians in West
    Bank, 12;
state of Israel, 74
jihad, 46, 78, 301. *see also*
    Islamic Jihad, 300.
John Paul ii, 389n7
Johns, L., 151
Johnson, P., vii, 148, 157, 168, *195*,
    197, *208*, *210*, *222*, 411
Johnston, 8, 407
Jordan, 75;
  -Israel conflict, 159;
  population, 145;
  PRIE of Egypt, 201
Joyce, K. A., 282, 407
Judaism, 3, 6, 12, 43, 74, 77, 82, 116,
    126, 134, 191, 388n1
Juergensmeyer, M., 64, 291–92,
    407–8, 413
July–August Crisis of 1914, 7

Kalyvas, S., 299, 304, 408
Kant, I., 8, 238, 392n10
Kantian culture, 240, 241, 242
Kaplan, J., 148, 157, 168, *195*, 197,
    208, *210*, *222*, 411
Karsh, E., 107, 403, 408
Kathman, J., 297, 408
Kashmir, *219*, *220*
Kemp, B. J., 5, 408
Keohane, R. O., 28, 32, 226, 229, 237,
    238, 311, 397, 408
Keshk, O., *195*, *202*, *204*, *205*, 244,
    398, 408
key cooperation variables, 254–56;
  combined cooperation, 255–56;
  economic cooperation, 255;
  institutional cooperation, 255;

key cooperation variables (*Continued.*)
  preferential trade agreements, 255;
  relative commitment variable, 255;
  security cooperation, 255
Khamenei, A., 39, 250
King, G., 311, 408
King, M. L. Jr., 313
Kinne, B. J., 233, 408
Kitchen, K. A., 74, 408
Knudsen T. L., 315, 414
Kono, D. Y., 249, 400
Korean War, 7, 8, *219*
Koremenos, B., 229, 235, 408
Koskinen, J., 281, 409
Kosovo, 194, 196;
  war, 12, *221*, 290, 345
Koubi, V., 290, 296, 305, 306, 408
Kurdish–Iraqi conflict, 341
Kuwait, 107, *221*

Lacina, B., 300–301, 408
Lai, B., 391n1, 395n1, 408
Laitin, D., 294, 323, 324, 327, 339, 343, 393n9, 402
Lancichientti, 275, 408–9
Laos, *220*
Latin America, 49, 89, 128, *140*, *142*, 160, 391n2
Lebanon, 57, *219*, *221*, *222*
Lebow, R. N., 388n4, 409
Leeds B. A., *195*, *207*, *210*, *211*, 232, 409
Leicht, E., 256, 275, 409
legitimacy, 38, 42, 77, 113;
  domestic, 349;
  ideational, 35;
  religious, 44
Lemke, D., 106, 157, 197, 389n12, 409
level of analysis 18, 21, 152, 153, 166, 167, 168, 169, 172, 173, 175, 182, *189*, 194, 196, 197, 198, 199, 222, 225, 253, 259, 260, *271*, 330, 339, 345, 350
Levy, J. S. 161, 312, 393n2, 397, 409
Li, Y., 308, 403
Libya, *221*, 341
Lichbach, M., 291, 304, 405, 409

Licklider, R., 292, 409
Lipson, C., 229, 235, 408
local religious issues, 45, 299
Locke, J., 8
Lockean culture, 240, 242
loyalty, 37, 66, 67, 76, 86, 164, 315, 316, 349
Lusher, D. 281, 409
Luttwak, E., 5, 286, 409
Lynch, C., 85, 409

Maccabees, 387n1
Mahayana family, 3
major world religions, 1945–2010:
  distribution, *123*;
  religious families, *142*
Mansfield, E. D., 225, 238, 274, 404, 409–10
Maoz, Z., 28, 98, 148, 150, 156–57, 159, 153, 166, 167, 168, 169, 180, 195, 199–200, 202–11, 213, 222, 230, 232, 234, 238, 244, 253, 257, 262, 264, 282, 287, 327, 358, 368, 389n12, 390n5, 391n8, 392n12, 404, 407, 409, 410–11;
  "ally's paradox," 234;
  community detection algorithm, 256, 257;
  definition of major and regional powers, 391n8;
  evolutionary versus revolutionary framework, 264;
  "fightaholism,"172, 173, 175, 182, *189*, 194, 196, 287;
  hostility scale, 168;
  IGO memberships, 255;
  "politically relevant dyads," 197–98, 391n6;
  politically relevant international environment, 106–8, 156–57, 170, 197, 321;
  rebel groups, 296, 320, 321, 335;
  reference group, 197, 243;
  regime score, 167, 358;
  religious polarization, 150, 326, 343

Marshall, M., 196, 209, 211, 351, 356, 357, 411
Martin, D., 350, 411
Martin L., 229, 237, 238, 408, 411
Marx, K., 9, 78
Marxism, 9, 28, 73, 300
Mason, T. D., 293, 411
mass mobilization, 37, 45, 78, 161, 309, 315
Matthews, J., 344, 411
Mazrui, A., 7, 49, 411
Mearsheimer, J. J., 11, 229, 234, 235, 244, 411
measuring religion, 115–22
Mecca, 74, 75
Melton, G., 170, *195*, 323, 356, 401
Meninga, E., 223, 281, 400
methodological issues, 43, 54, 55, 60, 153–54, 343
Metternich, W., 322, 418
Mexico, 201, 214, 216
Middle East, 5, 24, 49, 75, 124, 128, 200, 266, 290, 367, 395;
  Correlates of War, 199;
  government, 74, 391n1;
  Islam, 160;
  percent of regional population, *131*, 132;
  religious similarity, *135*, 136
MIDs. *see* militarized interstate disputes
Migdal, J., 395n1, 411
militarized interstate disputes (MIDs), 148, 150, 151, 154, 157, 174, 175, 181, 187, 188, 296, 329, 389n12;
  dyadic, 168, 198
Miller, B., 95, 295, 312, 389n9, 411
Mills, C., 392n10, 411
Milner, H. V., 230, 238, 274, 409, 410, 411
Min, B., 294, 399, 418
missing data, 44, 122;
  interpolation, and 136, 143–44
mobilization, 12, 37, 40, 42, 43, 45, 46, 78, 79, 101, 102, 106, 107, 108, 110, 111, 161, 165, 174, 175, 181, 190, 272, 301, 306, 309, 310, 313, 315, 316, 319, 320, 374, 380, 382;
  mass, 37, 45, 78, 161, 309, 315;
  political, 19, 20, 24, 71, 77, 81, 349, 382;
  racist, 310 (*see also* race/racial);
  religious, 80, 102, 103, 104, 106, *111*, 165, 305, 306, 327;
  resource, 304–305, 308, 309, 318;
  social mobilization, 19, 74, 77, 80, 81, 107, 183, 302
modernization, 9, 42, 366;
  economic, 90;
  and religion 27–35;
  revisionism, 28, 29;
  theory of, 19, 27–35, 47, 58;
  trends of, 137
Mollov, B., 32, 411
Mongolia, *219*
Montalvo, J. G., 294, 343, 411
Montesquieu, C., 8
Mooney, J., 217, 411
moral codes, 1, 2, 117
Morocco, *220*, *221*
Morrow, J. D., 71, 107, 225, 234, 399, 411, 412
Most, B., 303, 412
Mozambique, 290
Mubarak, Hosni, 39
Muehlenback, P., 33, 412
Mueller, J., 286, 412
Muhammad, 3, 64, 75, 77
Mullenbach, M., 301, 412
Murshed, S. M., 305, 412
Muslim Brotherhood, 38, 39, 53, *130–31*, 299
Muslims, 67, 92, 121, 270, 298, 307, 339, 353, 372, 385;
  Africa, 132, 137;
  Albania, 296;
  Asia, 133, 137;
  Bosnia, 52, 291;
  conflicts, 183, 192;
  definition, 64;
  Europe, 132;
  international cooperation, 259;

Muslims (*Continued.*)
  Kazakhstan, 136;
  Kyrgyzstan, 136;
  loans, 246;
  Middle East, 128;
  "other Muslims," 129;
  Palestine, 6;
  Philippines, 307;
  population, 123, 124, 128, 132, 137, 337;
  Saudi Arabia, 214;
  Sudan, 341;
  Sunni, 171, 214, 270, 379;
  Syria, 379;
  terrorism, 301;
  Turkey, 68;
  United States, 68;
  Yugoslavia, 341. *see also* Crusades; Sharia
Myanmar, 104, 317

Nafzinger, 304, 412
Nasserism, 387n3
nation-level analyses, 257–61, *258, 260, 261*
nation-state, 29, 45, 163, 164
Native American: lands, 64; shaman, 2
NATO, 229, 251, 264, 267, 270, 281, 290, 345
Nazi Germany, 7
Nehru, 387n3
neighborhood effects, 295–96
neoimperialim, 107, 389n8
neoliberalism, 11, 28, 32, 45, 318
neorealism, 11, 28, 45, 233
Netanyahu, B., 310
Netherlands, 6, *219, 220, 221*
networks: analytics, 17, 200, 213, 225, 253–54, 274–75, 278, 343;
  binary, 274;
  community, 274–75;
  cooperative, 254, 267–68, 276;
  definition, 253;
  dependence, 223;
  effects, 222–23, 280–82;
  hypothetical cooperative network with community assignments, *276, 277*;
  international trade, 346;
  polarization index, 343, 394n16;
  relational, 222
Neumayer, 151, 152, 304, 401, 412
Newman E., 350, 412
Newman, M. J., 254, 256, 275, 409, 412
New Testament, 4
New World, 387n2
New Zealand, *219*, 362
Nexon, D. H., 11, 32, 37, 38, 406, 412
Nkrumah, 387n3
Non-Aligned Movement, 86
nonstate religious actors, 45
Non-violent and Violent Campaigns and Outcomes (NAVCO), 323, 324, 393n9
Nordas, R., 301, 401
North Africa, 5, 75, 199
North America, 199
North Korea, *219, 220*, 362
Norton, D., 297, 414

OAS. *see* Organization of American States
Oceania, 86, 137
Ogunkoya, F., vii, 148, 157, 168, *195, 197, 208, 210, 222*, 411
Old Testament, 4, 5, 74, 387n1, 389n4
OLS. *see* ordinary least squares
Olson, M., 304, 412
Oman, *221*
Oneal, J. R., 28, 238, 414
opposition groups, 102, 108, 109, 110, 327, 335
ordinary least squares (OLS) models, 216, 257, 330, *338*
Oren, I., 11, 412
Organization of American States (OAS), 270, 281
Other (religions), *130–31*

Ottoman Empire, 7, 389n9
overemphasis on religious factors and religious actors, 59
Ozdamar, O., 317, 412

Pabst, A., 11, 413
Pakistan, 145, *219, 220, 221*;
  Indo–Pakistani wars, 7, 8, 12, 83, 159
Palestine, 5, 6, 74, 75, 78, 389n5
pan Arabism, 387n3
Paraguay, 213
Pateman, C., 392n10, 413
Paul, Saint, 77
Peace of Westphalia, 284
Pearce, S., 50, 51, 52, 116, 300, 322, 413
Peloponnesian Wars, 8
Pentagon, 12
Persian Gulf, 141, 199
perspective differentiation, 92–95
Peru, *221*
Pevehouse, J., *195, 208, 210, 211*, 229, 232, 238, 409, 413
PFLP. *see* Popular Front of the Liberation of Palestine
Philippines, *219, 220*, 307
Philpott, D., 28, 31, 36–38, 41, 42, 52, 56, 65, 83, 98, 103, 113, 193, 322, 324, 383, 387n3, 388n1, 388n8, 389n7, 390n3, 393n7, 413, 416, 417
Pierskalla, J., 299, 401
Pinker S., 286, 413
Plümper, T., 151, 152, 412
polemical writings, 19, 26, 58–59
political elites, 16, 19–20, 38, 39, 42, 71, 73, 77, 78, 79, 81, 83, 94, 102, 103, 104, 105, 106, 107, 108, 109, 113, 161, 162, 175, 193, 248, 291, 301, 310, 311, 316, 352, 370, 374, 379, 389n7
political history of world, 8
political instability, 22, 80, 82, 247, 337–38;
  cultural discrimination, 316;
  religion-state relations, 191–92;
  religious dissimilarities, 191;

religious factors as instruments of social mobilization, 183;
religious factors interaction with and their effects on conflict propensity of nations, *177*;
religious similarity, 250, 259, *261*, 262, 270;
risk of conflict, 185
politically relevant international environment (PRIE), 157, 175, 196, 295, 296, 321, 322, 327, 328, 336, 382–83, 389, 392n10;
  definition, 170–71;
  Egypt, 201, 213;
  Jordan, 201;
  religious homogeneity, 260;
  religious similarity, 108–9, 156, 170–71, 174, 177, 178, 179, 180, 201–2, 213, 258, 259, 260, *261*, 392n10;
  state-to-PRIE, 179;
  structure of the state, 106–7, 165, 166, 382
political survival, 19, 40, 71, 72, 73, 77, 79, 94, 98, 99, 110, 165, 237, 240, 249, 295, 349, 395n20
political theology, 36–37, 39, 69, 389n7
polytheistic beliefs, 5, 8
Popular Front of the Liberation of Palestine (PFLP), 300
Portugal, 49, 264
Posen, B., 291, 413
Powell, J. M., 171, *195, 196, 202*, 413
power, 8, 26, 27, 28, 34, 38, 46, 77, 84, 93m, 233, 239, 387n1;
  balance of, 80, 92, 236, 394n13;
  colonial, 163–64, 264;
  distribution of, 11, 235;
  economic, 30;
  and international relations, 10;
  military, 345;
  national, 235, 345;
  oppressive, 110;
  perception of, 64, 65;
  political, 19, 38, 73, 77, 85, 110, 329, 367, 394n13, 395n2;

power (*Continued.*)
  projection of, 197;
  of religion, 77, 98, 314–18;
  structure 26, 37
Powers, K., 229, 392n8, 393n15, 413
preferential trade agreements (PTAs), 228, 232, 243, 245, 249, 255, 259, 261, 262, 274, 392n8, 393n15;
  multilateral, 229
Preston, A., 33, 413
PRIE. *see* politically relevant international environment
primordialism, 63–71, 76, 81, 88, 94, *96*, 161, 318, 377–79, 380;
  proposition, 155–60;
  religion and international cooperation, 246–47
Prisoner's Dilemma, 231, 232, 234, 392n1
Protestant, 7, 33, *127*, 128, 129, 132, 139, *140*, *142*, 152, 171, 216;
  double counting of religious categories, 139;
  Europe, 6;
  exceptionalism, 33;
  population, 216;
  regional patterns, 129, 132;
  rise, 76;
  source data, 139, *see also* Protestantism
Protestantism, 3, 6, 38, 46, 76, 120, 160
proxy wars, 290
PTAs. *see* preferential trade agreements
public goods, 40, 66, 72, 231, 237
Putnam, R. 116, 413

Qatar, *221*
Quackenbush, S. L., 106, 413
quality of life and religion, 17, 22–23, 41, 94, 95, 111, 342, 344–67, 372, 377;
  appendix, 368–69;
  conclusion, 365–67;
  coorelations among dependent variables, *368*;
  correlations between measures of religious freedom and religion-state relations, *369*;
  descriptive statistics, *368*;
  human security, 376;
  human security, inequality, gender development, and political freedoms, *361*;
  human security, measuring the quality of life in societies, 348–52;
  human security, theoretical expectations, 352–55;
  human security, three-stage least-squares, *360*;
  introduction, 344–48;
  research design, 356–59;
  research design, control variables, 358;
  research design, data and units of analysis, 356;
  research design, dependent variables, 356–58;
  research design, estimation, 359;
  research design, independent variables, 358;
  results, 359–65;
  secularism, civil liberties, religious freedom, and human security, *364*

Rabin Y., 12
race/racial, 49, 84, 92, 284, 293, 296, 306;
  characteristics, 22, 100, 164, 297, 395n2;
  conflict, 394n10;
  discrimination, 340, 395n20;
  divisions, 298;
  equality, 348;
  persecutions, 87;
  slavery, 298;
  symbols, 291, 305;
racism, 389n3
Randall, V., 28–29, 414
Rasler, K.A., 159, 400
Rautsi, I., 107, 408
Ray, D., 305, 307, 326, 401, 402

Ray, J. L., 393n3, 414
realism, 27, 33, 58, 84, 389n3;
  classical, 28, 32, 45;
  international cooperation, 233–36;
  liberal, 32;
  neorealism, 45;
  Niebuhr's, 32
realpolitik, 8
Reed, W., 106, 157, 197, 389n12, 409
Reformation, 6, 37–38, 76, 91
Regan, P., 290, 292, 293, 297, 301, 391n1, 414
regional patterns, 129–36;
  distribution of major religions, *129–31*
relative deprivation, 289, 303, 305, 306, 307, 309, 314, 318
relative gains, 233–35, 272
religion: definition, 1–3, 20, 26, 116–22
religion and civil war, 283–343;
  appendix, 343;
  characteristics of civil violence in post–World War II era, 285–88;
  civil conflict attributes, 325, 330, 332–37, *333*;
  civil war duration, 300, 325;
  civil war occurrence, 325, 329, *331*, 332, *336*, 337;
  civil war severity, 325;
  conclusions, 340–42;
  debates and issues in research on civil conflict, 302–9;
  estimation, 329–30;
  ethnicity, linguistic, and religious factors, 302–9;
  extant literature problems, 309–12;
  external dimension of civil conflict, 319–22;
  introduction, 283–85;
  key themes in research on civil conflict, 288–302;
  mobilizing power of religion, 314–18;
  nation history, 337–40, *338*;
  proximate determinants of civil conflict, 318–19;
  religion and civil conflict, 312–22;
  religious structure of societies, 312–14;
  research design, 323–29;
  results, 330–40;
  theory and evidence on determinants of civil conflict, 288–312;
  war outbreak, 330–32
religion and international conflict, 146–223;
  appendix, 194–223;
  clash of civilizations, 164–65, *179* (*see also* clash of civilizations);
  constructivist propositions, 162–64, 192;
  determinants of international conflict, *188*;
  dyadic level of analysis, *182*, 182–90, *184, 185, 186, 187*;
  effects of religious characteristics of states, 1945–2020, *176*;
  effects of religious factors on conflict history of nations, *181*;
  effects of religious similarity and period on dyad history, *187*;
  effects of religious variables on conflict, *186*;
  empirical literature, 149–55;
  implications, 192–93;
  instrumentalist propositions, 161–62;
  integrative theory, 165–66;
  interaction between political instability and religion-state relations, 191–92;
  introduction, 146–49;
  national level of analysis, 175–81;
  political instability and effects on conflict propensity of nations, *177*;
  primordialist proposition, 155–60;
  religious homogeneity, 191;
  religious similarity, *187, 189*, 190–91;
  research design, 166–75;
  research design, estimation methods, 173–75;
  research design, key measures, 168–73;

religion and international conflict (*Continued.*)
  research design, units of analysis, 166–68;
  results, 175–90;
  secularism, 192;
  specific religions more conflict prone, 192;
  theory, 155–66;
  unstable regimes, 191
religion and international cooperation, 224–82;
  appendix, 274–82;
  clash of civilizations, 248;
  communities, 251–52;
  community cohesion matrix, *278*;
  conclusion, 269–73;
  constructivist paradigm, 239–42;
  cooperative international communities, 267–69, *268*;
  dyadic analyses, 261–65, *263*, *264*;
  empirical findings, *271*;
  hypothetical cooperative network with community assignments, *276*, *277*;
  instrumentalism, 247–48;
  integrative theory, 248–51;
  international cooperation—state of the art, introduction, 224–42;
  liberalism, 236–39;
  nation-level analyses, 257–61, *258*, *260*, *261*;
  network effects, 280–82;
  primordialism, 246–47;
  realism, 233–36;
  regional analyses, 265–66, *266*, 267;
  religious cohesion of cooperative communities, 256–57;
  research design, 252–57;
  research design, estimation, 257;
  religious similarity, *277*, *278*;
  research design, key variables, 254–55;
  research design, units of analysis, 253–54;
  results, 257–69;
  theories, 242–52
religion and quality of life, 17, 22–23, 41, 94, 95, 111, 342, 344–67, 372, 377;
  appendix, 368–69;
  conclusion, 365–67;
  correlations among dependent variables, *368*;
  correlations between measures of religious freedom and religion-state relations, *369*;
  descriptive statistics, *368*;
  human security, 376;
  human security, inequality, gender development, and political freedoms, *361*;
  human security, measuring the quality of life in societies, 348–52;
  human security, theoretical expectations, 352–55;
  human security, three-stage least-squares, *360*;
  introduction, 344–48;
  research design, 356–59;
  research design, control variables, 358;
  research design, data and units of analysis, 356;
  research design, dependent variables, 356–58;
  research design, estimation, 359;
  research design, independent variables, 358;
  results, 359–65;
  secularism, civil liberties, religious freedom, and human security, *364*
religion and state, 26, 41, 56, 104, 154, 169, 170, 172, 181, 189, 200, 311, 313, 323, 356, 389n2;
  national constitutions, 1946–2013, *57*;
  religion-state cohabitation, 70, 170, 172, *176*, 177, *177*, *182*, 186, *188*, 192, 196, *203*, *207*, *258*, *263*, *266*, *333*, *338*, 364, 378;
  separation, *57*, 66, 68, 105, 156, 162, 178, 316, 317

religion and world politics, theory and
  evidence, 1–24, 377–83;
    clash of civilization, 381–82 (*see also*
      clash of civilization);
    constructivism, 380–81 (*see also*
      constructivism);
    definition of religion, 1–3;
    history overview, 4–14;
    instrumentalism, 379–80 (*see also*
      instrumentalism);
    integrative theory, 382–83 (*see also*
      integrative theory);
    overview of book, 19–24;
    primordialism, 377–79 (*see also*
      primordialism);
    titles, 1945–2018, *10*;
    what is new and different about this
      study, 14–18
religion in world politics, 370–86;
    clash of civilizations, 374;
    constructivism, 374–75;
    implications for scholarship,
      383–85;
    introduction, 370–72;
    no particular religion is linked to
      bellicosity and conflict, 375;
    policy implications, 385–86;
    religions is key attribute of cultural
      identity of states, 374;
    religious factors affecting
      international relations and
      domestic politics is complex,
      376–77;
    religious factors are fairly stationary
      over time, 374;
    religious similarity between states and
      external environments, 376;
    religious wars label is problematic,
      375–76;
    secularism, 376;
    summary of key results, 372–77, *373*
religiosity, 15, 24, 26, 48, 49, 50,
  100, 101, 122–23, 126, 308, 356,
  358, 389n11
religious actors, 30, 31, 33, 34, 35, 36,
  37, 38, 39, 40, 41, 46, 47, 56, 57,
  60, 61, 79, 98–99, 100, 103, 113,
  301, 362;
    nonstate, 45;
    overemphasis on religious factors, 59;
    substate, 45
religious and non-religious conflicts,
  1946–2001, 52
religious characteristics, 20, 74, 107,
  116, 147, 148, 149, 153, 167, 175,
  176, 180–81, 182, 188, 196, 224,
  225, 258, *266*, 269, 297, 306, 318,
  332, 337, *338*, 342, 344, 348, 350,
  366, 383, 391n1
religious cohesion of cooperative
  communities, 256–57
religious conflict, 3, 6, 8, 20–21, 52,
  52–54, 69, 82, 88, 146, 162, 193,
  293, 297, 298, 300, 307, 311, 312,
  322, 326, 334, 335, 340, 341, 375;
    CoC, 184;
    definition, 50–51. *see also* religion and
      civil war; religion and international
      conflict
religious discrimination, 39, 41, 55, 68,
  153, 169, 170, 305, 308, 310, 311,
  314, 315, 316, 317, 319, 321, 334,
  339, 363, 366, 367
religious diversity, 48, 66, 93, 104, 169,
  190, 217, 252;
    civil war, 294, 318, 321, 326,
      340, 343;
    definition, 200;
    elites, 79, 352;
    Europe, 137, 152;
    global, *134*;
    human security, 355, 363, 366;
    international, 133, 134–35, 153,
      200–201;
    primordialism, 313;
    quality of life, 354, 358;
    religious discrimination, 317;
    religious freedom, 362, 364, 367;
    state, 103, 116;
    Trinidad, 214
religious families in Christianity and
  Islam, *127*

religious freedom, 23, 24, 40, 41, 56, 66, 70, 101, 105, 170, 317, 348, 353, 385, 395n3;
  civil liberties, 362–63;
  constitutional, 67, 68;
  dataset, 356, 358;
  elites, 79, 352;
  human security, 359, *360*, *361*, 366–67;
  Israel, 310;
  literature, 103;
  political stability, 354–55;
  religion-state relations, 364, 368, *369*;
  religious diversity, 367;
  religious persecution, 354
religious homogeneity, 20, 65, 66, 70–71, 101, 111, *177*, 201, 258, 259, 374;
  civil war, 300, 316, 318, 331, 332, 337, 339, 340;
  Cold War, 179;
  conflict, 181, 191, 193, 395n2;
  definition, 67;
  dyadic conflict, 183, 187, 261;
  independent variables, 172;
  international conflict, 191;
  international cooperation, 265;
  MIDs, 187;
  PRIE, 260;
  quality of life, 353;
  social structure, 99, 100;
  state, 100, 102, 103, 155, 156, 157, 158, 165, 166, 169, 175, 178, 213, 378
religious institutions, 2, 9, 12, 21, 29, 30, 40, 42, 45, 63, 65, 67, 70, 77, 79, 93, 94, 98, 99, 100, 101, 246, 325;
  collective action, 309;
  guidelines, 355;
  organizational characteristics, 310;
  pacifying effect, 299;
  political elites, 311;
  political leaders, 316;
  political violence, 311;
  relations with political institutions, 103–6, 112, 113, 165, 166, 167, 181, 183, 192, 249, 272, 318, 319, 335, 354, 378, 385;
  religious freedom, 353;
  religious leaders, 355;
  religious values, 366
religious legitimacy, 44
religious polarization, 150, 294, 300, 302, 307, 322, 326, 334, 335, *336*, 339, 340, 375, 382
religious policy, 1989–2008, *56*
religious practices, 5, 36, 70, 82, 105, 119, 311, 325, 363;
  noncitizens, 141
religious repression, 103–4
religious similarity, 7, 17, 20, 45, 67, 68, 69, 86, 88, 89, 112, 135, 150, 152, 162, 193, 225, 247, 250–51, 371–72, 374, 376, 378, 383;
  affinity, 246;
  Asia, 136, 265;
  average scores across regions, 1945–2010, *135*;
  civil war, 296, 321;
  clash of civilizations, 186, *187*, 187–88, 189, *189*, 190–91, 262, 270, 381;
  community-partitioned, *278*;
  cooperative communities, *268*;
  COW, 168, 391n1;
  definition, 390n9;
  distribution across warring dyads, *223*;
  dyadic, 136, 157, 158, 182, 183, *184*, 185, 201–2, 213, 214, 261;
  dyads in interstate wars, 1945–2007, *219–22*;
  economic transactions, 21;
  friends and foes, 41;
  hypothetical cooperative network, *277*;
  international conflict, *187*, *189*, 190–91;
  international cooperation, 267, 268, 269, 270, 272, 278, 281;
  political instability, 250, 259, *261*, 262, 270;

PRIE, 108, 109, 156, 170–71, 174, 177, 178, 179, 180, 201–2, 213, 259, 260, *261*, 392n10;
regional, 265–66;
religion and international conflict, *187*, *189*, 190–91;
religious families, *218*;
security cooperation, 379;
state-environment, 382;
within-community, 252, 257, 275, 276;
WRP, 116, 147
religious states, 44, 47, 332, 334, 376
religious values, 3, 19, 36, 42, 80, 82;
2010—selected states, *215*;
common, 272;
economic progress, 366;
effect, 355;
indicator of mutual interests or reliability, 108;
instrumentalism, 247;
justification of foreign adventure, 109;
manipulation, 247;
mobilization, 79, 102, 161, 162, 317;
non-, 353;
oppress political opposition, 110;
political elites, 77, 94;
political leaders at risk, 174;
political purposes, 104;
shared, 69;
threats, 43, 161, 162, 174;
unstable leaders, 191;
violation, 389n7
religious wars, 5, 6, 54, 64, 293, 297, 298, 301, 322, 325, 334, 335, 337, 375, 387n1;
definition, 299. *see also* religion and civil wars
religious worldviews, 44, 46, 47
Reuther, A. J., 82, 414
Reuther, H. J., 82, 414
revisionism, modernization, 28, 29
Revolutionary Guard, 250
Reynal-Querol, M. 294, 297, 343, 411, 414
Richardson, J., 388n3, 414

Richardson, L. F., 149, 150, 152, 414
Rittberger, V., 82, 405
rituals, 1, 9, 42, 47, 64, 117, 120, 352;
collective, 2, 63, 119;
religious, 4, 5, 40, 82, 348
Robins, G., 281, 409
Roeder, P., 282, 414
Rogan, E., 6, 414
Rohinyga, 104, 219
Roman Catholic Church, 2, 3, 128, 139;
power of, 78
Roman Empire, 5
Romania, *219*
Rorbaek, L. L., 315, 414
Rouhani, H., 250
Rousseau, J.-J., 8
Rudolph, S. H., 28, 414
Rummel, R., 290, 294, 414
Russett, B., 28, 106, 151, 152, 157, 197, *203*, 238, 358, *368*, 391n6, 410, 411, 413, 414
Russia, 7, 75, 126, 199, 291;
Revolution, 314. *see also* Soviet Union; USSR
Rwanda, 341

Sachar, H., 389n5, 415
Saggi, K., 228, 415
Saiya, N., 56, 414
Salafis, 39, 53, 299
Salehyan, I., 296, 400, 404, 415
Sambanis, N., 285, 291, 292, 293, 295, 297, 305, 400, 401, 405, 415
San-Akca, B., 70, 88, 108, 295, 296, 320, 321, 335, 407, 415
Sandal, 26, 34, 44, 45, 46, 47, 388n1, 415
Sandler, S., 30, 35, 36, 82, 98, 388n1, 401, 403, 413
Sarkees, M. R., 222, 286, *287*, 323, 415
Sarkissian, A., 103, 104, 353, 395n3, 415
Saudi Arabia, 53, *66*, 67, 88, 104, 107, 201, 214, 216, *220*, *221*, 316
Schelling, T. C., 226, 227, 415

scholarship on religion and world politics, 19, 25–63;
   central themes, 35–48;
   critical omission, 59–60;
   disaggregated empirical evidence, 60–61;
   empirical evidence, 48–58;
   introduction, 25–27;
   methodological issues, 60;
   modernization and classical paradigms of IR, 27–34;
   overemphasis on religious factors and religious actors, 59;
   polemical writings, 58–59
Schreiber, J. K., 387n2, 416
scriptures, 1, 46, 47, 119;
   definition, 2, 118. *see also* New Testament; Old Testament
Scroggins, D., 297, 415
secularism, 24, 26, 31, 34, 67, 101, 126, 192, 259, 261, 269, 316, 327, 331, 364, 385;
   civil war, 335, 338, 340, 342;
   dyads, 262;
   failure, 31;
   human security, 363, *364*, 364–65, 366, 367, 376, 377, 380;
   international conflict, 192;
   MIDs, 175;
   quality of life, 355, 359, 362;
   regional, 265;
   religious freedom, 362
security cooperation, 107, 108, 224, 227–28, 229, 234, 236, 238, 244, 250, 251, 252, 255, 256, 259, 261, 265, 266, 267–68, 269, 272, 273, 276, 376, 379, 381, 382, 392n8
Selway, J. S., 301, 404
Senese, P., 159, 415
September 11, 2001, 12, 32, 33, 45, 79, 147, 385
Serbia, 7, 52, 291, 345
Shah, T. 28, 29–30, 31, 36, 37, 38, 41, 42, 52, 56, 59, 65, 83, 98, 103, 113, 193, 322, 324, 383, 387n3, 388nn1–2, 390n3, 393n9, 406, 415–16

Shah of Iran, 389n7
Sharia law, 39, 246
Sharma, S. D., 347, 416
Shaw, I., 4, 416
Shi'ism, 3, 6, 91, 128;
   Iran, 67, 132;
   Iraq, 39, 132;
   Middle East, 132
Shreve, A. P., vii, 148, 157, 168, *195*, 197, *208*, *210*, *222*, 411
Singer, J. D., 116, 149, 152, 153, *195*, *203*, *207*, 229, 299, 393n1, 393n3, 393n5, 393n8, 398, 403, 405, 406, 407, 414, 416
Singer, M., 28
Sinic, 89, 391n2
Siverson, R. M., 71, 225, 303, 399, 412, 416
Six Day War, 387n3
Slovakia, 157, 197
Smart, N., 6, 416
Smith, A., 1, 71, 234, 399, 416
Smith, M. E., 387n2, 416
Snidal, D., 229, 235, 408
Snyder G. H., 108, 416
Snyder, J., 26, 32, 83, 388n1, 398, 412, 416
social structure, 9, 24, 99, 100–103, 104, 109, 111, 113, 245, 382
Söderbom, M., 300, 400
Somalia, *221*
South Africa, *219*, *220*, *221*
South America, 199
South Asia, 7, 132–33
South Korea *219*, *220*
Southwest Asia, 5
South Vietnam, *220*. *see also* Vietnam: War
Soviet Union, 11, 123, 126, 128, 157, 190, 199, 213, 391n7;
   US–Soviet rivalry, 159, 381. *see also* Russia; USSR
Spain, 49, 75, *220*
Spanish Civil War, 314
Stag Hunt Game, 231, 234, 392n1
Stam, A. III., 106, 197, 389n12

Starr, H., 303–4, 412, 416
state-nation model, 163, 164
state-to-national balance, 95, 295
state-to-PRIE, 179
stationarity, 153, 216–17, 371;
    bias, 173, 216, 222, 257
Stephan, A., 59, 286, *287*, 303, 315, 393n9, 400, 406, 415, 416, 417
Stewart, F., 306, 416
strategic rivalry 158, 159, 169, *196*, *206*
structure of the state-religion relations, 105, 200
structure of the state's environment, 99, 106, 109
structure of the state's PRIE, 165, 166, 382
sub-Saharan Africa, 199
Sudan, 52, 213, 297, 317, 341
Sudduth, J. K., 171, 172, *202*, 416
suicide bombing, 13, 57, 78, 306
Sunnism, 3, 6, 53, 67, 91, 102, 128, 132, 171, 201, 214, 270, 341, 379, 391n2
Sun Tzu: *The Art of War*, 8
survey of major world religions, *140–41*
Sutton, J. C., 315, 416
Svensson, I., 53–54, 298, 301, 315, 322, 324, 388n6, 416
syncretic religion, 121, 123, 124, 132, 141
Syria, 81, *219*, *220*, 221, 341;
    Alawites, 102, 379;
    civil wars, 67, 300;
    deserts, 75;
    Israel relations, 159;
    political elites, 107;
    population, 102;
    pre-civil war, 104;
    Sunni Muslims, 379;
    Turkey relations, 199;
    uprisings, 299
system, 27;
    anarchical, 11, 284;
    bipolar, 154;
    Cold War 154;
    communication, 27;
    communist, 126;
    economic, 27, 244, *339*;
    international (interstate, global), 11, 44, 55, 68, 84, 89, 91, 93, 98, 122–23, 133, 149, 157, 167, 180, 190, 194, 198, 235, 236, 237, 256, 265, 287, 345, 347, 349, 357, 371, 375;
    legal, 67, 100, 316, 317, 357, 358, 362, 389n10;
    membership in 122;
    military, 27;
    political, 27, 44, 68, 100, 175, 244, 300, 380, 395n1;
    size of, 55–56, 135–36, 256;
    state, 38, 76, 137, 323;
    tribal, 76

Tabares, T., 225, 412
Tabatabai, A., 250, 416
Tadjoeddin, M. Z., 305, 412
Taiwan *220*
Tanzania, *221*
Taydas, Z., 308, 397
terrorism, 13, 36, 37, 78–79, 152, 345;
    Global Terrorism Dataset, 57;
    "global war on terror," 12;
    international, 56, 151;
    ISIS, 385;
    Islamic perpetrators, 151;
    political, 301;
    religious, 45;
    United States, 11, 12, 33, 147
Thailand, 197, *219*, *220*
theoretical framework, 19–200, 62–114;
    civilizations, clash, 89–92;
    constructivism, 13, 33, 45, 58, 62, 83–89, 90, 94, *96*, 112, 239, 240, *253*, 263, 318, 380–81, 389n3;
    instrumentalism, 71–83, 94, *96*, 112, 161, 162, 379–80;
    instrumentalism, collective, 73, 74, 75, 77, 78;
    instrumentalism, elite, 73, 77, 78–79;
    instrumentalism and cooperation, 247–48;

theoretical framework (*Continued.*)
  integrative theory, 95–99 (*see also* integrative theory);
  integrative theory, effect of international environment, 106–9;
  integrative theory, political and religious institutions relationships, 103–6;
  integrative theory, religious influences on foreign and domestic policy, 109–12;
  integrative theory, social structure, 100–103;
  introduction 62–63;
  perspective differentiation, 92–95, *96–97*;
  primordialism, 63–71, *66*, 76, 81, 88, 94, *96*, 112, 155–60, 161, 247, 315, 318, 377–79, 380
Theravada, 3, *140, 142*
Thirty Years' War, 6, 37
Thomas, S.M., 291, 417
Thompson, W. R., 159, 169, *196, 204, 206, 208*, 210, 400, 409, 417
Thucydides: *Peloponnesian Wars*, 5, 8
Thyne, C. L., *195, 196, 202*, 413
Tickner, J., 344, 399, 417
Tilly, C., 304, 417
time-series cross-sectional (TSCS), 153, 196, 198, 216
time-series negative binomial regression, 330
Toft, M. D., 28, 31, 36, 37, 38, 41, 42, 52–54, 58, 59–60, 65, 83, 98, 103, 113, 193, 291, 297, 298, 301, 322, 324, 325, 383, 388n1, 388n8, 390n3, 393n9, 406, 415, 416, 417
trade, international, 7, 8, 72, 81, 85, 86, 87, 89, 102, 103, 227, 228, 232, 235, 238, 243, 244, 248, 253, 255, 256, 258–262, 265, 346, 349, 380, 390, 392n2, 392n8
transnational religious movements, 37, 45
Travelling Salesman algorithm, 275
treaty(ies) *195, 204*, 227–229, 238, 245, 272, 392n8;

  entente, 228;
  offensive 228;
  nonaggression/neutrality pact, 228, 244;
  security, 228, 251, 290;
  types of, 227–28. *see also* alliances
trends in world religions, 1945–2010, 122–36;
  average religious similarity scores across regions, 1945–2010, *135*;
  distribution of major world religions, 1945–2010, *123*;
  global patterns, 122–29;
  global religious diversity, 1945–2010, *134*;
  regional distribution of major religions, *129–31*;
  regional patterns, 129–36;
  religious families in Christianity and Islam, *127*;
  world population changes in relative share, *125*
tribal communities, 30, 74, 76, 298;
  rituals, 120
Trinidad, 201, 214, 216, 326
Trump, Donald, 12
trust, 242, 245–46
TSCS. *see* time-series cross-sectional
Tucker, R., 151, 152, 406
Turkey, 67–68, 199, *220, 221*, 317
Turkish Empire, 7
Tusicisny, A., 151, 391n3, 417
Type I states, 67, 70, 88, 156, 180, 316
Type II states, 67, 70, 88, 89, 180, 317
Type III states, 68, 70, 88, 180, 317
Type IV states, 68, 70, 89, 156, 180, 317

UCDP. *see* Uppsala Conflict Data Program
Uganda, *221*
Unger, L. K., vii, 238, 417
UN Human Development Index (HDI), 22, 346, 347–48, 356–57, 358, 359, 363, 364, 366, *368*, 395;

Gender-Adjusted, 357;
Inequality-Adjusted, 357, 417
United Arab Emirates, 141, *221*
United Kingdom, 213, *219, 220, 221, 222*, 264, 297. *see also* England
United States, 12, 24, *66*, 92, 194, *219, 220, 221, 222*, 317;
 Christian denominations, 390n4;
 civil conflicts, 394n10;
 democracy, 31;
 ethnicity, 297;
 international conflict, 213;
 Iran relations, 39, 250;
 Japan conflict, 7;
 Jews, 132;
 Muslims, 68;
 Protestants, 216;
 terrorism, 11, 12, 33, 57, 147;
 US–Soviet rivalry, 159, 381. *see also* America
UN Security Council, 235
unstable: dyads, 168;
 leaders, 191, 295;
 politically, 88, 162, 175, 185, 192, 259, 290;
 regimes, 191;
 regional religious homogeneity, 265;
 states, 187, 259
Uppsala, 286, 293
Uppsala Armed Conflict data (UCDP), 49, 50, 286, *287*, 323, 325, *331*, 332, *338*, 393n3, 417
Upper Egypt, 4
Uruguay, 213
USSR, 7, *219, 220*, 264. *see also* Russia; Soviet Union
US State Department Religion Freedom Reports, 358

validity scores, 121, *140–41*
Van Creveld, M., 286, 417
Vanhanen, T., 116, 297, 417
Vasquez, J. A., 159, 410, 415
Vietnam, 362;
 War, 7, 8, *220, 221*, 290, 394n10
Vijayaraghavan, V., 225, 238, 244, 417
Vullers, J., 299, 401

Waever, O., 345, 399, 418
Wahhabi Kingdom of Saudi Arabia, 67
Wallace, M. D., 229, 405, 418
Walter, B., 293, 418
Waltz, K., 8, 28, 86, 418
Ward, M. D. *207, 210, 211*, 281, 418
Warren, T. C., 281, 418
Warsaw Pact, 251, 281
war type, 322, 324, 325, *333*, 394n19, 394n19
Wasserman, S., 213, 418
Wayman, F. W., *222, 287*, 323, 415
Web of Science (WOS), 9, *10*, 387n2
Wendt, A., 83, 84, 85, 91, 240, 251, 392n9, 418
West Bank, 12, 57
Western Hemisphere, 128, 129, 266;
 Correlates of War, 199;
 regional distribution of major religions, *129*;
 religious similarity, 136
Wilson, P. H., 6, 418
Wilson S., 222, 405
Wimmer, A., 294, 296, 306, 329, 340, 394n17, 399, 418
winning coalition, 19, 72, 73, 81, 82, 98, 99, 108, 110, 165, 237, 249, 315, 355
within-community: cohesion scores, 279;
 cooperation, 267;
 density, 275;
 marriages, 6;
 religious similarity, 252, 257, 275, 276
women's rights, 82, 344, 367
world politics and religion, theory and evidence, 1–24, 377–83;
 clash of civilization, 381–82 (*see also* clash of civilization);
 constructivism, 380–81 (*see also* constructivism);
 definition of religion, 1–3;
 history overview, 4–14;
 instrumentalism, 379–80 (*see also* instrumentalism);
 integrative theory, 382–83 (*see also* integrative theory);

world politics and religion, theory and evidence (*Continued.*)
  overview of book, 19–24;
  primordialism, 377–79 (*see also* primordialism);
  titles, 1945–2018, *10*;
  what is new and different about this study, 14–18
world politics in religion, 370–86;
  clash of civilizations, 374;
  constructivism, 374–75;
  implications for scholarship, 383–85;
  introduction, 370–72;
  no particular religion is linked to bellicosity and conflict, 375;
  policy implications, 385–86;
  religions is key attribute of cultural identity of states, 374;
  religious factors affecting international relations and domestic politics is complex, 376–77;
  religious factors are fairly stationary over time, 374;
  religious similarity between states and external environments, 376;
  religious wars label is problematic, 375–76;
  secularism, 376;
  summary of key results, 372–77, *373*
World Religion Project (WRP), 20, 115–45, *195*;
  appendix, 138–45;
  average religious similarity scores across regions, 1945–2010, *135*;
  distribution of major world religions, 1945–2010, *123*;
  general logic, 115–22;
  global patterns, 122–29;
  global religious diversity, 1945–2010, *134*;
  introduction, 115;
  IQV measure, 343;
  major world religions and religious families, *142*;
  measuring religion, 115–22;
  regional distribution of major religions, *129–31*;
  regional patterns, 129–36;
  religious families in Christianity and Islam, *127*;
  survey of major world religions, *140–41*;
  trends in world religions, 1945–2010, 122–36;
  world population changes in relative share, *125*
world religion trends, 1945–2010, 122–36;
  average religious similarity scores across regions, 1945–2010, *135*;
  distribution of major world religions, 1945–2010, *123*;
  global patterns, 122–29;
  global religious diversity, 1945–2010, *134*;
  regional distribution of major religions, *129–31*;
  regional patterns, 129–36;
  religious families in Christianity and Islam, *127*;
  world population changes in relative share, *125*
World Trade Center, 12
World Values Survey (WVS), 48, 356, 358, 359, 362, 389n11
World War i, 7
World War ii, 7, 20, 56, 86, 98, 115, 136, 137, 159, 190, 238, 293, 307, 375;
  characteristics of civil violence, 285–88
WOS (Web of Science), 9, *10*, 387n2
WRP. *see* World Religion Project
WVS. *see* World Values Survey
Wucherpfennig, J. N., 322, 418
Wyn, Jones, 345, 418

Yugoslavia, 123, 145, 157;
  former, 52, 291, 341, 391n7;
  war, 290

Zionism, 82–83, 389n5